# Study Guide

Thomas M. Beveridge
*North Carolina State University*

Deborah Fretz
*McMaster University*

Michael R. Veall
*McMaster University*

Lonnie Magee
*McMaster University*

## PRINCIPLES OF
# macroeconomics

### SECOND CANADIAN EDITION

KARL E. CASE

RAY C. FAIR

J. FRANK STRAIN

MICHAEL R. VEALL

Prentice
Hall

Toronto

Original edition published by Prentice Hall, Inc., a division of Pearson Education, Upper Saddle River, New Jersey. © 1999 Prentice Hall, Inc. This edition is authorized for sale in Canada only.

ISBN 0-13-042249-5

Acquisitions Editor: Dave Ward
Developmental Editor: Maurice Esses
Production Editor: Julia Hubble
Production Coordinator: Janette Lush

1 2 3 4 5   06 05 04 03 02

Printed and bound in Canada.

# Contents

# Preface

This Study Guide accompanies the second Canadian edition of *Principles of Macroeconomics* by Karl Case, Ray Fair, J. Frank Strain, and Michael Veall. It draws on the Study Guide to the American edition by Thomas M. Beveridge and its graphing tutorial by Steven C. Pitts, and takes chapters 1 to 5, by Farrokh Zandi, directly from the companion Study Guide for *Principles of Microeconomics*. We thank the team at Pearson Education Canada: Maurice Esses, Developmental Editor, Deanne Walle, EMM Coordinator, Julia Hubble, Production Editor, and Dave Ward, Acquisitions Editor. This Guide has been devised to help you as you learn the concepts that are presented in the text. Most economics instructors stress the need to develop competence in three major areas—the application of economic concepts to real-world situations, the interpretation of graphs, and the analysis of numerical problems. This Guide gives you practice in developing these skills.

We believe that learning how to apply concepts creates a better and more long-lasting understanding of the material than mere memorization does. A reasonable goal for a non-economics major is to have absorbed enough insight to understand the economic content of an article in a publication like *The Globe & Mail* or *The National Post*.

## Study Guide Contents

The Study Guide contains one chapter for each chapter in the text. Each chapter has three main sections.

- The *Objectives: Point by Point* section summarizes what you should be able to accomplish after you've studied the material. These objectives match those given in the text. Each point is followed by some multiple choice questions to enable you to monitor how well you're understanding the concepts. You'll find some applications and examples, along with specific learning tips, graphing pointers, and "helpful hints." Many of these "tricks" have been suggested by students.

- The *Practice Test* section contains *Multiple Choice Questions* and *Application Questions*. These questions provide opportunities to practise the skills—graphing, numerical analysis, application of concepts—presented in the text. Think of each multiple choice question as four true/false statements. Don't just decide on the one "right" answer; determine why the other three options are wrong.

- The *Answers and Solutions* section contains the answers to the *Practice Test*. If you need more practice questions with answers, the answers to the even-numbered problems in the text are provided at the back of the text.

A conscientious and consistent use of this Guide, along with reading the text and regular class attendance (in mind as well as in body!), will improve your ability to use and apply economics.

Best wishes to you in your study of economics.

Deborah Fretz
Michael Veall
Lonnie Magee
McMaster University

# 1 The Scope and Method of Economics

## OBJECTIVES: POINT BY POINT

After completing this chapter, you should be able to accomplish the objectives listed below.

### General Comment

Much of this chapter is devoted to setting out the framework of economics. Don't be overwhelmed and don't try to remember it all. Chapter 1 is simply a good place to gather together this information, which will be dealt with more fully as the chapters go by.

### OBJECTIVE 1: State the importance of studying economics.

Summarize the importance of studying economic issues and describe how an economic way of thinking enables us to understand society and international affairs and thus become more informed voters. (page 2)

Other important concepts are marginalism and efficiency.

### Practice

1.  Which one of the following best describes the study of economics? Economics studies
    A.  how businesses can make profits.
    B.  how the government controls the economy and how people earn a living.
    C.  how society uses its scarce resources to satisfy its unlimited desires.
    D.  the allocation of income among different sectors of the economy.

    **ANSWER:** C. All of the options represent aspects of the study of economics. However, the most general statement is given in C—economics is the study of choice.

"Marginal" is a frequently used term in economics and it's important to understand it right away. "Marginal" means "additional" or "extra." "Marginal cost," then, means "additional cost."

Suppose you've bought a non-returnable, non-transferable ticket to the zoo for $10. This is a *sunk cost*. You've paid whether or not you visit the zoo.

Let's change the example a little. Suppose you win a free admission to the zoo and decide to go this Saturday. The trip is not entirely free, however. You still have to bear some costs—travel, for example. There is certainly an additional cost (caused by the trip to the zoo). It is a *marginal cost*. Suppose you always buy lunch on Saturdays. The cost of lunch is not a marginal cost since you'd have had lunch whether or not you went to the zoo. In this sense, the cost of lunch is not contingent on the trip to the zoo—it's not an extra cost.

You choose to visit the zoo this Saturday. The *opportunity cost* is the value of the activity you would have undertaken instead—that is, the next most-preferred activity. Perhaps it might be playing a round of golf or studying for a big economics test. The opportunity cost of the trip to the zoo is the value you attach to that *one* activity you would otherwise have chosen. (page 2)

**Opportunity Cost and Marginalism:** The "big concept" in this chapter is *opportunity cost*, with *marginalism* and *efficiency* a close second and third. You'll see all three repeatedly throughout the textbook. For practice on the concept of opportunity cost, try Application question 5 below. For practice on marginal thinking, look at Application question 8.

> **TIP:** Any time you make a choice, remember that an opportunity cost is involved.

## Practice

2. Your opportunity cost of attending university includes
   A. the money you spend on meals while at university.
   B. your tuition and the money you spend on travelling between home and university.
   C. the income you could have earned if you'd been employed full-time.
   D. Both B and C.

   **ANSWER:** A. You would have bought food whether or not you were at university. All the other expenses occur solely because of attending university.

3. _____ may be defined as the extra cost associated with an action.
   A. Marginal cost.
   B. Sunk cost.
   C. Opportunity cost.
   D. Action cost.

   **ANSWER**: A. See p. 3.

4. Jean owns a French restaurant—*La Crème*. Simply to operate this week, he must pay rent, taxes, wages, food costs, and so on. This amounts to $1000 per week. This evening, a diner arrives and orders some Chambolle-Musigny 1995 wine to go with her meal. Jean has none and sends out to the nearest liquor store for a bottle. It costs $40, and Jean charges his guest $60. Which of the following is true for Jean?
   A. The marginal cost of the wine is $40.
   B. The marginal cost of the wine is $60.
   C. The sunk cost of the meal is $1040.
   D. The sunk cost of the meal is $1060.

   **ANSWER:** A. The sunk cost is the up-front expense of $1000. The extra cost that Jean bears for buying the wine is $40.

## OBJECTIVE 2: Distinguish between the two main branches of economics.

Economics is split into two broad parts. *Microeconomics* focuses on the operation of individual markets and the choices of individual economic units (firms and households, for example). *Macroeconomics* deals with the broad economic variables such as national production, total consumer spending, and overall price movements. Economics also contains a number of subfields, such as international economics, labour economics, and industrial organization. (page 7)

## Practice

5.  **Macroeconomics** approaches the study of economics from the viewpoint of
    A.  individual consumers.
    B.  the government.
    C.  the entire economy.
    D.  the operation of specific markets.

    **ANSWER:** C. Macroeconomics looks at the big picture—the entire economy.

6.  **Microeconomics** approaches the study of economics from the viewpoint of
    A.  the entire economy.
    B.  the government.
    C.  the operation of specific markets.
    D.  the stock market.

    **ANSWER:** C. Microeconomics examines what is happening with individual economic units (households and firms) and how they interact in specific markets.

7.  Which of the following is most appropriately a microeconomic issue?
    A.  The study of the relationship between the unemployment rate and the inflation rate.
    B.  The forces determining the price in an individual market.
    C.  The determination of total output in the economy.
    D.  The aggregate behaviour of all decision-making units in the economy.

    **ANSWER:** B. Microeconomics examines what is happening with individual economic units (households and firms) and how they interact in specific markets.

## OBJECTIVE 3: Identify the roles played by theories, models, and empirical evidence in economics.

Economic theory is a statement (or a set of statements) about cause and effect. It attempts to generalize and explain what is observed. An economic model is a formal statement of an economic theory. A theory is accepted (or rejected) when it succeeds (fails) to explain what is observed. The observations that are based on the collection and use of data are empirical results. (page 14)

## OBJECTIVE 4: Describe the roles played by positive and normative economics in economic policy analysis.

Economists classify issues as either positive or normative. Positive questions explore the behaviour of the economy and its participants without judging whether the behaviour is good or bad. *Positive economics* collects data that describe economic phenomena (descriptive economics) and constructs testable—cause-and-effect—theories to explain the phenomena (economic theory). *Normative economic questions* evaluate the results of behaviour and explore whether the outcomes might be improved. (page 8)

## Practice

8.  A difference between positive statements and normative statements is that
    A.  positive statements are true by definition.
    B.  only positive statements are subject to empirical verification.
    C.  economists use positive statements and politicians use normative statements when discussing economic matters.
    D.  positive statements require value judgments.

**ANSWER:** B. A positive statement is not necessarily true by definition and can be disproved by empirical verification.

## Other Related Points.

## POINT 1: Explain the value of the *ceteris paribus* assumption within the context of economic modelling.

Economists (and other scientists) construct models—formal statements of relationships between variables of interest—that simplify and abstract from reality. Graphs, words, or equations can be used to express a model. In testing the relationships between variables within a model, it is convenient to assume *ceteris paribus*, that all other variables have been held constant. 
(page 12)

## Practice

9.    "An increase in the price of shampoo will cause less shampoo to be demanded, *ceteris paribus*." *Ceteris paribus* means that
    A.    there is a negative relationship between the price and quantity demanded of shampoo.
    B.    the price of shampoo is the only factor that can affect the amount of shampoo demanded.
    C.    other factors may affect the amount of shampoo demanded; these are assumed not to change in this analysis.
    D.    the price of shampoo is equal for all buyers.

    **ANSWER:** C. The price of shampoo is equal for all buyers, and there may be a negative relationship between the price and quantity of shampoo demanded, but *ceteris paribus* means that any other factors that may affect the amount of shampoo demanded are assumed to be constant.

## POINT 2: State the fallacies discussed in the text, give examples, and explain *why* such statements are fallacious.

Beware of false logic! The *fallacy of composition* involves the claim that what is good for one individual remains good when it happens for many. The fact that one farmer gains by having a bumper harvest *doesn't* mean that all farmers will gain if each has a bumper crop. The *post hoc, ergo propter hoc* fallacy occurs when we assume that an event that happens after another is caused by it. 
(page 13)

> Two examples of the fallacy of composition: One person who stands up to see a good play at a game derives a benefit—therefore all will benefit similarly if the entire crowd stands up. Running to the exit when there is a fire in a theatre will increase your chances of survival—therefore, in a fire, we should all run for the exit.

## Practice

10.    Which of the following is an example of the fallacy of composition?
    A.    Jane leaves work at 3:00 each day and avoids the rush-hour traffic. Therefore, if businesses regularly closed at 3:00, all commuters would avoid the rush-hour traffic.

B.  John stands up so that he can see an exciting football play. Therefore, if the entire crowd stands up when there is an exciting play, all spectators will get a better view.

C.  Since society benefits from the operation of efficient markets, IBM will benefit if markets become more efficient.

D.  Both A and B.

**ANSWER:** D. The example in C is arguing from the general to the specific. The fallacy of composition argues from the specific to the general. Therefore, D is correct.

## POINT 3: State and explain the four criteria used to assess the outcomes of economic policy.

Economists construct and test models as an aid to policy making. Policy makers generally judge proposals in terms of efficiency, equity (fairness), growth, and stability. (page 15)

## Practice

11. The nation of Arboc claims to have achieved an equitable distribution of income among its citizens. On visiting Arboc, we would expect to find that
    A.  each citizen receives the same amount of income.
    B.  Arbocali residents believe that the distribution of income is fair.
    C.  Arbocali residents believe that the distribution of income is equal.
    D.  each citizen receives the amount of income justified by the value of his or her contribution to production.

    **ANSWER:** B. Whether or not the distribution of income is equitable depends on what Arbocali citizens believe to be fair.

Use the following information to answer the next two questions.

Nicola and Alexander each have some dollars and some apples. Nicola values a kilo of apples at $3, while Alexander values a kilo of apples at $1.

12. In which of the following cases has an economically efficient trade taken place?
    A.  The market price of apples is $3 per kilo. Nicola sells apples to Alexander.
    B.  The market price of apples is $1 per kilo. Nicola sells apples to Alexander.
    C.  The market price of apples is $2 per kilo. Nicola sells apples to Alexander.
    D.  The market price of apples is $2 per kilo. Alexander sells apples to Nicola.

    **ANSWER:** D. When the market price of apples is $2 per kilo and Alexander is the seller, he gains $1. Nicola also gains because she receives goods she values at $3 for a payment of only $2.

13. In which of the following cases has an economically efficient trade not taken place?
    A.  The market price of apples is $3 per kilo. Alexander sells apples to Nicola.
    B.  The market price of apples is $1 per kilo. Nicola buys apples from Alexander.
    C.  The market price of apples is $4 per kilo. Alexander sells apples to Nicola.
    D.  The market price of apples is $2 per kilo. Nicola buys apples from Alexander.

    **ANSWER:** C. An efficient trade can occur only when some participant is better off and no participant is worse off. In Option A, Alexander gains and Nicola does not lose. In Option B, Nicola gains and Alexander does not lose. In Option D, Alexander and Nicola both gain. In Option C, Alexander gains but Nicola loses.

# OBJECTIVE 5: Appendix 1A, read and interpret graphs and linear equations.

Economic graphs depict the relationship between variables. A curve with a "rising" (positive) slope indicates that as one variable increases, so does the other. A curve with a "falling" (negative) slope indicates that as one variable increases in value, the other decreases in value. Slope is easily measured by "rise over run"—the extent of vertical change divided by the extent of horizontal change.                                    (page 19)

## Practice

> **TIP:** Economists almost automatically begin to scribble diagrams when asked to explain ideas, and you'll need to learn how to use some of the tools of the trade. In economics, graphs often feature financial variables like "price," "the interest rate," or "income." Usually the dependent variable is placed on the vertical axis and the independent variable on the horizontal axis. In graphing economic variables, however, it's a pretty safe bet that the financial variable will go on the vertical axis every time. Application questions 9 and 10 and the Tutorial offer some graphing Practice.

> **TIP:** Make a point of examining the graphs you see accompanying economics-based articles in the daily newspaper or news magazines. It's quite common to find examples of deceptive graphs, especially when variables are being compared over time. A graph comparing, say, the difference between government spending and tax revenues can be quite misleading if the vertical axis does not start at zero.

> **Graphing Pointer:** It is a natural tendency to shy away from graphs—they may seem threatening—but this is a mistake. To work with economic concepts, you must master all the tools in the economist's tool kit. Trying to avoid graphs is as unwise as trying to cut a piece of wood without a saw. See the Graphing Tutorial if you are uneasy.

Use the diagram below to answer the next four questions.

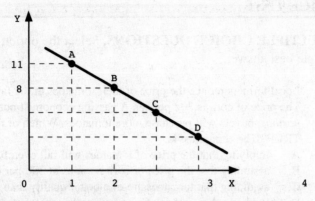

14. In the diagram above, the slope of the line is
    A. positive and variable.
    B. positive and constant.
    C. negative and variable.
    D. negative and constant.

    **ANSWER:** D. The diagram shows a straight line—straight lines have a constant slope. Visually, or by using the "rise over run" formula, the relationship is negative because, as one variable increases in value, the other decreases in value.

15. The slope of line between Point A and Point B is
    A. 3.
    B. 1/3.
    C. −3.
    D. −1/3.

    **ANSWER:** C. Use the "rise over run" formula. The rise is -3 (from 11 to 8), and the run is +1 (from 1 to 2).

16. At Point D, the value of Y is
    A. −3.
    B. 3.
    C. 5.
    D. 2.

    ANSWER: D. As X "steps up" in value by 1, Y "steps down" in value by 3. At Point B, X has a value of 2 and Y has a value of 8. Moving to Point D, X increases by 2 and Y decreases by 6, from 8 to 2.

17. In the diagram above, when the line reaches the vertical (Y) axis, the value of Y will be
    A. 3.
    B. 8.
    C. 11.
    D. 14.

    **ANSWER:** D. As X "steps down" in value by 1, Y "steps up" in value by 3. At Point A, X has a value of 1 and Y has a value of 11. X decreases by 1 and Y increases by 3, from 11 to 14.

**PRACTICE TEST**

**I.    MULTIPLE CHOICE QUESTIONS.** Select the option that provides the single best answer.

_____ 1.   Local farmers reduce the price of their tomatoes at the farmers' market. The price of corn is 30¢ per ear. A passing economist notes that, *ceteris paribus*, buyers will purchase more tomatoes. Which of the following is TRUE? The economist is
   A.   implying that the price of tomatoes will fall even further.
   B.   assuming that the price of corn remains at 30¢ per ear.
   C.   assuming that tomatoes are of a better quality than before.
   D.   implying that corn is of a poorer quality than before.

_____ 2.   Which of the following is **not** given in the textbook as a criterion for judging the results of economic policy?
   A.   Economic stability.
   B.   Energy conservation.
   C.   Efficiency.
   D.   Equity.

_____ 3.   Economic growth may occur if
   A.   more machines become available.
   B.   more workers become available.
   C.   workers become more efficient.
   D.   all of the above.

_____ 4.   Economics is the study of how
   A.   scarce resources are used to satisfy unlimited wants.
   B.   we choose to use unlimited resources.
   C.   limitless resources are used to satisfy scarce wants.
   D.   society has no choices.

_____ 5.   The opportunity cost of Choice X can be defined as
   A.   the cheapest alternative to Choice X.
   B.   the most highly-valued alternative to Choice X.
   C.   the price paid to obtain X.
   D.   the most highly-priced alternative to Choice X.

_____ 6.   In economics, efficiency means that
   A.   income is distributed equally among all citizens.
   B.   there is a low level of inflation and full unemployment of economic resources.
   C.   total productivity is increasing at a constant and equal rate within each sector of the economy.
   D.   the economy is producing those goods and services that citizens desire and is doing so at the least possible cost.

_____ 7.   Which of the following statements is true?
   A.   Microeconomics studies consumer behaviour, while macroeconomics studies producer behaviour.
   B.   Microeconomics studies producer behaviour, while macroeconomics studies consumer behaviour.
   C.   Microeconomics studies behaviour of individual households and firms, while macroeconomics studies national aggregates.
   D.   Microeconomics studies inflation and opportunity costs, while macroeconomics studies unemployment and sunk costs.

_____ 8. Which of the following statements is true?
  A. There is a positive relationship between the price of a product and the quantity demanded.
  B. There is a positive relationship between the number of umbrellas bought and the amount of rainfall.
  C. There is a negative relationship between height and weight.
  D. There is a negative relationship between sales of ice cream and noon temperature.

_____ 9. Oliver Sudden discovers that if he cuts the price of his tomatoes at the farmers' market, his sales revenue increases. Expecting similar results, all the other tomato sellers follow his example. They are guilty of committing
  A. the fallacy of composition.
  B. the fallacy of *post hoc, ergo propter hoc*.
  C. the fallacy of correlation.
  D. *ceteris paribus*.

_____ 10. The quantity of six-packs of Labatt Blue beer demanded per week (Qd) in Hometown is described by the following equation:
  $$Qd = 400 - 100P,$$
  where P (in dollars) is the price of a six-pack. This equation predicts that
  A. 300 six-packs will be bought this week.
  B. a $1 rise in price will cause 100 more six-packs to be bought this week.
  C. 300 six-packs will be bought per $100 this week.
  D. a 50¢ rise in price will cause 50 fewer six-packs to be bought this week.

_____ 11. The *ceteris paribus* assumption is used
  A. to make economic theory more realistic.
  B. to make economic analysis more realistic.
  C. to avoid the fallacy of composition.
  D. to focus the analysis on the effect of a single factor.

Use the diagram (not drawn to scale) below to answer the next four questions.

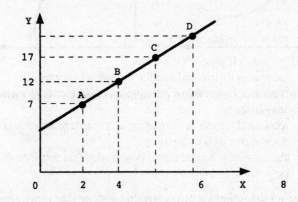

_____ 12. In the diagram above, the slope of the line is
  A. positive and variable.
  B. positive and constant.
  C. negative and variable.
  D. negative and constant.

_____ 13. The slope of the line between Point A and Point B is
A. 5/2.
B. 2/5
C. -2/5.
D. –5/2.

_____ 14. At Point D, the value of Y is
A. 5.
B. 8.
C. 19.5.
D. 22.

_____ 15. In the diagram above, when the line reaches the vertical (Y) axis the value of Y will be
A. 2.
B. 5/2.
C. 7.
D. 12.

Use the diagrams below (not drawn to scale) to answer the next four questions.

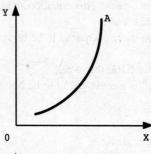
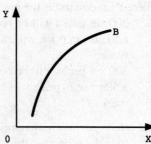
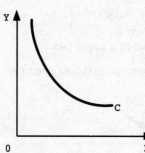
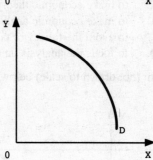

_____ 16. Of the four diagrams, which curve has a slope that is negative and decreasing in magnitude?
A. A.
B. B.
C. C.
D. D.

_____ 17. Of the four diagrams, which curve has a slope that is positive and increasing?
A. A.
B. B.
C. C.
D. D.

_____ 18. Of the four diagrams, which curve has a slope that is positive and decreasing?
  A.  A.
  B.  B.
  C.  C.
  D.  D.

_____ 19. Of the four diagrams, which curve appears to be described by the equation $y = x^2$?
  A.  A.
  B.  B.
  C.  C.
  D.  D.

_____ 20. During the debate about balancing the federal government budget, it has been proposed that transfer payments to provinces be reduced. This proposal has been criticized because it would force provinces to cut their respective social services, which would hurt the low-income families the most. This argument is based on concerns about
  A  economic growth.
  B  efficiency stability.
  C  economic stability.
  D  equity.

Use the following information to answer the next two questions. The Channel Tunnel, linking the United Kingdom and France, was originally planned to cost $100 million. After work had begun and the two excavators were under the English Channel, with $70 million already spent, the estimate of the total bill was revised to $150 million.

_____ 21. To an economist, the $70 million that had already been spent is best thought of as a
  A.  sunk cost that was important in determining whether to complete the project.
  B.  sunk cost that was not important in determining whether to complete the project.
  C.  marginal cost that was important in determining whether to complete the project.
  D.  marginal cost that was not important in determining whether to complete the project.

_____ 22. At this point the marginal cost of completion was best estimated as
  A.  $30 million.
  B.  $50 million.
  C.  $70 million.
  D.  $80 million.

## II.  APPLICATION QUESTIONS.

1.  The small nation of Smogland is unhappily situated in a valley surrounded by mountains. Smogland's Minister of the Environment has determined that there are 4000 cars, each of which pollutes the air. In fact, Smogland's air is so unhealthy that it is rated as "hazardous." If emission controls, costing $50 per car, are introduced, the air quality will improve to a rating of "fair." A survey has revealed that, of the 40 000 inhabitants, 10 000 would value the air quality improvement at $5 each, and the other 30 000 would value it at $7 each. The Minister of the Environment has asked you to analyze the issue and make a recommendation.

2. Refer to the following diagram.

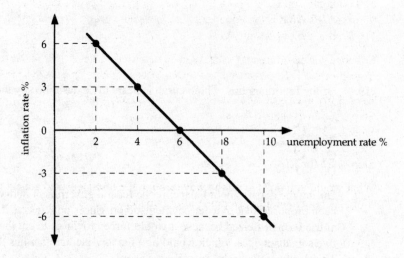

a. Construct a table from the data presented in the diagram.
b. Calculate the slope of the line.
c. Calculate the inflation rate when the unemployment rate is 9%.
d. Calculate the inflation rate when the unemployment rate is 5%.

3. What are some elements of the opportunity cost of "clean" air? In total, the "cost" of cleaner air increases as we remove more and more pollution. Do you think, however, that the extra (marginal) cost of cleaner air increases as we progressively remove pollution? Graph the behaviour of "extra cost" (vertical axis) and "cleanness of air" (horizontal axis).

4. Suppose that the opportunity cost of attending today's economics class is study time for a math test. By not studying you will lose fifteen points on your test. Attending the econ. class will increase your future econ. test score by no more than three points. Was your choice—to attend the econ. class—rational?

5. Suppose you had a summer internship in a bank just before your final year. You are "noticed" and are offered a full-time position in the bank, with a salary of $30 000 a year. A rival bank, also keen to attract you, offers you $32,000 for a similar position. After much thought, you decide to return to university to complete your economics degree. Based on the information given, what was the opportunity cost of your decision?

If you had chosen one of the banking jobs instead of resuming your studies, how could you have explained your decision to your parents, who would have pointed out that you would have "wasted" three years of university? How might "sunk costs" figure into your explanation?

6. Choose a local natural resource with which you are familiar, e.g., a hectare of farm land or a nearby lake.
a. List three alternative uses for your chosen raw material.
b. Choose one of the three uses. What is the opportunity cost of this use? Should you include the cost of clean-up (if this is appropriate) following use?
c. Is the resource renewable or not? If not, should this be factored into your calculations?
d. Describe how your community has chosen to use the resource so far, if at all. Who and what have determined that choice?

7. Suppose you're asked to choose one job out of three. Job A pays $30 000; Job B, $20 000; and Job C, $15 000. In all other respects, they are identical. Which would you choose? What is the opportunity cost of your choice? Is it rational to choose Job C? What is the opportunity cost of Job C?

8. Suppose you're offered three deals, each of which will give you $11 in return for $8. Your profit will be $3 in each case. *Deal A* is a straight swap—$11 for $8.

   *Deal B* involves four steps and you can quit at any point.
   Step 1. $5 in exchange for $2
   Step 2. $3 for $2
   Step 3. $2 for $2
   Step 4. $1 for $2

   What would you do? Go all the way through the four steps and collect a total of $3 profit? A better solution, stopping after two steps, would yield $4.

   *Deal C* also involves four steps.
   Step 1. $4 in exchange for $1
   Step 2. $4 for $2
   Step 3. $2 for $2
   Step 4. $1 for $3

   Would you collect your $3 profit or stop after two steps and gain $5?

   *Moral:* If the effects of extra (marginal) steps are assessed, you can raise your profits above $3. Without examining each step, the chance of greater profits would have been missed.

9. Using your own intuition, graph each of the following relationships in the space below.
   a. height and weight of males.
   b. (on the same graph) height and weight of females.

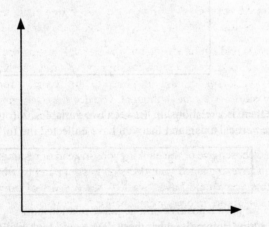

   c. Do these lines have a positive slope or negative slope?
   d. Have you drawn the relationships differently? If so, why? By referring to your own observations, you have constructed a model.
   e. Which factors have you "held constant"?
   f. i. Again using your own intuition, sketch in the space on the following page the relationship between the price of Ontario wine and the consumption of Ontario wine.
      ii. According to your theory and your diagram, is there any point, even if wine is free, at which consumers will not wish to buy any more wine?

iii.   Will the total number of dollars spent on wine remain the same at every price level?

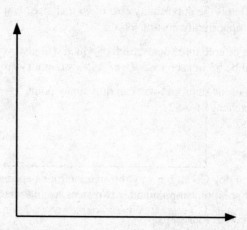

g.   i.   Using your own intuition, sketch in the space below the relationship between the interest rate and house purchases.
    ii.   According to your theory and your graph, is there any interest rate that will completely deter house purchases?

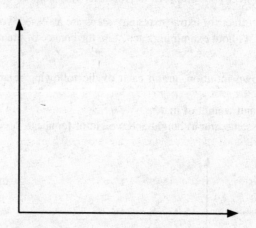

10.   Suppose there is a relationship between two variables, X (on the horizontal axis) and Y (on the vertical axis), and that you have collected the following data.

| X | 2 | 4 | 6 | 8 | 10 |
|---|---|---|---|---|----|
| Y | 5 | 6 | 7 | 8 | 9  |

a.   Do we have a positive or a negative relationship?
b.   Describe (in words) what these data would look like graphically.
c.   Calculate the slope (rise over run) of the line.
d.   Graph the relationship below.

11. Suppose that you have a new brand of low-alcohol, calorie-reduced beer, "Coors Light," that you intend to market. What variables do you think will be important in determining the amount of Coors Light that people will want to buy? You should be able to develop a fairly long list of variables. You have begun to construct an economic model of consumption behaviour. Now prune down your list to include, say, the five most important variables.

Now work out in which way each variable will impact the consumption of Coors Light. You should be able to work out a specific cause-and-effect pattern in each case. A higher price for Coors Light should cause less to be bought. A price hike for competing beers should increase the demand for Coors Light. Note that not all variables have been included in the model; an all-inclusive list would (1) be cumbersome and (2) distract from the major elements in the model.

The variables that you have compiled in your list will be continually changing their values. To isolate the effect of any one on the consumption of Coors Light you must invoke the *ceteris paribus* assumption. You might think of this as being the economic equivalent of the "standard temperature and pressure" conditions applied in the natural sciences.

Use the model that you developed for Coors Light beer. Putting "quantity demanded" on the horizontal axis, graph each of the relationships in the model.

12. Which of the following statements are positive and which are normative?
    a. The moon is made of green cheese.
    b. Provinces to the east of Quebec have lower provincial income tax rates than those to the west of Quebec.
    c. The federal government should be made to balance its budget.
    d. The most serious economic problem confronting the nation is unemployment.
    e. We should abolish the minimum wage.
    f. We should index-link the minimum wage to the rate of price inflation.
    g. If the federal budget deficit is reduced, then interest rates will decrease.

# ANSWERS AND SOLUTIONS

## PRACTICE TEST

### I.    SOLUTIONS TO MULTIPLE CHOICE QUESTIONS

1.    B. If the price of corn fell, perhaps very sharply, buyers might buy more corn and fewer tomatoes. Therefore, the economist is assuming that the price of corn is not going to change. That's what *ceteris paribus* implies.

2.    B. Energy conservation might be part of economic efficiency, but it is not one of the criteria for evaluating the results of economic policy. See p. 15.

3.    D. Growth will occur if resources become more plentiful or more productive.

4.    A. Economics is about choice—how we ration scarce resources to meet limitless wants.

5.    B. Price is not necessarily a reliable guide to value for a particular individual. Opportunity cost is the measure of the value placed on the next most-preferred item forgone as a result of Choice X.

6.    D. Efficiency means that producers are using the least costly method of production to supply those goods that are desired by consumers.

7.    C. To review the micro/macro distinction, see p. 7.

8.    B. There is a *negative* relationship between price and quantity demanded, so A is incorrect. The greater the rainfall, the larger the number of umbrellas bought.

9.    A. Just because an action done by one individual produces a given outcome, the same action done by many need not.

10.   D. Put in numbers. If P = $2, then Qd will equal 400 − 100(2), or 200. If the price rises by 50¢, then Qd will equal 400 − 100(2.5), or 150—a fall of 50.

11.   D. The *ceteris paribus* assumption freezes the effect of all but one change so that the effects of that change may be examined.

12.   B. The diagram shows a straight line—straight lines have a constant slope. Visually, or by using the "rise over run" formula, the relationship is positive because, as one variable increases in value, the other also increases in value.

13.   A. Use the "rise over run" formula. The rise is +5 (Y goes from 7 to 12) and the run is +2 (X goes from 2 to 4).

14.   D. As X "steps up" in value by 2, Y "steps up" in value by 5. At Point C, X has a value of 6 and Y has a value of 17. Moving to Point D, X rises by 2 and Y rises by 5, from 17 to 22.

15.   A. As X "steps down" in value by 2, Y "steps down" in value by 5. At Point A, X has a value of 2 and Y has a value of 7. X decreases by 2 and Y decreases by 5, from 7 to 2.

16.   C. As the X variable increases in value, the Y variable decreases in value—a negative relationship. The slope is decreasing in magnitude because, as X increases in value, the decrease in the value of Y becomes smaller and smaller.

17.   A. The relationship shows that as the X variable increases in value, the Y variable also increases in value—a positive relationship. The slope is increasing because, as X increases in value, the increase in the value of Y becomes larger and larger.

18.   B. The relationship shows that as the X variable increases in value, the Y variable also increases in value—a positive relationship. The slope is decreasing because, as X increases in value, the increase in the value of Y becomes smaller and smaller.

19.   A. As x assumes higher values, the values of y will increase more rapidly.

20.   D. For equity, read "fairness." Critics of this proposal argue that a cut in transfer payments, and thereby social spending, creates an unequitable redistribution of income against low-income families.

21. B. The $70 million had already been spent and was unrecoverable—a sunk cost. Sunk costs should have no impact on the decision to continue the project. See p. 3.

22. D. To complete the project would cost $80 million more than had already been spent.

## II. SOLUTIONS TO APPLICATION QUESTIONS

1. The (marginal) cost of the air quality improvement is valued at $50 x 4000, or $200 000. The benefit derived from the improvement is valued at ($5 x 10 000) + ($7 x 30 000), or $260 000. Smogland should proceed with the implementation of emission controls.

2. a.

| Unemployment Rate (%) | Inflation Rate (%) |
|---|---|
| 2.0 | 6.0 |
| 4.0 | 3.0 |
| 6.0 | 0.0 |
| 8.0 | -3.0 |
| 10.0 | -6.0 |

   b. Slope is –1.5.

   c. –4.5%.

   d. 1.5%.

3. In order to have cleaner (if not clean) air, we might wish to reduce emissions of cars, homes, and factories. The next most preferred use of the resources used to achieve this would be included in the opportunity cost. An initial 5% improvement in the quality of the air might be accomplished quite simply—perhaps by requiring more frequent car tune ups—but, progressively, the "cost" of achieving more stringent air cleanliness standards will rise. The marginal cost will increase. This will graph as an upward-sloping line that rises progressively more steeply.

4. The answer cannot be determined given the information. This choice may well have been rational. Perhaps the three extra points save you from flunking the course while, in the math class, you are confident of making an easy "A."

5. The opportunity cost is the salary forgone—$32 000 if you had chosen the rival bank. Presumably, the offer of the job at the bank was based on your abilities—some of which would have been developed while at university. That time, then, was not wasted. You could have taken the bank job and explained that the three years of university got you the internship and sufficient skills to be noticed in the first place. Also, the three university years cannot be relived—decisions should be based on the future, not the past.

6. This is an open question. The natural resource might be a river, a seam of coal, deer, a piece of wasteland used as a dump, prime agricultural land, or downtown lots. The main point is that using the resource one way means that it is not available for other uses. The final part of the question may lead you into a consideration of private property rights, social pressure, and the role of the government.

7. Choose Job A. The opportunity cost is $20 000 (the value of the next best alternative forgone—Job B). The opportunity cost of both Job B and Job C is $30 000—the value of the surrendered Job A. Choosing either B or C is not rational since the reward is less than the cost.

8. No answer necessary.

9. a. and b. See the diagram below.

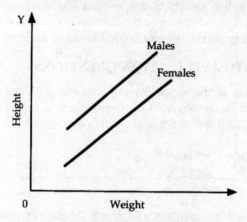

c.  Both positive—as height increases, so does weight.
d.  Probably the lines will be different. Perhaps, at any given height, males may weigh more than females, for example.
e.  Race, geographical location, and age are factors that have been ignored.
f.  i.  See the diagram below.
    ii.  Even if wine is free, consumers are likely to reach a point of satiation. This is shown on the diagram as the quantity at which the line reaches the horizontal axis.
    iii.  It depends on your demand for wine, of course, but probably not. We take up this issue in Chapter 5, when we consider elasticity of demand. In general, we'll find that total spending declines at high prices.

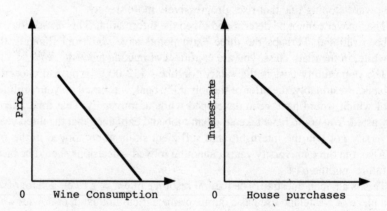

g.  i.  See the diagram above.
    ii.  It depends on the demand for houses, of course, and is shown as the point at which the line reaches the vertical axis.
10. a.  It's a positive relationship.
    b.  The line would be "rising" to the right.
    c.  Rise over run: Y rises by one unit every time X rises by two units, so the slope is +1/2.
    d.  See the diagram below.

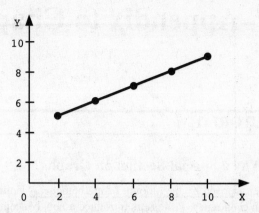

11. Your shortlist of variables probably will include the price of Coors Light, the prices of its competitors, advertising, the time of year, health attitudes, the income of potential buyers (launching a new product during an economic downturn might be difficult, for instance), and so on.

    The negative relationship you will have modelled (if not, why not?) between price and quantity demanded is called the demand curve. A movement along this curve indicates that price has changed causing a change in the amount of beer demanded, with all other variables held constant (*ceteris paribus*). (Keep this conclusion in mind when you read Chapter 4.)

12. Positive statements are testable; normative statements are opinions.
    a.  Positive. A statement need not be correct to be positive.
    b.  Positive. Data can be gathered and analysis undertaken.
    c.  Normative, as signalled by the use of "should".
    d.  Normative. This is an opinion, even during the Great Depression.
    e.  Normative. This is an opinion, as signalled by the use of "should".
    f.  Normative. This is an opinion, as signalled by the use of "should".
    g.  Positive. This statement can be tested.

# *1A* Appendix to Chapter 1

---

## GRAPHING TUTORIAL

---

### Introduction:  Why a Special Section on Graphs?

Many of you will be surprised by the amount of mathematics—geometry in particular—that you encounter in economics. Professors introduce a new concept and quickly draw a graph on the blackboard to illustrate the idea. Once past the initial chapter, the textbook reinforces the notion that economic theory and graphs are inseparable. This unexpected union of a social science course and mathematical methodology baffles some students. Often, you struggle so much with the techniques that you miss the powerful insights that economics has to offer. This section is designed to help you gain a working understanding of graphing techniques and to help you apply this knowledge to economics.

### Why Are Graphs Important?

Graphs are important for several reasons. First, graphs represent a compact way to convey a large amount of information. An old adage says that "one picture is worth one thousand words." This is particularly true in economics as the movement of an economic variable over time or the relationships between two economic variables can be quickly grasped through the use of graphs. Second, as this textbook mentions in the appendix to Chapter 1, economics uses quantitative (mathematical) techniques more than any other social science. Every academic discipline possesses its own "tool kit" that must be mastered in order to truly appreciate the content of the course. In an economic principles class, the primary "tool" is graphs. Third, there is a clear correlation between student success in economics and graphing skills. Research on student performance indicates that of the skills that lead to success (verbal, quantitative reasoning, graphing), graphing ability is vital. Fourth, an important component of a vibrant democratic society is *economic literacy*: a basic understanding of certain central economic concepts. Citizens who follow current events will constantly encounter graphs as prints and television journalists use the visual medium to communicate with their audience.

### Why Graphs Trouble Many Students

There are several factors that may cause you to have difficulty with graphs. Several years may have elapsed since you completed a high-school geometry course. Consequently, many graphing skills that were developed have been forgotten. More fundamentally, you read every day; however, you do not practise math every day. Therefore, most students will enter an economic principles class with a stronger reading ability than a mathematical ability. Because of this, you must remember that the graphs in this textbook are not photographs worthy of only a glance; *graphs must be studied*.

### General Tips for Studying Graphs

Here are some general tips that should assist you in developing your graphing skills:

1.  *Relax*! Remember that math is simply another language; therefore, graphs are just a specific form of communication;

2.  When studying a graph, first identify the labels that are on the graph axes and curves. These labels are like road signs that inform the reader;

3.  Once the labels are recognized, try to understand what economic intuition lies behind the curve (e.g., the demand curve indicates that as the product price falls, the amount that consumers wish to buy increases);

4.  Get into the habit of tracing the graphs that are in the text and copying the graphs as reading notes are taken; and

5.  *Draw, draw, draw*!!! The process of learning economics must be an active process. Graphing skills can be enhanced only by repeated attempts to graph economic concepts.

## What Are Graphs?

Graphs are a visual expression of quantitative information. Economic theory attempts to establish relationships between important concepts. If the value of a concept changes, the concept is considered a *variable*. Graphs illustrate the relationship between two variables. If two variables have a *direct* (positive) relationships, the value of one variable increases as the value of the other variable increases. If two variables have an *inverse* (negative) relationship, the value of one variable decreases as the value of the other variable increases.

**Example 1:** As children get older, they grow taller. Thus, there exists a direct relationship between a child's age and his or her height.

| AGE | 6 | 7 | 8 | 9 | 10 |
|---|---|---|---|---|---|
| HEIGHT (cm) | 120 | 125 | 130 | 135 | 140 |

This relationship can be graphed:

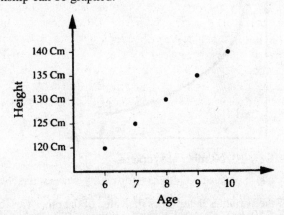

**Example 2:** After attending class, sleeping, eating, and working at a part-time job, a student has seven hours that can be used for studying or socializing. There exists an inverse relationship between time spent studying and time spent socializing.

| STUDYING | 7 | 5 | 3 | 1 | 0 |
|---|---|---|---|---|---|
| SOCIALIZING | 0 | 2 | 4 | 6 | 7 |

A graph of this relationship is shown below:

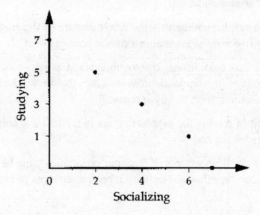

## Types of Graphs

There are two types of graphs. *Descriptive* graphs relate the observed association of two variables. The graphs in Examples 1 and 2 are descriptive graphs. Newspapers often express monthly unemployment data in descriptive graphs. *Analytical* graphs convey the hypothetical relationship, or association, between two variables. The existence of association is derived from economic theory, and its accuracy is the object of economic research.

**Example 3:** An understanding of a firm's goals and its constraints leads to the development of a hypothesis which states that as wages rise, a firm will hire fewer workers. Graphically, this relationship is expressed as:

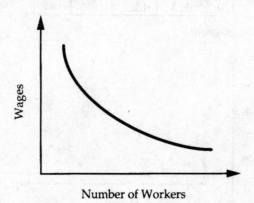

Often, the value of one of the variables determines the value of the other variable. In these cases, the former variable is called the *independent* variable; the latter variable is called the *dependent* variable. Normally (but not always), the independent variable is placed on the horizontal axis and the dependent variable is placed on the vertical axis.

## Drawing Graphs

Earlier, we examined the direct relationship between a child's age and his or her height. One would expect another direct relationship between a child's age and his or her weight.

| AGE | 6 | 7 | 8 | 9 | 10 |
|---|---|---|---|---|---|
| WEIGHT | 35 kg | 37.5 kg | 40 kg | 42.5 kg | 45 kg |

**Example 4:** Graph this relationship below:

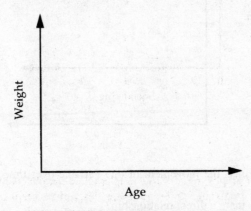

Combining the two series of data yields the table below:

| AGE | 6 | 7 | 8 | 9 | 10 |
|---|---|---|---|---|---|
| HEIGHT (cm) | 120 | 125 | 130 | 135 | 140 |
| WEIGHT (kgs) | 35 | 37.5 | 40 | 42.5 | 45 |

**Example 5:** Graph the height–weight combination for each age.

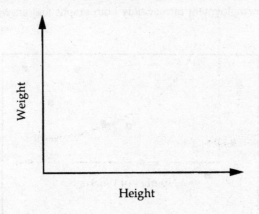

Is the relationship between height and weight direct or inverse? _____

Because the graph depicts the changes in two variables over time, it is called a *scatter diagram*.

**Example 6:** Graph the relationship between the annual Canadian unemployment rate (U%) and the years 1987–1996.

| YEAR | 87 | 88 | 89 | 90 | 91 | 92 | 93 | 94 | 95 | 96 |
|------|-----|-----|-----|-----|------|------|------|------|-----|-----|
| U(%) | 8.9 | 7.8 | 7.5 | 8.1 | 10.4 | 11.3 | 11.2 | 10.4 | 9.5 | 9.7 |

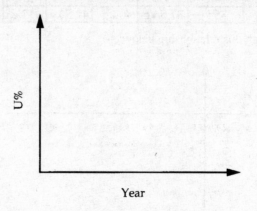

Because this graph depicts the movement of one variable over time, it is called a *time-series graph.*

Between what years is there a direct relationship? _____

Between what years is there an inverse relationship? _____

## Reading Graphs

In addition to graphing economic relationships, students must develop the skill of reading graphs. Below are a time-series graph of the movement of the poverty rates for Canadian families between 1987 and 1995 and a scatter diagram indicating the association between poverty rates and unemployment rates. Study both graphs and answer the questions that follow.

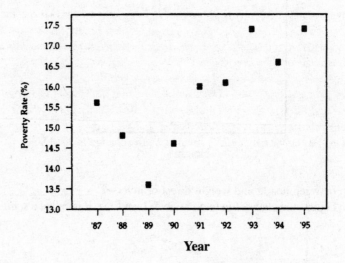

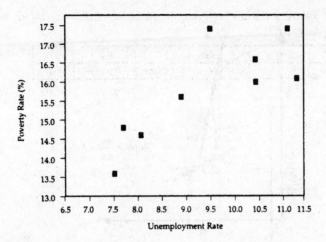

## Example 7:

1. What are the poverty rates in:
   a. 1988 _____
   b. 1992 _____
   c. 1995 _____

2. What are the poverty rate/unemployment rate combinations in:
   a. 1990 _____  _____
   b. 1993 _____  _____
   c. 1995 _____  _____

3. When is there a direct relationship between poverty rates and time?

4. Is there ever an inverse relationship between poverty rates and unemployment rates?

## Understanding and Calculating Slopes

The *slope* of a curve is one measure of the relationship between two variables. It indicates both the type of relationship (direct or inverse) and the rate of change of one variable as the other variable changes. For a straight line, the slope is constant. For a curve, the slope changes from one point along the curve to another. At any particular point, the slope of the curve is identical to the slope of the straight line that is tangent to that point. The slope of a line is calculated by identifying two points on the line and computing the ratio of the change in the variable on the vertical axis and the change in the variable on the horizontal axis. (In high school geometry, this was referred to as "the 'rise'; over the 'run'"; more formally, the slope was the "change in Y ($\Delta Y$) divided by the change in X ($\Delta X$)".)

## Example 8:

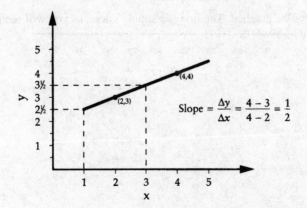

$$\text{Slope} = \frac{\Delta y}{\Delta x} = \frac{4 - 3}{4 - 2} = \frac{1}{2}$$

**Example 9:**

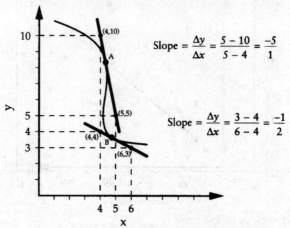

$$\text{Slope} = \frac{\Delta y}{\Delta x} = \frac{5-10}{5-4} = \frac{-5}{1}$$

$$\text{Slope} = \frac{\Delta y}{\Delta x} = \frac{3-4}{6-4} = \frac{-1}{2}$$

In Example 8, any two points along the line will show a slope of 1/2. In Example 9, the slope varies: at point A, the slope is –5; at point B the slope is –1/2. These slope numbers can be interpreted as indicating the unit change in the value of Y in response to a one unit change in X. For Example 8, Y will increase by 1/2 unit in response to a one unit change in X. At point A in Example 9, Y decreases by 5 units and, at point B, Y decreases by 1/2 unit in response to a one unit change in X. The fact that the slope is positive in Example 8 means that there is a direct relationship between X and Y (as X increases, Y increases). The negative slope in Example 9 illustrates an inverse relationship between X and Y (as X increases, Y decreases).

## Solving Equations

Often, the economic relationship between two concepts can be expressed algebraically with an equation. The advantage of this approach is that we can calculate the specific impact that a change in one variable has upon another variable.

**Example 10:** It is a reasonable assumption that as the price of a good rises, more of that good will be supplied. This positive relationship can be expressed with an equation. Let P represent price and Qs represent quantity supplied. For our purposes, let Qs = –10 + 80P. Thus, if P = 1, then Qs = 70. The table below captures this relationship:

| PRICE | 1 | 2 | 3 | 4 | 5 |
|---|---|---|---|---|---|
| QUANTITY SUPPLIED (Qs) | 70 | 150 | 230 | 310 | 390 |

1. What is Qs if P = 7? _____

2. What is Qs if P = 10? _____

The table can be graphed. The line is a supply curve, as you will see in Chapter 4—it is usually labelled "S".

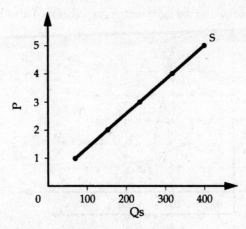

3.  What is the slope of the line? _____

    If the equation is $Qs = -10 + 50P$, the slope of the line will change. Below is a new table:

| PRICE | 1 | 2 | 3 | 4 | 5 |
|---|---|---|---|---|---|
| QUANTITY SUPPLIED (Qs) | 40 | 90 | 140 | 190 | 240 |

4.  Draw this new line on the graph below. Label it S1.

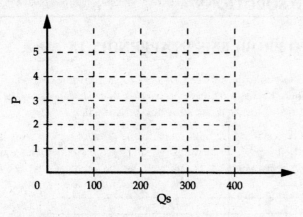

5.  What is the shope of this line? _____

    If the equation for the supply curve is $Qs = -20 + 75P$, answer the questions below.

6.  Complete the following table:

| PRICE | 1 | 2 | 3 | 4 | 5 |
|---|---|---|---|---|---|
| QUANTITY SUPPLIED (Qs) | | | | | |

7. Graph the line represented in the table on the graph below. Label it S2.

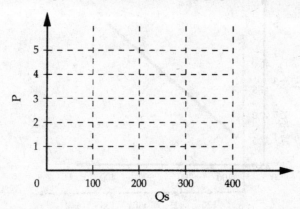

8. What is the slope of the line? _____

9. What is Qs if P = 8? _____

10. What is Qs if P = 20? _____

# ANSWERS AND SOLUTIONS

## SOLUTIONS TO PROBLEMS IN APPENDIX 1A

**Example 4:**

See the diagram below:

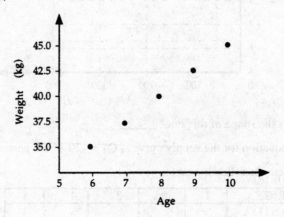

**Example 5:**

See the diagram below:

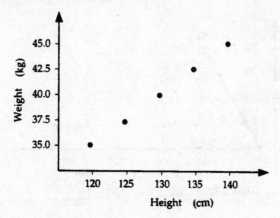

The relationship between height and weight is direct.

**Example 6:**

See the diagram below:

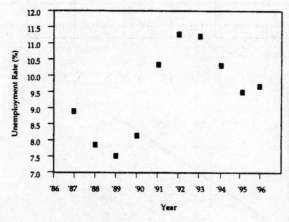

Between 1989 and 1992 there is a direct relationship.
Between 1992 and 1995 there is an inverse relationship.

**Example 7:**

1.  a.  14.8
    b.  16.1
    c.  17.4

2.  a.  14.6 and 8.1
    b.  17.4 and 11.2
    c.  17.4 and 9.5

3.  There is a direct relationship between poverty rates and time from 1989 to 1995.

4.  Yes, there is an inverse relationship between poverty rates and unemployment rates from 1992 to 1993.

**Example 10:**

1.  $Qs = -10 + 80P = -10 + 80(7) = 550$.

2.  $Qs = -10 + 80P = -10 + 80(10) = 790$.

3.    Slope = rise/run = 1/80. A 1 unit increase in P leads to an 80 unit increase in Qs.

4.    See the diagram below.

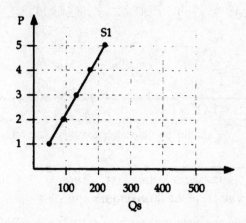

5.    Slope = rise/run = 1/50. A 1 unit increase in P leads to a 50 unit increase in Qs.

6.

| PRICE | 1 | 2 | 3 | 4 | 5 |
|-------|---|---|---|---|---|
| QUANTITY SUPPLIED (Qs) | 55 | 130 | 205 | 280 | 355 |

7.    See the diagram below:

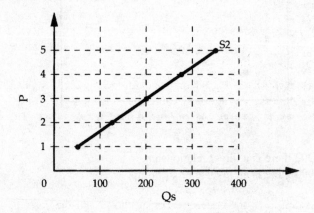

8.    Slope = rise/run = 1/75. A 1 unit increase in P leads to a 75 unit increase in Qs.

9.    $Qs = -20 + 75P = -20 + 75(8) = 580$.

10.   $Qs = -20 + 75P = -20 + 75(20) = 1480$.

# 2 The Economic Problem: Scarcity and Choice

## OBJECTIVES: POINT BY POINT

After completing this chapter, you should be able to accomplish the objectives listed below.

### OBJECTIVE 1: Define the three basic economic questions.

Economics studies the production and consumption choices that are made by society and the outcomes that occur. Solutions must be found to three "basic questions": *what* goods should be produced?; *how* should the goods be produced?; and *for whom* should the goods be produced?

### OBJECTIVE 2: State the significance of scarcity, choice, and opportunity cost.

Every economy (consisting of firms, households, and the government sector) must transform its scarce natural, capital, and human resources into usable production. In a complex society, the opportunity to cooperate and specialize offers great scope for increased production—but decisions must be made regarding the extent of cooperation, who specializes in what, and how goods are distributed. (page 27)

> **Opportunity Cost:** Economics has to do with making choices when constraints (scarcity) are present. Constrained choice occurs, for example, when you go to the grocery store with only a $5 bill in your pocket—you have to make choices based on this limitation. Unconstrained choice would be if you were allowed to take as many groceries home as you wanted, free of charge. Sadly, though, we know there's "no such thing as a free lunch."
>
> Practical examples of the consequences of choice and the costs of such choices include: present vs. future benefits (for example, do you study hard now so that, at exam time, reviewing is easier, or do you take it easy now and sweat it before the exam?), and capital vs. consumer production (for example, should we produce taxicabs or sports cars?).

> **TIP:** Everyone has been confronted with some version of the following scene: A favourite grandmother gives you a free choice from two or more items (ice cream sundaes, for example). From your viewpoint, is your chosen ice cream sundae free? Or is there an opportunity cost? If you have a range of sundaes from which to choose, what is the cost? The dollar amount of the chosen sundae? All the other sundaes you could have had? The opportunity cost is the next most favourite sundae.

## Practice

1. Which of the following statements about the operation of an economy is true? Each economy has a mechanism to determine
   A. what is produced and how much is produced.
   B. how to satisfy all of the desires of its citizens.
   C. how goods and services are distributed among its citizens.
   D. Both A and C.

   **ANSWER:** D. Because resources are limited, the economy cannot satisfy all the desires of its citizens. Therefore, B is incorrect. A and C are correct.

## LEARNING OBJECTIVE 3: Distinguish between absolute and comparative advantage and explain why comparative advantage is critical in the theory of specialization and exchange.

A producer has an absolute advantage over another producer if she can produce each and every product that both can make more efficiently (less costly).

A producer has a *comparative advantage* in the production of Good A if, compared with another producer, she can produce Good A at a lower opportunity cost.

The *theory of comparative advantage* provides the rationale for free trade. Given a two-country, two-good world, Ricardo showed that trading partners can benefit from specialization in the production of the good in which they have the comparative advantage. The increased production could be traded. In terms of the *production possibility frontier* (ppf) diagram, trade will be advantageous if the ppfs have differing slopes because differing slopes indicate differing costs. (page 29)

> **TIP:** If you're like most individuals, you'll need several numerical examples to strengthen your grasp of comparative advantage. The Applications take you through all the steps included in the text.

**Comparative advantage** hinges on the concept of opportunity cost. The producer (person, firm, or country) with the lowest opportunity cost will hold the comparative advantage in that product. Don't be misled—it is irrelevant whether or not the producer can produce *more* of the good. The issue revolves around the relative opportunity costs.

## Practice

Use the following information to answer the next five questions. Arboc and Arbez are two economies that produce computer chips and VCRs. In Arboc, a one-unit increase in computer chips requires a four-unit decrease in VCR production. In Arbez, a one-unit increase in computer chips requires a three-unit decrease in VCR production. In each economy, costs remain constant.

2. Which of the following statements is false?
   A. In Arboc, the opportunity cost of 1 computer chip is 4 VCRs.
   B. In Arbez, the opportunity cost of 1 computer chip is 3 VCRs.
   C. The opportunity cost of 1 computer chip is greater in Arboc than in Arbez.
   D. An increase in the Arbocali production of computer chips requires a decrease in the Arbezani production of VCRs.

**ANSWER:** D. An increase in the Arbocali production of computer chips requires a decrease in the Arbezani production of VCRs. In fact, both independent economies might choose to increase computer-chip production.

3.  Which of the following statements is true?
    A.   In Arboc, the opportunity cost of 1 VCR is 4 computer chips.
    B.   In Arbez, the opportunity cost of 1 VCR is 3 computer chips.
    C.   The opportunity cost of 1 VCR is greater in Arbez than in Arboc.
    D.   Arbez can produce more VCRs than Arboc can produce.

    **ANSWER:** C. We don't know whether Arbez has an absolute advantage in VCRs (Option D). The information tells us only about relative performance. Arbez, in fact, may be a very small country capable of producing only a few VCRs. In Arboc, the opportunity cost of a VCR is 1/4 of a computer chip, and in Arbez, the opportunity cost of a VCR is 1/3 of a computer chip.

4.  In _____, the opportunity cost of 1 computer chip is _____ VCRs, which is less than the opportunity cost of 1 computer chip in _____.
    A.   Arboc, 1/4, Arbez.
    B.   Arboc, 4, Arbez.
    C.   Arbez, 3, Arboc.
    D.   Arbez, 1/3, Arboc.

    **ANSWER:** C. In Arboc, each computer chip "costs" 4 VCRs. In Arbez, each computer chip "costs" 3 VCRs. Computer chips cost less in Arbez.

5.  In _____, the opportunity cost of 1 VCR is _____ computer chips, which is less than the opportunity cost of 1 VCR in _____.
    A.   Arboc, 1/4, Arbez.
    B.   Arboc, 4, Arbez.
    C.   Arbez, 3, Arboc.
    D.   Arbez, 1/3, Arboc.

    **ANSWER:** A. In Arboc, each VCR "costs" 1/4 of a computer chip. In Arbez, each VCR "costs" 1/3 of a computer chip. VCRs cost less in Arboc.

6.  According to the information above,
    A.   Arboc has a comparative advantage in the production of both goods.
    B.   Arboc has a comparative advantage in producing computer chips, and Arbez has a comparative advantage in producing VCRs.
    C.   Arboc has a comparative advantage in producing VCRs, and Arbez has a comparative advantage in producing computer chips.
    D.   Arbez has a comparative advantage in the production of both goods.

    **ANSWER:** C. Arboc has a comparative advantage in the production of VCRs (1 VCR costs 1/4 of a computer chip), and Arbez has a comparative advantage in the production of computer chips (1 computer chip costs 3 VCRs). Note: No country can be relatively better at producing both goods.

# OBJECTIVE 4: Define and use the production possibility frontier.

The ppf shows all the combinations of Good A and Good B that can be produced when all resources are employed efficiently. Points inside the ppf represent unemployment and/or inefficiency, while points outside are currently unattainable. An outward movement of the ppf represents growth. Growth occurs if more resources become available or if existing resources become more productive (e.g., through better education, more efficient techniques of production, or technological innovations). (page 32)

**Production and Economic Efficiency:** The thought of a great volume of production, with all resources employed, is an attractive one. For this reason, it's often difficult to understand that, in serving the needs of consumers, producing the right goods is more important than mere quantity. This distinction lies at the heart of most confusion about productive and economic efficiency. Having the Inuit economy fully employed and producing refrigerators may help you see the point. It would be "better" (more efficient) for the Inuit to have some unemployment but be producing warm clothing. Turning out the refrigerators is productively efficient, while making the warm clothing is economically efficient. Ideally, you'd want to be on the ppf (being productively efficient) and producing the economically efficient mix of output.

**TIP:** Think of the ppf as a way to depict opportunity cost and constrained choice. In general, you want to be somewhere on the curve because any production combination inside the curve means that you're losing production, which is inefficient. Production on the curve means that resources are being used to the maximum (no unemployment). The inefficiency of a mismatch between an "efficient" production mix and society's needs is easily explained—just because we're producing "on the line" doesn't mean we're meeting society's needs as effectively as possible. Employing all our resources to produce taxicabs, for example, is unlikely to be desirable!

**Graphing Pointer:** Suppose we are on the ppf and, at one point, can produce 16 cars and 5 pickups while, at another point, we can produce 12 cars and 7 pickups. Note that the opportunity cost is calculated by looking at the change in production levels—2 extra trucks cost 4 cars.

**Graphing Pointer:** Reducing unemployment does not shift the ppf. Remember the underlying assumptions. The ppf is drawn *given* a set of resources (whether or not the resources are being used). Unemployment represents a situation where the resources are not fully utilized. If unemployment is reduced, the economy moves closer to the ppf.

## Practice

7. Which of the following is an assumption underlying the ppf?
   A. Technological knowledge is fixed.
   B. Resources are not fully employed.
   C. Resources are efficiently employed.
   D. Both A and C.

**ANSWER:** B. When drawing a ppf, all resources are assumed to be fully employed.

8. The production possibility frontier represents
   A. the maximum amount of goods and services that can be produced with a given quantity of resources and technology.
   B. those combinations of goods and services that will be demanded as price changes.
   C. the maximum amount of resources that are available as the wage level changes.
   D. those combinations of goods and services that will be produced as the price level changes.

   **ANSWER:** A. The production possibility frontier represents what it is "possible to produce" given the available resources and technology.

9. The Arbezani economy is operating at a point inside its ppf. This may be because
   A. the economy has very poor technological know-how.
   B. Arbez is a very small nation and can't produce much.
   C. poor management practices have led to an inefficient use of resources.
   D. Arbez has only a small resource base.

   **ANSWER:** C. Very poor technological know-how or a small resource base will result in a ppf that is close to the origin. Fully and efficiently employed resources would still be on the ppf.

Choosing to employ resources for one use prevents them from being employed for other uses—there is an *opportunity cost* involved in the choice. The *production possibility frontier* portrays graphically the opportunity cost of transferring resources from one activity to another in a two-good environment. Assuming that all resources are fully employed, as more of Good A is produced, fewer resources are available to produce Good B. (page 33)

**Why Does the ppf Slope Downward?:** The production possibility frontier is the key piece of economic analysis in this chapter. It's always presented as having only two goods or bundles of goods. It slopes downward because "the more you get of one thing, the less you get of the other." The more you study economics, the less time you have for other activities. The opportunity cost of an extra hour of studying economics is the value of an hour of other activities.

**Graphing Pointer:** When drawing a ppf, remember that the frontier extends from the vertical axis to the horizontal axis. It is a mistake to leave the frontier unconnected to the axes. If the frontier is not connected, it implies that an infinitely large quantity of either good could be produced, which is exactly the opposite message that the ppf is intended to give.

**Graphing Pointer:** Don't be concerned with which goods should be placed on the vertical axis and which goods should be placed on the horizontal axis. This is a case (one of many) where the geometry (a negative slope) is directly linked to economic theory (scarce resources). Recognizing these linkages helps graphical understanding.

## Practice

10.  Along the production possibility frontier, trade-offs exist because
     A.  buyers will want to buy less when price goes up, but producers will want to sell more.
     B.  not all production levels are efficient.
     C.  at some levels, unemployment or inefficiency exists.
     D.  the economy has only a limited quantity of resources to allocate between competing uses.

     **ANSWER:** D. Along the ppf, resources are fully and efficiently employed. However, since resources are scarce, an increase in the production of Good A requires that resources be taken from the production of Good B.

## Other Related Points:

## POINT 1: Explain why increasing opportunity costs occur and how this relates to the production possibility frontier diagram.

Increasing opportunity costs are present when the production possibility frontier bulges outward from the origin. Increasing costs occur if resources are not equally well suited to the production of Good A and Good B.                    (page 34)

## Practice

11. There are increasing costs in the economy of Arbez. To portray this fact in a production possibility diagram, we should
    A. move the ppf outward (up and to the right).
    B. draw the ppf bulging outward.
    C. shift the ppf's end point on the horizontal axis to the right.
    D. shift the ppf's end point on the vertical axis upward.

    **ANSWER:** B. The slope of the ppf represents the behaviour of opportunity cost as production level changes. A straight ppf represents constant costs. To show increasing costs the ppf is bowed outward from the origin.

## POINT 2: Identify ways in which economic growth may occur.

Economic growth may occur if an economy increases the quantity or quality of its resources—the production possibility frontier shifts outward. Additionally, technological change and innovation can increase productivity.                                    (page 35)

> **Investment and Capital:** "Investment" and "capital" are two terms that have very specific meanings in economics. Beware! Investing doesn't just mean buying something. To an economist, investing means only the creation of capital. What, then, is capital? Capital refers to man-made resources usable in production. A hammer is capital; a share of Bell Canada stock is not. A nail is capital; a dollar is not. Buying a hammer or nail is capital investment; buying Bell Canada stock is not.
>
> If this capital/non–capital distinction is giving you problems, ask yourself if the purchase of the item in question increases the economy's ability to produce. If it does, it's an investment in capital.

## OBJECTIVE 5: Identify the two main types of economic systems and describe the strengths and weaknesses of each.

The two "pure" types of economic systems are the command economy and the *laissez-faire* economy. A *command (planned) economy* has a central agency that coordinates production and finds answers for the three basic questions. In a *laissez-faire (market) economy*, the three basic questions are answered through the operation of individual buyers and sellers following their own self-interest in markets.

All economies, in fact, are driven by a mixture of market forces and government intervention and regulation. Government intervention is felt to be necessary to correct *laissez-faire* "mistakes" such as an excessive inequality in the distribution of income, inadequate provision of public goods, and periodic spells of unemployment or inflation.    (page 38)

## Practice

12. Advocates comparing the performance of a pure *laissez-faire* system with that of a command economy would claim that a pure *laissez-faire* system would do all of the following except
    A. promote efficiency.
    B. stimulate innovation.
    C. achieve an equal income distribution.
    D. be directed by the decisions of individual buyers and sellers.

**ANSWER:** C. A pure *laissez-faire* system, which rewards those who contribute most, would have an unequal income distribution.

---

 **PRACTICE TEST**

**I.    MULTIPLE CHOICE QUESTIONS.** Select the option that provides the single best answer.

_____ 1.    Since the nation of Arboc is operating at a point inside its ppf, it
   A.    has full employment.
   B.    has unemployed or inefficiently employed resources.
   C.    must cut output of one good to increase production of another.
   D.    will be unable to experience economic growth.

_____ 2.    Arboc commits more of its resources to capital production than does Arbez. _____ should experience a(n) _____ rapid rate of economic growth.
   A.    Arboc, more.
   B.    Arbez, more.
   C.    Arboc, less.
   D.    Both, equally.

_____ 3.    Which of the following does not count as a productive resource?
   A.    Capital resources, such as a tractor.
   B.    Natural resources, such as a piece of farmland.
   C.    Financial resources, such as a twenty-dollar bill.
   D.    Human resources, such as a hairdresser.

Use the following diagram to answer the next four questions.

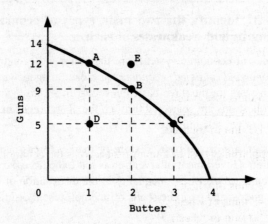

_____ 4.    Point E might become attainable if this economy
   A.    becomes more efficient.
   B.    reduces wages.
   C.    improves the quality of its workforce.
   D.    encourages emigration.

_____ 5. A movement from A to B and then to C indicates that
    A. the cost of additional butter is decreasing.
    B. the cost of additional guns is increasing.
    C. the economy is becoming more efficient.
    D. the cost of additional butter is increasing.

_____ 6. To move from D to A indicates that
    A. the opportunity cost would be zero.
    B. some butter would have to be given up.
    C. there would have to be an increase in the quantity of resources.
    D. the opportunity cost would be 7.

_____ 7. The opportunity cost of producing another unit of butter is
    A. higher at B than at C.
    B. lower at D than at C.
    C. higher at A than at B.
    D. equal at D and at C.

_____ 8. A production possibility frontier illustrates the following concepts
    A. scarcity.
    B. unlimited wants.
    C. opportunity cost as well as scarcity.
    D. both A and C.

_____ 9. Of the following, the least serious problem for _laissez-faire_ economies is
    A. unemployment.
    B. income inequality.
    C. provision of public goods.
    D. satisfaction of consumer sovereignty.

Use the following production possibility table to answer the next three questions. Suppose that wheat is on the Y-axis.

| Alternative | A | B | C | D | E | F |
|---|---|---|---|---|---|---|
| Wheat | 0 | 1 | 2 | 3 | 4 | 5 |
| Tobacco | 15 | 14 | 12 | 9 | 5 | 0 |

_____ 10. The opportunity cost of a unit of wheat as the economy moves from C to D is
    A. –3 units of tobacco.
    B. 3 units of tobacco.
    C. –1/3 unit of tobacco.
    D. 1/3 unit of tobacco.

_____ 11. The opportunity cost of a unit of tobacco as the economy moves from C to B is
    A. 2 units of wheat.
    B. –2 units of wheat.
    C. 1/2 unit of wheat.
    D. –1/2 unit of wheat.

_____ 12. An output of 3 units of wheat and 7 units of tobacco indicates that
    A. this economy has poor technology.
    B. resources are being used inefficiently.
    C. tobacco is preferred to wheat.
    D. it is not possible for this economy to produce at a point on the production possibility frontier.

_____ 13. Which of the following is most likely to shift the production possibility frontier outward?
A. A sudden expansion in the labour force.
B. An increase in stock prices.
C. A shift of productive resources from capital goods to consumer goods.
D. A general increase in the public's demand for goods.

_____ 14. Which of the following is *least* likely to be a public good?
A. Medical treatment for cancer patients.
B. The National Park system.
C. The police force.
D. National defence.

_____ 15. Private markets work best when
A. they are competitive.
B. they are regulated by a government agency.
C. a monopolist is present.
D. public goods are demanded.

_____ 16. The opportunity cost along an increasing-cost ppf must be
A. positive and increasing.
B. positive and decreasing.
C. negative and increasing.
D. negative and decreasing.

_____ 17. For Jill to have a comparative advantage in the production of pins means that, relative to Jack, with the same resources
A. Jill is relatively better at producing pins than at producing needles.
B. Jill is relatively better at producing both pins and needles.
C. Jill can produce fewer needles than Jack can produce.
D. Jill can produce more pins than Jack can produce.

_____ 18. Each of the following is a basic concern of any economic system except
A. the allocation of scarce resources among producers.
B. the mix of different types of output.
C. the distribution of output among consumers.
D. all of the above.

The table below shows the maximum output of each good in each country, e.g., maximum Arbezani production of goat milk is 3 units.

|           | Arbez | Arboc |
|-----------|-------|-------|
| Goat Milk | 3     | 6     |
| Bananas   | 5     | 2     |

_____ 19. According to the table above,
A. Arbez has a comparative advantage in producing both goods.
B. Arbez has a comparative advantage in the production of bananas, and Arboc has a comparative advantage in the production of goat milk.
C. Arbez has a comparative advantage in the production of goat milk, and Arboc has a comparative advantage in the production of bananas.
D. Arboc has a comparative advantage in the production of both goods.

_____ 20. The nation of Regit has a bowed-out production possibility frontier with potatoes on the vertical axis and steel on the horizontal axis. A movement down along the ppf will incur _____ costs; a movement up along the ppf will incur _____ costs.

A. increasing, increasing.
B. increasing, decreasing.
C. decreasing, increasing.
D. decreasing, decreasing.

## II. APPLICATION QUESTIONS.

1. Farmer Brown has four fields that can produce corn or tobacco. Assume that the trade-off between corn and tobacco within each field is constant. The maximum yields are given in this table:

| Field | A | B | C | D |
|---------|----|----|----|----|
| Corn | 40 | 30 | 20 | 10 |
| Tobacco | 10 | 20 | 30 | 40 |

   a. Draw Farmer Brown's ppf.
   b. To be on the ppf, what conditions must hold true?
   c. Brown is currently producing only corn. If he wants to produce some tobacco, in what order would he switch his fields from corn to tobacco production?
   d. Explain your answer to c.

2. Two countries, Arboc and Arbez, produce wine and cheese, and each has constant costs of production. The maximum amounts of the two goods for each country are given in the table below.

| Arboc | Arbez | Goods |
|-------|-------|--------|
| 40 | 120 | wine |
| 20 | 30 | cheese |

   a. Draw the production possibility frontier for each country.

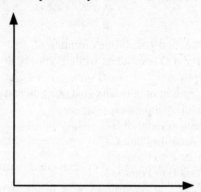

   b. Calculate the opportunity cost of wine in Arboc and in Arbez.
   c. In which country, then, is wine production cheaper?
   d. Answer questions b. and c. for cheese production—remember that the opportunity costs are reciprocals of one another.
   Note that Arbez has an advantage in both goods in terms of total production, but a comparative advantage only in wine production.
   Now assume that Arboc becomes more efficient and can double its output of both wine and cheese.
   e. Graph the new ppf on the diagram above.
   f. Which good should Arboc now produce?
   Suppose, instead, that Arbez has a specific technological advance that permits it to increase cheese production to a maximum of 90.
   g. Now which nation should produce wine?

3. In a national contest, the first prize is a town. The winner receives a furnished house, a general store and gasoline station, a pick-up truck, and 100 hectares of land. The store comes fully stocked with everything you might find in a country general store. The town is located 100 kilometres from a small city. It is the shopping centre for about a thousand families who live in the countryside. In addition, the road through the town is fairly well travelled. Suppose you win the contest and decide to try running the town as a business for at least a year.

  a. Describe the resources available to the economy of your town. What is the potential labour force? What are the natural resources?

  b. Describe the capital stock of your town.

  c. List some of the factors that are beyond your control that will affect your income.

  d. List some of the decisions you must make that could affect your income, and explain what their effects might be.

  e. At the end of the year, you must decide whether to stay or go back to university. How will you decide? What factors will you weigh in making your decision? What role do your expectations play?

4. The following data give the production possibilities of an economy that produces two types of goods, cloth (horizontal axis) and wheat (vertical axis).

| Production Possibilities | Cloth | Wheat |
|---|---|---|
| A | 0 | 105 |
| B | 10 | 100 |
| C | 20 | 90 |
| D | 30 | 75 |
| E | 40 | 55 |
| F | 50 | 30 |
| G | 60 | 0 |

  a. Graph the production possibilities frontier.

  b. Explain why Point D is efficient while Point H (30 units of cloth and 45 units of wheat) is not.

  c. Calculate the per-unit opportunity cost of an increase in the production of cloth in each of the following cases.

    i. From Point A to Point B?
    ii. From Point B to Point C?
    iii. From Point E to Point F?
    iv. From Point F to Point G?

  d. Calculate the per-unit opportunity cost of an increase in the production of wheat in each of the following cases.

    i. From Point G to Point F?
    ii. From Point D to Point C?
    iii. From Point C to Point B?
    iv. From Point B to Point A?

5. Draw a production possibilities frontier with farm goods (x-axis) and manufacturing goods (y-axis) on the axes. In each of the following cases, explain what will happen to the production possibilities frontier.

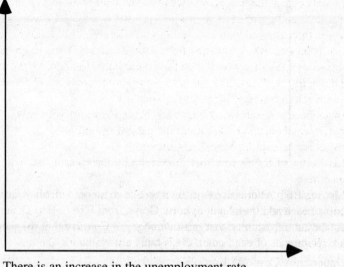

a. There is an increase in the unemployment rate.
b. There is an improvement in farming techniques.
c. There is a decrease in quantity of physical capital.
d. The productivity of workers doubles.
e. The government requires farmers to slaughter a portion of their dairy herds.

6. Consider the following ppf diagram.

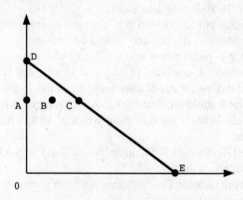

a. Which point is "best" and which is "worst"?
b. Now suppose that you're told that the axes measure food (horizontal) and moonshine whisky (vertical). Would your answer be different?
c. Point B may be preferable to Point D, although Point B is productively less efficient. Why might it be preferable?

7. The nation of Arbez can produce two goods, corn and steel. The table shows some points on the Arbezani ppf.

| Alternative | A | B | C | D | E | F |
|-------------|-----|-----|-----|-----|-----|-----|
| Corn | 0 | 1 | 2 | 3 | 4 | 5 |
| Steel | 20 | 16 | 12 | 8 | 4 | 0 |

a. Draw the ppf in the space below.

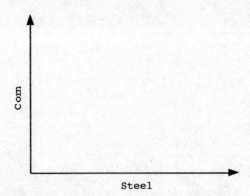

b.   Moving from Alternative A to B, B to C, and so on, calculate the opportunity cost of each additional unit of corn. Going from F to E, E to D, and so on, calculate the opportunity cost *per unit* of steel. Confirm that the pairs of values are reciprocals of each other. (This must always be true.)

Opportunity Cost of 1 Unit of:

| Alternative | Corn | Steel |
|---|---|---|
| A – B | | |
| B – C | | |
| C – D | | |
| D – E | | |
| E – F | | |

c.   Consider each of the following situations.
Situation X: Arbez is producing 4 units of corn and no steel. What is the opportunity cost of 1 extra unit of corn and 1 extra unit of steel?
Situation Y: Arbez is producing 4 units of corn and 4 units of steel.  What is the opportunity cost of 1 extra unit of corn and 1 extra unit of steel?

d.   Why do you find a different set of answers in Situation X and Situation Y?

e.   Now consider a new situation, Situation Z: Arbez is producing 3 units of corn and 5 units of steel. What is the opportunity cost of 1 extra unit of corn and 1 extra unit of steel?

f.   Which Situation (X, Y, or Z) is the most productively efficient and which is the least productively efficient?

g.   On the Arbezani ppf, what is the cost of each unit of corn and what is the cost of each unit of steel?
The nation of Arboc also produces corn and steel. The following table shows some points on the Arbocali ppf.

| Alternative | A | B | C | D | E | F |
|---|---|---|---|---|---|---|
| Corn | 0 | 1 | 2 | 3 | 4 | 5 |
| Steel | 20 | 16 | 12 | 8 | 4 | 0 |

h.   On the Arbocali ppf, what is the cost of each unit of corn and what is the cost of each unit of steel?

i.   Point to ponder: Because steel is relatively cheaper to produce in Arboc/Arbez and corn is relatively cheaper to produce in Arboc/Arbez, might mutually beneficial trade be possible?

8.  Refer to the following diagram.

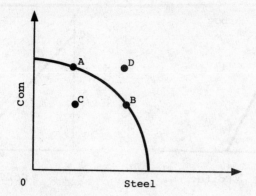

a.  Which point is unattainable?
b.  To achieve this currently unattainable production combination, what must happen (two possible answers)?
c.  Which point represents unemployment or inefficiency?
d.  Will a movement from B to A increase corn production or steel production?
e.  What is the opportunity cost of moving from C to B?

9.  Draw the axes of a ppf. Use corn (on the vertical axis) and steel (on the horizontal axis) as the two goods.

Choose a point, A, that represents some corn and some steel production. Suppose that this point is on the ppf—it's a maximum point. Split the diagram up into quarters, with Point A in the centre.

a.  Is a production mix to the south-west possible?
b.  Would such a mix be productively efficient?
c.  Would such a mix be economically efficient?
d.  Is a move to the north-east quadrant possible? What do you know about it?

Only the north-west and south-east quadrants are possible locations in which productively efficient output alternatives can occur.

e.  What would happen if the present level of corn production (at Point A) was reduced?

If steel production does not change, unemployment occurs. The unemployed resources can be absorbed by the steel industry and more steel can be produced. A parallel case can be made given cutbacks in steel production. Can you see how the ppf must have a negative slope and that it portrays the concept of opportunity cost?

10. Use the diagrams below to answer this question.

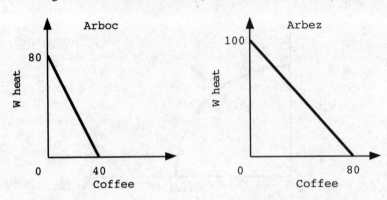

a. What is the opportunity cost of one unit of coffee in Arboc?
b. What is the opportunity cost of one unit of coffee in Arbez?
c. Which country has a comparative advantage in the production of coffee?
d. What is the opportunity cost of one unit of wheat in Arboc?
e. What is the opportunity cost of one unit of wheat in Arbez?
f. Which country has a comparative advantage in the production of wheat?
g. *Ceteris paribus*, ignoring other issues, which good should Arboc produce and which good should Arbez produce?

11. Draw a production possibility curve. Put cloth on the vertical axis and wheat on the horizontal axis. Suppose that the technology for producing wheat improves but the technology for producing cloth does not. Describe how your diagram would change. In general, how will this technological advance affect the opportunity cost of producing cloth?

12. Jennie has set 10 hours this weekend to study for an Economics test and a Physics test. She believes that, with no studying at all, she would score 40 points on each test. Suppose that for each hour studying Economics, she can raise her Economics score by 10 points, and that for each hour studying Physics, she can raise her Physics score by five points.

a. Draw a production possibility frontier graph and show all the points that are feasible if Jennie has 10 hours to divide between Economics and Physics. Put "hours of study for Economics" on the vertical axis and "hours of study for Physics" on the horizontal axis.

b.  Show Point A, where Jennie studies Econ. for 5 hours and Physics for 5 hours.

c.  Show Point B, where Jennie studies Econ. for 0 hours and Physics for 10 hours.

d.  True or false? Jennie can score 60 on the Econ. test and 80 on the Physics test.

e.  True or false? Jennie is lying when she tells us that, in fact, she scored 80 on both tests.

f.  Jennie decides to spend 4 hours studying for the Econ. test. What's the highest score she can expect to get on the Physics test?

g.  If Jennie was satisfied with 60 on both tests, how many hours would she have had to study?

h.  True or false? If Jennie scored 70 on both tests, we know that she did not study for the full 10 hours.

i.  Draw a line (labelled EE) showing all the points which have exactly 2 hours of study time for the Econ. test.

---

## ANSWERS AND SOLUTIONS

## PRACTICE TEST

### I.  SOLUTIONS TO MULTIPLE CHOICE QUESTIONS

1.  B. To be on the ppf, Arboc must have all of its resources fully and efficiently employed. Since it is operating inside the ppf, at least one of these conditions must have been violated.

2.  A. If Arboc produces relatively more capital, then it is expanding its resource base more rapidly and, *ceteris paribus*, it will grow more rapidly.

3.  C. Financial resources may be used to purchase real productive resources but are not themselves productive. Note that, to an economist, "investment" is the creation of real productive capacity, not merely the purchase of stock in a company.

4.  C. To reach Point E the economy must grow, shifting out its ppf. This could occur if the labour force became more efficient.

5.  D. This is an increasing cost ppf. As we increase the production of one good (butter), the cost in terms of the other good increases. In this case, a one-unit increase in butter (A to B) costs three guns; the move from B to C costs more (four guns).

6.  A. Opportunity cost is defined (loosely) as the quantity of Good B given up to increase production of Good A. The quantity of butter remains at one unit while gun production is increased.

7.  B. See the answer to Question 6. Opportunity cost of one unit of butter is zero at Point D. The opportunity cost of one unit of butter at Point C is five guns.

8.  D. The ppf depicts what it is possible to produce but nothing about what is wanted. Therefore B is the odd one.

9.  D. *Laissez-faire* economies respond well to the needs of private consumers, in general. One exception worth noting is the provision of public goods.

10. B. The opportunity cost is positive. A one-unit increase in wheat results in a three-unit decrease in tobacco production.

11. C. A two-unit increase in tobacco results in a one-unit decrease in wheat.

12. B. This point is inside the ppf. (We could be producing two more units of tobacco with the same amount of wheat production, for example.) This indicates that our resources are unemployed and/or inefficiently employed.

13. A. The labour-force expansion represents an increase in productive resources. Note that the ppf depicts what can be supplied—demand is not reflected in the diagram.

14. A. Parks, police, and defence, which become available to all once they become available, do not lend themselves to private sale and purchase as readily as cancer treatment. The benefits of treatment can be retained exclusively by the purchaser.

15. A. A general theme in economics is that private competition is highly efficient in providing most goods.

16. A. Opportunity cost is *always* positive. With a curving ppf, the cost of producing one good in terms of the other accelerates as production level increases.

17. A. Comparative advantage is a relative concept. If, relative to Jack, Jill is better at producing pins, then she has a comparative advantage in this.

18. D. The first three answers are statements of the three "basic" questions. They are all correct.

19. B. The cost of one unit of goat milk in Arbez is 1 and 2/3 unit of bananas while the cost of one unit of goat milk in Arboc is 1/3 unit of bananas. Arboc has the advantage here. One unit of bananas in Arbez costs 3/5 unit of goat milk while one unit of bananas in Arboc costs 3 units of goat milk. Arbez has the advantage in bananas.

20. A. A bowed-out ppf indicates increasing costs; the costs increase whether the movement is down along the ppf or up along the ppf.

## II. SOLUTIONS TO APPLICATION QUESTIONS

1. a.    Your ppf should include the following points:

| Corn    | 100 | 90 | 70 | 40 | 0   |
|---------|-----|----|----|----|-----|
| Tobacco | 0   | 40 | 70 | 90 | 100 |

There will be a straight line between each of the points.

b.    Resources must be fully employed, and employed in the more efficient activity. For example, Field A may be producing its maximum output of tobacco, but (since the opportunity cost of tobacco production in that field is high) it should be used to produce tobacco only after the other fields have been switched over to tobacco production. If it is switched before Field B, for instance, Brown will be producing inefficiently and inside his ppf.

c.    D, C, B, A.

d.    See the explanation for b.

2. a, e.    See the diagrams below.

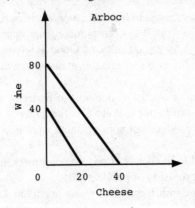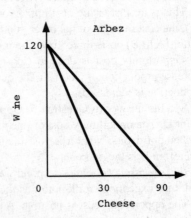

b.    1 wine = 1/2 cheese, 1 wine = 1/4 cheese.

c.    Arbez.

d.    1 cheese = 2 wine (Arboc), 1 cheese = 4 wine (Arbez). Arboc can produce cheese more cheaply than Arbez can.

f.    Arboc should still produce cheese since the comparative costs have not changed.

g.  Arboc. Recompute the opportunity costs. Note that the relative steepness of the ppfs has changed.

3.  a-b.  This question is intended to get you to think about all of the decisions that must be made in an economic system. The owner has land, labour, and capital at his/her disposal. The capital stock includes the store, the gas station, inventories, trucks, the house, and so forth. The road is also capital even though it was produced by the government. We are not told much about the natural resources of the town. These would include the fertility of the land. The potential labour force includes some fraction of those who live nearby.

c.  The people who travel the road, the general economic circumstances of the people who live nearby, the weather, gasoline prices, the potential for competition from other stores, and so forth.

d.  What to sell, whether to advertise, what prices to change, whether to fix up the town, how many people to hire, and so forth.

e.  I will add up all the future income I will earn, net of costs. I must consider all the alternatives and my expectations about them. How much will I earn here? How much will university cost? What am I likely to earn when I have graduated from university? I also need to consider carefully the personal pleasure I will derive from the two situations.

4.  a.  See the diagram below.

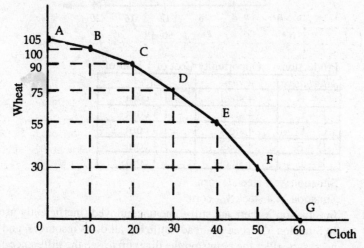

b.  Point D is on the ppf, indicating full employment of resources, while Point H is inside the curve, indicating underproduction and an underutilization of scarce resources.

c.  i.    1/2 unit of wheat.
    ii.   1 unit of wheat.
    iii.  21/2 units of wheat.
    iv.   3 units of wheat.

d.  i.    1/3 units of cloth.
    ii.   2/3 units of cloth.
    iii.  1 unit of cloth.
    iv.   2 units of cloth.

5.  a.  No change in the position of the ppf.

b.  The end of the ppf on the x-axis will shift out. The end on the y-axis will not move.

c.  The ppf would shift inward.

d.  The ppf would shift outward.

e.  The end of the ppf on the x-axis will shift in. The end on the y-axis will not move.

6. a. You might think C and A are "best" and "worst," respectively—but the question is a trap. What do we mean by "best"? Perhaps a particular point inside the ppf is better than a particular point on it. There's not enough information to give a complete answer.

   b. Clearly, all points on the ppf are not created equal, and Point E might be the "best" choice of those depicted.

   c. The "best" output mix depends on what best meets society's wants. If you think about it, what society *wants* isn't shown on a ppf diagram—only what can be *produced*.

7. a. See the diagram below.

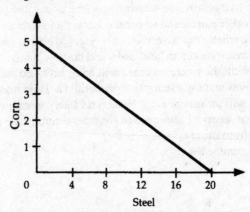

   b.
   | Production | Opportunity Cost of 1 Unit of: | |
   |---|---|---|
   | Alternative | Corn | Steel |
   | A – B | 4 steel | 1/4 corn |
   | B – C | 4 steel | 1/4 corn |
   | C – D | 4 steel | 1/4 corn |
   | D – E | 4 steel | 1/4 corn |
   | E – F | 4 steel | 1/4 corn |

   c. Situation X: 0 steel; 0 corn.
   Situation Y: 4 steel; 1/4 corn.

   d. In Situation X there are still some unemployed (inefficiently used) resources. In Situation Y, Arbez is already utilizing all of its resources, and a trade-off is necessary. (Plot the points on the diagram to see the difference.)

   e. Situation Z: 1 steel; 0 corn.

   f. Situation Y is the most productively efficient. Either X or Z is the least productively efficient—we don't have enough information.

   g. Each unit of corn costs 4 units of steel; each unit of steel costs 1/4 unit of corn.

   h. Each unit of corn costs 2 units of steel. Each unit of steel costs 1/2 unit of corn.

   i. Arbez; Arboc. Yes, trade can be mutually beneficial.

8. a. D.

   b. The economy must either grow (more resources) or experience a technological improvement.

   c. C.

   d. Corn.

   e. There is no opportunity cost; more steel is produced without any reduction in corn production. Note that there are "free lunches" if the economy is operating at an inefficient point.

9. a. Yes.

   b. No, because it is possible to produce more of each good. Also some resources are unemployed.

  c.  No, not relative to Point A, where consumers would have more of each good available to them.

  d.  It is beyond the maximum level of production, given current resources and technology.

  e.  Resources would be released and transferred to steel production.

10. a.  2 units of wheat.

  b.  1 1/4 units of wheat.

  c.  Arbez.

  d.  1/2 unit of coffee.

  e.  8/10 unit of coffee.

  f.  Arboc.

  g.  Arboc should specialize in wheat production and Arbez should specialize in coffee production.

11. The ppf would pivot at its "cloth" end point and become flatter, which indicates that it is possible to produce a greater maximum quantity of wheat than before, while still producing the same maximum quantity of cloth. The slope of the ppf represents opportunity cost. Producing only cloth means that we surrender a larger quantity of wheat than before—the opportunity cost of cloth has increased (and the opportunity cost of wheat has decreased).

12. a.  See the diagram below.

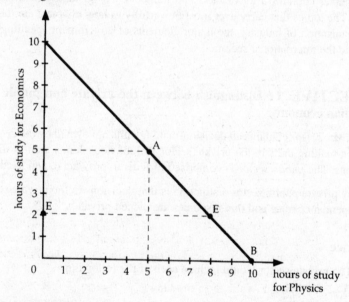

  b.  See the diagram above.

  c.  See the diagram above.

  d.  True. Economics: 40 + (10 x 2) = 60. Physics: 40 + (5 x 8) = 80.

  e.  True. Economics: 40 + (10 x 2) = 60. Physics: 40 + (5 x 8) = 80. If she gets 80 on the Physics test, 60 is the maximum she can get on the Economics test.

  f.  She has 6 hours for Physics. Physics: 40 + (5 x 6) = 70.

  g.  Economics: 40 + (10 x 2) = 60. Physics: 40 + (5 x 4) = 60. This totals 6 hours.

  h.  True. Economics: 40 + (10 x 3) = 70. Physics: 40 + (5 x 6) = 70. This totals 9 hours.

  i.  See the diagram above.

# 3 The Structure of the Canadian Economy: The Private, Public, and International Sectors

## OBJECTIVES: POINT BY POINT

After completing this chapter, you should be able to accomplish the objectives listed below.

### General Comment

This chapter contains a lot of facts and numbers. Try to look past these to the broader issues. The topics that carry over most powerfully to later chapters are those dealing with the organization of industry, the major elements of government spending and tax collection, and the international sector.

### OBJECTIVE 1: Distinguish between the private and public sectors of the Canadian economy.

The *private sector* contains all decision-making units not owned by the government. These decision-making units in the private sector include households, non-profit organizations, and firms. The *public sector* is comprised of federal, provincial, and local governments.

The key private/public sector distinction is that decisions in the private sector are subject to independent choice and that resources are owned privately. (page 49)

### Practice

1.  The private sector would include each of the following
    A.  Nortel.
    B.  Noranda.
    C.  Canada Post.
    D.  Both A and B.

    **ANSWER:** C. Canada Post is a Crown corporation. Although a Crown corporation is different from a government department, it is still accountable to its respective federal or provincial government, and therefore not part of the private sector.

2.  The public sector would include each of the following organizations except
    A.  the United Way, a charitable organization.
    B.  the Federal Department of Finance.
    C.  the office staff of your local MP.
    D.  both B and C.

    **ANSWER:** D. The United Way is a private non-profit organization, and not part of the public sector. Both B and C are.

## OBJECTIVE 2: Describe the diversity of consumption and production activities engaged in by Canadian households.

As consumers, Canadian households purchase a wide variety of goods and services dictated by their diverse tastes, preferences, and income. There are thousands of occupations in Canada. Some are high-paying jobs and some low-paying jobs. Furthermore, many Canadians earn income because of their ownership of real and financial assets, which are not evenly distributed.

When we look at the productive activities of Canadian households we notice even more dramatic diversity. There are as many specialized jobs requiring specialized tools or intellectual powers, as there are workers. (page 49)

## Practice

3. The most popular category of occupation of Canadians, in 1996 was
   A. Arts, Culture, Recreation and Sport.
   B. Business, Finance, and Administrative Occupations.
   C. Sales and Service Occupations.
   D. Health Occupation.

   **ANSWER:** C. There are over 3.7 million working in this sector, more than any other sector in this country, in 1996.

4. The highest income earners in Canada, in 1999 are
   A. Lawyers.
   B. Investment Dealers.
   C. Plumbers.
   D. Physicians.

   **ANSWER:** D. The average income of physicians in that year was more than $107,000—more than other income groups.

## OBJECTIVE 3: Describe the three main legal forms taken by Canadian business firms.

*Sole proprietors* have the disadvantage of unlimited liability—their personal assets, outside the firm, might be taken if their company runs up sufficiently high debts. Advantage: The sole proprietors are their own boss and are free to follow their business instincts. Also, they keep all of the profits they make. Usually, *partnerships* have the same unlimited liability drawback. Indeed, perhaps it's worse—partners may be held responsible not only for their own debts, but also for those of their partners. Advantage: greater expertise and financial resources. *Corporations* have the advantage of limited liability because they exist as separate legal entities—XYZ, Inc. can be taken to court. If the firm runs up debts, the owners' maximum liability is the value of their stock investment. After-tax profits may be distributed as dividends or held by the company as retained earnings. A major disadvantage is that the corporation's management structure may become cumbersome. Also, owners of corporations are subject to double taxation. (page 52)

## Practice

5. The most common form of business organization is
   A. the proprietorship.
   B. the partnership.
   C. perfect competition.
   D. the corporation.

   **ANSWER:** A. See page 52.

6. In terms of total economic activity, the most important form of business organization is
   A. the proprietorship.
   B. the partnership.
   C. monopoly.
   D. the corporation.

   **ANSWER**: D. See page 53.

7. The Cumfy Chair Corporation has a net income of $300 000 in 1998. Of this income, $160 000 is paid in taxes and $40 000 is retained to buy capital. The Cumfy Chair Corporation will pay dividends of
   A. $140 000.
   B. $120 000.
   C. $100 000.
   D. more than $100 000 but less than $140 000.

   **ANSWER:** C. Net income—the profits of a corporation—may be split up into corporate income tax payments, dividends, and retained earnings.

## OBJECTIVE 4: State the main characteristics of the Canadian public sector.

The Canadian public sector is organized on a federal basis. The Canadian federal system has two levels of government, federal and provincial, enjoying a special constitutional status. The federal government has jurisdiction over national defence and an integrated economy and is responsible for employment insurance, old age security, and the Canadian Pension Plan. Provincial governments are responsible for medical care, social welfare and education.

There is a third level of government—municipal governments. Municipal governments do not have constitutional power and are subordinate to provincial governments. (page 56)

## OBJECTIVE 5: Outline the sources of government revenue and the main areas of government expenditure.

The government is a major employer of resources and purchaser of goods. The federal government is the largest branch of government. Today, the largest components of federal spending are the interest payment on the national debt and transfers to persons and other levels of government; however, spending on goods and services—education, health and hospitals, and highways—is the main expenditure category for provincial and local governments.

The main sources of federal revenue, in order of importance, are personal income tax, general sales taxes, health and insurance levies, and corporate income tax. At the provincial and local levels, property taxes are immediately behind personal income tax. See Table 3.9.
(page 59)

> **TIP:** Note the important distinction between government purchases and transfer payments—the former is a payment for goods and services received by the government; the latter is not. A welfare cheque is given precisely because the recipient is *not* providing a service.

## Practice

8. The salary of your local MP is classified as
   A. a government transfer payment.
   B. a government interest payment.
   C. government spending.
   D. a government subsidy payment.

   **ANSWER:** C. Your local MP's salary (which he or she has earned for work performed) is government spending. A transfer payment is a payment that requires no good or service in return. Your member of Parliament would strongly resent the implication if you answered Option A.

9. The largest single source of federal revenue is
   A. sales taxes.
   B. property taxes.
   C. health and insurance levies.
   D. personal income tax.

   **ANSWER:** D. See Table 3.9 and p. 60.

10. The largest single source of provincial and local revenue is
    A. sales taxes.
    B. property taxes.
    C. corporate taxes.
    D. personal income taxes.

    **ANSWER:** D. See Table 3.9 and p. 60.

## Other Related Points:

## POINT 1: Describe and give reasons for the changing expenditure patterns within the three levels of government over the past decade.

A study of the structure of the Canadian public sector brings out three important features. First, the provincial/local/hospital sector is a much more important provider of goods and services than the federal government. The provincial governments have primary responsibility for health, social services, and roads. Second, the federal government is more active in directly transferring income than other levels of government combined. Finally, debt charges are most significant at the federal level. (page 57)

## OBJECTIVE 6: Discuss the importance of international trade to Canada.

International trade has always played an important role in the growth of the Canadian economy. This role has become more significant in recent years. Canada's trade pact with Mexico and the United States, NAFTA, has contributed to the growth of our trade. (page 61)

## Practice

11. In 1995 exports were _____ of GDP and imports were _____ of GDP.
    A. 25%, 18%.
    B. 28%, 20%.
    C. 30%, 15%.
    D. 43%, 40%.

    **ANSWER:** D. See p. 61.

## PRACTICE TEST

**I.   MULTIPLE CHOICE QUESTIONS.** Select the option that provides the single best answer.

_____ 1.   Which of the following would not be included in the private sector?
A.   The bookstore chain "Chapters."
B.   Alcan Aluminum Ltd.
C.   University of Victoria.
D.   The local charity organization "Meals on Wheels."

_____ 2.   The type of business organization with limited liability from debt for its owner(s) is a
A.   proprietorship.
B.   partnership.
C.   corporation.
D.   company.

_____ 3.   Statement 1: "After all the corporation's expenses have been paid, the retained earnings are distributed to the stockholders."
Statement 2: "Welfare cheques are a part of transfer payments."
Statement 1 is _____; Statement 2 is _____.
A.   false, false.
B.   true, true.
C.   false, true.
D.   true, false.

_____ 4.   Government expenditures are made up of
A.   government purchases, transfer payments, and interest payments.
B.   government purchases, welfare payments, and national defence.
C.   transfer payments, national defence, and employment benefits (EI).
D.   transfer payments, tax payments, and interest payments.

_____ 5.   The biggest single revenue earner for the federal government is the
A.   personal income tax.
B.   corporate income tax.
C.   sales tax.
D.   payroll tax.

_____ 6.   As a percentage of GDP, the federal interest payment on the public debt _____ between 1970 and 1995.
A.   has increased.
B.   has decreased.
C.   has remained unchanged.
D.   has not been considered as a government outlay.

_____ 7.   Which of the following is not a government transfer payment?
A.   Old Age Security payments.
B.   Employment insurance payments (EI).
C.   Payments to the widow of a war veteran.
D.   Payroll taxes payment by an employee.

## II.    APPLICATION QUESTIONS.

1.  Are your local radio broadcasts a public good? Are Céline Dion's concerts a public good? Of the two goods, why is the market system more likely to underproduce radio broadcasts? In practice, how has radio reduced the problem of non-payers?

2.  Suppose that you are a senior advisor to Federal Minister of Finance, Paul Martin. The government has committed to balancing the budget before the next election, and Mr. Martin asks you how this can be achieved. (Remember, if the current government is not returned to office, you lose your job!)

    Come up with three distinct policy recommendations. If the government cuts expenditures, where should the cuts fall? Be specific. Who would be hurt by such a proposal? Would it affect particular social or regional groups? Does the political power of a province, such as Ontario or Quebec, have any bearing on the political decision process? If taxes are to be raised, which ones? Again, who might be hurt by a specific tax hike? Should producers be taxed, or should consumers? Wage earners or investors? Are there any parts of the budget that are "not negotiable" (education or health care, for example)?

3.  Give the advantages and disadvantages of organizing a firm as a
    a.   proprietorship.
    b.   partnership.
    c.   corporation.
    d.   Give an example of each form of business organization.

4.  You are considering setting up a small business. Which factors would you take into account when deciding whether to establish a single proprietorship or a partnership?

5.  Think up a simple business enterprise—such as doing yard work, typing term papers, opening a hot dog stand, or selling vitamins—and decide which would be the most appropriate form of legal organization for your firm. Why is this form of organization the best choice? List the drawbacks that might occur. How might you solve the problems? What advantages do the other forms of organization offer, for example? If you have a proprietorship, how would you feel about giving up control/ownership of "your" business to a group of unknown shareholders and about making decisions by committee?

    Major point: No single legal organization is always "best"—it depends upon the particular circumstances of the business and the objectives of the owner(s).

6.  In a sense, the three levels of government specialize. For the federal government, Revenue Canada and Foreign Affairs and International Trade are major sources of employment. Why? Because there's a need for a "national" organization. At the provincial level, education, health, and highways are the main sources of employment. At the local level, fire, police, and sanitation (all "local" issues) are prominent.

    Now do a thought experiment: Try to imagine what would happen if Ottawa tried to control fire, police, and sanitation, while turning national defence over to local government. Not very efficient! Also, observe that the public sector can *complement* private endeavours through the provision of public goods (roads and education, for example) and through the enforcement of compliance with a legal system designed to protect the rights of private consumers and firms.

7.  What are the three kinds of legal organization for the firm? List them and give your own example of the sort of firm you'd expect to find in each category.

8. List the four factors used in defining market organization. Into which market structure is entry easiest?

9. Which form of legal organization is most likely for each of the following businesses?
   a. Coca-Cola _____
   b. an accounting firm _____
   c. a legal firm _____
   d. a plumbing firm _____
   e. a car manufacturer _____
   f. a small corn grower _____
   g. a small convenience store _____
   h. the Music Channel _____
   i. a law firm _____
   j. McDonald's _____

In each case, which factors led you to your answer, and what do you think is the main advantage that each firm derives from this form of organization?

# ANSWERS AND SOLUTIONS

## PRACTICE TEST

### I. SOLUTIONS TO MULTIPLE CHOICE QUESTIONS

1. C. Universities in Canada are financed by the government.
2. C. Corporations have limited liability. See p. 52. Note that a partnership may have limited liability, but only in some cases.
3. C. Retained earnings are just that—retained (by the corporation). Welfare cheques are payments that do not require a service in return—i.e., transfers.
4. A. National defence is an element in government purchases, and welfare payments as well as EI are included in the more general category of "transfer payments."
5. A. Personal income taxes are now the largest component of federal revenues. See Table 3.9.
6. A. See Table 3.7.
7. D. This is a tax payment by an individual to the government.

### II. SOLUTIONS TO APPLICATION QUESTIONS

1. Local radio broadcasts are a public good—my consumption does not diminish your consumption. A public concert is not a public good—if I buy a seat, fewer seats are available for others. The market system is likely to underproduce local radio because it is impossible to exclude non-payers. In practice, commercial radio does not sell programming to listeners; it sells listeners to advertisers who pay for advertising time.
2. The answer to this question is open to opinion. Most economists would claim that, to cut the deficit, the government must increase taxes or reduce transfer payments and expenditures.
3. a. proprietorship: advantages—the proprietor is his own boss, keeps all the profits, the firm is flexible, possible tax breaks
   disadvantages—unlimited liability, no pool of specialized experience at the top

b. partnership:    advantages—pool of expertise
disadvantages—unlimited liability, less flexibility, greater need
for consultation between partners

c. corporation:    advantages—limited liability, market power, political power
disadvantages—possible lack of communication and coordination

d. proprietorship—corner grocery store; partnership—law firm; corporation—Petro-Canada.

4.  The most important consideration is likely to be financial—can the business be started without outside help. Additionally, can the business be run effectively with only one individual in control—can a manager be hired?

5-6. The answer to each question is open to opinion.

7.  Proprietorship, a family grocery store; partnership, a legal firm; corporation, a manufacturing firm.

8.  Market organization (the way an industry is structured) is defined by how many firms there are in the industry, whether products are differentiated or are virtually the same, whether or not firms in the industry can control prices or wages, and whether or not competing firms can enter and leave the industry freely.

9.  a. corporation.
    b. partnership.
    c. partnership.
    d. proprietorship.
    e. corporation.
    f. proprietorship.
    g. proprietorship.
    h. corporation.
    i. partnership.
    j. corporation.

# 4 Demand, Supply, and Market Equilibrium

## OBJECTIVES: POINT BY POINT

After completing this chapter, you should be able to accomplish the objectives listed below.

### General Comment

The single best piece of advice, particularly for this essential chapter, is "practise, practise, practise." A second piece of advice must be "draw, draw, draw." Don't be put off by the graphs—try to develop a solid intuitive feel for demand and supply by talking your way through how the market should behave.

In most of the multiple choice questions in this chapter, the *first* thing to do is to start to sketch a demand and supply picture.

Get into the habit of asking "What should happen to demand?" and "Will this make supply increase or decrease?" Predict whether price should rise or fall in a given circumstance (common sense should carry you a long way here). Don't try to avoid graphs—they'll make your course a lot easier *and* more rewarding. If you have some initial problems, check the Appendix to Chapter 1 and the "Graphing Pointers" sections in this Guide.

### OBJECTIVE 1: Describe the relationship between input and output markets in a simple market economy.

To produce goods and services, firms buy resources or inputs. The markets in which the resources (inputs) used to produce products (output) are exchanged are called input or factor markets. The markets in which goods and resources are exchanged are called product or output markets. (page 66)

### OBJECTIVE 2: Explain the role of price and other factors in the basic theory of demand.

The willingness and ability of a household to buy units of a good (quantity demanded) are likely to depend principally on the price of the good itself. Other factors—including the household's income and wealth, the prices of other products, tastes and preferences, and expectations about price, income, and wealth—will influence demand.

> **Comment:** This section of the textbook will probably be your most frustrating section. Be patient—time spent understanding demand/ supply analysis will serve you well in future chapters.

*Quantity demanded* is the amount of a product that a household would buy, in a given period, if it could buy all it wanted at the current price. The *law of demand* states that there is a negative relationship between the price and the quantity demanded of a product. When the price of McDonald's fries increases, we buy less.

A *demand schedule* is a table showing how much of a given product households would be willing and able to buy at different prices in a given time period; a *demand curve* shows this relationship graphically. Demand curves slope downward. (page 69)

> **Graphing Pointer:** These graphs *always* have price on the vertical axis and quantity (demanded or supplied, as appropriate) on the horizontal axis. It is a bad, though common, mistake to reverse the variables.

> **Graphing Pointer:** Learn to draw the demand and supply graphs quickly. A demand curve slopes down; a supply curve slopes up. Practise to increase your speed. Label each curve as you go. In diagrams where there are several curves, clear, consistent labelling is critical.

## Practice

1.

| Price per apple | Quantity demanded |
|---|---|
| 60¢ | 30 |
| 50¢ | 35 |
| 40¢ | 50 |
| 30¢ | 55 |
| 20¢ | 70 |
| 10¢ | 80 |

Suppose the above is your demand schedule for apples. In the blank space to the right of the demand schedule, draw vertical (price) and horizontal (quantity) axes. Plot your monthly demand curve for apples. Label the curve $D_1$.

**ANSWER:** This line is unlikely to be smooth like those in the textbook, but it should have a general downward slope—the lower the price, the more you're likely to buy. You should have the horizontal axis labelled "quantity demanded" and the vertical axis labelled "price."

When you constructed your demand schedule and demand curve with varying price levels in Practice Question 1, you made assumptions about your income level, wealth, prices of other goods, and so on. Change the assumptions and you will change the diagram. The curve shifts position—*a change in demand*.

Factors that can cause a change in demand are:
a.  income.
b.  wealth.
c.  prices of related products.
d.  tastes or preferences of the household.
e.  expectations.

Increases in income and wealth, improved preferences, or expectations of a higher price, income, or wealth will increase demand for normal goods. An increase in the price of a substitute product or a decrease in the price of a complementary product will also increase demand, i.e., the entire demand curve shifts to the right. Graphically, an increase in demand ($D_1$ to $D_2$) appears as shown below:

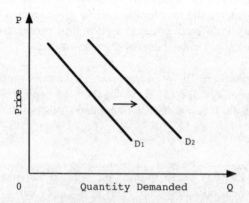

**TIP:** When shifting the demand or supply curve, think in terms of the curve sliding *left* for a decrease (demand less or supply less) and *right* for an increase (demand more or supply more), *not* up and down.

**Graphing Pointer:** You might naturally associate "rise" and "fall" with a vertical shift. This causes no problems in the case of demand, and you'd expect to be correct in using the same approach in the case of supply—but you'd be wrong.

# OBJECTIVE 3: Distinguish between changes in quantity demanded (movements along the demand curve) and changes in demand (shifts in the demand curve).

When important factors other than the price of the product change, such as tastes or income, the entire demand curve shifts position. This is called a *change in demand* to distinguish it from a movement along the demand curve, which represents a *change in quantity demanded* and which can be caused *only* by a change in the price of the commodity.

(page 73)

**Graphing Pointer: Changes in Quantity Demanded (Supplied) vs. Changes in Demand (Supply).** Some students experience confusion regarding the distinction between a "change in quantity demanded" and a "change in demand." Perhaps the distinction is rather artificial; the six factors (listed on page 75) that affect demand do include price of the product. However, we regard the price–quantity demanded relationship as the most important and draw the demand curve with these two variables on the axes, assuming that all other factors are fixed at a "given" level. This is the *ceteris paribus* assumption.

Look at a demand curve; price and quantity demanded can have a range of values while all other variables (income, other prices, etc.) are fixed at a particular level. If price changes, we move along the curve; if another factor changes, our *ceteris paribus* assumption is broken and we must redraw the price–quantity demanded relationship.

The *only* thing that can cause a "change in the quantity demanded" of Pepsi is a change in the price of Pepsi—a movement from one point on the demand curve to another point on the same demand curve.

**Pointer, continued:** If any other factor on the list changes, we will have to redraw the entire diagram—a "change in demand"—because the "all else being equal" assumption has been broken.

Similarly, a "change in the quantity supplied" of chicken can only be caused by a change in the price of chicken. A change in any other factor on the list on page 88 of the text causes a "change in supply."

**Graphing Pointer:** Remember—if you would do more of the activity (buying more, producing more) because of the change in a factor (demand, supply), draw a new curve to the right of the original curve. If you reduce the activity, draw the new curve to the left of the original curve.

**TIP:** Here is an example that points out the difference between a "change in quantity demanded" and a "change in demand." In the diagram below, we have a demand curve for Ford Rangers on the left and a demand curve for Dodge Rams on the right.

Initially, the price of the Ranger is $17 000 and 2000 are demanded per week. The Ram sells for $16 000 and has 2500 demanders at that price. (Note: It's irrelevant whether the Ram's price is above, below, or equal to that of the Ranger—at any realistic price, each truck will have some enthusiasts.)

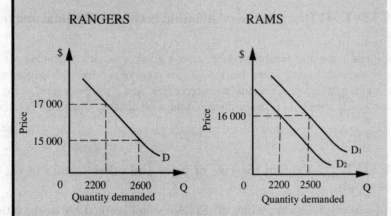

Suppose that the price of Rangers decreases to $15 000. More truck buyers will order Rangers—an increase in quantity demanded as there is a movement along the demand curve from *A* to *B*. Some of those new Ford customers would have bought the Dodge Ram but now will not. At the same price ($16 000) as before, demand for Rams has decreased, perhaps to 2200. The entire demand curve for Rams has shifted.

## Practice

2. Return to Practice Question 1. Suppose that the prices of other fruits you might buy increase. What would happen to the number of apples you demand per month? Sketch this change on your diagram. Label the demand curve $D_2$. What is likely to happen to the price of apples?

    **ANSWER:** See your diagram for Practice Question 1. Presumably, you'd demand more apples at each price. The demand curve shifts right, to $D_2$. Because apples are more popular now, the price of apples will likely rise.

3. A "change in demand" means
    A. the quantity demanded changes as price changes.
    B. a movement along a given demand curve or schedule.
    C. a shift in the position of the demand curve.
    D. a change in the shape of a demand curve.

    **ANSWER:** C. A "change in demand" means that, at every price level, more or less is being demanded. This is represented as a shift in the position of the demand curve. See p. 73.

4. Which of the following will cause a decrease in the demand for tennis rackets?
    A. A rise in the price of squash rackets.
    B. A rise in the price of tennis rackets.
    C. A rise in the price of tennis balls.
    D. A fall in the price of tennis shoes.

    **ANSWER:** C. A decrease in the demand for tennis rackets will occur if a complement (tennis balls) increases in price because fewer tennis balls will be bought. See p. 72.

## OBJECTIVE 4: Describe the relationship between individual and market demand.

*Market demand* is the sum of all the quantities of a good or service demanded per period by all the households buying in the market for that good or service. The *market demand curve* is a summing of all the individual demand curves. At a given price level, the quantity demanded by each household is determined and the total quantity demanded is calculated.

(page 75)

## OBJECTIVE 5: Explain the role of price and other factors in the basic theory of supply.

The decision to supply is affected by the ability to earn profits (that is, the difference between revenues and costs). The willingness and ability of a firm to offer units of a good for sale (quantity supplied) are likely to depend principally on the price of the good itself. If other factors important to producers change, then the supply curve diagram will change. The supply curve shifts position—a *change in supply*.

The quantity supplied is the amount of a product that a firm would be willing and able to offer for sale at a particular price during a given period of time. The law of supply states that there is a positive relationship between the price and the quantity supplied of a product. When McDonald's raises its hourly wage, we want to work more hours there.

A supply *schedule* is a table listing how much of a product a firm will supply at alternative prices in a given period; a supply curve shows this relationship graphically. A *supply curve* slopes upward.

(page 78)

Factors that can cause a change in supply are:
a.    changes in costs of production (input prices)
b.    new costs and market opportunities
c.    changes in prices of related products.                              (page 78)

Improvements in technology, decreases in the costs of inputs and other costs of production, or increases in the price of complementary products will increase supply. Decreases in the price of substitute products will also increase supply, i.e., the entire supply curve will shift to the right. Graphically, an increase in supply ($S_1$ to $S_2$) appears as shown below:

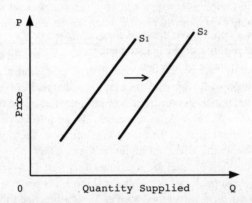

**Graphing Pointer:** At first glance, a leftward shift of a supply curve looks like the supply curve has moved up, but it's still a *decrease* in supply—at each price level, less is being supplied. Second, when considering if a given factor will cause supply to increase or decrease, ask "Will this change increase or decrease profits?" Producers will want to supply more if their profits are rising—so, if the answer to the question is "increase profits," you should predict an increase (rightward shift) in supply.

**TIP:** These lists of factors that can change demand or supply should be kept in a place very close to your heart. Write them on an index card and review them frequently.

**Demand:** Pick a good that you buy frequently (preferably a name brand), such as Petro-Canada gasoline. Do "thought experiments." What would your demand do if Petro-Canada hiked the price of its gas? If your income fell? If the price of engine oil (a complement) increased? If the price of Esso gas (a substitute) decreased?

**Supply:** Perhaps you have a part-time job—that is, you supply labour. Think of factors that would affect how many hours you would work per week. The wage (price) you earn would affect the quantity of labour you supply. What other factors would make you more or less willing and able to work?

**TIP, continued:** Note the reference to the *short run* and the *long run* on page 78. These are important economic concepts that you'll meet later on. Essentially, suppliers will be more responsive to demand-side changes in a longer time period than they will be in a shorter time period.

**Graphing Pointer:** The "change in demand" and "change in supply" concepts are tough; ask yourself, what would you do if the price of a good (say, steak) remains constant and your income rises substantially? If you would buy more steak, this is an increase in demand. To graph this change, draw a hypothetical (negatively sloped!) demand curve for steak ($D_1$). Choose a point ($A_1$) on the curve and identify the associated quantity demanded. Choose another price and repeat the operation with point $B_1$. To construct the new demand curve which results from the higher income, pick a point immediately to the right of $A_1$ and label it $A_2$. This point represents the additional purchases due to the additional income. Draw a point directly to the right of $B_1$ which will indicate the effects of higher income. Label this point $B_2$. Draw a line through $B_1$ and $B_2$ and label this line $D_2$—your new demand curve. Repeat this graphing exercise for each of your "thought experiments" mentioned above. As you practise this for all of the factors which change demand and supply, your mastery of graphical analysis will develop.

(These "thought experiments" will be easier for demand factors than for supply factors because you buy things every day while most of you are not producers. Once again, be patient and ask yourself: if you were a business owner committed to maximizing profits, how would you respond if your product's price remained the same but one of the supply factors changed?)

**Graphing Pointer:** Many students feel that a "curve" must be curved. Our demand and supply curves are models, however. Keep it simple—draw straight lines.

**TIP:** When you are told to imagine that income or some other variable has changed, imagine an *enormous* change—this will help you work out the effects. If a can of Pepsi has risen in price, suppose that it has tripled in price—it's easier to see what will happen to the quantity demanded or supplied of Pepsi and to the demand for Coke.

## Practice

5. In the diagrams below, match each of the numbers with the appropriate term below to produce a correct demand or supply diagram for apples.
   - A. Price of apples demanded.
   - B. Price of apples supplied.
   - C. Quantity of apples supplied.
   - D. Quantity of apples demanded.
   - E. Demand curve.
   - F. Supply curve.

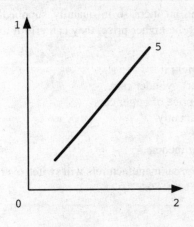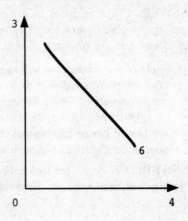

**ANSWER:**    1. B    4. D
                      2. C    5. F
                      3. A    6. E

6. A decrease in the supply of domestic cars might be caused by
    A. an increase in the price of imported Japanese cars.
    B. an increase in the wages of Canadian car workers.
    C. an increase in demand that causes car prices to rise.
    D. a reduction in the cost of steel.

    **ANSWER:** B. The supply of domestic cars will decrease if input prices, such as the wages of Canadian car workers, increase. See p. 79.

7. Energizer and Duracell's Coppertop batteries are substitutes. The Energizer Bunny increases the price of its batteries. Equilibrium price will _____ and quantity exchanged will _____ in the market for Duracell.
    A. rise, rise.
    B. fall, rise.
    C. fall, fall.
    D. rise, fall.

    **ANSWER:** A. If Energizer increases the price of its batteries, consumers will switch over to substitutes such as Duracell, increasing the demand for Duracell. This will raise both equilibrium price and quantity. See p. 85.

8. Bicycles and bicycle helmets are complements. The producers of helmets notice a decrease in the quantity of their products demanded (a movement along their demand curve). This could have been caused by
    A. a decrease in the income of helmet producers' customers.
    B. an increase in the price of these helmets.
    C. an increase in the price of bicycles.
    D. an increased expectation that manufacturers of bicycles will reduce the price of their bicycles in the near future.

    **ANSWER:** B. This is a change in quantity demanded, not a change in demand. The only thing that can cause a change in quantity demanded is a change in price. See p. 73.

9. As the price of oranges increases, orange growers will
    A. use more expensive methods of growing oranges.
    B. use less expensive methods of growing oranges.
    C. increase the supply of oranges.
    D. decrease the supply of oranges.

**ANSWER:** C. An increase in price results in an increase in quantity supplied. Suppliers are able to produce more because, at the higher price, they can afford to hire more expensive resources. See p. 80.

10. The supply of 4-cylinder cars will shift to the right if
    A.  consumers switched over to 6 (and higher)-cylinder cars.
    B.  manufacturers of 4-cylinder cars see the price of larger cars (6-cylinder and higher) decreasing permanently.
    C.  the cost of labour inputs stays constant.
    D.  consumers experience an increase in their income.

    **ANSWER:** D. B. As the price of larger cars drop, car manufacturers will switch over to another production option: 4-cylinder cars. See p. 86.

## OBJECTIVE 6: Distinguish between changes in quantity supplied (movements along the curve) and changes in supply (shifts in the supply curve).

When important factors other than price change for a producer, the amount of a given product offered for sale will change even if the price level is unchanged. This is a *change in supply*. If *only* the price of the product itself changes, there will be a movement along the original supply curve—a *change in quantity supplied*.                    (page 80)

## Practice

11. If the firms producing fuzzy dice for cars must obtain a higher price than they did previously to produce the same level of output as before, then we can say that there has been
    A.  an increase in quantity supplied.
    B.  an increase in supply.
    C.  a decrease in supply.
    D.  a decrease in quantity supplied.

    **ANSWER:** C. Draw the supply curve. At the same output level and at a higher price, the supply curve has shifted to the left—a decrease in supply. See p. 80.

12. The market supply curve for wheat depends on each of the following except
    A.  the price of wheat-producing land.
    B.  the price of production alternatives for wheat.
    C.  the tastes and preferences of wheat consumers.
    D.  the number of wheat farmers in the market.

    **ANSWER:** C. Tastes and preferences are determinants of demand, not supply. See p. 78.

## Other Important Points

## POINT 1: Provide explanations for the slope of a typical demand curve.

Demand curves slope down—as price rises, quantity demanded falls. We know this intuitively, but economists have explored this important relationship ("social law") more analytically. The higher the price of a good, low-fat milk, for instance, the higher the opportunity cost of buying it, (i.e., the more of other goods we will give up, and the less willing we will be to buy low-fat milk).

*Utility* is a conceptual measure of satisfaction. Successive units of a good bestow satisfaction, but typically at a decreasing rate—the second cup of coffee may be less enjoyable than the first. Accordingly, the price we will be willing to pay will decrease.

As the price of steak rises, you become poorer because your food dollar can't stretch as far as it did before (this is called the *income effect*), and you seek cheaper substitutes such as chicken (this is called the *substitution effect*). Both effects result in a decrease in the quantity demanded of steak as its price increases. (page 69/70)

## Practice

13. The demand curve has
    A. "price" on the vertical axis, "quantity demanded per time period" on the horizontal axis, and an upward sloping demand curve.
    B. "price" on the horizontal axis, "quantity demanded per time period" on the vertical axis, and an upward sloping demand curve.
    C. "price" on the vertical axis, "quantity demanded per time period" on the horizontal axis, and a downward-sloping demand curve.
    D. "price" on the horizontal axis, "quantity demanded per time period" on the vertical axis, and a downward-sloping demand curve.

    **ANSWER:** C. See p. 70.

14. We are trying to explain the law of demand. When the price of pretzels rises,
    A. the opportunity cost of pretzels increases along the demand curve.
    B. sellers switch production and increase the quantity supplied of pretzels.
    C. income rises for producers of pretzels.
    D. the opportunity cost of other goods increases.

    **ANSWER:** A. See p. 69.

## POINT 2: Distinguish the relationship that exists between two goods that are substitutes and the relationship that exists between two goods that are complements.

If, when the price of Good A rises, the demand for Good B also rises, then A and B are *substitutes*; however, if the demand for B falls when the price of A rises, then A and B are *complements*. (page 72)

> **TIP:** Think of several ready-made examples of substitute goods and complementary goods from your own life. Working with your own examples (e.g., during an exam) makes it easier to work through the analysis correctly. Here are a few examples:
>
> **Substitutes:** Coke and Pepsi, pre-recorded audiotapes and CDs.
>
> **Complements:** peanut butter and jelly, CDs and CD players, cars and gasoline, cameras and film, left and right shoes.

## Practice

15. The demand for Kraft peanut butter will decrease if there is
    A. an increase in the price of Kraft peanut butter.
    B. an increase in the price of Equality, the Dominon Store brand of peanut butter.
    C. a decrease in the demand for jelly.
    D. an increase in the price of bread.

    **ANSWER:** D. Bread and peanut butter are complements. An increase in the price of bread will result in less bread being bought and a lower demand for Kraft to spread on it. See p. 72.

16. Good A and Good B are substitutes for one another. An increase in the price of A will
    A. increase the demand for B.
    B. reduce the quantity demanded of B.
    C. increase the quantity demanded of B.
    D. reduce the demand for B.

    **ANSWER:** A. Suppose A is Coke and B is Pepsi. If Coke rises in price, we would buy less Coke (a fall in quantity demanded of Coke) and more of Pepsi (an increase in the demand for Pepsi). See p. 71-72.

## POINT 3: Distinguish between a good that is normal and a good that is inferior.

When income increases, demand increases for *normal* goods. If demand for a good decreases when income increases, then the good is *inferior*.                      (pages 71-72)

> **TIP:** Think of several ready-made examples of both normal goods and inferior goods from your own life. Working with your own examples (during an exam, for instance) makes it easier to work through the analysis correctly. Here are a few examples:
>
> **Normal goods:** movie tickets, steak, and more expensive imported beers.
>
> **Inferior goods:** second-hand clothes, store-brand (versus name-brand) foods, generic medicines, rice, beans, bus rides.

## Practice

17. You expect your income to rise. For a normal good, this would result in
    A. an increase in quantity demanded and a fall in price.
    B. an increase in demand and a fall in price.
    C. an increase in quantity demanded and a rise in price.
    D. an increase in demand and a rise in price.

    **ANSWER:** D. If you expect your income to rise, you will demand more of a normal good. This will cause the price to increase. See p. 71.

18. The demand for Good A has been increasing over the past year. Having examined the following facts, you conclude that Good A is an inferior good. Which fact led you to that conclusion?
    A. The price of Good A has been increasing over the past year.

B.   An economic slowdown has reduced the income of the traditional buyers of Good A.

C.   Good B, a substitute for Good A, has cut its price over the past twelve months.

D.   Household wealth has increased among the traditional buyers of Good A.

**ANSWER:** B. Inferior goods experience increasing popularity as income levels fall. See p. 72.

19.   Turnips are available in both Canada and in Mexico. During the past year, incomes have grown by 10% in each country. The demand for turnips has grown by 12% in Canada and 3% in Mexico. We can conclude that turnips are

A.   normal goods in Canada and normal goods in Mexico.

B.   normal goods in Canada and inferior goods in Mexico.

C.   inferior goods in Canada and normal goods in Mexico.

D.   inferior goods in Canada and inferior goods in Mexico.

**ANSWER:** A. In each case, demand has increased as income has increased. See p. 72.

# OBJECTIVE 7: Describe the relationship between individual and market supply.

The market supply is a horizontal summing of all the supply curves for a given product.

(page 83)

# OBJECTIVE 8: Describe the three market outcomes: excess demand, excess supply, and equilibrium.

If the quantity demanded is greater than the quantity supplied of a good, there is *excess demand*, and we would expect the price of that good to rise. If quantity supplied is greater than the quantity demanded of a good, there is an *excess supply*, and we would expect the price of that good to fall.

(pages 81–86)

## Practice

20.   When there is an excess supply, quantity supplied _____ quantity demanded. Price will _____.

A.   exceeds, rise.

B.   is less than, fall.

C.   is less than, rise.

D.   exceeds, fall.

**ANSWER:** D. An excess supply occurs when quantity supplied exceeds quantity demanded. This excess supply will force price down. See p. 84.

21.   The equilibrium price of a litre of unleaded gas is 50¢. At a price of 45¢

A.   quantity supplied will be less than quantity demanded, causing an excess demand for unleaded gas.

B.   quantity supplied will be greater than quantity demanded, causing an excess supply of unleaded gas.

C.   quantity supplied will be greater than quantity demanded, causing an excess demand for unleaded gas.

D.   quantity supplied will be less than quantity demanded, causing an excess supply of unleaded gas.

**ANSWER:** A. If the current price is less than the equilibrium price, an excess demand will occur (quantity supplied will be less than quantity demanded). This excess demand will force price to increase.

## OBJECTIVE 9: Use the demand/supply market equilibrium model to analyze the impact of market changes on market prices, sales, and expenditures.

In the market for a particular good or service, quantity demanded may be greater than, less than, or equal to quantity supplied. *Equilibrium* occurs when quantity demanded equals quantity supplied. There is no tendency for the price to change because, at that price, there is a perfect match between the quantity of the good demanded and the quantity supplied.

(page 81)

Example: Demand decreases and supply increases.

> **TIP: Equilibrium.** The notion of equilibrium is important throughout the remainder of the course. The simple, less analytical, way to think about this concept is as "the point where the lines cross." It will help your understanding if you remember that equilibrium is the "balance" situation in which there is no tendency for change—unless some outside factor intervenes.

> **Graphing Pointer:** Sometimes demand and supply will change position simultaneously. If the magnitudes of the shifts are unknown, then either the effect on equilibrium price or on equilibrium quantity *must* be uncertain. It's easy to forget this important fact, particularly when demand and supply are still new concepts to you. See the following Tip for assistance.

> **TIP: Changes in Equilibrium Price and Quantity.** If demand and supply change position simultaneously, break down each situation into two separate graphs, one for the "demand shift" and the other for the "supply shift." In each case, decide the direction of change in price and quantity, and then add them together.

|  | **Price Change** | **Quantity Change** |
|---|---|---|
| Demand-side effect | decrease | decrease |
| Supply-side effect | decrease | increase |
| Total effect | decrease | uncertain |

In this case, where demand decreases and supply increases, we predict a certain decrease in price and an uncertain change in equilibrium quantity.

**Graphing Pointer:** A change in price does not cause the demand curve or the supply curve to shift position. Analyze the following sequence of events for errors. "Demand goes up. That makes price go up, which encourages sellers to supply more. But, when more is supplied, price goes down. When price goes down, demand goes up again, and so on."

**ANSWER:** A demand increase from $D_1$ to $D_2$ will make price rise from $P_1$ to $P_2$. Sellers will supply more from $Q_1$ to $Q_2$ —an increase in *quantity supplied*, not an increase in supply, as the statement claims. Price, therefore, will *not* go back down. The remainder of the statement is incorrect. Draw this example.

## Practice

22. Equilibrium quantity will certainly decrease if
    A.   demand and supply both increase.
    B.   demand and supply both decrease.
    C.   demand decreases and supply increases.
    D.   demand increases and supply decreases.

    **ANSWER:** B. A decrease in demand will decrease equilibrium quantity. Similarly, a decrease in supply will decrease equilibrium quantity.

23. The market for canned dog food is in equilibrium when
    A.   the quantity demanded is less than the quantity supplied.
    B.   the demand curve is downsloping and the supply curve is upsloping.
    C.   the quantity demanded and the quantity supplied are equal.
    D.   all inputs producing canned dog food are employed.

    **ANSWER:** C. A market is in equilibrium when price has adjusted to make the quantity demanded and the quantity supplied equal. See p. 81.

24. Equilibrium price will certainly increase if
    A.   demand and supply both increase.
    B.   demand and supply both decrease.
    C.   demand decreases and supply increases.
    D.   demand increases and supply decreases.

    **ANSWER:** D. An increase in demand will increase equilibrium price. Similarly, a decrease in supply will increase equilibrium price.

25. In the market for mushrooms, the price of mushrooms will certainly increase if
    A.   the supply curve shifts right and the demand curve shifts right.
    B.   the supply curve shifts right and the demand curve shifts left.
    C.   the supply curve shifts left and the demand curve shifts right.
    D.   the supply curve shifts left and the demand curve shifts left.

    **ANSWER:** C. When demand increases and supply decreases, both shifts are prompting a price increase.

## OBJECTIVE 10 (APPENDIX 4A): Use simple algebra to represent demand, supply, and market equilibrium.

As the Appendix shows, supply and demand can be analyzed using algebra. Application Question 5 below is an example.

## PRACTICE TEST

**I.     MULTIPLE CHOICE QUESTIONS.** Select the option that provides the single best answer.

_____ 1.   Households are
A.   suppliers in the input market.
B.   demanders in the labour market.
C.   suppliers in the product market.
D.   demanders in the input market.

_____ 2.   Good C increases its price. The demand for Good D increases. The goods are
A.   complements.
B.   substitutes.
C.   normal.
D.   inferior.

_____ 3.   The demand for CDs is down-sloping. Suddenly the price of CDs rises from $8 to $10. This will cause
A.   demand to shift to the left.
B.   demand to shift to the right.
C.   quantity demanded to increase.
D.   quantity demanded to decrease.

_____ 4.   Which of the following will cause a movement along the supply curve of Frisbees?
A.   an increase in price of Frisbees.
B.   an improvement in the production processes used to manufacture Frisbees.
C.   a reduction in the price of plastic from which Frisbees are made.
D.   an improvement in storage resulting in fewer defective Frisbees.

_____ 5.   Along a given supply curve for eggs
A.   supply increases as price increases.
B.   supply increases as technology improves.
C.   quantity supplied increases as price increases.
D.   quantity supplied increases as technology improves.

_____ 6.   Price is currently below equilibrium. There is a situation of excess _____. We would expect price to _____.
A.   demand, rise.
B.   demand, fall.
C.   supply, rise.
D.   supply, fall.

_____ 7. You expect income to rise. For a normal good, this would result in
   A. an increase in quantity demanded and a fall in price.
   B. an increase in demand and a fall in price.
   C. an increase in quantity demanded and a rise in price.
   D. an increase in demand and a rise in price.

_____ 8. The price of Frisbees (a normal good) will definitely increase if
   A. there is an improvement in the technology of making Frisbees and Frisbees become more popular.
   B. the cost of plastic used to produce Frisbees increases and people have more leisure time to throw Frisbees.
   C. Frisbee workers negotiate a wage increase and boomerangs (a Frisbee substitute) decrease in price.
   D. a sales tax is imposed on Frisbees and (because of widespread unemployment) incomes fall.

_____ 9. A rightward shift in the supply of domestic cars might be due to
   A. an increase in the price of steel.
   B. a reduction in foreign competition.
   C. the introduction of cost-saving robots.
   D. increased popularity of foreign cars.

_____ 10. If the market is initially in equilibrium, a technological improvement will cause price to _____ and quantity demanded to _____.
   A. fall, fall.
   B. rise, rise.
   C. fall, rise.
   D. rise, fall.

_____ 11. The price of beans rises sharply. Which of the following cannot be true?
   A. The supply of beans may have decreased with no change in the demand for beans.
   B. The demand for beans may have increased with no change in the supply of beans.
   C. The demand for beans may have increased with an increase in the quantity supplied of beans.
   D. The supply of beans may have increased with an increase in the quantity demanded of beans.

_____ 12. The market for peas is experiencing an excess supply. You should predict that
   A. price will increase, quantity demanded will fall, and the quantity supplied will rise.
   B. price will increase, quantity demanded will rise, and the quantity supplied will fall.
   C. price will decrease, quantity demanded will rise, and the quantity supplied will fall.
   D. price will decrease, quantity demanded will fall, and the quantity supplied will rise.

_____ 13. Equilibrium price will certainly decrease if
   A. demand and supply both increase.
   B. demand and supply both decrease.
   C. demand decreases and supply increases.
   D. demand increases and supply decreases.

_____ 14. If a demander demands less of a product at each possible price, there has
been
A.   a decrease in the quantity demanded.
B.   a decrease in demand.
C.   an increase in demand.
D.   an increase in the quantity demanded.

_____ 15. Frito Lay Chips and Knorr's Dip are complements. Costs of chip produc-
tion fall. At the same time, a government health report alleges that dip con-
sumption causes bone cancer. For Knorr's Dip, the equilibrium price will
_____, and the equilibrium quantity will _____.
A.   fall, be indeterminate.
B.   be indeterminate, rise.
C.   be indeterminate, fall.
D.   be indeterminate, be indeterminate.

_____ 16. Suppose there is a simultaneous increase in the demand for legal secretaries
and a decrease in the supply of legal secretaries. If there is no change in the
wage paid to legal secretaries
A.   there will be an excess demand for legal secretaries.
B.   there will be an excess supply of legal secretaries.
C.   law firms will have no difficulty in hiring the desired number of legal
secretaries at the current wage.
D.   the supply of legal secretaries will decrease even more.

Use the diagram below to answer the next six questions. The diagram refers to the demand
for and supply of hot dogs. The hot dog market is initially in equilibrium at Point A.
Assume that hot dogs are a normal good.

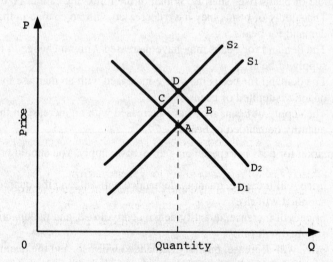

_____ 17. The hot dog market moves from Point A to a new equilibrium at Point B.
There has been
A.   an increase in demand and an increase in supply.
B.   an increase in demand and an increase in quantity supplied.
C.   an increase in quantity demanded and an increase in quantity supplied.
D.   an increase in quantity demanded and an increase in supply.

_____ 18. The movement from Point A to Point B might have been caused by
A. an increase in the price of hamburgers (a substitute for hot dogs).
B. an increase in the price of fries (a complement for hot dogs).
C. a new widespread belief that meat products are bad for the heart.
D. a decrease in the price of ketchup (an ingredient used in making hot dogs).

_____ 19. The hot dog market moves from Point A to a new equilibrium at Point C. There has been
A. a decrease in demand and a decrease in supply.
B. a decrease in demand and a decrease in quantity supplied.
C. a decrease in quantity demanded and a decrease in quantity supplied.
D. a decrease in quantity demanded and a decrease in supply.

_____ 20. The movement from Point A to Point C might have been caused by a
A. decrease in the price of hamburgers (a substitute for hot dogs).
B. tightening of sanitary regulations required for the preparation of hot dogs.
C. decrease in the wages of workers in the hot dog industry.
D. decrease in the price of hot dog buns.

_____ 21. The hot dog market moves from Point A to a new equilibrium at Point D. There has been
A. an increase in demand and an increase in supply.
B. an increase in demand and a decrease in supply.
C. a decrease in demand and an increase in supply.
D. a decrease in demand and a decrease in supply.

_____ 22. The movement from Point A to Point D might have been caused by
A. an increase in the price of hot dogs and no change in the equilibrium quantity of hot dogs.
B. an expected increase in the income of hot dog consumers and a hike in the wages of hot dog preparers.
C. an expected decrease in the price of hot dogs and an increase in the cost of making hot dogs.
D. a decrease in the income of hot dog consumers and a reduction in the cost of making hot dogs.

_____ 23. Generic aspirin is an inferior good. As Pierre's income decreases, we would expect
A. a decrease in Pierre's demand for generic aspirin.
B. an increase in Pierre's quantity demanded of generic aspirin.
C. an increase in Pierre's demand for generic aspirin.
D. a decrease in Pierre's quantity demanded of generic aspirin.

_____ 24. The supply of computer software packages increases. As a result, the demand for personal computers rises. These two goods are _____. The price of microchips, used to produce personal computers, will

_____.
A. substitutes, increase.
B. substitutes, decrease.
C. complements, increase.
D. complements, decrease.

_____ 25. Along a given demand curve for corn, which of the following is not held constant?
- A. The price of corn.
- B. The income of corn farmers.
- C. The income of corn demanders.
- D. The price of wheat.

_____ 26. The law of demand is best illustrated by
- A. the price of Pepsi rising, leading consumers to buy more Coke.
- B. increased purchases of Coke as the price of Coke decreases.
- C. an increase in income which results in reduced purchases of store-brand soft drinks.
- D. an increase in income which results in increased purchases of Coke.

Use the table below to answer the next three questions. The table refers to the demand for and supply of tuna.

| Price of Tuna | Quantity Demanded | Quantity Supplied |
|---|---|---|
| 90¢ | 30 | 80 |
| 80¢ | 45 | 70 |
| 70¢ | 60 | 60 |
| 60¢ | 75 | 50 |
| 50¢ | 90 | 40 |
| 40¢ | 105 | 30 |

_____ 27. The equilibrium price is _____ and the equilibrium quantity is _____.
- A. 70¢, 60.
- B. 60¢, 75.
- C. 60¢, 50.
- D. 70¢, 70.

_____ 28. There would be an excess demand for tuna if the price were at
- A. 90¢.
- B. 80¢.
- C. 70¢.
- D. 60¢.

_____ 29. If the price were 80¢, there would be
- A. an excess demand of 70.
- B. an excess demand of 25.
- C. an excess supply of 25.
- D. an excess supply of 70.

_____ 30. New costly regulations to protect workers are introduced in the production of tuna. We would expect the equilibrium price of tuna to _____ and the equilibrium quantity of tuna to _____.
- A. increase, increase.
- B. increase, decrease.
- C. decrease, increase.
- D. decrease, decrease.

## II.  APPLICATION QUESTIONS.

1. Consider the following information regarding the quantity of cardboard demanded and supplied per month at a number of prices.

| Price per square metre | Quantity demanded | Quantity supplied |
|---|---|---|
| 40¢ | 39 000 | 83 000 |
| 35¢ | 48 000 | 78 000 |
| 30¢ | 58 000 | 74 000 |
| 25¢ | 67 000 | 67 000 |
| 20¢ | 75 000 | 62 000 |
| 15¢ | 81 000 | 59 000 |

a. What is the equilibrium price? What is the equilibrium quantity?

b. Describe the situation when the price is at 40¢ per square metre and predict what will happen.

c. Describe the situation when the price is at 15¢ per square metre and predict what will happen.

d. Explain what would happen if a serious transport strike reduced cardboard quantity supplied (at each price) by 30 000 square metre.

2. Pita bread is a normal good. What will happen to the equilibrium price and quantity of pita bread in each of the following situations?

a. Due to a recession, households which buy pita bread experience a decrease in income.

b. The cost of wheat used in pita bread increases significantly.

c. Bakeries buy improved ovens that reduce the costs of pita bread.

d. The prices of other types of bread fall.

e. Consumers become health conscious and switch to low-calorie breads.

3. How will each of the following changes affect the supply of hamburgers?

a. There is an increase in the price of hamburger buns (used in the production of burgers).

b. There is an increase in the price of hamburgers.

c. Producers discover that the price of cheeseburgers is increasing.

4. Pietro Cavalini sells ice cream at the beach. He is in competition with numerous other vendors. How will each of the following changes affect the demand for Pietro's ice cream?

a. Hot dog vendors reduce the price of hot dogs. Hot dogs are substitutes for ice cream.

b. The cost of refrigeration decreases.

c. Fine weather attracts record crowds to the beach.

5. The market for video cassettes has supply and demand curves given by $Qs = 3P$ and $Qd = 60 - 2P$, respectively.

a. Complete the following table.

| Price | Quantity Demanded | Quantity Supplied |
|---|---|---|
| $30 | _____ | _____ |
| $25 | _____ | _____ |
| $20 | _____ | _____ |
| $15 | _____ | _____ |
| $10 | _____ | _____ |
| $ 5 | _____ | _____ |
| $ 0 | _____ | _____ |

b. Calculate the equilibrium price and quantity. You can do this either by graphing the curves or algebraically.

c. Suppose that the current market price is $20. Calculate the number of units that will be traded.

d. Suppose that the demand equation changed to Qd = 80 – 2P. Is this an increase or a decrease in demand? Suggest what might have caused such a change.

e. Calculate the new equilibrium price and quantity.

6. Here is a demand and supply schedule for bread in Lethbridge, Alberta.

| Price ($) | Quantity Demanded | Quantity Supplied |
|---|---|---|
| 5.00 | 1000 | 6000 |
| 4.50 | 1300 | 4500 |
| 4.00 | 1600 | 4000 |
| 3.50 | 2000 | 3500 |
| 3.00 | 3000 | 3000 |
| 2.50 | 3200 | 2700 |
| 2.00 | 4000 | 2200 |
| 1.50 | 4500 | 1800 |
| 1.00 | 5400 | 1400 |
| .50 | 7000 | 1200 |

a. Find equilibrium price and equilibrium quantity.

b. Graph the demand (D₁) and supply (S₁) schedules in the space below and confirm the equilibrium values.

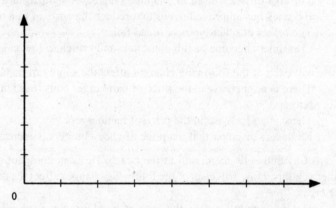

c. At a price of $1, is there an excess demand or supply? How great is the excess? Suppose supply increases by 1800 units at each price level.

d. Draw the new supply curve (S₂) on the graph in b. above.

e. At the original equilibrium price level, is there an excess demand or an excess supply?

f. What will now happen to price, quantity demanded, and quantity supplied?

7. The diagram below shows the labour market. D is the demand for labour and S is the supply. The minimum wage is $6.85, and unemployment is 150 workers.

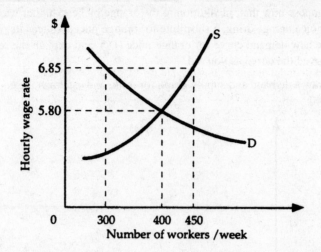

If the minimum wage law was revoked, the wage would fall to an equilibrium level of $5.80, and there would be no unemployment because quantity demanded would be equal to quantity supplied. However, the number of workers demanded would rise by only 100, not 150. Reconcile this apparent contradiction.

8. Here are the demand schedules for orange juice for 3 buyers in the orange juice market and the supply schedules for 3 sellers in the orange juice market.

| Price/ | Quantity demanded by: | | | Quantity supplied by: | | |
|--------|-------|-------|-------|------|-------|----------|
| litre | Brown | Black | White | Gray | Green | Scarlett |
| $5.00 | 1 | 0 | 0 | 5 | 10 | 14 |
| $4.00 | 3 | 2 | 0 | 4 | 7 | 9 |
| $3.00 | 7 | 5 | 4 | 3 | 6 | 7 |
| $2.00 | 9 | 9 | 5 | 0 | 4 | 5 |
| $1.00 | 11 | 12 | 7 | 0 | 0 | 1 |

a. Graph market demand ($D_1$) and market supply ($S_1$).

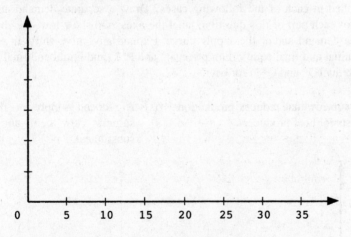

b. Show equilibrium price (P*) and quantity (Q*).
c. Now suppose the farm workers who pick oranges are given a higher wage rate. Show on your graph the changes that will occur in the orange juice market. Label any new demand curve $D_2$ and supply curve $S_2$. Discuss why curves shift, why price changes, and the significance of excess demand or excess supply. Note that you don't have the data to draw precise curves.

d.   Suppose now that, in addition to the orange pickers' higher wage rate, Master Choice orange drink, a substitute for orange juice, reduces its price. Sketch in the new demand curve for orange juice ($D_3$), and explain the reason why you moved the curve as you did.

9.   a.   Draw a demand and supply graph for milk, and establish the equilibrium price ($P^*$).

b.   There is an increase in demand for milk (from $D_1$ to $D_2$). How will this change affect the equilibrium price?

c.   In terms of the diagram you just sketched, what is the only way that the equilibrium price can increase, if the supply curve doesn't shift?

d.   Draw in the new demand curve. Now trace through the process by which a new equilibrium is established.

On one diagram, you can display the distinction between a change in demand and a change in quantity demanded.

10.   Assume that beef is a normal good. What happens to the amount of beef demanded or supplied in each of the following cases? Draw a separate demand and supply graph for each part of this question, label the axes, and show how the change will shift the demand and/or the supply curve. Explain any curve shifts in each case. Show initial and final equilibrium price ($P^*$ and $P^{**}$) and initial and final equilibrium quantity ($Q^*$ and $Q^{**}$) for beef.

a.   A subsidy that reduces production costs for beef producers.

b.   A reduced supply of fish (consumers view beef and fish as substitutes).

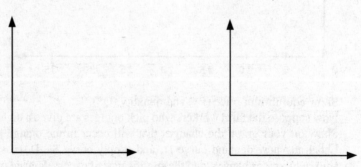

c. A rise in the wage rate in the beef industry.

d. A rise in income.

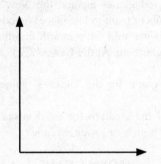
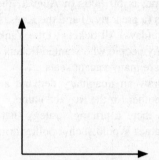

e. An improvement in the productivity of producing beef.

f. A bad tomato crop (beef and ketchup are complements and tomatoes are used to produce ketchup).

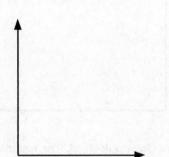

11. Think of some commodity that you like. Try to avoid "lumpy" things, like cars or houses, and pick something like coffee, movies, CDs, or long-distance phone calls.
    a. Roughly sketch your demand curve for this good. Does it intersect the price axis? Where? How much of this commodity would you buy at a zero price?

    b. Are there substitutes for this commodity? How does the availability of substitutes affect the shape of your curve?
    c. How would your demand curve change in response to an increase in the price of a substitute?
    d. How would your demand curve change if you won the lottery and were to receive $2 million?

12. Assume that the Toronto Blue Jays baseball team charges $15 per ticket for all seats at all regular season games. Assume also that the capacity of their stadium, SkyDome, is 50 000. In August, the Jays played games against the New York Yankees (a great rival) and the Kansas City Royals (a team in last place) on consecutive Sundays. All tickets to the Yankees game were sold out a month in advance, and many people who wanted tickets could not get them. At the Kansas City game, there were many vacant seats.

   a. Draw an imaginary demand and supply graph for the Yankees' game and another for the Royals' game.

   b. Is there a pricing strategy that would fill the stadium for the Kansas City game? Would such a policy bring the Jays higher or lower revenue?

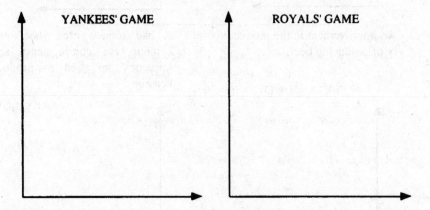

YANKEES' GAME          ROYALS' GAME

13. During the 1980s, home prices in the Southern Ontario doubled. The result was a significant increase in new home construction and a large increase in the demand for labour in the region. At the same time, though, high home prices caused a drop in the supply of labour as people found it too expensive to live in the region. Draw a diagram of the labour market and discuss the impact of these events on wages and thus on the costs of doing business in this region.

14. In London, England, cabbies must be able to demonstrate a knowledge of at least 400 streets in order to obtain a licence. This is quite difficult, so the number of cabbies is rather limited.

   a. Draw a demand and supply diagram for taxi service in London. How has this diagram been affected by the presence of the test?

b. How has the presence of the test affected usage of other forms of public transport—for example, the red double-decker buses and the "tube" (subway)? How have these prices responded?

c. If the effect of restricting the numbers of cabbies is to reduce the number of customers, why might cab drivers favour the restriction?

15. Indicate in each case whether demand for steak (a normal good) will increase (I), decrease (D), or remain unchanged (U) in the following cases.

   a. _____ Pork, a substitute for steak, decreases in price.

   b. _____ High levels of unemployment sweep the nation.

   c. _____ The price of steak falls.

   d. _____ The price of steak sauce increases dramatically.

   e. _____ A government report establishes a conclusive link between the consumption of steak and cancer.

   f. _____ New refrigeration techniques reduce spoilage of steaks before they reach the market.

   g. _____ It is expected that the price of steak will skyrocket within two months.

16. Indicate in each case whether the supply of beer will increase (I), decrease (D), or remain unchanged (U) in the following cases.

   a. _____ Wine coolers become more popular with consumers.

   b. _____ Beer decreases in price.

   c. _____ Provinces impose a new tax on beer producers.

   d. _____ Beer workers' wages increase.

   e. _____ The price of hops, an important ingredient in brewing, decreases.

   f. _____ Costs of transportation decrease.

   g. _____ Improved technology results in less waste of beer.

   h. _____ The economy enters a downturn, and many beer drinkers become unemployed.

   i. _____ Fuel costs rise at the brewery.

17. Indicate in each case whether the market price and quantity of popcorn will increase (I), decrease (D), or be uncertain (U) in the following cases. Assume that popcorn and lemonade are normal goods.

   *Price Quantity*

   a. _____ _____ The price of lemonade, a complement of popcorn, rises while the harvest of popping corn is unusually poor this year.

   b. _____ _____ Consumers' income falls; lower farm wages this year cause the cost of popping corn to decline.

c. _____ _____ Oil, used in popcorn production, falls in price; consumers expect an imminent rise in the price of popcorn.

d. _____ _____ Eating popcorn is shown to be healthy; new hybrid corn is less expensive to produce and provides higher yields.

18. Chatham is a small city in Ontario. Work out what will happen to the amount of corn supplied in each of the following cases and explain your answer.

*Result A* = increase in the supply of corn.

*Result B* = decrease in the supply of corn.

*Result C* = increase in the quantity supplied of corn.

*Result D* = decrease in the quantity supplied of corn.

a. _____ A new government tax is imposed on corn production.

b. _____ Landlords raise the rent on land, but only if it is used for growing corn.

c. _____ A new spray, effective in controlling insects harmful to corn plants, is made available.

d. _____ The local MP campaigns effectively for an increase in the price of corn, which can be grown in Chatham.

e. _____ The local MP campaigns effectively for a rise in the price of beets, which are grown in Chatham.

f. _____ Many corn-growing farmers suffer bankruptcy.

g. _____ The cost of diesel fuel, used in farm machinery, falls.

h. _____ The wages of agricultural workers increase.

i. _____ Cornflakes (which are made from corn) become much more popular. (Careful!)

## ANSWERS AND SOLUTIONS

### PRACTICE TEST

### I.    SOLUTIONS TO MULTIPLE CHOICE QUESTIONS

1. A. In the input market, firms demand inputs and household supply inputs.

2. B. To check your answer, put in a pair of substitutes, such as Pepsi and Coke. If Pepsi increases in price, we will buy less Pepsi, and the demand for Coke will increase.

3. D. A change in price leads to a movement along the demand curve. This is a "change in quantity demanded." An increase in price causes a decrease in quantity demanded.

4. A. A change in price leads to a movement along the supply curve. See p. 80.

5. C. A movement along a supply curve (a change in quantity supplied) can only be caused by a change in the price of the good itself. See p. 80.

6. A. Draw the demand and supply diagram. In equilibrium, quantity demanded equals quantity supplied. At lower prices, quantity demanded exceeds quantity supplied.

7. D. For a normal good, higher income will stimulate additional demand. Higher demand will cause the equilibrium price to rise. See p. 79.

8. B. If the cost of plastic increases, supply will decrease. If buyers have more leisure time, demand for leisure goods (like Frisbees) will increase. A decrease in supply, coupled with an increase in demand, will push up the price.

9. C. A rightward shift—an increase in supply—will occur if costs are reduced.

10. C. A technological improvement will increase supply. This will drive down the equilibrium price. As the price decreases, quantity demanded will increase.

11. D. If the price of beans rises, then it cannot have been caused by an increase in the supply of beans.

12. C. An excess supply means that quantity supplied is greater than the quantity demanded. To reduce the excess supply, sellers will accept lower prices. As price falls, quantity demanded will increase and quantity supplied will decrease.

13. C. A decrease in demand will drive down price; an increase in supply will drive down the price. Draw the diagram to confirm the result.

14. B. Try drawing this. At each price level, the demand curve will be further to the left.

15. D. Frito Lay's supply increases because costs have fallen. This will increase chip (and dip) demand. The health report will reduce demand for dip. Because we don't know which has the stronger effect on the demand for dip, the change in both equilibrium price and quantity is indeterminate.

16. A. Higher demand and less supply will lead to an excess demand if the wage level doesn't increase.

17. B. The demand curve has shifted right from $D_1$ to $D_2$. As the price increased, quantity supplied increased.

18. A. There has been an increase in demand. This could have been due to an increase in the price of hamburgers because consumers would wish to buy fewer hamburgers and would switch over to demanding hot dogs.

19. D. The supply curve has shifted left, from $S_1$ to $S_2$. As the price increased, quantity demanded decreased.

20. B. There has been a decrease in supply. This could have been due to a tightening of the sanitary regulations required for the preparation of hot dogs (which would have increased costs and/or reduced the number of sellers).

21. B. The demand curve has shifted right, from $D_1$ to $D_2$, and the supply curve has shifted left, from $S_1$ to $S_2$.

22. B. An expected increase in the income of hot dog consumers will increase demand for a normal good, and a hike in the wages of hot dog preparers will increase costs and reduce supply. Option A is incorrect—it describes the effect rather than the cause.

23. C. As income changes, it changes the *demand* for a good. A decrease in income results in a decrease in the demand for a normal good. A decrease in income results in an increase in the demand for an inferior good. See p. 71.

24. C. If the supply of software increases, the price will fall. As one might expect, software and computers are complements—the evidence in the question bears this out. As the quantity of computers traded increases, the demand for microchips will increase, which pushes up their price. See Figure 4.12, graph 6.

25. A. A movement along a demand curve is a change in quantity demanded. The only factor that can cause such a change is a change in the price of the good. See p. 68.

26. B. The law of demand relates the relationship between the price of a good and the quantity demanded. See p. 69.

27. A. Equilibrium occurs where quantity demanded equals quantity supplied. See p. 81.

28. D. At 60¢, quantity demanded is 25 units greater than quantity supplied.

29. C. At 80¢, quantity supplied is 25 units greater than quantity demanded.

30. B. The new regulations will decrease the supply of tuna which, in turn, will increase the equilibrium price and decrease the equilibrium quantity.

## II. SOLUTIONS TO APPLICATION QUESTIONS

1. a. 25¢. 67 000 square metres.
   b. There is an excess supply of 44 000 square metres at a price of 40¢ per square metre. Pressure is present to force price down.
   c. There is an excess demand of 22 000 square metres at a price of 15¢ per square metre Pressure is present to force price up.
   d. Supply would shift to the left by 30 000 square metres. Equilibrium price would increase to 35¢ per square metre and the equilibrium quantity would be 48 000 square metres.

2. a. A decrease in income will reduce demand. Equilibrium price will fall and equilibrium quantity will fall.
   b. An increase in the cost of wheat will decrease supply. Equilibrium price will rise and equilibrium quantity will fall.
   c. A decrease in the cost of wheat will increase supply. Equilibrium price will fall and equilibrium quantity will rise.
   d. A fall in the price of a substitute will reduce the demand for pita. Equilibrium price will fall and equilibrium quantity will fall.
   e. There will be a decrease in demand. Equilibrium price will fall and equilibrium quantity will fall.

3. a. Supply will decrease—cost of inputs has increased.
   b. Supply will not change. A change in the price of a good results in a change in quantity supplied.
   c. Supply of hamburgers will decrease—producers will switch resources to cheeseburger production.

4. a. Hot dogs are substitutes for ice cream. Demand for ice cream will decrease.
   b. No effect on demand. Changes in the cost of refrigeration will affect supply.
   c. Demand will increase as the number of buyers increases.

5. a.

| Quantity Price | Quantity Demanded | Quantity Supplied |
| --- | --- | --- |
| $30 | 0 | 90 |
| $25 | 10 | 75 |
| $20 | 20 | 60 |
| $15 | 30 | 45 |
| $10 | 40 | 30 |
| $ 5 | 50 | 15 |
| $ 0 | 60 | 0 |

   b. Equilibrium price is $12 and equilibrium quantity is 36.
      In equilibrium, Qd = Qs, therefore,
      $$60 - 2P = 3P$$
      $$60 = 5P \text{ and } P = 12.$$
      If P = 12, then Q = 60 – 2(12) = 36.
   c. At $20, there is an excess supply of 40 units. It's a buyers' market—only 20 units will be traded.
   d. This is an increase in demand. Tastes might have changed, consumer incomes may have risen (if video cassettes are a normal good), and so on.
   e. Equilibrium price is $16 and equilibrium quantity is 48.
      In equilibrium,    Qd = Qs, therefore,
      $$80 - 2P = 3P$$
      $$80 = 5P \text{ and } P = 16.$$
      If P = 16, then Q = 80 – 2(16) = 48.

6. a. $3; 3000.
   b. See the diagram below.

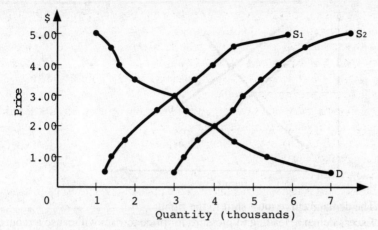

c. There is an excess demand equal to 4000 units (5400 – 1400).
d. See the diagram above ($2, 4000).
e. There will be an excess supply of 1800 units.
f. Price will fall to $2; quantity demanded and supplied will move to 4000 units.

7. The unemployment was removed because 100 extra jobs were created (increase in quantity demanded) and, because the wage had become too low, 50 workers decided to cease offering themselves for employment (decrease in quantity supplied).

8. a. See the diagram below.
   b. $P^* = \$3; Q^* = 16$.

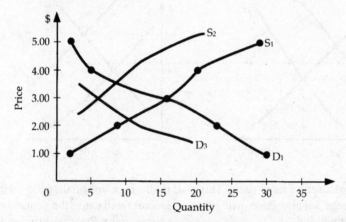

   c. See the diagram above. There will be no change in demand. Costs have risen, reducing profits, so supply will shift to the left (although we can't say how far). At $3, an excess demand now exists, which will push prices higher.
   d. See the diagram above. Demand for orange juice will fall (although we can't say by how much). Consumption of Master Choice orange drink will rise, and some consumers of orange juice will substitute the relatively cheap Master Choice orange drink.

9. a. See the diagram below.
   b. Increase.

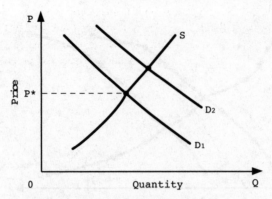

c. The demand curve must shift to the right.

d. Excess demand, leading to pressure for price to rise, will cause a reduction in the quantity demanded and an increase in the quantity supplied. This will continue until a new equilibrium is established.

10.

a. The subsidy will increase supply. Price will fall and output will rise.

b. The price of fish will increase and consumers will switch to beef. The demand for beef will increase. Price will rise and output will rise.

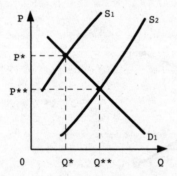

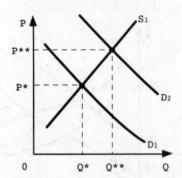

c. Costs of production have risen. This will decrease supply. Price will rise and output will fall.

d. Beef is a normal good. Higher incomes will cause the demand curve to shift right. Price will rise and output will rise.

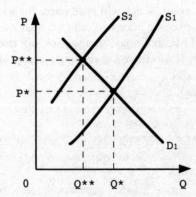

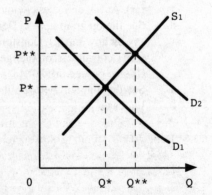

e. Costs of production will fall. Supply will shift to the right. Price will fall and output will rise.

f. A poor tomato crop will drive up the price of tomatoes (and ketchup). Less ketchup will be used so less beef will be demanded. Price and output will fall.

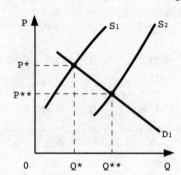

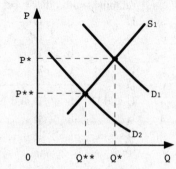

11. a. Presumably, your demand curve is downsloping and intersects the price axis at some point.

    b. With a greater number of substitutes, you will be more sensitive to changes in the price of your good. The curve will tend to be flatter.

    c. Presumably, the demand curve would shift to the right.

    d. If this is a normal good, demand would increase. If it is an inferior good, demand would decrease.

12. a. The supply curves are the same (vertical at 50 000). In the Yankees' case, at a price of $15 per ticket, there is an excess demand. In the Royals' case, at a price of $15 per ticket, because demand is so low, there is an excess supply. See the diagram below.

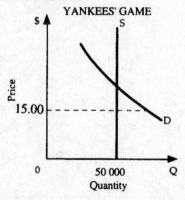

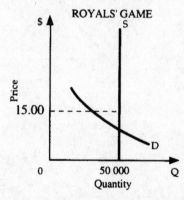

    b. To fill the stadium, let the ticket price fall to the equilibrium level. Whether this strategy will bring in more revenue will depend on the elasticity of the demand curve—see *Principles of Microeconomics* Chapter 5 for more on the concept of elasticity. Another strategy would be to charge $30 for a combined pass to both games. Fans wanting to see the Yankees would probably pay out more money and might also come to the second game.

13. Demand for labour would increase and, as workers moved away from the region, supply of labour would decrease. Wages, then, would increase and the costs of doing business in Southern Ontario would rise.

14. a. The test has reduced the supply of cabbies. This has forced up the price of taxi rides in London.

b. Given the raised price of cab rides, the demand for substitutes will have increased. Other forms of public transportation will have been able to increase their prices.

c. Cabbies who have passed the test and earned their licence like the scheme because it reduces competition. This is especially true if the degree of substitutability with other types of public transportation is slight.

15. a. D  b. D  c. U  d. D
    e. D  f. U  g. I
16. a. U  b. U  c. D  d. D
    e. I  f. I  g. I  h. U
    i. D
17. a. U and D  b. D and U  c. U and I  d. U and I
18. a. B  b. B  c. A  d. C
    e. B  f. B  g. A  h. B
    i. C

# 5 The Price System and Supply and Demand

## OBJECTIVES: POINT BY POINT

After completing this chapter, you should be able to accomplish the objectives listed below.

### OBJECTIVE 1: Describe the role of price as a rationing device.

The price system has two important functions—it rations scarce output and determines how productive resources are allocated. Because of scarcity, rationing always occurs. Price rationing operates to distinguish those who are "willing and able" to buy from those who are only able but no longer willing, i.e., it allocates according to the willingness and ability of consumers to pay—those who are willing and able to pay as the price increases will get the good. Demand is constrained by income and wealth but, within those limits, individual preferences will prevail. If demand increases, price rises, signalling producers that profits may be made. More of the good will be produced with resources being switched from other lines of production.

(page 97)

> **TIP:** Note the lobster example in the textbook, which describes the rationing and allocative roles that prices play in the market place.
>
> Note, too, that the profit motive is highly durable. Limitations (such as price ceilings or rationing) placed on the operation of the market can lead to black markets so that demand can be serviced.

## Practice

1.  In a free market, non-price rationing must occur when _____ exists.
    A.  an excess demand.
    B.  an excess supply.
    C.  a perfectly horizontal demand.
    D.  a perfectly vertical demand.

    **ANSWER**: A. Given an excess demand, either price will increase (price rationing) or non-price rationing must be enforced.

2.  In a free market the rationing mechanism is
    A.  price.
    B.  quantity.
    C.  demand.
    D.  supply.

    **ANSWER**: A. Given an imbalance between quantity demanded and quantity supplied, a free market will adjust price to achieve equilibrium.

## OBJECTIVE 2: Descrive the alternative rationing mechanisms.

Price rationing may be considered "unfair"—poor people might be priced out of the market for some essentials—so other non-price-rationing methods, including queuing, ration coupons, favoured customers, and lotteries, are applied. Such schemes usually involve hidden costs (queuing costs time, for example) that may make them inefficient. Note that different types of rationing benefit different groups of people. (page 100)

At some U.S. universities, basketball tickets are distributed on a first come first served basis—meaning that students must queue, perhaps for days, to get tickets to the big game. Not-so-hidden costs include the inconvenience, loss of study time, and possible health effects. As an example of a lottery, universities may allocate dorm rooms, not by price or need, but by random number selection.

> **TIP:** Remember that a price ceiling stops the price going higher (just like a ceiling in a room), while a price floor is a lower limit. To have an effect on equilibrium price, a ceiling must be set below the equilibrium price and a floor above the equilibrium price.

> **Comment:** The conceptual companion of a price ceiling is a price floor. A price ceiling sets a maximum price; a price floor sets a minimum price. The minimum wage is a price floor. An effective price ceiling creates an excess demand; an effective price floor creates an excess supply. This may seem confusing—to have a ceiling below the equilibrium price.

> **Graphing Pointer:** It is not true that a price ceiling must be established below the equilibrium price, although a ceiling set above the equilibrium has no effect. If demand and/or supply conditions change however, the ceiling could become effective. For instance, in the U.S., the adjustable rate mortgages have "caps" on how high the interest rate can move in response to market conditions—this is a price ceiling.

### Practice

3.  A price ceiling is established below the equilibrium price. We can predict that
    A.  quantity demanded will decrease.
    B.  quantity supplied will be greater than quantity demanded.
    C.  demand will be less than supply.
    D.  quantity supplied will decrease.

    **ANSWER: D.** Price will be reduced by the price ceiling. A decrease in price causes quantity supplied to decrease (not a shift in the supply curve).

4.  A price ceiling is established below the equilibrium price. We can predict that
    A.  there will be a leftward shift in the demand curve.
    B.  there will be a leftward shift in the supply curve.
    C.  quantity demanded will be greater than quantity supplied.
    D.  quantity supplied will be reduced to equal quantity demanded.

    **ANSWER: C.** A change in price does not cause the demand and/or supply curve to shift position. If price is "too low," an excess demand (quantity demanded greater than quantity supplied) will occur.

5. Ticket scalping will be successful if
   A. demand is relatively flat.
   B. demand is relatively steep.
   C. the official price is below the equilibrium price.
   D. the official price is above the equilibrium price.

   **ANSWER:** C. The steepness of the demand curve is irrelevant in this case. The important issue is that an excess demand for tickets exists because the official price has been set too low.

## OBJECTIVE 3: Apply the demand and supply model in a variety of situations.

The text offers the gasoline market and the developments since February of 1999 that caused a dramatic surge in the price of gasoline as an example of the usefulness of demand and supply analysis. The analysis shows that the agreement by OPEC and two non-OPEC (Mexico and Norway) nations to lower crude oil production along caused the supply of crude oil to drop. This in turn resulted in a drastic jump in the price of crude oil and a decline in the quantity demanded. Furthermore, the subsequent surge in the world demand for oil caused the demand to rise resulting in a further jump in the price.

The higher price of oil, however, tends to generate further developments. While such increases offer significant gains for oil-producing countries in the short term, by encouraging the development of alternative sources of energy and possibly causing a worldwide recession they tend to breed their own downfall. (page 105)

## Practice

Refer to the following diagram for the next four questions. The world price of oil in this hypothetical situation is $20 per barrel.

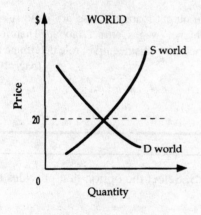 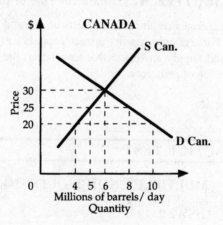

6. If the world price is the market price in Canada, then there will be an _____ of _____ million barrels per day.
   A. excess supply, 10.
   B. excess supply, 6.
   C. excess demand, 10.
   D. excess demand, 6.

   **ANSWER:** D. At $20 per barrel, quantity supplied is 4 million and quantity demanded is 10 million.

7.   Suppose that Canada imposes a $5 per barrel import fee. This will result in each of the following except
   A.   a decrease in imports to 3 million barrels per day.
   B.   an increase in the quantity supplied of oil in Canada to 5 million barrels per day.
   C.   a decrease in the quantity demanded of oil in Canada to 8 million barrels per day.
   D.   a decrease in Canadian imports of oil by 2 million barrels per day.

   **ANSWER:** D. Oil imports had been 6 million barrels per day. After the imposition of the fee, oil imports are 3 million barrels per day. Imports decreased by 3 million barrels per day.

8.   An import fee of $5 per imported barrel of oil will generate a tax revenue of
   A.   $3 million per day.
   B.   $5 million per day.
   C.   $8 million per day.
   D.   $15 million per day.

   **ANSWER:** D. Imports are 3 million barrels per day. Each barrel yields a tax revenue of $5.

9.   Suppose that Canada wishes to become self-sufficient in oil. This could be done by
   A.   establishing a price ceiling (maximum price) of $15 per barrel of oil.
   B.   establishing a price ceiling (maximum price) of $30 per barrel of oil.
   C.   imposing a fee of $10 per barrel on foreign oil.
   D.   imposing a fee of $7 per barrel on foreign oil.

   **ANSWER:** C. A fee of $10 per barrel on foreign oil will result in equilibrium in the Canadian market.

# OBJECTIVE 4: Explain the role of prices in the allocation of resources.

Price changes resulting from shifts of demand in output markets cause profits to rise or fall. For example, profits attract capital, and higher wages attract labour. Therefore, demand, supply, and prices that tend to play the incentive (disincentive) role determine the allocation of resources.                                                                                          (page 105)

## PRACTICE TEST

**I.   MULTIPLE CHOICE QUESTIONS.** Select the option that provides the single best answer.

_____  1.   A ticket to a concert by the Boys from North costs $35. Just before the concert, however, tickets are being exchanged for $100. To a ticket holder, the opportunity cost of actually attending the concert is
   A.   $35.
   B.   $65.
   C.   $100.
   D.   $135.

_____  2.   Assume that in a free labour market, the quantity demanded equals the quantity supplied at 500 000 youth jobs and the equilibrium wage rate is

equal to $5/hour. Now the government decides that the market wage is too low and imposes a wage floor (minimum wage) at $6.50. Everything else remaining equal,
A.    more jobs will be created.
B.    fewer people will be looking for a job.
C.    the demand curve will shift to the right.
D.    there will be a persistent surplus of youth workers.

Use the diagram below to answer the next three questions. The world price for gasoline is 35¢ per litre. The equilibrium price in the Canadian market is 55¢.

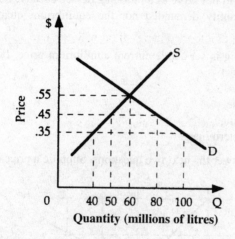

_____ 3.    Assume that Canada neither imports nor exports gasoline. At the world price for gasoline, there is an _____ of gas in the Canada market of _____ million litres.
A.    excess supply, 60.
B.    excess supply, 100.
C.    excess demand, 60.
D.    excess demand, 100.

_____ 4.    Assume that Canada imports gasoline. The government imposes an import tax that raises the price of gas to 45¢ per litre. Imports in millions of litres are
A.    30.
B.    40.
C.    50.
D.    60.

_____ 5.    The government has decided that the free market price for baby formula is "too high." Which of the following rationing proposals will result in the **least** misallocation of baby formula resources?
A.    Proposal A: establish an official price ceiling, then let sellers decide how to allocate baby formula among customers.
B.    Proposal B: issue coupons for baby formula that cannot be resold.
C.    Proposal C: issue coupons for baby formula that can be resold.
D.    Proposal D: establish a price ceiling and require purchasers to queue.

_____ 6.    A government-imposed ceiling on apartment rents, if set above the equilibrium rent level, would
A.    have no effect on the housing market.
B.    lead to a persistent shortage of apartments.
C.    lead to a persistent surplus of apartments.
D.    shift the supply curve for apartments to the right.

_____ 7.  The supply curve of bottled water on an island is completely vertical. The market for bottled water is in equilibrium. A ferryload of thirsty holiday-makers arrives and the demand for bottled water increases. Which of the following statements is true?

 A. Price will serve as a rationing device.
 B. Price will not serve as a rationing device because the quantity supplied cannot change.
 C. Price will not serve as a rationing device because the equilibrium quantity demanded cannot change.
 D. Price will not serve as a rationing device because neither the equilibrium quantity demanded nor the equilibrium quantity supplied can change.

_____ 8.  A price ceiling is set above current equilibrium price. If supply decreases, price would

 A. increase.
 B. decrease.
 C. not change.
 D. be indeterminate.

Use the graph below to answer the next two questions. Suppose a price ceiling of $1 is set.

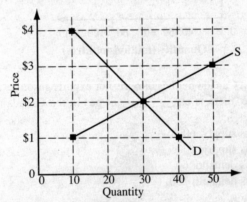

_____ 9.  The price ceiling will cause an

 A. excess supply of 40 units.
 B. excess demand of 40 units.
 C. excess demand of 30 units.
 D. excess supply of 40 units.

_____ 10.  If the price ceiling is left in place, we would predict that, eventually,

 A. Demand would decrease until quantity demanded and quantity supplied were equal at a price of $1.
 B. Demand would increase until quantity demanded and quantity supplied were equal at a price of $1.
 C. The market participants will be convinced that $1 is the equilibrium price.
 D. A persistent excess demand would lead to the emergence of non-price rationing practices such as queuing.

## II.  APPLICATION QUESTIONS.

1.  Consider the following diagram which shows the market for fluid milk. Quantity is in thousands of litres.

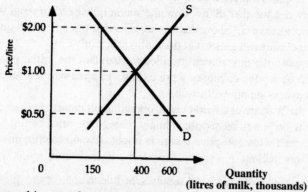

a. Calculate total income for dairy farmers.

b. Suppose that this income level is felt to be inadequate, and that a political decision is made to boost farm income to $1 200 000. Suppose the provincial government establishes a price floor at $2.00, with the government buying the excess supply. How much milk will be supplied?

c. Who gets the milk?

d. The plan achieves the income objective, but what else has it done? There are costs involved with tampering with the price mechanism. What are they?

Now suppose the government establishes a price ceiling of 50¢ per litre.

e. How much milk would consumers actually receive?

f. Which plan is better for a milk consumer who pays no provincial tax? Why?

2. In the *Applications* section of Chapter 4, we examined the market for video cassettes where the supply and demand curves are given by $Qs = 3P$ and $Qd = 60 - 2P$, respectively.

a. If the government imposes a price ceiling of $5 in this market, what will happen to the positions of the demand and supply curves?

b. Given the price ceiling, determine the extent of excess demand or supply that is present.

c. Suppose the government increases the price ceiling to $15. Determine the extent of excess demand or supply that is present.

3. Consider the egg market in the city of Warsaw.

a. Draw a demand and supply diagram below for the Warsaw egg market. Label the curves $D_1$ and $S_1$ respectively. Show the equilibrium price ($P_1$) and quantity ($Q_1$).

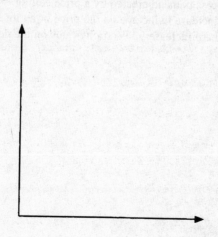

b. In August, the price of eggs tripled because of a decrease in supply caused very hot weather. Show how the market changed in August. Label the new supply curve $S_2$. Show the new equilibrium price $(P_2)$ and quantity $(Q_2)$.

c. Is the Warsaw egg market operating efficiently?

d. Suppose the government decided to maintain the initial price $(P_1)$. Should it impose a price ceiling or a price floor? Explain whether an excess demand or an excess supply will result.

e. Is the Warsaw egg market now operating efficiently?

f. How do you think suppliers might react to the price ceiling?

g. Suggest what non-price methods might develop to circumvent the imbalance in this market.

4. Use the following demand and supply schedule to answer the questions.

| Price | Quantity Demanded | Quantity Supplied |
|-------|-------------------|-------------------|
| $6 | 10 | 70 |
| $5 | 20 | 60 |
| $4 | 30 | 50 |
| $3 | 40 | 40 |
| $2 | 50 | 30 |
| $1 | 60 | 20 |

a. Calculate the equilibrium price and the equilibrium quantity.

b. Now the government establishes a price ceiling of $2. Will this cause an excess supply or an excess demand? An excess of how many units?

c. What will happen to the quantity supplied?

d. Given this change, will there be an overallocation or an underallocation of resources to the production of this good?

e. Such a price ceiling interferes with which function of the price system?

5. The freeze that destroyed a good portion of the South American coffee crop in the mid-1970s increased the price of tea. Demonstrate why, using supply and demand diagrams.

6. Illustrate each of the following with demand and/or supply curves.

a. A situation where the quantity supplied is completely unresponsive to changes in price.

b. A labour demand curve, with wage on the vertical axis, where, as the wage decreases the increase in the number of workers demanded progressively decreases.

c. A situation of excess demand created by a price ceiling.

d. The effect of an increase in income on the price of an inferior good.

e. The effect of a sharp increase in electricity rates on the demand for and price of air conditioners.

## ANSWERS AND SOLUTIONS

### PRACTICE TEST

## I. SOLUTIONS TO MULTIPLE CHOICE QUESTIONS

1. C. The opportunity cost is the value of the next best alternative given up, i.e., in monetary terms, whatever the $100 offered price would buy.

2. D. A minimum wage, set above the equilibrium price, increases the quantity of labour supplied and at the same time, reduces the quantity demanded. This results in a surplus.

3. C. The price is below the equilibrium price, with quantity demanded being 100 and quantity supplied being only 40. An excess demand of 60 exists.

4. A. Domestic demand will be 80 and domestic supply 50.

5. C. Issuing coupons that can be resold will lead to a market for coupons with those willing and able to pay the most receiving the right to buy baby formula.

6. A. To be effective, a price ceiling must be set below the equilibrium price.

7. A. Demand has increased, causing an excess demand. Price will rise to remove the imbalance.

8. A. A price ceiling above the equilibrium price will have no effect. A decrease in supply will therefore result in a higher price.

9. C. An effective price ceiling (set below the equilibrium price) will create an excess demand. Quantity demanded is 40, but quantity supplied is only 10 , so an excess demand of 30 exists.

10. D. Demand and supply curves do not shift in response to changes in price!

## II. SOLUTIONS TO APPLICATION QUESTIONS

1. a. $400 000.
   b. 600 000 litres.
   c. 150 000 litres for the consumer, and the rest is taken by the government.
   d. Many things—milk is now more expensive and less plentiful for consumers. Taxpayers—who needn't be milk consumers—will have to pick up the subsidy tab. There will be storage and administrative costs, too. Also, there is an over-allocation of resources toward milk production.
   e. Consumers will receive 150 000 litres. In this case, there will be an excess demand.
   f. The second plan is better in that the price of milk is lower.

2. a. Nothing. A change in price leads to movements along the given demand and supply curves.
   b. Equilibrium price (without the price ceiling) is $12. Therefore the price ceiling is effective. At a price of $5 the quantity demanded will be $50 and the quantity supplied will be $15. Excess demand will be 35.
   c. The price ceiling is set above the equilibrium price and will have no effect on the original market conditions.

3.  a.  See the diagram below.

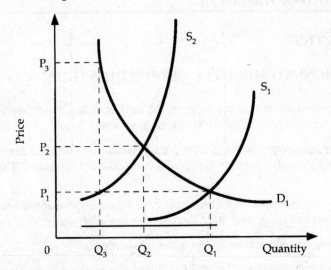

b.  See the diagram above.
c.  The market is efficient in that it is reflecting the change in supply and equalizing quantity demanded and quantity supplied.
d.  The government should impose a price ceiling to place an upper limit on price. Quantity demanded will exceed quantity supplied—there will be an excess demand.
e.  This is now a seller's market. Output is restricted to $Q_3$. At that output, an excess demand exists.
f.  Suppliers may withdraw eggs from the controlled Warsaw market—selling them either outside Warsaw or on the black market within the city. Sub-standard (small or damaged) eggs may be offered for sale. Egg quality may be sacrificed.
g.  Other rationing methods, such as queuing or preferred customers, might be used. Black markets with higher prices are likely to develop. Eggs may be sold as part of a "package" of commodities.

4.  a.  $3; 40.
    b.  excess demand; 20.
    c.  Quantity supplied will decrease.
    d.  Given demand and the reduction in supply, fewer resources than society would desire are being allocated to the production of this good.
    e.  The allocative function is constrained.

5.  Higher coffee prices increased the demand for tea (a substitute). See the diagrams below.

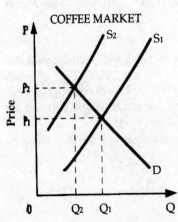

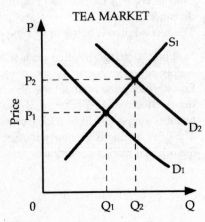

6. See the diagrams below.

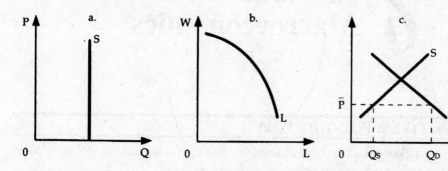

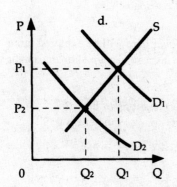

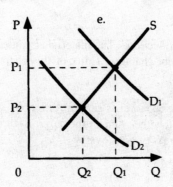

# 6 Introduction to Macroeconomics

## OBJECTIVES: POINT BY POINT

After completing this chapter, you should be able to accomplish the objectives listed below.

### General Comment

This chapter is an "introduction." The material skimmed over here will be explored more completely in subsequent chapters. Think of this chapter as a road map showing major points of interest.

> **TIP:** Different economists support different interpretations of how the economy fits together. One of the purposes of this course is to help you identify the areas of controversy.

### OBJECTIVE 1: Describe the development of Keynesian macroeconomic theory and policy within the context of the Great Depression and more recent macroeconomic events.

Macroeconomics was born out of the dark days of the Great Depression in the 1930s when the labour market didn't clear in the way that the classical model predicted it should— wages were "sticky" and unemployment persisted for years. A theoretical re-think was performed by John Maynard Keynes, who argued that the level of employment is not determined by prices and wages, but by the level of aggregate demand for goods and services. Macroeconomics remains a controversial area of study.                    (page 114)

> **TIP:** Refer to Chapter 1 to refresh your memory on the distinction between micro- and macroeconomics.

**Evolution:** Macroeconomics evolves in light of new information and phenomena. Keynes's economic theory was a product of, and response to, his own (unemployment-ridden) era. Existing theory couldn't analyze the conditions that he observed. Later developments have followed the same pattern—an orthodox view; some fresh, "awkward" real-world facts; a revision of the theory.

The 1960s had high levels of demand and a booming economy. Employment levels and job opportunities were high. This environment differed from the one that prompted Keynes to rethink economic analysis. Inflation, which became a serious issue in the 1970s, hadn't been a critical factor for him. A new controversy arose—between Keynesians and "monetarists." More on this in Chapter 18.

The soaring oil prices in the 1970s and the phenomenon of stagflation led to the development of supply-side economics. See Chapter 18.

**Practice**

1. The classical economists assumed that wages were _____ upward and _____ downward.
   A. flexible, flexible.
   B. flexible, not flexible.
   C. not flexible, flexible.
   D. not flexible, not flexible.

   **ANSWER:** A. The classical economists believed that the wage would respond to shifts in the demand for, and supply of, labour. See p. 114.

2. Aggregate behaviour refers to
   A. the behaviour of all individuals in a group taken together.
   B. the calculation of average values by adding together and dividing.
   C. forecasting future values, based on past data.
   D. the development of the microeconomic foundations of macroeconomics.

   **ANSWER:** A. See p. 114.

3. The classical economists predicted that, if the demand for labour fell, then
   A. the wage would increase, the supply of labour would increase, and unemployment would occur.
   B. the wage would decrease, the supply of labour would decrease, and unemployment would occur.
   C. the wage rate would fall to clear the market, resulting in higher unemployment.
   D. the wage rate would fall to clear the market, reducing the quantity of labour supplied and eliminating unemployment.

   **ANSWER:** D. Try drawing the labour market using demand and supply curves. The classical economists used microeconomic tools. They did not take into account contracts, minimum wages, and the possibility that the wage level could become stuck.

4. Keynes believed that the level of employment is determined by
   A. the wage level.
   B. the aggregate (overall) price level.
   C. aggregate demand.
   D. stock prices.

   **ANSWER:** C. Keynes's macroeconomic model is driven by aggregate demand. When there is an increase in the demand for goods and services, there is an increase in employment.

5. At the beginning of 1996, the Lifeguards' Union negotiates a wage contract of $8 per hour for lifeguards. The summer of 1996 is especially bleak, with little bathing. Although the demand for lifeguards decreases, their hourly wage rate does not. This is an example of a
   A. macroeconomic price.
   B. price control.
   C. sticky price.
   D. price ceiling.

   **ANSWER:** C. If the price of lifeguard services were influenced by changes in market conditions, the price (wage) should have fallen. The contractual agreement made the price "sticky."

## OBJECTIVE 2: Define inflation, aggregate output, and unemployment rate.

Major topics of concern in macroeconomics are: inflation (a general increase in the aggregate price level); aggregate output of the economy and the business cycle; and the level of employment (and the rate of unemployment, which is the proportion of the labour force that is unemployed). (page 115)

## Practice

6. _____ occurs when there are extremely rapid increases in the overall price level.
   A.  Inflation.
   B.  Stagflation.
   C.  Hyperinflation.
   D.  Superflation.

   **ANSWER:** C.  See p. 116.

7. A prolonged and deep recession is called a
   A.  stagflation.
   B.  hyperinflation.
   C.  boom.
   D.  depression.

   **ANSWER:** D.  See p. 118.

8. In a recession we expect to see unemployment _____ and aggregate output _____.
   A.  increasing, increasing.
   B.  increasing, decreasing.
   C.  decreasing, increasing.
   D.  decreasing, decreasing.

   **ANSWER:** B.  A recession is a period of decreasing output. As output decreases (usually because of falling aggregate demand), the unemployment lines lengthen.

## OBJECTIVE 3: Define fiscal policy, monetary policy, and growth (supply-side) policy.

Macro problems may be attacked through the use of fiscal, monetary, and supply-side policy actions. *Fiscal policy* involves manipulating the amount of taxation and government spending; *monetary policy* involves adjusting the quantity of money available; and *growth* or *supply-side policy* is intended to manipulate aggregate supply. (page 119)

## Practice

9. Fiscal policy is best described as government policy regarding
   A.  taxes and expenditure.
   B.  interest rates.
   C.  exchange rates.
   D.  the money supply.

   **ANSWER:** A.  See p. 119.

10. The economy is in a recession. Using fiscal policy tools, the government might
_____ government spending and _____ taxes.
   A. increase, increase.
   B. increase, decrease.
   C. decrease, increase.
   D. decrease, decrease.

   **ANSWER:** B.   Raising government spending will increase aggregate demand.
   Cutting taxes will also increase aggregate demand.

11. Cutting taxes and/or increasing government expenditure is _____ policy.
   A. expansionary fiscal policy.
   B. contractionary fiscal policy.
   C. expansionary monetary policy.
   D. contractionary monetary policy.

   **ANSWER:** A.   See p. 119.

12. Policies designed to control the amount of money in circulation are known as
   A. fiscal policies.
   B. monetary policies.
   C. incomes policies.
   D. supply-side policies.

   **ANSWER:** B.   See p. 120.

13. The government initiates a new policy designed to stimulate production directly
rather than to operate on aggregate demand. Such a policy is a(n)
   A. incomes policy.
   B. growth or supply-side policy.
   C. fiscal policy.
   D. monetary policy.

   **ANSWER:** B.   Rather than affect demand, the government's policy is intended to
   influence the economy's ability to supply. See p. 120.

## OBJECTIVE 4: Describe circular flow.

The circular flow model represents the linkages among the four different sectors of the
economy—households, firms, the government, and the rest of the world. There are three
major markets—goods-and-services, labour, and money—and the four sectors interact in
each of these.                                                              (page 120)

> **TIP:** Note that the circularity makes an important point—each dollar
> spent is also a dollar earned as income by producers. You will see this
> concept again.

## OBJECTIVE 5: Distinguish the goods-and-services market, the labour market, and the money market.

The goods-and-services market is where households purchase goods and services from
firms. The labour market is where firms purchase labour from households. The money market (or the financial market) is where households purchase stocks and bonds from firms and
also borrow from firms. Note that there are numerous markets within each "market"—the
goods-and-services market contains the market for cars, coffee, corn flakes, and cotton
swabs, for example. Each "market" is a macroeconomic aggregation.                (page
122)

## Practice

14. Households are
    A. only demanders in the money market.
    B. only suppliers in the money market.
    C. both demanders and suppliers in the money market.
    D. neither demanders nor suppliers in the money market—banks are.

    **ANSWER:** C. Households deposit (supply) funds and borrow (demand) funds. See p. 122.

15. The main point to draw from the circular flow diagram is that
    A. saving will always equal investment.
    B. every dollar of expenditure is also a dollar of income.
    C. exports equal imports.
    D. wages equal income.

    **ANSWER:** B. Option D is incorrect—other payments (rent and dividends, for example) are part of income. Because Canada typically has a trade surplus, we know that exports and imports are not necessarily equal. Saving and investment are not mentioned explicitly in the diagram—more about them later.

16. In our model of the macroeconomy, each of the following is a market arena in which households, firms, the government, and the rest of the world interact except
    A. the goods-and-services market.
    B. the foreign trade market.
    C. the labour market.
    D. the money market.

    **ANSWER:** B. Modelling in economics, as in other sciences, involves selection. Our model chooses to exclude the foreign trade market as a separate arena. See p. 122.

## OBJECTIVE 6: Use aggregate demand and aggregate supply curves to describe movements of aggregate output and the price level.

Aggregate demand (AD) and aggregate supply (AS) can be depicted in a diagram.

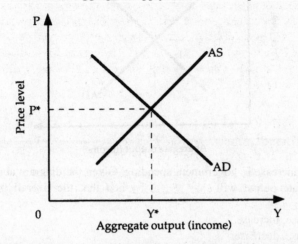

The overall price level (P) is on the vertical axis and aggregate output (Y) is on the horizontal axis. At the price level (P*) where AD and AS are equal, the economy is in equilibrium—equilibrium output is Y*. Keynesian fiscal and monetary policy is intended to shift the aggregate demand curve; supply-side policies aim to shift the aggregate supply curve. If we can shift one or both of these curves, output (and employment) and the price level (inflation) can be adjusted.                                                    (page 123)

> **Graphing Pointer:** Note that P and Y are aggregate values—the AS/AD diagram is not the same as, say, a graph showing the demand and supply of a single good like coffee.

## Practice

17.  Aggregate demand is the demand for goods and services by
     A.   households.
     B.   the private sector (households and firms).
     C.   the public  (government) sector.
     D.   all sectors in the economy.

     **ANSWER:** D.   Aggregate demand is the *total* demand by all sectors.


Use the following diagram and your intuition to answer the next three questions.

Note: These questions extend further than the material covered in the text, but you should be able to see your way to the correct answer.

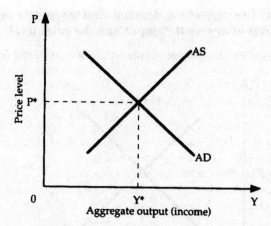

18. There is an increase in government spending. Given the diagram above, we predict that aggregate output will _____ and that the overall price level will _____.
    A. increase, increase.
    B. increase, decrease.
    C. decrease, increase.
    D. decrease, decrease.

    **ANSWER: A.** An increase in government spending increases aggregate demand. As demand shifts right, equilibrium output and price level will increase.

19. There is an increase in government spending. Given the diagram above, we predict that unemployment will _____ and that inflation will _____.
    A. increase, increase.
    B. increase, decrease.
    C. decrease, increase.
    D. decrease, decrease.

    **ANSWER: C.** As aggregate output increases, job opportunities will open up. As the overall price level rises, inflation occurs.

20. Refer to the diagram. Which of the following situations would permit stagflation to occur?
    A. An increase in aggregate demand.
    B. A decrease in aggregate demand.
    C. An increase in aggregate supply.
    D. A decrease in aggregate supply.

    **ANSWER: D.** If aggregate supply decreases (shifts left), aggregate output level will fall, causing unemployment to increase and the overall price level to increase, stimulating inflation. Inflation that occurs during periods of high and persistent unemployment is called stagflation (see p. 115).

21. In an aggregate demand/aggregate supply diagram, _____ is plotted on the vertical axis and _____ is plotted on the horizontal axis.
    A. price, quantity.
    B. overall price level, aggregate output.
    C. quantity, price.
    D. aggregate output, overall price level.

    **ANSWER: B.** This is an "aggregate" diagram—aggregate measures are called for. As in Chapter 4, though, the "price" variable goes on the vertical axis. See the diagram on p. 124.

## OBJECTIVE 7: List three main determinants of long-run growth. Distinguish between long-run growth and the business cycle.

Figure 6.7 in the text is striking because it emphasizes how important long-run growth has been in Canadian macroeconomic history. Earlier in the chapter (p. 118), it is noted that growth depends on (1) growth in the number of workers and their abilities, (2) the growth in the stock of physical capital (e.g., equipment and factories) and (3) technological progress.

But while the Canadian economic record has shown a long-term underlying expansion (growth trend), there have been fluctuations around this trend. Economists call these fluctuations "business cycles"—the Great Depression being the most grave example. Each cycle consists of four phases—peak, recession, trough, and expansion. One goal of government economic policy has been to smooth out business cycles and have the economy stay on a more even keel. (page 124)

## Practice

22. Which of the following government policies can affect output growth?
    A. Immigration policy.
    B. Education policy.
    C. Health policy.
    D. All of the above.

    **ANSWER:** D. See p. 120.

Use the following diagram of a business cycle in an economy with zero long-run trend growth to answer the next two questions.

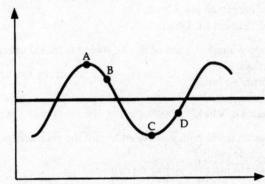

23. In the diagram of a business cycle, _____ is on the vertical axis; _____ is on the horizontal axis.
    A. inflation, unemployment.
    B. unemployment, inflation.
    C. gross domestic product, time.
    D. time, gross domestic product.

    **ANSWER:** C. The diagram plots the output level over time. Add this information to the diagram above. See the diagram on p. 126.

24. In the diagram above, the expansion of the business cycle occurs at point _____ and the recession occurs at point _____.
    A. A, B.
    B. A, C.
    C. B, C.
    D. D, B.

**ANSWER:** D. The peak is at point A, the recession at point B, the trough at point C, and the expansion at point D.

25. Inflation in Canada
    A. has been stable since 1970.
    B. was typically higher in the 1970s than in the 1990s.
    C. was typically lower in the 1970s than in the 1990s.
    D. has risen steadily since 1970.

    **ANSWER:** B. See p. 129.

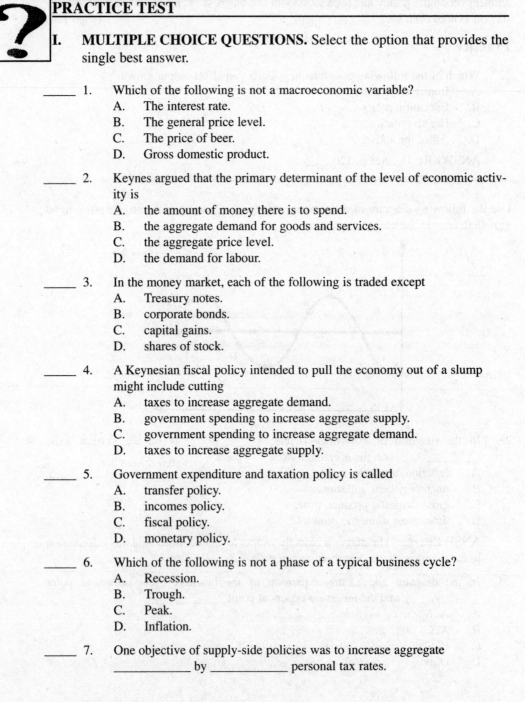

# PRACTICE TEST

**I.** **MULTIPLE CHOICE QUESTIONS.** Select the option that provides the single best answer.

_____ 1. Which of the following is not a macroeconomic variable?
    A. The interest rate.
    B. The general price level.
    C. The price of beer.
    D. Gross domestic product.

_____ 2. Keynes argued that the primary determinant of the level of economic activity is
    A. the amount of money there is to spend.
    B. the aggregate demand for goods and services.
    C. the aggregate price level.
    D. the demand for labour.

_____ 3. In the money market, each of the following is traded except
    A. Treasury notes.
    B. corporate bonds.
    C. capital gains.
    D. shares of stock.

_____ 4. A Keynesian fiscal policy intended to pull the economy out of a slump might include cutting
    A. taxes to increase aggregate demand.
    B. government spending to increase aggregate supply.
    C. government spending to increase aggregate demand.
    D. taxes to increase aggregate supply.

_____ 5. Government expenditure and taxation policy is called
    A. transfer policy.
    B. incomes policy.
    C. fiscal policy.
    D. monetary policy.

_____ 6. Which of the following is not a phase of a typical business cycle?
    A. Recession.
    B. Trough.
    C. Peak.
    D. Inflation.

_____ 7. One objective of supply-side policies was to increase aggregate
    _____ by _____ personal tax rates.

A. demand, increasing.

B. demand, decreasing.

C. supply, increasing.

D. supply, decreasing.

_____ 8. Employment often rises during

A. a period of stagflation.

B. a period of inflation.

C. a recession.

D. the period from the peak to a trough in a business cycle.

_____ 9. Each of the following is an example of a transfer payment except

A. a welfare cheque.

B. social security benefits.

C. interest on a Treasury bond.

D. unemployment compensation.

_____ 10. In the labour market, suppliers are

A. households.

B. households and firms.

C. firms and government.

D. firms.

_____ 11. In the circular flow model

A. households purchase transfer payments.

B. firms and government purchase households.

C. government sells goods and services.

D. households purchase goods and services.

_____ 12. As the economy moves into a recession, we typically see inflation
_____ and unemployment _____.

A. increasing, increasing.

B. increasing, decreasing.

C. decreasing, increasing.

D. decreasing, decreasing.

_____ 13. Governments in Canada reduced their spending levels during the 1990s.
This was an example of a(n)

A. fiscal policy.

B. monetary policy.

C. incomes policy.

D. supply-side policy.

_____ 14. Stagflation is characterized by _____ unemployment and a
_____ price level.

A. high, rising.

B. high, falling.

C. low, rising.

D. low, falling.

_____ 15. At the peak of the business cycle _____ will be low while at the
trough _____ will be slow or negative.

A   employment; unemployment

B   unemployment; economic growth

C. inflation; unemployment

D. economic growth; employment

_____ 16. Consider the aggregate demand and aggregate supply diagram on p. 121 of the textbook. If aggregate supply shifted to the left, the economic result is best described as
A. inflation.
B. hyperinflation.
C. stagflation.
D. recession.

_____ 17. A government introduces a new training program for the unemployed. Such a policy is a(n)
A. incomes policy.
B. growth or supply-side policy.
C. fiscal policy.
D. monetary policy.

_____ 18. "Sticky" prices in a given market suggest that excess demand _____ be sustained and excess supply_____ be sustained.
A. can, can.
B. can, cannot.
C. cannot, can.
D. cannot, cannot.

_____ 19. Which of the following statements is true?
A. During a period of hyperinflation, we would expect an increase in the value of savings, because everyone needs to have more money.
B. During a period of high inflation, Keynesian fiscal policy would call for an increase in the money supply.
C. Stagflation is defined as a rapid increase in the overall price level.
D. Government expenditure on infrastructure may enhance productivity.

_____ 20. In sequence, the four phases of a business cycle are
A. the trough, the expansion, the peak, and the recession.
B. the recession, the peak, the expansion, and the trough.
C. the trough, the expansion, the recession, and the peak.
D. the trough, the recession, the expansion, and the peak.

## II.   APPLICATION QUESTIONS

1.   Devise a hypothesis about the link between household income and household spending. As one increases, does the other increase or decrease? Which variable is the "cause" and which the "effect"? Why is your theory an abstraction? Is your theory invalidated if one household behaves differently?

2.   How do you personally participate in the markets for goods and services, labour and finance?

3.   Our aggregate demand and supply analysis is not yet theoretically rigorous, but let us use the model anyway. An aggregate demand and aggregate supply diagram follows. Equilibrium output is Y*. Suppose that, at this output level, there are large quantities of unemployed resources in the economy and that the more production there is the higher employment will be.

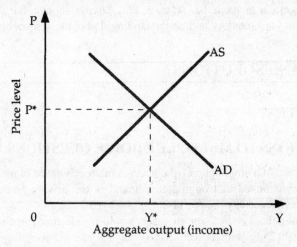

a. What comprises total demand for goods in the economy?
b. Given the income level, what will happen to the level of consumption spending by households if saving increases?
c. How will aggregate demand be affected by an increase in saving?
d. How could you represent this change in aggregate demand on the diagram?
e. In terms of output (and employment), what would be the impact of the change in aggregate demand?
f. Ignoring the foreign sector of the economy, how could such a shift in aggregate demand be prevented?
g. Suppose the government reduced income taxes on households. What effect is this likely to have on consumption, aggregate demand, output level, employment, unemployment, and the aggregate price level?

4. Draw an aggregate demand and aggregate supply graph for the economy. Suppose aggregate demand increases. What happens to aggregate output? What should happen to employment? If the government managed to increase aggregate demand (and cut unemployment), what other problems might it face?

5. Identify the following topics as either predominantly macroeconomic (MAC) or microeconomic (MIC).
   a. _____ gross domestic product.
   b. _____ the demand for beer
   c. _____ inflation
   d. _____ the price of gold relative to the price of silver
   e. _____ unemployment among economics professors
   f. _____ wages in regulated public utilities
   g. _____ economic growth
   h. _____ stagflation
   i. _____ price of medical care
   j. _____ job discrimination
   k. _____ recession
   l. _____ apartment rents
   m. _____ total employment
   n. _____ household income
   o. _____ national income
   p. _____ business cycles
   q. _____ the budget deficit
   r. _____ the money supply

6. A flow diagram is given in the text on p. 121. After going over the section in the text, draw it from your memory and understanding. Label the arrows between sectors.

## ANSWERS AND SOLUTIONS

## PRACTICE TEST

## I. SOLUTIONS TO MULTIPLE CHOICE QUESTIONS

1. C. The price of a single good (like beer) is microeconomic in nature.
2. B. Keynes believed that aggregate demand is the driving force in determining macroeconomic activity. See p. 114.
3. C. Capital gains occur when an asset is sold at a higher price than its purchase price. See p. 123.
4. A. Keynesian fiscal policy focuses on aggregate demand. To move the economy out of a slump, the government could cut taxes. This would give taxpayers more income to spend. See p. 119.
5. C. See p. 119 for a discussion of the types of policy.
6. D. A business cycle reflects changes in production level. The missing phase is the expansion. See p. 126.
7. D. Supply-side policies affected aggregate supply. A cut in tax rates was intended to increase production as some economists argue that high taxes may discourage effort, saving and investment. See p. 124.
8. B. See the discussion of Canadian business cycles since 1970, beginning on p. 126. Note however that if aggregate supply decreases, the economy can experience inflation and increasing unemployment—i.e., stagflation.
9. C. Transfers are payments that require no good or service in return. Interest on a bond is a fee (reward) for lending the government money. See p. 120.
10. A. See p. 122.
11. D. See the circular flow diagram on p. 121.
12. C. When the economy is slowing down, it is harder to sell goods (harder to raise prices) and harder to find a job. Note that if a decrease in aggregate supply has caused the recession, inflation will increase—i.e., stagflation.
13. A. See p. 119.
14. A. Stagflation combines stagnation (high unemployment) with inflation (rising aggregate price level). See p. 115.
15. B. See p. 126.
16. C. As aggregate supply shifts left, aggregate output decreases and economic growth falters. Also, the aggregate price level will increase (inflation). It is true that inflation occurs (Option A) and that a recession occurs (Option D) but, for a description of the complete situation, stagflation is more comprehensive. See p. 115 for the definition of stagflation.
17. B. This policy, which increases the quality of the workforce, can influence the economy's ability to supply. See p. 120.
18. A. When prices are sticky (not very responsive to demand or supply changes), a situation of excess demand or excess supply can persist because, in either case, price does not move to eliminate the market imbalance. See p. 114.
19. D. See p. 120. Answer A is incorrect because during hyperinflation, the value of currency is decreasing rapidly. The worst thing to do is hold money—it is better to spend it before it falls further in value. Answer B is incorrect because increasing the money supply is not fiscal policy. Answer C is not correct because stagflation is more than just inflation.
20. A. See p. 126.

## II.    SOLUTIONS TO APPLICATION QUESTIONS

1.    There is a positive relationship between household income (independent variable) and household spending (dependent variable). The theory is an abstraction because it excludes all other factors that might affect household spending. If, in general, households behave as predicted by the theory, it is supported, exceptions notwithstanding.

2.    In the market for goods and services, you are probably a buyer (e.g., groceries); in the market for labour you are probably a seller; and, in the money market, you are a seller if you save and a buyer if you borrow (e.g., student loans).

3.    a.    Consumption, investment, government spending, and net exports.
      b.    Consumption will decrease.
      c.    Aggregate demand will fall because consumption has fallen.
      d.    The AD curve would shift to the left.
      e.    Equilibrium output would decrease. Because fewer goods are being produced, we can predict increased unemployment.
      f.    Such a decrease in aggregate demand may be prevented by increasing investment spending or increasing government spending. Another possibility is that another factor could make consumption increase again.
      g.    If the government reduced income taxes on households, after-tax income would increase, and consumption would increase (making AD shift right). Output level and employment would increase, unemployment would decrease, and the aggregate price level would increase.

      Note: One way, perhaps, to alleviate unemployment is through fiscal policy actions—changing the levels of government spending and/or taxes.

4.    Refer to the diagram on p. 124 of the textbook. An increase in aggregate demand would cause the equilibrium output level to increase. As more is being produced, more workers will be hired. An increase in demand, though, will cause the overall price level to increase (inflation). A government fiscal policy to increase aggregate demand might involve cutting taxes and/or increasing government spending—these measures would increase the federal budget deficit.

5.    
| a. | MAC | f. | MIC | k. | MAC | p. | MAC |
|----|-----|----|-----|----|-----|----|-----|
| b. | MIC | g. | MAC | l. | MIC | q. | MAC |
| c. | MAC | h. | MAC | m. | MAC | r. | MAC |
| d. | MIC | i. | MIC | n. | MIC | | |
| e. | MIC | j. | MIC | o. | MAC | | |

6.    Refer to the text for the solutions to this exercise.

# 7 Measuring National Output, National Income, and the Price Level

## OBJECTIVES: POINT BY POINT

After completing this chapter, you should be able to accomplish the objectives listed below.

### General Comment

Most students find this chapter a bit of a chore. Memorize the important definitions: GDP, the components of the expenditure approach, depreciation, saving, and disposable income.

### OBJECTIVE 1: Define GDP. Explain the difference between GDP and GNP.

There is a family of national income accounts, but the key measure of current domestic economic activity is *gross domestic product*. GDP is the market value of all final goods and services produced within the economy. Second-hand sales, sales of intermediate goods, public and private transfers payments, and the value of financial transactions are all excluded. (page 132)

> **TIP:** There's no substitute for learning the rationale behind the concept of GDP. Productive economic activity within the economy results in new final goods and services. Sales of final goods plus (or minus) change in inventories will capture this. Compare this idea of new productive activity with the items that are excluded from GDP.

> **TIP:** Consider the logic behind the exclusion of some items from GDP calculations, such as transfer payments (public and private), intermediate goods, second-hand sales, and financial transactions. We're measuring current production of goods and services. Why are these categories excluded?
>
> Moonlighting, "do-it-yourself" activities, barter, and illegal activities don't show up either, although current goods and services are provided through these activities. How much would GDP change if, for example, the sale of drugs were decriminalized?

GDP is the value of output produced by factors of production located within a country, while GNP is the value of output produced by factors owned by a country's residents. In *principle*, this means that agricultural production attributed to Jamaican migrant workers harvesting peaches in Ontario should not be counted in Canadian GNP but should be counted in GDP. But in *practice*, in calculating the official statistics, Statistics Canada does not make an adjustment for labour income; hence such output will count in both Canadian GNP and GDP. Statistics Canada does make the adjustment for investment income so that, for example, the value of production in Canada attributed to Shell, a foreign-owned oil company, does not count in Canadian GNP but does count in Canadian GDP, both in principle and in practice.

## Practice

1. Canada's gross domestic product for 1998 is defined as the total market value of all
   A. final goods and services sold in 1998.
   B. goods and services produced in 1998 by productive resources owned by Canadian citizens.
   C. final goods and services produced in 1998 within Canadian boundaries by productive resources owned by Canadian citizens.
   D. final goods and services produced in 1998 within Canadian boundaries.

   **ANSWER:** D. Ownership of resources is irrelevant in GDP calculations; the location of production is—it must be within Canadian boundaries. See p. 134.

2. _____ goods are goods that are not resold to someone else.
   A. Intermediate.
   B. Final.
   C. Transfer.
   D. Consumer durable.

   **ANSWER:** B. Consumer durables may not be resold (except as second-hand goods)—they are final goods. Goods that are resold are intermediate goods or second-hand goods. See p. 133.

3. Jean, an avid gardener, buys a packet of carrot seeds. The packet of seeds _____ counted in GDP as a final product; the carrots Jean grows and consumes _____ counted in GDP as a final product.
   A. is; are.
   B. is; are not.
   C. is not, are.
   D. is not, are not.

   **ANSWER:** B. The seeds are sold to the final user. Because Jean grows and eats the carrots, they never reach a market and will not be counted (although they do represent a part of production). This is one of the limitations of the GDP concept.

4. Many Arbezani workers cross the border to work in Arboc although few Arbocalis work in Arbez. We should expect that Arbezani GDP will be _____ than its GNP and that Arbocali GDP will be _____ than its GNP.
   A. greater, greater.
   B. greater, smaller.
   C. smaller, greater.
   D. smaller, smaller.

   **ANSWER:** C. GDP measures production by location. More resources are producing in Arboc. GNP measures production by ownership. See p. 134. Note this answer assumes that Arboc and Arbez make adjustments for labour income in calculating GDP.

## OBJECTIVE 2: Explain how to use the expenditure approach when calculating GDP. Define value added.

Two methods, the *expenditure approach* and the *income approach*, are used to calculate GDP. The two methods produce the same result, because a dollar spent is also a dollar received as income. The expenditure approach is summed up by:

$$GDP = C + I + G + (EX - IM)$$

where      C = personal consumption expenditures
               I = gross private domestic investment
               G = government purchases
               (EX − IM) = net exports              (page 136)

> **TIP:** The market value of production is the equivalent of price times quantity and can be visualized in two ways. We can measure the market value by focusing on the aggregate demand side (expenditure) or by focusing on the aggregate supply side (income of producers). We'll see later (in Chapter 14) that aggregate demand is made up of C + I + G + (EX − IM).

*Gross private investment* includes residential investment, non-residential investment, and *changes* in the level of business inventories—not financial transactions, or putting money in your savings account. Depreciation is the allowance made by businesses for the deterioration of capital as time passes. This is certainly a cost of production. Net investment is gross investment minus depreciation.           (page 136)

> Tip: "Change in inventories" is an important part of the analysis. What would happen to (total) inventories if (total) demand in the economy was bigger than (total) supply? Inventories would fall. Unexpected inventory change is an important part of the economy's signalling mechanism. Falling inventories tell producers to increase production; unpleasantly high inventory levels tell producers to cut back production. Watch for this point in Chapter 9.

Consumption expenditures are divided among spending on durable goods (e.g., a car), non-durable goods (e.g., gasoline), and services (e.g., an oil change).

Value added is the difference between the value of goods as they leave a stage of production and the cost of the goods as they entered that stage. We cannot calculate GDP as the value of all goods and services that are produced but only as the value of final goods. (To count both the value of the bread sold at the grocery store and the value of the flour used to make the bread would be double-counting.) However we can calculate GDP as the value added of all goods and services at each stage of production.

## Practice

5.     Wheat is used in the production of bread. Wheat is a(n) _____ good; bread is a(n) _____ good.
      A.    final, final.
      B.    final, intermediate.
      C.    intermediate, final.
      D.    intermediate, intermediate.

      **ANSWER:** C.   The wheat is used in producing the bread. To count both it and the bread as final products would be double-counting. See p. 133.

6. The expenditure approach equation is
   A. C + I + G + (EX + IM).
   B. C + I + G − (EX + IM).
   C. C + I + G + (EX − IM).
   D. C + I + G − (EX − IM).

   **ANSWER:** C. Net exports (EX − IM) are added to the total. See p. 136.

7. A developer has some apartment buildings built. This expenditure is best described as
   A. residential consumption.
   B. residential investment.
   C. durable consumption.
   D. inventory investment.

   **ANSWER:** B. All new construction is classified as investment. See p. 136.

8. Gross private investment has three components:
   A. Business investment in plant and equipment, residential construction, and inventory investment.
   B. Business investment in plant and equipment, residential construction, and net exports of machinery.
   C. Stocks, bonds, and real estate.
   D. Purchases of new firms, purchases of existing firms, and purchases of residential housing stock.

   **ANSWER:** A. See p. 136.

9. Having totalled the other components of GDP, Arbez finds that (i) business inventories have fallen during the last year while (ii) imports have exceeded exports. (i) will _____ GDP; (ii) will _____ GDP.
   A. increase, increase.
   B. increase, decrease.
   C. decrease, increase.
   D. decrease, decrease.

   **ANSWER:** D. A decrease in inventories is a reduction in investment spending. If imports have exceeded exports, net exports are negative.

10. GDP is 1200, consumption is 900, gross private domestic investment is 150, exports are 50, and imports are 125. Depreciation is 40. Government spending is
    A. 15.
    B. 75.
    C. 225.
    D. 265.

    **ANSWER:** C. GDP = C + I + G + (EX − IM). 1200 = 900 + 150 + G + (50 − 125). Depreciation is not relevant in this calculation.

11. The capital stock at the end of 1998 is equal to the capital stock at the beginning of 1998
    A. plus depreciation.
    B. minus depreciation.
    C. plus net investment.
    D. plus gross investment.

    **ANSWER:** C. The change in the capital stock is net investment. See p. 137.

## OBJECTIVE 3: Explain how to use the income approach when calculating GDP.

The *income approach* totals the income payments of the productive resources (labour income [wages and salaries, mostly], interest income, farm income, unincorporated business income, and corporate profits before taxes) plus two other non-income charges (depreciation and indirect taxes minus subsidies) that affect the market value of production. Income payments of productive resources are called *net domestic income*.

Note that GDP adds in payments to foreign factors and subtracts payments earned abroad by Canadian citizens. GNP does not count either of these factor payments and, to get to GNP from GDP, we must *subtract* payments to foreign factors and *add* payments earned abroad by Canadian citizens.

> **TIP:** Think of saving as non-consumption. You don't have to put money into the bank for an economist to consider as "saved" the income left over after you've bought what you want.

> **TIP:** Keep reminding yourself that investment involves purchases of real productive plant and equipment (and changes in inventory), but not financial investments. The buying and selling of stocks and bonds does not, in itself, constitute investment.

## Practice

12. The best measure of the total income of households is
    A. GDP.
    B. GNP.
    C. net domestic income.
    D. personal income.

    **ANSWER:** D.   Net domestic income measures the income earned by productive resources. Some income, though, doesn't reach households—net investment income. Some income received by households is unearned—transfer payments such as welfare. Personal income records the income received by all households after these adjustments have been made.

13. Using the income approach, GDP is equal to
    A. Net domestic income + Depreciation + (Indirect Taxes + Subsidies)
    B. Net domestic income + Depreciation + (Indirect Taxes – Subsidies)
    C. Net domestic income – Depreciation – (Indirect Taxes + Subsidies)
    D. Net domestic income – Depreciation + (Indirect Taxes – Subsidies)

    **ANSWER:** B.   The value of production equals the costs of resources plus other production costs (depreciation and indirect taxes) minus offsetting subsidies. See p. 139.

14. GDP minus _____ and minus _____ equals net domestic income.
    A. net investment income outflows; depreciation.
    B. net investment income outflows; indirect taxes less subsidies.
    C. indirect taxes less subsidies; depreciation.
    D. net investment income inflows; indirect taxes less subsidies.

    **ANSWER:** C.   GDP includes depreciation. Net domestic product subtracts these costs. Net domestic income subtracts indirect taxes less subsidies from net domestic product.

15. If a country's personal income is $680 billion, personal taxes are $170 billion, and personal savings are $20 billion, then the saving rate is
    A. 2.9%.
    B. 3.9%.
    C. 11.8%.
    D. 27.9%.

    **ANSWER:** B. The saving rate is the percentage of disposable income that is saved. Disposable income is personal income minus personal taxes = $680b – $170b = $510b, so the saving rate = $20b/$510b = .039 = 3.9%.

# OBJECTIVE 4: Distinguish between real GDP and nominal GDP.

*Nominal GDP* measures production in current dollars, meaning that the dollar value of the production of a given year is calculated using the prices from that year, while *real GDP*, a measure of output that controls for price changes, is calculated using prices from a base year.                                                                    (page 142)

> **TIP:** A common mistake in macroeconomics is failing to distinguish between real and nominal values, as in the case of GDP. *Real* values correct for the effect of price changes, *nominal* values don't. Example: Your nominal wage is simply the number of dollars in your pay cheque; your real wage (spending power) also depends on prices in the grocery store. When your grandmother tells you how wonderfully cheap things were back in the good old days, she's comparing nominal values that shouldn't be compared. Ask her about hourly wage levels back in those same good old days.

# OBJECTIVE 5: Explain how the GDP price deflator and the consumer price index are calculated.

Because changes in nominal GDP include the effect of price changes and real GDP does not, the GDP deflator = (Nominal GDP ÷ real GDP) × 100 is an index of the overall price level. Because it is based on comparing the value of current production at current prices to its value at base-year prices, the "weights" change each year as the mix of current production changes. The consumer price index (CPI) is an example of a fixed-weight price index. It is calculated by comparing the cost of the same fixed basket of goods in different years. Thus one reason that the GDP deflator will yield a different measure of inflation than the CPI is that the former uses a changing basket of goods (current production) while the latter uses a fixed basket.

> **TIP:** Note that the formula
> GDP deflator = (Nominal GDP ÷ real GDP) × 100
> can be rearranged to get
> Real GDP = (Nominal GDP ÷ GDP deflator) × 100.

## Practice

16. If real GDP decreases from 1997 to 1998, we can conclude that
    A. production levels are lower in 1998.
    B. price levels are lower in 1998.
    C. there is less unemployment in 1998.
    D. we need more information before commenting.

    **ANSWER:** A. Real GDP measures the level of real production.

Use the following information about prices of goods in Arboc to calculate the economy's production for the next three questions.

| | Production | | | Prices | | |
|---|---|---|---|---|---|---|
| Good | Year 1 | Year 2 | Year 3 | Year 1 | Year 2 | Year 3 |
| Goat Milk | 200 | 180 | 160 | 2.00 | 2.40 | 2.50 |
| Bananas | 80 | 90 | 100 | 3.00 | 3.20 | 3.10 |

17. Nominal GDP in Year 1 is _____ and nominal GDP in Year 2 is _____.
    A. 640, 720.
    B. 640, 736.
    C. 630, 720.
    D. 630, 736.

    **ANSWER:** A. Nominal GDP for Year 1 = $(200 \times 2.00) + (80 \times 3.00) = 640$. Nominal GDP for Year 2 = $(180 \times 2.40) + (90 \times 3.20) = 720$.

18. In Year 1 prices, real GDP in Year 2 is _____ and real GDP in Year 3 is _____.
    A. 640, 620.
    B. 640, 630.
    C. 630, 640.
    D. 630, 620.

    **ANSWER:** D. Real GDP for Year 2 = $(180 \times 2.00) + (90 \times 3.00) = 630$. Real GDP for Year 3 = $(160 \times 2.00) + (100 \times 3.00) = 620$.

19. The GDP deflator in Year 3, with Year 1 as the base year, is
    A. 82.9.
    B. 87.3.
    C. 114.5.
    D. 120.6.

    **ANSWER:** C. Nominal GDP for Year 3 = $(160 \times 2.50) + (100 \times 3.10) = 710$. Real GDP for Year 3 = $(160 \times 2.00) + (100 \times 3.00) = 620$. GDP price index = (nominal GDP/real GDP) $\times 100 = (710/620) \times 100 = 114.5$.

20. In Arbez, between 1998 and 1999, nominal GDP rose by 3.9% while real GDP fell by 1.3%. We can conclude that the overall price level
    A. rose by about 5.2% between 1998 and 1999.
    B. rose by about 2.6% between 1998 and 1999.
    C. fell by about 2.6% between 1998 and 1999.
    D. fell by about 5.2% between 1998 and 1999.

    **ANSWER:** A. If real GDP had been unchanged, the increase in nominal GDP would tell us that prices had risen by 3.9%. Because real GDP did fall, the increase in price level must have been even greater. For small changes, the percentage increase in nominal GDP is approximately equal to the sum of the percentage increase in real GDP and the percentage change in the price level (as measured by the GDP deflator). Hence 3.9% = −1.3% + the percentage change in the price level, implying the percentage change in the price level is 5.2%.

21. In Arboc, nominal GDP is 4000 opeks and real GDP is 3000 opeks. The GDP price index is
    A.  25.
    B.  33.33.
    C.  75.
    D.  133.33.

    **ANSWER:** D.  To find the GDP price index, divide nominal GDP by real GDP and then multiply by 100.

Use the following information about prices of goods in Arboc to calculate measures of price change for the next two questions.

|  | **Production** | | **Prices** | |
| --- | --- | --- | --- | --- |
| Good | Year 1 | Year 2 | Year 1 | Year 2 |
| Goat Milk | 200 | 180 | 2.00 | 2.40 |
| Bananas | 80 | 90 | 2.80 | 3.00 |

22. The GDP deflator in Year 2, when Year 1 is the base year, equals
    A.  112.5.
    B.  114.7.
    C.  115.4.
    D.  117.6.

    ANSWER:  B.   The GDP deflator in Year 2 = 100 times (nominal GDP in Year 2) divided by (real GDP in Year 2). Nominal GDP in Year 2 is Year 2 production valued at Year 2 prices = 702. Real GDP in Year 2, with Year 1 as the base year, is Year 2 production at Year 1 prices = 612. (702/612) × 100 = 114.7.

23. The fixed-weight price index in Year 2, when Year 1 is both the base year and the source of the weights, equals
    A.  112.5.
    B.  114.7.
    C.  115.4.
    D.  117.6

    ANSWER:  C.   The value of Year 1 quantities at Year 1 prices is 624. The value of Year 1 quantities at Year 2 prices is 720. The fixed-weight price index in Year 2 is 100 times 720 divided by 624 or 115.4. Note the consumer price index is a fixed-weight price index.

## OBJECTIVE 6: Outline the shortcomings of per capita GDP as a measure of social well-being.

It's tempting to equate a rising GDP, or even a rising per capita GDP, with greater well-being, but the limitations of the national income measure disallow this. GDP measures the "market value" of production; but not all goods and services affecting our well-being reach a market—the "underground economy" is a significant example. GDP doesn't count "bads" such as pollution, and changes in GDP simply might be due to activities such as child care or house work being recorded in the market when they previously weren't. GDP also ignores the distribution of spending power, and what kinds of goods are being produced—all of these factors can affect the well-being of individuals in society. (page 147)

## Practice

24. GDP includes
    A. the market value of goods and services produced in the underground economy.
    B. the value of satisfaction derived from amusement parks.
    C. the expenditures involved in changing aerosol production away from the use of CFCs (chlorofluorocarbons).
    D. purchases of illegal substances that are produced in Canada.

    **ANSWER:** C. The expenditures needed to change production of aerosols would be represented in investment expenditures.

## The Family of Accounts

Collected below is the entire family of national income and production accounts, showing how to move from one account to another. Applications 4 and 6, below, give you practice in calculating the different values.

| | |
|---|---|
| Gross Domestic Product (GDP) | C + I + G + (EX – IM) |
| Net Domestic Product | GDP – Depreciation |
| Net Domestic Income | Net domestic product – (Indirect taxes – Subsidies) |
| Gross National Product (GNP) | GDP – Net investment income outflows |
| Net National Income | Net domestic income – Net investment income outflows |
| Personal Income | Net national income + (Transfers – Retained earnings) |
| Personal Disposable Income | Personal income – Personal taxes |

## PRACTICE TEST

### I.     MULTIPLE CHOICE QUESTIONS. Select the option that provides the single best answer.

_____ 1.    The value of GDP can be found by adding together
    A. government spending, consumption, net exports, and gross private investment.
    B. wages, consumption, gross private investment, and imports.
    C. consumption, government spending, transfer payments, and net exports.
    D. wages, investment, government spending, and depreciation.

_____ 2. For national accounting purposes, which of the following is not considered to be investment?
   A. Accumulation of inventories on a grocery shelf.
   B. Construction of a residential housing scheme.
   C. Purchase of 100 shares of Quebecor stock by Prof. Veall from Prof. Strain.
   D. Purchase of a new machine by the Case and Fair Manufacturing Corp.

_____ 3. Which of the following would have been entirely included in 1998 GDP?
   A. The purchase in 1998 of a 1997-model car.
   B. The purchase in 1998 of a share of GM common stock.
   C. The purchase in 1998 of a car produced in 1998.
   D. Two of the above would be counted.

_____ 4. Nominal GDP is higher this year than last. We can conclude that
   A. production levels are higher this year.
   B. price levels are higher this year.
   C. there is less unemployment this year.
   D. we need more information before commenting.

_____ 5. GDP minus _____ and minus _____ equals net domestic income.
   A. investment, depreciation.
   B. indirect taxes less subsidies, depreciation.
   C. indirect taxes less subsidies, net investment.
   D. depreciation, net investment.

_____ 6. Which one of the following most accurately reflects the amount of income actually received by households after taxes?
   A. Gross domestic product.
   B. Net national income.
   C. Personal disposable income.
   D. Personal income.

_____ 7. Real gross domestic product
   A. refers only to manufacturing production.
   B. includes government transfers.
   C. excludes services.
   D. eliminates the effect of overall price change on GDP.

_____ 8. Which of the following items would be included in Canada's gross domestic product?
   A. The value of a German camera brought back to Canada by a Canadian tourist.
   B. The output of a Canadian-owned family farm in Nova Scotia.
   C. The value of clean air.
   D. The value of imports into Canada.

_____ 9. One problem of incorporating the government sector into GDP is that
   A. we must include transfer payments, so double-counting occurs.
   B. some government production, such as national defence, is not sold.
   C. taxes reduce consumption and investment expenditures.
   D. the government adds nothing to the value of production.

_____ 10. The value of imports is subtracted in the expenditure approach, because
   A. imports are included when the value of consumption and the other components of expenditure are calculated.
   B. imports take away from domestic production.
   C. imports are bought by foreigners.
   D. imports must be bought with foreign currency.

_____ 11. The most likely immediate response to an unforeseen surge in demand for a firm's product would be to
   A. cut the price of the final product.
   B. reduce inventory levels.
   C. build up inventory levels.
   D. reduce depreciation.

_____ 12. Cambium and Xylem Timber Company of New Jersey produces wooden furniture in a facility located in Ontario, and sells its product in Canada. The profits of this U.S.-owned company are included in
   A. Canada's GDP and Canada's GNP.
   B. Canada's GDP but not Canada's GNP.
   C. Canada's GNP but not Canada's GDP.
   D. neither Canada's GDP nor Canada's GNP.

_____ 13. Net investment is
   A. depreciation plus inventory levels.
   B. depreciation minus inventory levels.
   C. gross investment plus depreciation.
   D. gross investment minus depreciation.

_____ 14. The personal saving rate is the percentage of _____ that is saved.
   A. GDP.
   B. personal income.
   C. national income.
   D. personal disposable income.

_____ 15. Transfer payments are _____ in national income and _____ in personal income.
   A. included, included.
   B. included, not included.
   C. not included, included.
   D. not included, not included.

_____ 16. In Arboc, nominal GDP is 12 000 opeks and the GDP price index is 80. Real GDP is
   A. 150 opeks.
   B. 1500 opeks.
   C. 9600 opeks.
   D. 15 000 opeks.

_____ 17. Which of the following would not be counted in Canada's GNP?
   A. $10 million worth of newly produced Honda automobiles produced in Ontario that Honda can't sell.
   B. A $1000 fee charged by a lawyer to plead a court case which she does not win.
   C. The salary of a player playing in the NBA for the Toronto Raptors.
   D. The purchase of Nortel stock just before its price increases.

_____ 18. Which of the following would be included in Canada's GNP but not Canada's GDP?
   A. Profit earned in Canada by Honda Corporation, a Japanese-owned company.
   B. Wages paid to Jamaican migrant workers harvesting peaches for a Canadian-owned company.
   C. Rent paid to Sean Thornton, the Canadian owner of a piece of land in Ireland.
   D. Dividends paid to Canadian citizens on stock in Honda Corporation, a Japanese-owned company.

_____ 19. Which of the following statements about net investment is true?
   A. Net investment equals gross investment plus depreciation.
   B. When net investment is negative, the stock of capital has decreased.
   C. When net investigation is negative, inventory levels are decreasing.
   D. When net investment is negative, inventory levels are increasing.

_____ 20. In Arbez, nominal GDP is one billion opeks in both 1991 and 2001. The GDP price index is 50 in 1991 and 120 in 2001. We can conclude that
   A. prices and real GDP have both risen from 1991 to 2001.
   B. prices have risen and real GDP has fallen from 1991 to 2001.
   C. prices have fallen and real GDP has risen from 1991 to 2001.
   D. prices and real GDP have both fallen from 1991 to 2001.

## II. APPLICATION QUESTIONS

1. Examine the following list of goods and services. Which goods and services should be included in Freedonian GDP in 2002, which should be excluded, and why?

   2500 quarter-pounder hamburgers produced in 2002
   100 tons of coal taken from the mines in the Freedonian mountains in 2002
   2 Freedonian Drof automobiles, sold in 2002, produced in 2001
   3 Freedonian Drof automobiles, sold in 2003, produced in 2002
   3 Canadian-built Fords produced in 2002 and sold in 2002
   Welfare benefits for Freedonian citizens paid in 2002
   625 pounds of beef used in hamburgers made in 2002
   Wages of employees at the company that produces the hamburgers in 2002

2. Below are some nominal GDP figures for the nation of Regit.

| Year | Nominal GDP | Percentage Change | GDP Price Index | Real GDP | Percentage Change |
|------|-------------|-------------------|-----------------|----------|-------------------|
| 1 | 4268.6 | | 0.9700 | _____ | _____ |
| 2 | 4539.9 | _____ | 1.0000 | _____ | _____ |
| 3 | 4900.4 | _____ | 1.0390 | _____ | _____ |
| 4 | 5244.0 | _____ | 1.0840 | _____ | _____ |
| 5 | 5513.8 | _____ | 1.1310 | _____ | _____ |
| 6 | 5672.6 | _____ | 1.1760 | _____ | _____ |

   a. Calculate the percentage change in nominal GDP from one year to the next, i.e., divide the difference in GDP by the GDP in the first year.
   b. Calculate real GDP.

c. Use the real GDP figures to calculate the percentage change in real GDP from one year to the next.

d. Write a brief report on the similarities and differences between the "percentage change" columns.

3. In Macrovia, the only two goods produced are bread and wine. In 1995, bread cost 90¢ a loaf and wine cost $4.00 a bottle. 800 loaves of bread and 180 bottles of wine were produced. In 2000, bread cost $1.00 a loaf and wine cost $5.00 a bottle. 1000 loaves and 200 bottles of wine were produced. In 2005, bread cost $1.20 a loaf and wine cost $5.50 a bottle. 1200 loaves and 220 bottles of wine were produced.

a. Calculate the nominal GDP for each of the three years.

b. Calculate the real GDP for each of the three years. Use 2000 as the base year.

c. Calculate the GDP deflator for each of the three years. Use 2000 as the base year.

d. Repeat b. and c. using 1995 as the base year.

e How much has real GDP changed from 1995 to 2005? Compare the results using 1995 and 2000 as base years.

4. You are given the following information by a colleague who is doing research on the Macrovian economy. Since she has never taken an economics course, she has turned to you for help using the information she has found.

| | |
|---|---|
| Macrovian exports of goods and services | 94.4 |
| Depreciation | 160.8 |
| Personal consumption expenditures | 878.2 |
| Net investment income outflows | 17.1 |
| Personal taxes | 304.0 |
| Government purchases of goods and services | 400.4 |
| Indirect taxes less Subsidies | 187.4 |
| Gross private investment | 322.7 |
| Transfers less Retained earnings | 224.6 |
| Macrovian imports of goods and services | 70.5 |

Use the information above to calculate

a. GDP _____

b. Net Domestic Product _____

c. Net Domestic Income _____

d. Net National Income _____

e. Personal Income _____

f. Personal Disposable Income _____

5. a. A Macrovian farmer produces 2000 bushels of wheat which he sells to a miller for 20¢ a bushel. The farmer receives payment of $_____ from the miller. The value added by the farmer is $_____.

b. The miller grinds the wheat into flour. She makes 1200 pounds of flour which she sells to a baker for 40¢ a pound. The miller receives payment of $_____ from the baker. The value added by the miller is $_____.

c. The baker bakes the flour into 1000 loaves which he sells for 50¢ apiece to a food distributor. The baker receives a payment of $_____ from the distributor. The value added by the baker is $_____.

d. The distributor sells 200 loaves to a local restaurant (Loafers) for $1.00 each. The remainder are sold to grocery stores at 80¢ each. The distributor receives payments totalling $_____. The value added by the distributor is $_____.

e.   At the retail level, Loafers sells 180 loaves at $1.50 each. 20 loaves are unsold and must be discarded. The grocery stores sell all of their consignment for $1.00 each. Retailers receive payments totalling $_____. The value added by the retailers is $_____.

f.   The total value added by all participants in the production process is $_____.

6.   Given the following national income and product accounts data, compute:

a.   Gross private investment   _____
b.   Net exports   _____
c.   Gross domestic product   _____
d.   Net domestic income   _____
e.   Depreciation   _____
f.   Net national income   _____
g.   Personal income   _____
h.   Disposable income   _____

| | |
|---|---|
| Imports | 110.2 |
| Fixed capital formation | 61.0 |
| Farm income | 1.6 |
| Net investment income outflows | 12.8 |
| Transfers less Retained earnings | 53.0 |
| Indirect taxes less Subsidies | 48.4 |
| Inventory valuation adjustment | 0.3 |
| Labour income | 210.5 |
| Corporate profits before taxes | 33.4 |
| Unincorporated business income | 23.0 |
| Inventory change | −2.6 |
| Exports | 121.9 |
| Interest income | 28.4 |
| Personal consumption | 230.7 |
| Government purchases | 78.8 |
| Personal taxes | 91.2 |

7.   Arboc and Arbez are two neighbouring nations. Each produces only corn. Last year, final sales of corn in each country were 500 units. Inventory rose by 50 in Arboc and fell by 25 in Arbez. Calculate GDP for:

a.   Arboc _____
b.   Arbez _____

Suppose depreciation runs at 10% of GDP in each country. Calculate Net domestic product for:

c.   Arboc _____
d.   Arbez _____

Indirect taxes and subsidies are a greater percentage of GDP in Arboc (12%) than in Arbez (5%). Calculate Net domestic income for:

e.   Arboc _____
f.   Arbez _____

8.   Use the table overleaf to answer the following questions:

a.   Calculate the percentage increase in nominal GDP from one year to the next.
b.   Use the GDP deflator to derive real GDP.
c.   Calculate the percentage increase in real GDP from one year to the next.

| Year | Nominal GDP | Nominal GDP (% increase) | GDP Deflator | Real GDP | Real GDP (% increase) |
|---|---|---|---|---|---|
| 1981 | 1212.8 | — | 46.5 | | |
| 1986 | 1990.5 | | 67.3 | | |
| 1991 | 3166.0 | | 100.0 | | |
| 1996 | 4486.2 | | 117.3 | | |

9. The nation of Arboc produces pencils and notepads. Using the following information, calculate:

| | Pencils | Notepads |
|---|---|---|
| Year 1 | 2000 at 10¢ each | 75 at $1.00 each |
| Year 2 | 2400 at 15¢ each | 60 at $1.10 each |

    a. Nominal GDP for Year 1     _____

    b. Nominal GDP for Year 2     _____

    c. Real GDP for Year 1 (Year 1 as base)     _____

    d. Real GDP for Year 2 (Year 1 as base)     _____

10. Should each of the following be included in Canada's GDP? Write Y for "yes" and N for "no."

    1. _____ the purchase of a new Canadian-made camera by Joe Blow

    2. _____ the gift of the same camera from Joe to Flo Blow

    3. _____ the purchase of the same camera by Barbara Ann Stop at a yard sale

    4. _____ the purchase of a new camera by the RCMP

    5. _____ the services of a photographer hired by the RCMP

    6. _____ the services of a photographer hired by Joe and Flo Blow on the occasion of their wedding

    7. _____ the services of Cousin Bo Blow (amateur photographer extraordinaire) to photograph the wedding

    8. _____ the production of a camera that remains unsold at the factory in Alberta

    9. _____ the purchase of a Japanese-made camera by Joe Blow

    10. _____ the use of welfare money by Moe Blow to buy a new camera

    11. _____ the provision of welfare money to Moe Blow

    12. _____ the use of welfare money to buy a second-hand camera

    13. _____ the use of welfare money to open a bank account

    14. _____ the use of welfare money to buy Kodak stock on the stock exchange

    15. _____ the purchase of in-store surveillance equipment for "The Camera Cabin"

    16. _____ the purchase of a camera for display in "The Camera Cabin"

    17. _____ the purchase of film by Joe Blow

    18. _____ the purchase of a Canadian-made camera by Joseph von Blau (a German tourist)

    19. _____ the purchase, in Germany, of a Canadian-made camera, by Josef von Blau

20. _____ the payment for the services of a camera repairman hired by Joe Blow who fails to repair the broken camera

21. _____ the payment for the services of the garbage collector who takes the broken camera to the city dump

---

# ANSWERS AND SOLUTIONS

## Practice Test

### I.   SOLUTIONS TO MULTIPLE CHOICE QUESTIONS

1. A   This is the expenditure approach. See the equation on p. 136.

2. C.   The stock transfer does not represent the production of any additional goods or services.

3. C.   We are interested in measuring how much has been produced in 1998 (whether or not it is sold in that year). The stock purchase adds no production, so it is not counted.

4. D.   Nominal GDP measures the current value of production. This value might have increased because more goods and services were produced this year than last (possibly with correspondingly lower unemployment), or because prices are higher this year than last. In short, we must be wary of reading too much into the change in this single figure. See p. 142.

5. B.   See Figure 7.1.

6. C.   This is the after-tax income of all households. See p. 142.

7. D.   Real GDP certainly includes manufacturing production, but it includes other forms of production too, including services. "Real" variables are variables that have had the effects of price changes removed. See p. 142.

8. B.   The German camera is not Canadian production. The value of clean air is intangible. Imports are included in the value of consumption purchases, etc., and then subtracted from GDP.

9. B.   GDP measures the market value of production—this is difficult when there is not an explicit market. Note that transfer payments are not included in GDP.

10. A.   See p. 139.

11. B.   If the demand for orange juice surges at the Food Tiger grocery store, the shelves begin to empty even before the management decides to raise the price.

12. B.   The profits of a foreign-owned company are included in Canada's GDP (which is concerned with the location of production) but not in Canada's GNP (which is concerned with ownership of resources).

13. D.   See p. 137.

14. D.   See p. 142.

15. C.   National income records payments to productive resources. Because a transfer is not a payment to a productive resource, it is excluded. Personal income measures income to households from all sources.

16. D.   Real GDP = (nominal GDP divided by the GDP price index) × 100 = (12 000 / 80)100 = 15 000.

17. D.   The purchase of stock is a financial transaction that does not reflect productive activity. Note that goods that are produced but not sold are included in inventory.

18. C.   GNP measures production by resources owned by Canadian citizens, regardless of where output is produced.

19. B.   Net investment will be negative if gross investment is less than depreciation. In that case, the addition to the capital stock is less than the reduction due to wear and tear. Note that net investment is gross investment minus depreciation. See the equation on p. 137.

20. B. Rising prices are indicated by the higher GDP price index in 2001. Real GDP = nominal GDP/GDP price index; therefore the real GDP is lower in 2001, (833 333 333 opeks instead of 2 billion opeks in real terms).

## II. SOLUTIONS TO APPLICATION QUESTIONS

1. 2500 quarter-pounder hamburgers produced in 2002, 100 tons of coal from the mines in the Freedonian mountains, and 3 Freedonian Drof automobiles sold in 2003 but produced in 2002 are final items that would qualify for inclusion in 2002's GDP.

   The 2 Freedonian Drof automobiles produced in 2001 were not produced in 2002. The 3 Canadian-built Fords were not produced in Freedonia. Welfare benefits for Freedonian citizens are transfer payments. The beef used in hamburgers and the wages of hamburger employees are costs of intermediate goods and services that are captured in the price of the hamburgers.

2. a.

| Year | Nominal GDP | Percentage Change | GDP Price Index | Real GDP | Percentage Change |
|------|-------------|-------------------|-----------------|----------|-------------------|
| 1 | 4268.6 | | 0.9700 | 4400.6 | |
| 2 | 4539.9 | 6.36 | 1.0000 | 4539.9 | 3.17 |
| 3 | 4900.4 | 7.94 | 1.0390 | 4716.5 | 3.89 |
| 4 | 5244.0 | 7.02 | 1.0840 | 4837.6 | 2.57 |
| 5 | 5513.8 | 5.14 | 1.1310 | 4875.2 | 0.77 |
| 6 | 5672.6 | 2.88 | 1.1760 | 4823.6 | −1.06 |

   b–c. See the table above.

   d. The "percentage change" figures display similarities, e.g., year 3 is the best year and year 6 is the worst year in each case. Notably, the real values are consistently lower than the nominal values because of rising prices. The nominal result for year 6 is the most misleading—recording 2.88% growth while the economy in fact shrank in size.

3. a.

| | 1995 | 2000 | 2005 |
|---|------|------|------|
| bread | 800 × $0.90 = $720 | 1000 × $1.00 = $1000 | 1200 × $1.20 = $1440 |
| wine | 180 × $4.00 = $720 | 200 × $5.00 = $1000 | 220 × $5.50 = $1210 |
| Nominal GDP | $1440 | $2000 | $2650 |
| bread | 800 × $1.00 = $800 | 1000 × $1.00 = $1000 | 1200 × $1.00 = $1200 |
| wine | 180 × $5.00 = $900 | 200 × $5.00 = $1000 | 220 × $5.00 = $1100 |
| Real GDP, 2000 base | $1700 | $2000 | $2300 |
| GDP deflator, 2000 base | .8471 | 1.0000 | 1.1522 |
| bread | 800 × $0.90 = $720 | 1000 × $0.90 = $900 | 1200 × $0.90 = $1080 |
| wine | 180 × $4.00 = $720 | 200 × $4.00 = $800 | 220 × $4.00 = $880 |
| Real GDP, 1995 base | $1440 | $1700 | $1960 |
| GDP deflator, 1995 base | 1.0000 | 1.1765 | 1.3520 |

b–d. See the table opposite.

e.     Real GDP has grown by 35.29% from 1995 to 2005 when 2000 is the base year, and by 36.11% when 1995 is the base year.

4.    a.    GDP = C + I + G + X = 878.2 + 322.7 + 400.4 + (94.4 – 70.5) = 1625.2.

     b.    Net domestic product = GDP – Depreciation = 1625.2 – 160.8 = 1464.4.

     c.    Net domestic income = Net domestic product – (Indirect taxes less Subsidies) = 1464.4 – 187.4 = 1277.0.

     d.    Net national income = Net domestic income – Net investment income outflows = 1277.0 – 17.1 = 1259.9.

     e.    Personal income = Net national income + (Transfers less Retained earnings) = 1259.9 + 224.6 = 1484.5

     f.    Personal disposable income = Personal income – Personal taxes = 1484.5 – 304.0 = 1180.5

5.    a.    $400, $400.

     b.    $480, $80.

     c.    $500, $20.

     d.    $840, $340.

     e.    $1070, $230.

     f.    $1070.

6.    a.    Gross private investment = Fixed capital formation + Inventory change = 61.0 + (–2.6) = 58.4.

     b.    Net exports = Exports – Imports = 121.9 – 110.2 = 11.7.

     c.    Gross domestic product = Personal consumption + Gross private investment + Government purchases + Net exports = 230.7 + 58.4 + 78.8 + 11.7 = 379.6.

     d.    Net domestic income = Labour income + Corporate profits before taxes + Interest income + Farm income + Unincorporated business income + Inventory valuation adjustment = 210.5 + 33.4 + 28.4 + 1.6 + 23.0 + 0.3 = 297.2.

     e.    Since Gross domestic product = Net domestic income + Depreciation + Indirect taxes less Subsidies, then Depreciation = Gross domestic product – Net domestic income – Indirect taxes less Subsidies = 379.6 – 297.2 – 48.4 = 34.0.

     f.    Net national income = Net domestic income – Net investment income outflows = 297.2 – 12.8 = 284.4.

     g.    Personal income = Net national income + Transfers less Retained earnings = 284.4 – 53.0 = 231.4.

     h.    Personal disposable income = Personal income – Personal taxes = 231.4 – 91.2 = 140.2.

7.    a.    GDP = Final sales + Inventory change = 500 + 50 = 550 units.

     b.    GDP = Final sales + Inventory change = 500 – 25 = 475 units.

     c.    Depreciation = 10% of GDP = 55. Net domestic product = GDP – Depreciation = 550 – 55 = 495 units.

     d.    Depreciation = 10% of GDP = 47.5. Net domestic product = GDP – Depreciation = 475 – 47.5 = 427.5 units.

     e.    Net domestic income = GDP – Depreciation – (Indirect taxes – Subsidies) = 550 – 55 – 550(.12) = 429 units.

     f.    Net domestic income = GDP – Depreciation – (Indirect taxes – Subsidies) = 475 – 47.5 – 475(.05) = 403.75 units.

8. See the table below.

| Year | Nominal GDP | Nominal GDP (% increase) | GDP Deflator | Real GDP | Real GDP (% increase) |
|------|------------|--------------------------|--------------|----------|-----------------------|
| 1981 | 1212.8 | — | 46.5 | 2608.2 | — |
| 1986 | 1990.5 | 64.1 | 67.3 | 2957.7 | 13.4 |
| 1991 | 3166.0 | 59.1 | 100.0 | 3166.0 | 7.0 |
| 1996 | 4486.2 | 41.7 | 117.3 | 3824.6 | 20.8 |

Note: Rearrange the formula
GDP price index = (Nominal GDP ÷ Real GDP) × 100 to get:
Real GDP = (Nominal GDP ÷ GDP price index) × 100

9. a. Nominal GDP for Year 1     $275
   b. Nominal GDP for Year 2     $426
   c. Real GDP for Year 1 (Year 1 as base)     $275
   d. Real GDP for Year 2 (Year 1 as base)     $300

10.

| | | | |
|---|---|---|---|
| 1. Y | 7. N | 12. N | 17. Y |
| 2. N | 8. Y | 13. N | 18. Y |
| 3. N | 9. N | 14. N | 19. Y |
| 4. Y | 10. Y | 15. Y | 20. Y |
| 5. Y | 11. N | 16. Y | 21. Y |
| 6. Y | | | |

# 8 Macroeconomic Problems: Unemployment and Inflation

After completing this chapter, you should be able to accomplish the objectives listed below.

### OBJECTIVE 1: Explain how the unemployment rate is measured.

The *labour force* totals the employed and unemployed. The *employed* include any person 15 years of age or older who:

    a.    works for pay or profit,

    b.    works without pay in a family enterprise, or

    c.    has a job but is temporarily absent from work.

The *unemployed* must be available and looking for work. Otherwise, they are considered to be out of the labour force. Some workers, *discouraged* by their inability to find jobs, stop looking for work and drop out of the labour force.     (page 154)

The *unemployment rate* is the ratio of unemployed persons (who have no job and are actively seeking employment) to the labour force. An analysis of unemployment reveals large differences in unemployment rates across demographic groups.     (page 155)

## Practice

The population of Arbez is 150 000, of which 100 000 are aged 15 or older. Of this 100 000, 60 000 have jobs, and 40 000 do not. 20 000 are unemployed but actively seeking jobs, and there are 20 000 who have given up the job search in frustration.

1.    What is the unemployment rate? _____

2.    What is the labour-force participation rate? _____

    **ANSWERS:** The unemployment rate is 25%; the labour-force participation rate is 80%. Of the 150 000 Arbezanis, only 100 000 are of an age that qualifies them to be in the labour force. Of the 100 000, 60 000 are employed, and an additional 20 000 are unemployed (without jobs, seeking work). The remaining 20 000 discouraged workers have dropped out of the labour force. There are, then, 80 000 workers in the labour force.

    Unemployment rate = Unemployed / Labour force = 20 000 / 80 000 = 25%.

    Labour-force participation rate = Labour force / Population (15+)= 80 000 / 100 000
        = 80%.

3.  During a recession, we expect to see output _____ and unemployment
    _____.
    A.  increasing, increasing.
    B.  increasing, decreasing.
    C.  decreasing, increasing.
    D.  decreasing, decreasing.

    **ANSWER:** C.  By definition, a recession occurs when real GDP falls for two or
    more quarters. As output falls, more workers are laid off. See p. 154.

4.  Typically, workers in a fish-packing factory have a high rate of absenteeism. Phyllis
    the Filleter has been "off sick" this week. She is correctly classified as
    A.  employed.
    B.  unemployed.
    C.  a discouraged worker.
    D.  not in the labour force.

    **ANSWER:** A.  If Phyllis is temporarily absent, with or without pay, she is consid-
    ered employed. See p. 154.

5.  The labour force is comprised of
    A.  the employed plus the unemployed.
    B.  the employed minus the unemployed.
    C.  the employed, the unemployed, and discouraged workers who could work.
    D.  the employed plus the unemployed minus discouraged workers who could
        work.

    **ANSWER:** A.  Discouraged workers are not counted as part of the labour force.

6.  In Arbez, there are 80 000 persons in the labour force and the unemployment rate is
    25%. As the economy moves out of a long recession and job openings increase, 5000
    discouraged workers become "encouraged" and begin searching for a job. The
    unemployment rate will become
    A.  18.75%.
    B.  23.5294%.
    C.  29.4118%.
    D.  31.25%.

    **ANSWER:** C.  Initial unemployment rate = 25% = unemployed / 80 000. The num-
    ber unemployed is 20 000. When 5000 new (unemployed) workers enter the labour
    force, the unemployment rate = 25 000 / 85 000 = 29.4%.

7.  The nation of Regit has a population of 1 million citizens age 15 or over. The labour-
    force participation rate is 80%. The number of Regitians with jobs is 728 000. The
    unemployment rate is
    A.  7.20%.
    B.  8.00%.
    C.  9.00%.
    D.  9.89%.

    **ANSWER:** C.  The unemployment rate = unemployed ÷ labour force = 72 000 /
    800 000 = .09. Labour force = participation rate × population = .8 × 1 000 000 =
    800 000. Unemployed = 800 000 – 728 000 = 72 000.

8. The nation of Noil has a population of 1 million citizens age 15 or over. The labour-force participation rate is 80%. 50 000 persons are unemployed in March. By June, 10 000 persons have given up seeking employment. This is the only change over the quarter. We can conclude that the unemployment rate was
   A. 6.25% in March and 7.50% in June.
   B. 6.25% in March and 6.25% in June.
   C. 6.25% in March and 5.06% in June.
   D. 5.00% in March and 6.25% in June.

   **ANSWER:** C. In March, the unemployment rate = unemployed ÷ labour force = 50 000 / 800 000 = .0625. In June, the unemployment rate = unemployed ÷ labour-force = 40 000 / 790 000 = .05063 = 5.06%.

## OBJECTIVE 2: Distinguish among frictional, structural, and cyclical unemployment. Describe the economic and social costs of unemployment.

The three types of unemployment are:

*frictional*—short-run unemployment due to the movement of individuals between jobs, while seeking a better match for their skills.

*structural*—longer-term unemployment, caused by changing tastes or changing technology that make some job skills less desirable. Automation or change in public preferences (foreign cars instead of Canadian-made cars) might cause structural unemployment.

*cyclical*—caused by recessions and depressions.                     (page 159)

The first two types of unemployment are inevitable in a healthy, dynamic economy. Together, they comprise the rather imprecise concept of the *natural rate of unemployment*—the rate of unemployment that occurs during the normal operation of the economy. Full employment doesn't imply zero percent unemployment.                     (page 160)

Recessions and cyclical unemployment result in lost output and adverse social consequences (broken homes, alcoholism, and suicide), and lower investment and economic growth. However, such downturns may weed out inefficient firms and reduce inflation.                     (page 162)

> **TIP:** Think of full employment as 100% employment minus the natural rate of unemployment.

## Practice

9. Unemployment caused by short-run job/skill matching problems is
   A. frictional unemployment.
   B. structural unemployment.
   C. cyclical unemployment.
   D. natural unemployment.

   **ANSWER:** A. See p. 159.

10. Recessions may have all of the following effects except
    A. inflation is reduced.
    B. efficiency is improved.
    C. investment is increased.
    D. the balance of payments improves because imports decrease.

    **ANSWER:** C. Typically, investment falls during a recession. See p. 162.

11.  During the Great Depression of the 1930s, many labourers found great difficulty finding a job. They were
A.  frictionally unemployed.
B.  structurally unemployed.
C.  cyclically unemployed.
D.  discouraged workers.

**ANSWER:** C.  In the 1930s, aggregate demand was low throughout the economy. See p. 160.

12.  The unemployment rate that occurs as a normal consequence of the efficient functioning of the economy is the
A.  frictional rate of unemployment.
B.  structural rate of unemployment.
C.  cyclical rate of unemployment.
D.  natural rate of unemployment.

**ANSWER:** D.  See p. 159. This rate includes both frictional and structural unemployment.

13.  For many years, Noil was a traditional agrarian economy, specializing in rice production. In the past few years, however, due to loans from the World Bank, Noil has developed a thriving industrial sector, and farming (although increasingly mechanized) has declined. We could expect that, over the past few years, frictional unemployment has _____ and structural unemployment has _____.
A.  increased, increased.
B.  increased, decreased.
C.  decreased, increased.
D.  decreased, decreased.

**ANSWER:** A.  As the economy's structure is changing, new skills are being required and old skills are becoming obsolete—structural unemployment is increasing. As skills become more specific and more complex, the search time to find a suitable job increases—frictional unemployment increases.

## OBJECTIVE 3: Define inflation. Outline the problems of price indexes such as the Consumer Price Index.

*Inflation* is a rise in the overall price level. It can be measured by a price index (such as the Consumer Price Index). The CPI and most other price indexes are based on a typical "basket" of commodities, and measure how the price of the basket changes over time. The effectiveness of a price index depends on how well its basket of commodities reflects the economy as time passes and prices change.                                      (page 163)

> **TIP:** Each price index has a *base year* that is assigned an index value of 100. Use the following formula to calculate the price index for a given year:
>
> $$\frac{\text{price of bundle in given year}}{\text{price of bundle in base year}} \times 100 = \text{given year's index}$$
>
> In the base year itself, this becomes $1.00 \times 100$. An index of more than (less than) 100 in a given year indicates that prices are more than (less than) those in the base year.

## Practice

14. If the CPI is 135 in Year 2 and 120 in Year 1, what is the percentage change in the price level between the years?
    A.  12.5%.
    B.  15%.
    C.  20%.
    D.  35%.

    **ANSWER:** A.  The price index changes by 15 relative to the initial price of 120. (15 / 120) × 100 = 12.5%.


## OBJECTIVE 4: Distinguish between anticipated and unanticipated inflation. Define real interest rate. Indicate who gains and who loses from inflation.

The costs of inflation are difficult to measure. Some inefficiencies occur, administrative costs may increase and there are "menu costs" (the costs of changing price tags, printing new catalogues, etc.). Unanticipated inflation is more troublesome than anticipated inflation. Losers include those on fixed incomes and lenders (creditors), while winners include borrowers (debtors). Indexation can reduce the impact of inflation. The real interest rate is the interest rate minus the rate of inflation.                    (page 166)


## Practice

15. Inflation is expected to run at 10% during 2004. Instead, it slows to 3%. This change will hurt
    A.  creditors.
    B.  debtors.
    C.  creditors and debtors equally, because it's the same for both parties.
    D.  neither, because inflation is lower.

    **ANSWER:** B.  If inflation is higher than expected, creditors lose because they will fail to compensate themselves through a higher interest rate. When inflation is lower than expected, debtors lose because they are paying an interest rate that is "too high."

16. Inflation is expected to run at 10% during 2004. Instead, it slows to 3%. During 2004, there has been
    A.  an anticipated deflation.
    B.  an unanticipated deflation.
    C.  an anticipated reduction in inflation.
    D.  an unanticipated reduction in inflation.

    **ANSWER:** D.  The change was not expected. This is not deflation—the price level is still rising at 3% a year. A deflation occurs when the price level (not the rate of increase in the price level) falls.

17. The real interest rate is 4%. Inflation is expected to run at 10% during 2004. During 2004, the market interest rate is _____. If, during 2004, the actual inflation rate is 4%, _____ lose.
    A.  6%, lenders.
    B.  6%, borrowers.
    C.  14%, lenders.
    D.  14%, borrowers.

    **ANSWER:** D.  The interest rate = expected inflation rate + real interest rate = 10% + 4% = 14%. Unanticipated reductions in inflation hurt borrowers.

18. Which of the following statements is false?
    A.  When interest rates are high, the opportunity cost of holding cash is high.
    B.  The more difficult it becomes to predict the rate of inflation, the more the level of investment decreases.
    C.  Individuals on fixed incomes gain during periods of deflation.
    D.  In the mid-1970s, prices were lower than in the 1990s, and, therefore, inflation was lower too.

    **ANSWER:** D.   Historically, Option D is false; inflation rates were higher in the mid-1970s than in the 1990s. See Figure 8.4 in the textbook. Option D is false theoretically, too. The fact that the price level is low doesn't imply that the rate of increase will also be low.

19. The difference between the interest rate on a loan and the inflation rate is
    A.  the profit margin.
    B.  the real interest rate.
    C.  the anticipation markup.
    D.  the nominal interest rate.

    **ANSWER:** B.  See p. 166.

---

**?** **PRACTICE TEST**

**I.   MULTIPLE CHOICE QUESTIONS. Select the option that provides the single best answer.**

_____ 1.   A newly-qualified dental school graduate, Shelly McCafferty, is looking for a place to set up practice. She is _____ unemployed.
           A.  frictionally.
           B.  structurally.
           C.  cyclically.
           D.  residually.

_____ 2.   The unemployment rate will fall if
           A.  there is an increase in the number of discouraged workers.
           B.  there is a recession.
           C.  the number in the labour force decreases.
           D.  there is a decrease in the population.

_____ 3.   Francine loses her job because of the introduction of labour-saving machinery. Because she has few marketable skills, she stops looking for work. We would consider her to be _____ unemployed.
           A.  cyclically.
           B.  frictionally.
           C.  structurally.
           D.  none of the above.

_____ 4. Labour-saving robots are introduced into a car assembly line. The resulting unemployment is
A. frictional.
B. structural.
C. mechanical.
D cyclical.

_____ 5. Arbez is producing at the full-employment level of production. There is
A. no unemployment.
B. some frictional and structural unemployment.
C. some cyclical unemployment.
D. a maximum participation rate.

_____ 6. Recently, a flood of cheap computer chips has poured over the border from Arboc to Arbez. Thousands of workers in the Arbezani computer chip industry have lost their jobs. This unemployment is best described as
A. frictional.
B. structural.
C. competitive.
D. cyclical.

_____ 7. The natural rate of unemployment
A. is inevitable.
B. is always at a desirable level.
C. is constant.
D. may be reduced by retraining policies.

_____ 8. A fully anticipated increase in the inflation rate can lead to
A. increased efficiency.
B. greater speculative activity.
C. higher market interest rates.
D. a decrease in barter.

_____ 9. Unanticipated inflation erodes the purchasing power of money.
_____ is hurt least by unanticipated inflation.
A. A person on a fixed income.
B. A lender.
C. A creditor.
D. A borrower.

_____ 10. The Consumer Price Index has risen from 110 to 121 during the last year. We should estimate the annual inflation rate for the last year at about
A. 9.1%.
B. 10%.
C. 11%.
D. 12%.

_____ 11. With unanticipated inflation, there will be all of the following except
A. greater risks involved in long-term contracts.
B. a reduction in the purchasing power of fixed incomes.
C. harm to debtors.
D. falling real rewards for lenders.

_____ 12. Your real wage has risen by 3% while the inflation rate was 7%. Your nominal wage must have
   A. risen by 4%.
   B. risen by 10%.
   C. fallen by 4%.
   D. fallen by 10%.

_____ 13. As the economy moves out of a recession, the discouraged-worker effect will tend to _____ the unemployment rate.
   A. increase.
   B. decrease.
   C. leave unaffected.
   D. have no influence on.

_____ 14. Which of the following statements about the labour market is true?
   A. Discouraged workers are those workers who have voluntarily chosen to become unemployed.
   B. The labour force includes everyone over the age of 16, including those who are unemployed.
   C. The labour-force participation rate is the ratio of employed persons to the total labour force.
   D. The natural rate of unemployment is usually taken to be the sum of frictional and structural unemployment.

_____ 15. Which of the following statements about inflation is false?
   A. The real interest rate is equal to the nominal interest rate plus the anticipated inflation rate.
   B. Changes in the CPI tend to overstate changes in the cost of living.
   C. During periods of unanticipated inflation, debtors benefit at the expense of creditors.
   D. "Inflation" is an increase in the overall level of prices; when the overall level of prices decreases, it's called "deflation."

_____ 16. As a result of access to the Internet, there is an increase in the speed with which unemployed workers are matched with suitable jobs. This will
   A. increase the natural rate of unemployment.
   B. decrease the natural rate of unemployment.
   C. not affect the natural rate of unemployment but reduce structural unemployment.
   D. not affect the natural rate of unemployment but reduce frictional unemployment.

Use the following information to answer the next two questions. The Arbocali Bureau of Labour Statistics provides you with the following information about those aged 15+:

| | |
|---|---|
| Employed | 360 000 |
| Unemployed | 40 000 |
| Not in the labour force | 100 000 |
| Population (aged 15 or over) | 500 000 |

_____ 17. The Arbocali unemployment rate is
   A. 8%.
   B. 10%.
   C. 11.11%.
   D. 40%.

_____ 18. The labour-force participation rate is
   A. 36%.
   B. 40%.
   C. 72%.
   D. 80%.

_____ 19. We would expect to see each of the following during a recession except
   A. decreased production.
   B. an increase in inflation.
   C. an increased incidence of psychological disorder and stress.
   H decreased capacity utilization rates.

_____ 20. In an economy where inflation is usually unpredictable, the degree of risk associated with investment
   A. increases.
   B. decreases.
   C. depends on the nominal interest rate.
   D. is not affected.

_____ 21. Hester Investor wishes to earn a 6% real return on a $500 loan that she is planning to make to Buck Poor. Last year the inflation rate was 2%, but Hester expects the inflation rate to rise to 4%. She should charge an interest rate of
   A. 3%.
   B. 4%.
   C. 10%.
   D. 12%.

_____ 22. The nation of Arboc has recently been at the trough of a business cycle and is moving through the next phase. The unemployment rate is rising. Which of the following is a plausible explanation?
   A. After the trough, Arboc will move into the recession phase, and unemployment rises during recessions.
   B. After the trough, different sectors of the Arbocali economy will recover at different rates, so the average unemployment rate may increase.
   C. Firms will not hire extra workers until the recovery is assured; therefore the numbers of workers employed will be artificially reduced.
   D. The expansion phase will encourage previously discouraged workers to re-enter the labour force, leading to an initial increase in the number without jobs.

## II.  APPLICATION QUESTIONS

1. Can you think of any adaptations that have been made in our economy to alleviate the redistributional effects of inflation?

2. a. The market interest rate on a savings account is 5%. The inflation rate is 2%. Calculate the real interest rate that savings account depositors will earn.
   b. Suppose that the nominal interest rate that banks charge on loans is subject to a price ceiling of 7%. To be worthwhile, banks require a real interest rate of 4% or more. The inflation rate is currently 5%. Describe what will happen in this market.

3. The following table provides information on inflation rates and unemployment rates for Arboc over a seven-year period.

| Year | Inflation Rate | Unemployment Rate |
|------|----------------|-------------------|
| 1992 | 0.0 | 7.5 |
| 1993 | –2.0 | 9.0 |
| 1994 | 4.0 | 5.0 |
| 1995 | 6.0 | 4.0 |
| 1996 | 10.0 | 2.5 |
| 1997 | 2.0 | 6.0 |
| 1998 | –4.0 | 10.5 |

Each year, Arboc has a population of 1 000 000 people age 15 and over. The labour-force participation rate is 90%.

a. Calculate the number of workers unemployed in 1992.

b. Calculate the number of workers employed in 1998.

Assume that the citizens of Arboc, when trying to determine the inflation rate for the next twelve months, base their calculations solely on the current inflation rate.

c. During the period from 1993 to 1996, will borrowers be gaining or losing?

d. In 1996, the market interest rate was 12%. Calculate the real interest rate.

e. Use the aggregate demand–aggregate supply analysis to suggest how the economy has adjusted from 1996 to 1998.

4. Gilligan is a small island economy containing six individuals. In each of the following cases, determine if the individual is employed, unemployed, or not in the labour force.

a. Krystal Krazy, Ph.D., 32, works 20 hours per week and is looking for a full-time job.

b. Lisa Looney, 20, is a student who is not working.

c. Maggie Madd, 74, works 10 hours a week doing accounting services for her son, Norman Neurotic.

d. Norman Neurotic, 50, works full-time but hates his job and really wants a new job.

e. Olivia Opprest, a housewife, does not work outside the home and isn't looking for other employment.

f. Pete Paranoid, 40, used to work as a fisherman but believed that everyone hated him and has given up in disgust.

g. Calculate the labour-force participation rate.

h. Calculate the unemployment rate.

5. Using the figures below, calculate the economic quantities for each year.

| | 1993 | 1998 |
|---|------|------|
| Total population aged 15 and over | 200 million | 210 million |
| Labour force | 130 million | 144 million |
| Employed | 120 million | 125 million |

a. the labour-force participation rate  _____  _____

b. the number unemployed  _____  _____

c. the unemployment rate  _____  _____

d. There is more likely to have been a recession in which year?

e. The Prime Minister, denying that unemployment is growing, claims that:

  i. "We've created more jobs," and

  ii. "Some of the unemployed in the statistics have stopped seeking work."

How would you respond to these points?

6. Answer the questions, based on the following information.

| Year | Nominal GDP (bill.) | Price Index | Real GDP (bill.) | Nominal Wage ($) | Real Wage |
|------|------|------|------|------|------|
| 2002 | 4486.0 | 108 | | 40 000 | |
| 2003 | 4710.3 | 112 | | 40 800 | |

a. Between 2002 and 2003, nominal GDP has _____ by _____%.

b. Between 2002 and 2003, the price level has _____ by _____%.

c. Frank lent Freda $500 in 2002 to be paid back in 2003. He guessed inflation would run at 5% and increased accordingly the interest rate on the loan. In the circumstances, who won?

d. Calculate the real GDP figures.

e. Now calculate the real wage of the typical worker in each year.

f. To have maintained her/his 2002 standard of living, the typical worker would need to have received a nominal wage of _____ in 2003.

7. Calculate the annual rates of inflation and complete the table below.

| Year | Price Index | Rate of Inflation |
|------|------|------|
| 2001 | 100.00 | |
| 2002 | 113.00 | |
| 2003 | 121.50 | |
| 2004 | 126.70 | |
| 2005 | 125.10 | |

8. The following table shows the market value of a given basket of goods in a number of selected years. The hourly nominal wage is also given.

| Year | Value of Market Basket | Price Index | Rate of Increase | Nominal Wage/ Hour | Rate of Increase | Real Wage/ Hour |
|------|------|------|------|------|------|------|
| 1994 | $ 887.00 | | — | $4.55 | — | |
| 1995 | $ 993.44 | | | $5.01 | | |
| 1996 | $1132.52 | | | $5.61 | | |
| 1997 | $1245.78 | | | $6.40 | | |
| 1998 | $1320.52 | | | $6.98 | | |

a. Use the table above to calculate the price index values, with 1996 as the base year.

b. Using the price index values, calculate the real hourly wage.

c. For 1995 to 1998, work out the rate of increase in the price index (what does it measure?), and the rate of increase in nominal wage/hour.

d. Compare the two "rates of increase" and the behaviour of real wage/hour. Make up a rule of thumb linking these variables.

9. a. Distinguish between frictional, structural, and cyclical unemployment. Give an example of each.

   b. Suppose you've just become unemployed because of company cutbacks. Are you frictionally unemployed? Is it a good idea to accept the first job offer that comes along? Can you see any disadvantages to doing so?

## ANSWERS AND SOLUTIONS

## PRACTICE TEST

### I. SOLUTIONS TO MULTIPLE CHOICE QUESTIONS

1. A. Job openings exist for Shelly. It's merely a case of tracking down a position. See p. 159 for a discussion of the types of unemployment.

2. A. If there are more discouraged workers, the numbers on the unemployment rolls will decrease because workers who have ceased looking for a job (discouraged workers) no longer meet the definition of being "unemployed." See p. 158.

3. D. Francine has stopped seeking work—she is not classified as unemployed. See p. 158 on discouraged workers.

4. B. The skills of a group of workers have become obsolete, either through a change in demand or, as in this case, through a technological change. See p. 159.

5. B. The concept of full employment assumes that some (frictional and structural) unemployment will be present. See p. 160.

6. B. The new Arbocali computer chip industry represents a structural change. Canadian car- and steel-workers have experienced similar unemployment.

7. D. See p. 160.

8. C. The nominal interest rate is the real interest rate plus the anticipated inflation rate. See p. 166.

9. D. A borrower pays a lower rate of interest than he or she should have if inflation had been fully anticipated. In fact, if inflation is very high, the cost of a loan may be zero or negative. See p. 166.

10. B. The inflation rate = (change in CPI / initial CPI) × 100 = (11 / 110) × 100 = 10%.

11. C. Unanticipated inflation hurts lenders but helps debtors.

12. B. If the nominal wage rose by 7% and the inflation rate was 7%, the real wage would not have changed. For the real wage to have risen by 3%, the nominal wage must have risen by more than 7%—10%, in fact.

13. A. Discouraged workers, seeing an improving economy, will begin to look for jobs—and will be counted as unemployed, whereas, previously, they were not.

14. D. See p. 158. Discouraged workers aren't classified as unemployed.

15. A. The real interest rate is equal to the nominal interest rate minus the anticipated inflation rate.

16. B. Structural and frictional unemployment should both be reduced, as will the natural rate (the sum of structural and frictional unemployment).

17. B. The labour force is the population minus those not in the labour force (500 000 – 100 000). The unemployment rate equals the number unemployed divided by the labour force. In this case, the unemployment rate equals 40 000 / 400 000, or 10%.

18. D. The labour-force participation rate equals the number in the labour force (400 000) divided by the population (500 000). See p. 155.

19. B. Inflation tends to fall during recessions. See p. 162.
20. A. The more unpredictable a situation is, the riskier it is. See p. 167.
21. C. The nominal interest rate is the real interest rate (6%) plus the expected inflation rate (4%).
22. D. See p. 158.

## II. SOLUTIONS TO APPLICATION QUESTIONS

1. Adjustable-rate mortgages, indexation of the tax system, and indexation of pension benefits are a few of the changes.

2. a. The real interest rate (3%) equals the market interest rate (5%) minus the inflation rate (2%).
   b. There will be an excess demand for loans. In fact, loans will dry up. The maximum nominal interest rate is 7%; with inflation of 5%, the maximum real interest rate is 2%, which is insufficient to induce banks to lend.

3. a. $900\ 000 \times .075 = 67\ 500$.
   b. $900\ 000 \times .895 = 805\ 500$.
   c. Inflation is increasing—borrowers gain and creditors lose.
   d. The market interest rate is based on the real interest rate plus the inflation rate. In 1996, the market interest rate was 12% and the inflation rate was 10%. The real interest rate was 2%.
   e. Inflation has decreased while unemployment has risen. The simplest explanation is that aggregate demand has declined from 1996 to 1998.

4. a. Employed.
   b. Not in labour force.
   c. Employed.
   d. Employed.
   e. Not in labour force.
   f. Not in labour force.
   g. $3 / 6 = .5$.
   h. No one is unemployed in this economy.

5. a. The labour-force participation rate is labour force / population aged 15 and over. In 1993, $130 / 200 = 65\%$; in 1998, $144 / 210 = 68.57\%$.
   b. Labour force equals the number employed plus the number unemployed. In 1993, the number unemployed = 130 million – 120 million = 10 million; in 1998, the number unemployed = 144 million – 125 million = 19 million.
   c. The unemployment rate = number unemployed / labour force. In 1993, number unemployed / labour force = $10 / 130 = 7.69\%$; in 1998, number unemployed / labour force = $19 / 144 = 13.19\%$.
   d. 1998, because the unemployment rate is higher in 1998.
   e. i. It is possible for a growing economy to experience rising employment and rising unemployment but, if the increase in the participation rate is sufficiently higher than the increase in job openings, the unemployment rate will rise.
      ii. If, indeed, some individuals have stopped seeking work, then they would have dropped off the unemployment rolls. Admitting the presence of discouraged workers, on top of the listed unemployed, actually makes the Prime Minister's performance worse!

6.  a.  risen; 5%. Percentage change = (change in nominal GDP / initial GDP) × 100 = (224.3 / 4486) × 100 = 5%.

    b.  risen; 3.7%. Percentage change = (change in price index / initial price index) x 100 = (4 / 108) × 100 = 3.7%.

    c.  Frank as creditor, because anticipated inflation was greater than the actual inflation rate.

    d.  See the table below. Real GDP = (nominal GDP / price index) × 100. Example: Real GDP for 2002 = (4486 / 108) × 100 = 4153.7.

| Year | Nominal GDP (bill.) | Price Index | Real GDP (bill.) | Nominal Wage ($) | Real Wage |
|------|---------------------|-------------|------------------|------------------|-----------|
| 2002 | 4486.0 | 108 | 4153.7 | 40 000 | 37 037.04 |
| 2003 | 4710.3 | 112 | 4205.6 | 40 800 | 36 428.57 |

    e.  See the table above. Real wage = (nominal wage / price index) × 100. Example: Real wage for 2002 = (40 000 / 108) × 100 = 37 037.04.

    f.  Real wage in 2002 was $37 037.04 ($40 000 / 1.08). To maintain the same value in 2003, (x / 1.12) = $37 037.04. Therefore, x = $37 037.04(1.12) = $41 481.48.

7.  See the table below.
    Example: rate of inflation for 2003 = [(121.5 – 113) / 113] × 100 = 7.52%.

| Year | Price Index | Rate of Inflation |
|------|-------------|-------------------|
| 2001 | 100.00 | — |
| 2002 | 113.00 | 13.00% |
| 2003 | 121.50 | 7.52% |
| 2004 | 126.70 | 4.28% |
| 2005 | 125.10 | –1.26% |

8.  a.  See the table below.
        Example: price index for 1995 = (nominal value 1995 / nominal value in base year) × 100 = (993.44 / 1132.52) × 100 = 87.72.

| Year | Value of Market Basket | Price Index | Rate of Increase | Nominal Wage/ Hour | Rate of Increase | Real Wage/ Hour |
|------|------------------------|-------------|------------------|--------------------|------------------|-----------------|
| 1994 | $ 887.00 | 78.32 | — | $4.55 | — | $5.81 |
| 1995 | $ 993.44 | 87.72 | 12.0% | $5.01 | 10.1% | $5.71 |
| 1996 | $1132.52 | 100.00 | 14.0% | $5.61 | 12.0% | $5.61 |
| 1997 | $1245.78 | 110.00 | 10.0% | $6.40 | 14.1% | $5.82 |
| 1998 | $1320.52 | 116.60 | 6.0% | $6.98 | 9.1% | $5.98 |

    b.  See the table above. Example: real hourly wage for 1995 = (nominal wage 1995 / price index) × 100 = ($5.01 / .8772) × 100 = $5.71.

    c.  Inflation. See the table above. Example: rate of increase in nominal wage for 1995 = [(nominal wage 1995 – nominal wage 1994) / nominal wage 1994] × 100 = (.46 / 4.55) × 100 = 10.1%.

    d.  When inflation is greater than the rate of increase in the nominal wage, the real wage will fall.

9. a. See the definitions on pp. 159–160. A graduate in economics or business entering the job market is frictionally unemployed. The graduate has desirable qualifications; it's only a matter of tracking down an acceptable job. Many workers in the manufacturing sector have become structurally unemployed due to technological changes since the early 1980s. Cyclical unemployment occurred during the recession of 1991 as consumer confidence plummeted and demand declined.

b. If the company cutbacks are due to a fall in demand that is being felt nationwide, you are cyclically unemployed. If this one industry is affected, perhaps due to aggressive foreign competition, you are structurally unemployed. Whether you should accept the first job that is offered depends on the costs and benefits of staying unemployed. If you think it is unlikely that a sufficiently better job offer will materialize that will cover the costs of a continued search, you should accept.

# 9 Aggregate Expenditure and Equilibrium Output

## OBJECTIVES: POINT BY POINT

After completing this chapter, you should be able to accomplish the objectives listed below.

### General Comment

Give yourself plenty of time to understand the model developed in this chapter—it's the basis for what comes later. To keep things simple at the beginning, for this chapter only it is assumed that there is no government (and hence no taxes) and no exports or imports. In this simple context, can you confirm that income must equal consumption plus saving? Given the consumption function diagram, can you draw the related saving function diagram? Can you derive the consumption and saving equations? Can you see how unplanned inventory changes "balance" expenditures and output? Can you see why a $100 increase in investment is "multiplied"? If not, go back and work through this chapter again.

### OBJECTIVE 1: Explain why aggregate output is equal to aggregate income.

In Chapter 7, gross domestic product (GDP) was introduced as a measure of aggregate output (Y). Because output can be measured by what is spent on it, Y is the sum of all expenditures on final goods and services. But because every dollar that is spent must end up in someone's hands as income (if it is not paid out as wages, rent or interest then it must be profit), aggregate output must always equal income. (page 176)

### OBJECTIVE 2: Define the marginal propensity to consume and the marginal propensity to save.

For households, income (Y) is split between consumption (C) and saving (S). Determinants of aggregate *consumption* include
  i.   household income,
  ii.  household wealth,
  iii. interest rates, and
  iv.  household expectations about the future.

If your wage increases by $100 each month, your consumption will rise too, but by something less than $100. The rest will be saved. How much of the extra $100 you choose to spend depends on your *marginal propensity* to consume (MPC). If you spend $80, MPC is 80 / 100 = 0.8. *Marginal propensity to save* (MPS) is 20 / 100 = 0.2 because any income not spent is saved ($20 out of $100). Clearly, MPC + MPS must sum to one (100% of any extra income must be spent or saved). (page 179)

> **TIP:** In Chapter 10 we introduce taxes. This affects the definition of MPC and MPS. You'll find the transition easier if you read the denominator term, "change in income," as "change in disposable income." In this chapter, the former term is identical with the latter (with no taxes, all income is disposable income); in Chapter 10, MPC and MPS will be derived using the change in disposable income.

The consumption function shows the relationship between consumption spending and income; its slope ("rise" over "run") is the value of MPC ("change in consumption" over "change in income"). Algebraically, the consumption function is:

$$C = a + bY \qquad \qquad \text{(page 178)}$$

A similar function, the saving function, can be developed because consumption and saving are related activities.

## Practice

1.  Aggregate consumption will increase if
    A.  income increases and wealth decreases.
    B.  income increases and interest rates decrease.
    C.  interest rates increase and household wealth increases.
    D.  interest rates increase and consumer confidence about the future strengthens.

    **ANSWER:** B. Lower interest rates reduce the cost of borrowing. See p. 177.

2.  Given the income level, saving is directly (positively) related to
    A.  interest rates and wealth, and inversely (negatively) related to households' expectations about future income.
    B.  interest rates, and inversely (negatively) related to wealth and households' expectations about future income.
    C.  households' expectations about future income, and inversely (negatively) related to interest rates and wealth.
    D.  wealth, and inversely (negatively) related to interest rates and households' expectations about future income.

    **ANSWER:** B. Higher interest rates encourage saving. As wealth increases and households become richer, and/or as households' expectations about the future improve, consumption increases. Given the income level, though, saving must decrease if consumption increases. See p. 177.

3.  When MPC is .75, MPS is
    A.  .25.
    B.  .75.
    C.  3.00.
    D.  4.00.

    **ANSWER:** A. MPC + MPS = 1. See p. 179.

4.  The consumption function is $C = 200 + .9Y$. The saving function is
    A.  $S = 200 - .1Y$.
    B.  $S = -200 - .1Y$.
    C.  $S = 200 - .9Y$.
    D.  $S = -200 + .1Y$.

    **ANSWER:** D. Recall that $Y = C + S$. The equations must sum to Y. The first term must be negative because consumption is positive. Also, recall that saving increases as income increases—the second term must be positive.

Use the following diagram (not drawn to scale) to answer the next three questions.

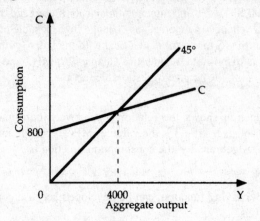

5.  When income equals 4000, consumption equals _____ and saving equals
    _____.
    A.  4000, 0.
    B.  3200, 800.
    C.  4000, 4000.
    D.  2000, 2000.

    **ANSWER: A.** The 45° line shows all the points at which the variable on the vertical axis equals the variable on the horizontal axis, in this case, where C = Y. If Y = 4000, C = 4000. If all income is being spent, saving must be zero.

6.  The equation for this consumption function is
    A.  C = 800 + .75Y.
    B.  C = 800 + .8Y.
    C.  C = 4000 + .75Y.
    D.  C = 4000 + .8Y.

    **ANSWER: B.** The intercept term (a) is 800. As income increases from 0 to 4000, consumption increases from 800 to 4000, an increase of 3200. MPC = change in consumption/change in income = 3200 / 4000 = .8.

> **Graphing Pointer:** Note the answer to Practice Question 6. When the consumption function intercepts the vertical axis, the associated value indicates the level of consumption that is independent (or autonomous) of income. Your instructor may call this intercept "autonomous consumption." According to the model, if income = 0, this spending would still exist, out of past savings or borrowing.

7.  If income is 6000, consumption is _____ and saving is _____.
    A.  4800, 1200.
    B.  5600, 400.
    C.  5200, 1000.
    D.  6000, 0.

    ANSWER: B. When Y = 4000, C = 4000 and S = 0. MPC = .8. As income increases by 2000 (from 4000 to 6000), consumption will increase by 2000 × .8, or 1600. Consumption will total 5600 (4000 + 1600). We know that Y = C + S; therefore S = Y – C. S = 6000 – 5600 = 400.

## OBJECTIVE 3: Define investment, as economists use the term. Distinguish between actual and planned investment.

The amount of planned investment is assumed to remain constant as output changes—investment will graph as a horizontal line. *Actual investment* can differ from *planned investment* because of unplanned changes in the level of inventories.          (page 183)

> **TIP:** Investment is one of the most difficult concepts to learn. Economists use the word differently from others. Investment does *not* mean saving, not even financial investment. Investment is the purchase of new machinery and buildings (productive capacity) and changes in inventory levels.

Note that firms buy more than investment goods. They hire workers, for example. To count this expenditure would be double-counting—the wages are used by households for consumption and saving.

> **TIP:** Keep in mind that, in this model, actual investment will *always* equal saving. In equilibrium, planned investment will equal saving, and unplanned inventory investment will be zero.

If aggregate output exceeds (is less than) consumption plus planned change in inventory, there will be an unplanned increase (decrease) in inventory. (For an example of this, see Application Question 3 below.)          (page 183)

> **Unplanned Inventory Change and Equilibrium:** Unplanned changes in inventory draw the economy into equilibrium. Call expenditures "demand" and output "supply" for the moment. When "demand" is more than current "supply," firms are forced to reduce their previously accumulated inventory. Emptying shelves are the signal to increase production.
>
> When "demand" is less than "supply," unsold production is piling up—the signal to cut output.
>
> Firms feel no pressure to adjust production levels (i.e., there will be equilibrium), only when "demand" equals "supply."
>
> Also, when unplanned inventory change is not zero (either positive or negative), the actual level of investment differs from the level managers planned to have. If, for example, actual investment is "too low," managers will boost production to compensate.

> **TIP:** An economic system requires some mechanism to drive it towards equilibrium. In the market for coffee, the equilibrium mechanism is price. In our model, the price is fixed and the equilibrating mechanism is unplanned inventory change. When unplanned inventory change occurs, it is a signal to adjust output.

## Practice

8. Investment refers to
   A. the purchase of new stock in a company.
   B. the purchase of new or existing stock in a company.
   C. the creation of capital stock.
   D. the stock of accumulated saving.

   **ANSWER:** C.   Investment is addition to the capital stock. Financial transactions are excluded from GDP—review Chapter 7.

9. The change in inventories is
   A. production minus sales.
   B. sales minus production.
   C. a value equal to or greater than zero, but cannot be negative.
   D. consumption minus saving.

   **ANSWER:** A.   See p. 183.

## OBJECTIVE 4: Describe equilibrium in the simple Keynesian model of national income determination. Explain the adjustment process if planned aggregate expenditure differs from aggregate output.

Planned aggregate expenditure is the sum of consumption and investment at each income level. Because investment is constant at each income level, the AE function is an upward-sloping line whose slope equals MPC.                                                         (page 183)

> **TIP:** Sometimes you'll find understanding easier if you talk about "output," and sometimes about "income." For example, "When unplanned inventory reductions occur, output will rise" is more obvious than "when unplanned inventory reductions occur, income will rise." However, "output is split between consumption and saving" is much less intuitive than "income is split between consumption and saving."

Equilibrium occurs when planned aggregate expenditure equals aggregate output (income)—i.e., when C + I = C + S. Only in this case will planned investment equal actual investment—there will be no unplanned inventory change. If expenditures exceed output, inventory levels are unexpectedly depleted. Firms respond by increasing production. Higher production results in higher income and, given MPC, more consumption spending. Spending rises, but at a slower rate than output rises. Eventually, the two will be equal. How big an increase in output level is needed to achieve equilibrium depends on the value of the multiplier.                                                         (page 187)

The conditions necessary for equilibrium can be stated in different ways.

   a.   If there is a difference between actual and planned investment, the economy is not in equilibrium. Equilibrium condition: Planned investment equals actual investment.
   b.   Aggregate planned expenditure must equal aggregate output (income). Therefore, C + I = C + S. Equilibrium condition: Planned investment must equal saving.

Note that there's no requirement that the equilibrium level of production be enough to provide full employment to the economy's workers.

**Graphing Pointer:** Planned investment is assumed constant at all output levels—the graph linking planned investment and aggregate income is a line parallel to the horizontal axis. Consequently, the curve representing aggregate expenditures (the sum of consumption and planned investment in this model) is a line which is parallel to the consumption curve. (See the graph for Questions 18–22.)

## Practice

Use the following table to answer the next six questions.

| Output | Consumption | Investment | Planned Aggregate Expenditure | Unplanned Change in Inventory |
|--------|-------------|------------|-------------------------------|-------------------------------|
| 2000 | 2100 | 400 | _____ | _____ |
| 3000 | 2850 | 400 | _____ | _____ |
| 4000 | 3600 | 400 | _____ | _____ |
| 5000 | 4350 | 400 | _____ | _____ |
| 6000 | 5100 | 400 | _____ | _____ |
| 7000 | 5850 | 400 | _____ | _____ |

10. Complete the planned aggregate expenditure column in the table above.

    **ANSWER:** See the *Answers and Solutions* section.

11. Equilibrium output is
    A. 3000.
    B. 4000.
    C. 5000.
    D. 6000.

    **ANSWER:** B. Equilibrium occurs where output equals planned aggregate expenditure.

12. Complete the unplanned change in inventory column in the table above.

    **ANSWER:** See the *Answers and Solutions* section. Unplanned changes in inventory is the difference between output and planned aggregate expenditure.

13. In the table above, MPC is
    A. .6.
    B. .75.
    C. .8.
    D. .9.

    **ANSWER:** B. Every time income rises by 1000, consumption rises by 750.

14. When income is 0, consumption is
    A. 0.
    B. 250.
    C. 600.
    D. 1000.

    **ANSWER:** C. When income is 2000, consumption is 2100. If income decreases by 2000 and MPC is .75, consumption will decrease by 1500.

15. When output is 6000, firms will
    A. increase production.
    B. decrease production.
    C. increase planned investment.
    D. decrease planned investment.

    **ANSWER:** B. Output exceeds planned aggregate expenditure and inventories are too high. Firms would cut production.

## OBJECTIVE 5: Analyze how a change in planned investment affects output in the model. Explain the concept of the spending multiplier.

The *spending multiplier* measures the extent to which the output level will change given a particular initial change in the level of spending. It is calculated by the formula: 1 / (1 − MPC) or 1 / MPS. (page 188)

> **TIP:** You might find subsequent material easier if you focus more on the 1 / MPS formula. The strength of the multiplier depends on how rapidly spending power leaks out of the circular flow diagram. This is even more obvious when leakages other than saving (taxes, imports) make their appearance.

> **TIP:** One way to visualize the multiplier is to use the following circular flow diagram.

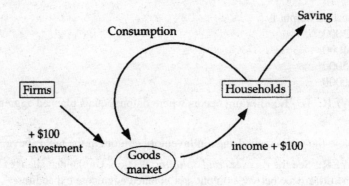

> You know that households split their income into consumption expenditures and saving. Some investment also takes place. Suppose MPC is .9 and MPS is .1. Suppose that an extra $100 of investment spending occurs and income rises by $100. Trace through the circular flow—consumption rises by $90, then by $81, then by $72.90, and so on. Where is the rest going? It's leaking away into saving (non-spending).
>
> The same $100 increase in investment, with a lower MPC, such as .5, gives a less-substantial expansion in spending because the extra income drains away more quickly. The multiplier is smaller, right?
>
> The force of the expansion is lessened if spending power drains away more rapidly—as MPS increases. The multiplier value, then, is linked negatively to MPS and positively to MPC.

An increase in investment (or consumption) generates extra income. Extra income, however, stimulates consumption and saving—MPC and MPS determine how much consumption and saving will rise. Extra consumption generates more new income. The process of "spend–earn income–spend" runs out of steam as progressively more of the extra dollars leak away into saving. (page 190)

> **TIP:** As shown in the textbook, the multiplier model works given a change in investment, but it is more general than that. The analysis works for any component of planned aggregate expenditure—in this chapter, consumption and investment and, in Chapter 10, government spending.

> **Graphing Pointer:** Note that, graphically, equilibrium must occur where the AE function crosses the 45° line. The 45° line plots all the points where spending equals output—i.e., all the points where equilibrium might occur.

Example: If planned investment increases, the AE line shifts upwards. At the current output level, inventories unexpectedly fall. As firms raise production to restore desired inventory levels, income and consumption will rise, and the economy will move to the point where the new (higher) AE function crosses the 45° line. This same story can be told in terms of the saving-investment diagram that contains similar information.

> **TIP:** You may want to memorize the two multiplier formulas on p. 191. But remember these only work for the simple model of this chapter. A sure way to calculate an investment spending multiplier in any numerical example is to (1) calculate equilibrium national income (2) increase planned investment spending by 1 and recalculate equilibrium national income. The increase in equilibrium national income between steps (1) and (2) will be the multiplier. See practice question 20 for an example.

## OBJECTIVE 6 (Appendix 9A): Derive the multiplier algebraically.

Even if you do not study this appendix, you should understand that an initial increase in planned investment spending increases income which stimulates consumption which in turn increases income again which stimulates more consumption and so on, although each round of spending is smaller and smaller because of saving at each stage. Here is an example that you should be able to follow even if you have not studied the appendix.

In Arboc, MPC is .9. The economy is in equilibrium. Suddenly, there is a 100-opek increase in investment spending. This creates 100 opeks of extra income. The income is split 90:10 between new consumption and new saving. The new consumption generates additional income.

| New Expenditure | New Income | = | New Saving | + | New Consumption |
|---|---|---|---|---|---|
| 100.00 | 100.00 | = | 10.00 | + | 90.00 |
| 90.00 | 90.00 | = | 9.00 | + | 81.00 |
| 81.00 | 81,00 | = | 8.10 | + | 72.90 |
| 72.90 | 72.90 | = | 7.29 | + | 65.61 |
| 65.61 | 65.61 | = | 6.56 | + | 59.05 |
| • | • | | • | | • |
| • | • | | • | | • |
| • | • | | • | | • |
| 1000.00 | 1000.00 | = | 100.00 | + | 900.00 |

This process goes through many "rounds," only the first five of which are given. The final row gives the total results.

Notes

A.   The initial "injection" of spending is 100; ultimately this will all become new saving. Indeed, the opeks will continue to circulate (generating more income and expenditure) until all of the "extra" 100 opeks have leaked away. *The leakage must equal the injection.* The multiplier's strength depends on how rapidly the injection of extra spending leaks away.

B.   We know that income equals consumption plus investment. Income increased by 1000, consumption increased by 900, and investment increased by 100.

## Practice

16.   In Arbez, MPC is .8. The economy is in equilibrium. Suddenly, there is a 100-bandu increase in investment spending. This creates 100 bandu of extra income. Income is split 80:20 between new consumption and new saving. Complete the following table.

| New Expenditure | New Income | = | New Saving | + | New Consumption |
|---|---|---|---|---|---|
| 100.00 | ___ | = | ___ | + | ___ |
| ___ | ___ | = | ___ | + | ___ |
| ___ | ___ | = | ___ | + | ___ |
| ___ | ___ | = | ___ | + | ___ |
| ___ | ___ | = | ___ | + | ___ |
| • | • | | • | | • |
| • | • | | • | | • |
| • | • | | • | | • |
| 500.00 | 500.00 | = | 100.00 | + | 400.00 |

Notes

A.   As in the Arboc example, the initial "injection" of spending leaks aways to saving; ultimately all of this ends up as new saving.

B.   Income increased by 500, consumption increased by 400, and investment increased by 100.

C    The expansion in income is less in Arbez (the multiplier is smaller) because MPC is smaller (MPS is greater). The extra 100 units of spending leak away more slowly in the Arboc example.

**ANSWER:** See the *Answers and Solutions* section.

17.   The formula for the multiplier in the simple model of this chapter is
A.    1 / MPC.
B.    1 / MPS.
C.    1 / (1 – MPS).
D.    1 / (1 + MPC).

**ANSWER:** B.   See p. 191.

Use the following diagram (not to scale), which builds on the previous diagram for Questions 5 to 7, to answer the next five questions.

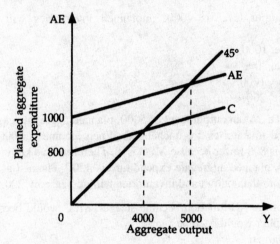

18.   The level of investment in this economy is
A.    200.
B.    800.
C.    1000.
D.    5000.

**ANSWER:** A.   AE = C + I. When Y = 0, AE = 1000 and C = 800.

19.   The slope of the AE function is
A.    .6.
B.    .75.
C.    .8.
D.    .9.

**ANSWER:** C.   The slope of the AE function depends on MPC. Question 6 above determined that MPC is .8. If we refer to the AE function by itself, we get the same result. Spending increases by 4000 (from 1000 to 5000) as income increases from 0 to 5000.

20.   The multiplier has a value of
A.    4.
B.    5.
C.    8.
D.    10.

**ANSWER:** B.   The multiplier formula is 1 / (1 – MPC). MPC is .8. Alternatively note that here C = 800 + .8Y and planned investment spending I = 200. Hence in equilibrium Y = C + I or Y = 800 + .8Y + 200 which implies Y = 1000 + .8Y or .2Y = 1000 or Y = 5000 as above. If I is increased to 201, Y = 800 + .8Y + 201 or .2Y = 1001 or Y = 5005. An increase in planned investment spending by 1 has increased output by 5 and hence the multiplier is 5.

21. If planned investment increases by 100, equilibrium output will increase by _____. In equilibrium, saving will equal _____.
    A. 100, 200.
    B. 100, 300.
    C. 500, 200.
    D. 500, 300.

    **ANSWER:** D. The multipler is .5. Equilibrium output will increase by 500 (100 × 5). In equilibrium, saving will equal investment. Recall that investment was 200 and rose further by 100.

22. When the output level is 4000, unplanned inventories will _____ by _____.
    A. increase, 1000.
    B. increase, 200.
    C. decrease, 1000.
    D. decrease, 200.

    **ANSWER:** D. At an output level of 5000, planned aggregate expenditure is 5000 and unplanned inventories are unchanged. When income is 1000 lower, at 4000, consumption is 800 lower because MPC is .8. Therefore, we know that, at an output level of 4000, planned aggregate expenditure is 4200. Planned aggregate expenditure is 200 more than output and inventories will decrease by 200.

23. If the slope of the AE function became steeper, MPC would become _____ and the multiplier would become _____.
    A. larger, larger.
    B. larger, smaller.
    C. smaller, larger.
    D. smaller, smaller.

    **ANSWER:** A. Compare the multiplier in Arbez in question 16 with the multiplier in Arboc in the table under Objective 6.

    > **Graphing Pointer:** Remember: The steeper the AE curve, the higher the value of the multiplier.

24. Refer to the table used in Practice Question 10. The economy is in equilibrium. If saving initially increases by 100, equilibrium output will decrease by _____ and consumption will decrease by _____.
    A. 100, 100.
    B. 100, 400.
    C. 400, 100.
    D. 400, 400.

    **ANSWER:** D. MPC is .75 (Question 13); the multiplier is 4. If saving increases by 100, consumption decreases initially by 100 and after the multiplier effect, output decreases by 400 (100 × 4). When output (income) decreases by 400, consumption is reduced by an additional 300. The total decrease in consumption is 400.

## SUMMARY: EQUILIBRIUM CONDITIONS

Equilibrium can be described in several ways. Learn them all!

Planned aggregate expenditure  =  aggregate output (income)

$$C + S \;=\; C + I$$

$$S \;=\; I$$

planned investment  =  actual investment

unplanned inventory change  =  0

Note: As the model is extended in later chapters, the second and third of these conditions will be modified.

## PRACTICE TEST

**I.    MULTIPLE CHOICE QUESTIONS. Select the option that provides the single best answer.**

_____  1.    MPC is _____ divided by _____.
    A.    consumption, income.
    B.    change in consumption, income.
    C.    change in consumption, change in income.
    D.    consumption, change in income.

_____  2.    The larger the MPC, the
    A.    larger the value of the multiplier.
    B.    steeper the slope of the saving function.
    C.    smaller the value of the multiplier.
    D.    flatter the slope of the consumption function.

Use the following table to answer the next three questions.

| Income | Consumption | Investment |
|--------|-------------|------------|
| 2000 | 1800 | 1000 |
| 3000 | 2600 | 1000 |
| 4000 | 3400 | 1000 |
| 5000 | 4200 | 1000 |
| 6000 | 5000 | 1000 |
| 7000 | 5800 | 1000 |

_____  3.    The equilibrium income level is _____ and the equilibrium saving level is _____.
    A.    7000, 200.
    B.    greater than 7000, 1000.
    C.    6000, 1000.
    D.    1000, 100.

_____ 4. The MPS is _____ and the multiplier is _____.
   A. .1, 10.
   B. .2, 5.
   C. .2, 10.
   D. .1, 5.

_____ 5. If planned saving suddenly rises by 100, then, at the new equilibrium, income will _____, and, compared to its original level, saving will _____.
   A. fall by 100, fall by 100.
   B. fall by 500, not change.
   C. fall by 500, fall by 100.
   D. fall by 100, not change.

Use the following table to answer the next three questions.

| Income | Consumption |
|--------|-------------|
| 0 | 100 |
| 100 | 180 |
| 200 | 260 |
| 300 | 340 |
| 1000 | 900 |
| 2000 | 1700 |

_____ 6. Referring to the equation $C = a + bY$, the value of "a" is _____.
   A. 0.
   B. 20.
   C. 80.
   D. 100.

_____ 7. Marginal propensity to consume is _____.
   A. 80.
   B. .2.
   C. .8.
   D. .9.

_____ 8. An increase in investment of 100 would _____ income, at the new equilibrium, by _____.
   A. raise, 500.
   B. raise, 100.
   C. lower, 500.
   D. lower, 100.

_____ 9. The economy is in equilibrium at an output level of 2000. Now planned investment increases. At the initial output level, all of the following are true except
   A. aggregate expenditure is greater than aggregate output.
   B. saving is less than planned investment.
   C. inventory levels are rising unexpectedly.
   D. consumption level has remained unchanged.

_____ 10. A decrease in MPS would
   A. cause the consumption function to shift upwards, all along its length.
   B. cause the consumption function to shift downwards, all along its length.
   C. cause the consumption function to shift upwards, pivoting where it meets the vertical axis.
   D. have no effect on the consumption function.

_____ 11. In our model, MPC must be less than _____ and MPS must exceed _____.
   A. one, one.
   B. one, zero.
   C. zero, one.
   D. zero, zero.

_____ 12. If planned investment suddenly decreases, the AE line will shift _____ and equilibrium saving will _____.
   A. upwards, increase.
   B. upwards, decrease.
   C. downwards, increase.
   D. downwards, decrease.

_____ 13. Equilibrium occurs when aggregate output is equal to planned _____ plus planned _____.
   A. consumption, saving.
   B. consumption, investment.
   C. investment, saving.
   D. inventories, investment.

_____ 14. Aggregate output is currently less than planned aggregate expenditure. We can predict that inventory levels are unexpectedly _____ and saving is _____ than planned investment.
   A. increasing, greater.
   B. increasing, less.
   C. decreasing, greater.
   D. decreasing, less.

_____ 15. Which of the following statements is true?
   A. Savings is the difference between current income and current consumption.
   B. When expenditures are high, saving is less than actual investment.
   C. Saving is a flow variable; savings is a stock variable.
   D. When the interest rate falls, saving increases and consumption decreases.

_____ 16. If income is zero, consumption will be
   A. positive.
   B. zero, because you can't spend what you don't have.
   C. zero, because the sum of consumption and saving must equal income.
   D. unknown—it depends on the slope of the consumption function.

_____ 17. As consumer uncertainty about the future increases, consumption will _____ and saving will _____ at a given income level.
   A. increase, increase.
   B. increase, decrease.
   C. decrease, increase.
   D. decrease, decrease.

_____ 18. Firms have the least control over
A.   inventory levels.
B.   production levels.
C.   planned investment.
D.   purchases of new equipment.

_____ 19. MPC equals .9. Consumers receive an extra $100 of income. We can say that, prior to any multiplier effect,
A.   the consumption function has moved upwards.
B.   the consumption function has moved downwards.
C.   consumption spending increases by $100.
D.   saving increases by $10.

_____ 20. MPC = .9. Planned investment = 100 and equilibrium income level is 1000. If income were at 800, what would be the level of saving?
A.   100.
B.   90.
C.   80.
D.   70.

Use the following diagram to answer the next five questions.

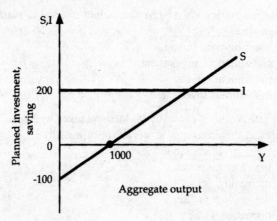

_____ 21. The equation for this consumption function is
A.   C = 100 + .8Y.
B.   C = 100 + .9Y.
C.   C = 200 + .8Y.
D.   C = 200 + .9Y.

_____ 22. The multiplier value is
A.   .9.
B.   8.
C.   9.
D.   10.

_____ 23. The equilibrium output level is
A.   200.
B.   1000.
C.   3000.
D.   4000.

_____ 24. If investment decreases by 50, equilibrium output will decrease by
_____ and consumption will decrease by _____.
A. 200, 450.
B. 200, 500.
C. 500, 450.
D. 500, 500.

_____ 25. The equation for this saving function is
A. S = 100 + .1Y.
B. S = 100 + .9Y.
C. S = –100 + .1Y.
D. S = –100 + .9Y.

## II. APPLICATION QUESTIONS

1. The Arbezani Minister of Macroeconomics gives you the following data about Arbez:

(1) C = 300 + .75Y.
(2) I = 200
(3) AE = C + I
(4) AE = Y

a. Calculate the marginal propensity to consume and the marginal propensity to save.
b. Derive the algebraic formula for the saving function.
c. What are the four conditions necessary for the economy to be in equilibrium?
d. Using your knowledge of the model, confirm that each equilibrium condition is consistent with the others.
e. Calculate equilibrium income.
f. Graph equations (3), which is the AE function, and (4) below.

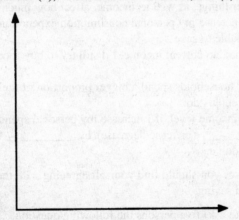

g. If GDP were 1200, unplanned inventory accumulation would be how much?
h. If GDP were 2200, unplanned inventory accumulation would be how much?
i. Based on these results, make up a rule relating the direction of unplanned inventory change, the 45° line, and the expenditure function.
j. How much saving will occur if GDP is 1200?
k. How much saving will occur if GDP is 2200?
l. Calculate the value of the multiplier.

When the economy is at the natural rate of unemployment, the output level is 2800.

m.  How much would investment have to change to create full employment?

The economy is at its original equilibrium income level. Now, because of a surge in consumer optimism, consumption increases by 100 at each income level.

n.  Inventories are changing by how much at the original income level? Are they rising or falling?
o.  Calculate the new equilibrium income level.
p.  Calculate the new equilibrium consumption level.
q.  Calculate the new equilibrium saving level.
r.  Calculate the new equilibrium investment level.
s.  Explain the result that has emerged regarding the net amount of change in the level of saving.

2.  Most of the ideas associated with the consumption function are quite intuitive. Try to prove to yourself that the theory reflects common sense. The following questions cover many of the main points about consumption and saving that are dealt with in this chapter.
a.  Suppose you have received a $100 per week wage increase (after tax). Would you spend
    i.   all of the extra $100?
    ii.  some of the extra $100?
    iii. none of the extra $100?
b.  Would you save
    i.   all of the extra $100?
    ii.  some of the extra $100?
    iii. none of the extra $100?
c.  The level of disposable income affects the amount spent and saved. Do you agree or disagree with the following statements?
    i.   Other things, as well as income, affect how much I spend and save.
    ii.  If I increase my personal consumption expenditures, I will have less available to save.
    iii. If I had no current income, I'd still try to buy food and other necessities.
    iv.  Poor households spend a bigger proportion of their income than rich households do.
d.  Given my income level, if I increase my personal spending by $1, my saving will _____ (increase/decrease) by _____ (more than/less than/exactly) a dollar.

In most other cases you should find yourself agreeing with the textbook's theory of consumption and saving.

3.  Ask (or pretend to ask) five persons the following question:
    "You are a typical consumer with an income of $100 per week. How much of your income will you set aside as saving?"

Now ask yourself (the owner of a small business):
    How much of your expected value of production (which you forecast to be $500 per week) will you plan to plow back into the firm? (Remember you have employees and other bills to pay!)

Enter the results of the two questions in the table.

| Saving | Investment |
|--------|------------|
|        |            |

There's no single "right" answer—it depends on preferences, income level, wealth, and so on. It's unlikely saving and planned investment will be equal. Suppose saving totals $15 and planned investment equals $20.

a. Which is greater: C + I or C + S?

b. Which is greater: planned aggregate expenditure or aggregate output?

c. Will firms be able to meet the planned demand for output, given their current level of production?

d. What will happen?

e. Write the formula for actual investment.

f. Calculate actual investment.

So actual investment is forced to the saving level!

4. "Planned Investment is equal to 100. Consumption is equal to income. MPC equals .9."

a. Saving is equal to _____.

b. "Currently, the marginal propensity to save equals zero." (True/False)

c. Currently, the economy _____ (is/is not) in equilibrium. Aggregate expenditure is _____ (greater than/less than) aggregate output.

d. Calculate the value of the multiplier.

e. Unplanned inventory change is _____ (positive/negative)

f. To establish equilibrium, output level will have to _____ (rise/fall) by _____, in which case consumption will _____ (rise/fall) by _____ and saving will _____ (rise/fall) by _____.

Now suppose that the income level (where consumption equals income) is 1000.

g. When income equals zero, consumption will equal _____ and saving will equal _____.

h. Calculate the formula for the consumption function.

i. Algebraically, confirm your results from (f) above, and calculate the equilibrium income level.

j. Sketch the saving-investment diagram, showing the slope of the saving function, the present income level (1000) and the equilibrium income level.

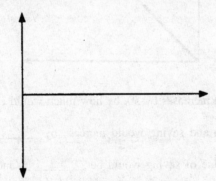

5. a. Fill in the blanks in the following table, based on the model given in the text.

| Income | Consumption | Saving | Investment | Expenditures |
|--------|-------------|--------|------------|--------------|
| 0 | | | | |
| 100 | 180 | | | |
| 200 | 260 | | | |
| 300 | | | 20 | |
| 400 | | | | |
| 500 | | | | |
| 600 | | | | |

MPC _____    MPS _____
multiplier = _____

b. The equilibrium output level is _____.
c. Algebraically, determine the consumption function.
d. Confirm your answer to (b) algebraically.
e. When income is 300, there will be an unplanned inventory _____ (increase/decrease) while, at an income level of 700, inventories will unexpectedly _____ (increase ≠ decrease).
f. Graph the AE function on the 45° line diagram below. Show the income range in which inventories will be rising unexpectedly and the income range in which they will be falling.

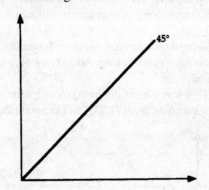

g. If investment increases by 50, by how much would equilibrium output level increase?
h. Consumption and saving would increase by _____ and _____ respectively.
i. The final value of saving would be _____ and investment would be _____.
j. Confirm your results for (g), (h), and (i) algebraically.
k. The economy's equilibrium income level is 850. Suppose that 1000 is the level of production that would provide full employment. How much more would investment have to rise in order to achieve full employment?

6.

> **Graphing Pointer:** Suppose that the consumption function does *not* graph as a straight line, but rather increases at a decreasing rate (flattening off). Given your knowledge of the relationships between consumption, saving, and income, could you now draw the saving function? What sort of slope would it have? What would be happening to the value of the multiplier as income level increased?

7.

> **Graphing Pointer:** We have modelled investment as remaining constant as output increases. Suppose, more realistically, that investment increases as income rises. What would happen to the slope of the AE curve? What would happen to the value of the multiplier?

## ANSWERS AND SOLUTIONS

### ANSWERS TO PRACTICE QUESTIONS

10 and 12.

| Output | Consumption | Investment | Planned Aggregate Expenditure | Unplanned Change in Inventory |
|--------|-------------|------------|-------------------------------|-------------------------------|
| 2000 | 2100 | 400 | 2500 | −500 |
| 3000 | 2850 | 400 | 3250 | −250 |
| 4000 | 3600 | 400 | 4000 | 0 |
| 5000 | 4350 | 400 | 4750 | +250 |
| 6000 | 5100 | 400 | 5500 | +500 |
| 7000 | 5850 | 400 | 6250 | +750 |

16.

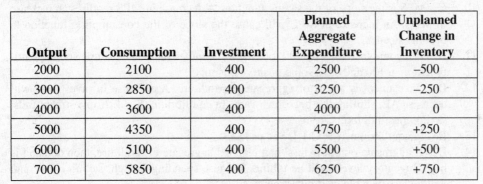

| New Expenditure | New Income | = | New Saving | + | New Consumption |
|-----------------|------------|---|------------|---|-----------------|
| 100.00 | 100.00 | = | 20.00 | + | 80.00 |
| 80.00 | 80.00 | = | 16.00 | + | 64.00 |
| 64.00 | 64.00 | = | 12.80 | + | 51.20 |
| 51.20 | 51.20 | = | 10.24 | + | 40.96 |
| 40.96 | 40.96 | = | 8.19 | + | 32.77 |
| • | • | | • | | • |
| • | • | | • | | • |
| • | • | | • | | • |
| 500.00 | 500.00 | = | 100.00 | + | 400.00 |

# I. SOLUTIONS TO MULTIPLE CHOICE QUESTIONS

1. C. See p. 178.
2. A. The multiplier formula is 1 / (1 – MPC). See p. 191.
3. C. Equilibrium occurs where income equals consumption plus investment, at 6000. In equilibrium, S = I, so saving must equal 1000. Alternatively, when income is 6000 and consumption is 5000, saving must be 1000.
4. B. When the income level changes by 1000 (from 3000 to 4000, for example), consumption increases by 800 (from 2600 to 3400). The additional 200 is saved. MPS = change in saving/change in income = 200 / 1000 = .2. The multiplier = 1 / MPS = 1 / .2 = 5.
5. B. If saving rises by 100, consumption must fall initially by 100, given the income level. The multiplier is 5. The final change in equilibrium income is 500 (i.e., 100 x 5). If income falls by 500 and the MPC is .8, consumption will fall by an additional 400. The total decrease in consumption is 500.
6. D. In the equation, "bY" is the portion of consumption that responds to changes in income. When income is zero, consumption is 100.
7. C. When the income level changes by 100 (from 200 to 300, for example), consumption increases by 80 (from 180 to 260). MPC = change in consumption/change in income = 80 / 100 = .8.
8. A. If expenditure increases, then equilibrium income will increase. The multiplier is 5 because MPC is .8. The multiplier equals 1 / (1 – MPC). Income, then, will increase by 500 (i.e., 100 × 5).
9. C. Because the demand for goods has risen, inventory levels will be decreasing.
10. C. MPS is the slope of the saving function. A decrease in MPS requires an increase in MPC. An increase in MPC will cause the slope of the consumption function to become steeper.
11. B. If income increases by 100, our theory assumes that we consume some quantity less than 100 and save some positive quantity.
12. D. Investment is a part of aggregate expenditure. A decrease in investment will decrease AE, shifting the line downward. In equilibrium, S = I. If investment falls, saving must fall too.
13. B. In equilibrium, Y = C + I. See p. 184.
14. D. If aggregate output is less than planned aggregate expenditure, then demand is high. Inventory levels will be falling. Because spending is high, saving is low and will be less than planned investment.
15. C. Savings is the accumulation of saving from past periods; it is a stock, while saving is a process (a flow). Saving always equals actual investment. When the interest rate falls, saving decreases and consumption increases.
16. A. The slope of the consumption function is irrelevant in this question. Consumption is positive even when income is zero because it is necessary to buy food, housing, and other staples of life. Without income, this is financed by "dissaving."
17. C. When future prospects are less clear, households tend to hold back on purchases, saving more of their current income.
18. A. Firms choose output levels and set up investment programs, but their inventory levels are affected by sales which are dependent upon the whims of their customers.
19. D. An increase in income will not shift the consumption function—there will be a movement along it. If MPC is .6, MPS is .1. A $100 increase in income will generate a $10 increase (100 × .1) in saving.
20. C. Equilibrium income is 1000 and planned investment is 100. In equilibrium, consumption must be 900 and saving must be 100. If income falls by 200, consumption falls by 180 (200 × .9) and saving falls by 20 (200 × .1). Saving will be 80.

21. B. The intercept term (a) is 100 because income is zero at that point, and C + S must equal this. As income increases from zero to 1000, saving increases from –100 to 0, an increase of 100. MPS = change in saving/change in income = 100 / 1000 = .1. MPC = 1 – MPS.

22. D. The multiplier equals 1 / (1 – MPC).

23. C. In equilibrium, saving must equal investment and, therefore, must equal 200. For saving to increase by 300 (from –100 to 200), income must increase by 3000 (from zero) if MPS is .1.

24. C. Expenditure initially decreases by 50. The multiplier is 10. Equilibrium output will decrease by 500 (50 x 10). Because MPC is .9, consumption will decrease by 450 (500 × .9). Saving will fall by 50 (500 x MPS), causing saving to be 150 and to be equal to investment.

25. C. S = Y – C = Y – (100 + .9Y) = –100 + .1Y.

## II. SOLUTIONS TO APPLICATION QUESTIONS

1. a. MPC = .75. Equation 1 tells us that, as income (Y) increases by 100, consumption increases by 75. MPS = .25. Recall that MPC + MPS = 1. Alternatively, as income (Y) increases by 100 and consumption increases by 75, the remaining 25 must be saved.

   b. S = –300 + .25Y.

   c. The equilibrium conditions are:

      (1) Planned aggregate expenditure = aggregate output (income)

      $$C + S = C + I$$

      (2) saving = planned investment

      $$S = I$$

      (3) planned investment = actual investment

      (4) unplanned inventory change = 0

   d. If, in equilibrium, equation (1) holds, then (2) must also hold because AE is defined as consumption plus investment and Y is defined as consumption plus saving. Similarly, cancelling the "consumptions," we can derive (3). We know that actual investment always equals planned investment plus unplanned inventory change, so unplanned inventory change must equal zero.

   e. $$Y = C + I \text{ (in equilibrium)}$$
      $$Y = 300 + .75Y + 200 = 500 + .75Y$$
      $$Y - .75Y = 500$$
      $$.25Y = 500 => Y = 2000.$$

   f. See the diagram below (not drawn to scale).

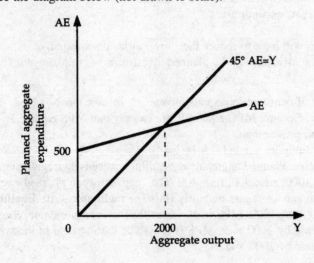

g.    200 decrease in inventories. Demand (1400) exceeds production (1200).

h.    50 increase in inventories. Production (2200) exceeds demand (2150).

i.    At income levels where the AE line is above the 45° line, unplanned inventory change will be negative (e.g., when Y = 1200); at income levels where the AE line is below the 45° line, unplanned inventory change will be positive (e.g., when Y = 2200).

j.    C = 300 + .75Y. Y = 1200. C = 300 + .75(1200) = 1200. S = Y – C = 0.

k.    C = 300 + .75Y. Y = 2200. C = 300 + .75(2200) = 1950. S = Y – C = 250.

l.    An autonomous 100-unit increase in expenditure causes a 400 increase in equilibrium income. The multiplier is 4.00.

Check: Multiplier = 1 / (1 – MPC) = 1 / .25 = 4.00.

m.    $\Delta Y = m \times \Delta I$, where m is the multiplier. m = 4 and $\Delta Y$ = 800, therefore $\Delta I$ = 200.

n.    Inventories are falling by 100 as producers use previously produced output to meet the unexpected demand.

o.
$$Y = C + I \text{ (in equilibrium)}$$
$$Y = 400 + .75Y + 200 = 600 + .75Y$$
$$Y - .75Y = 600$$
$$.25Y = 600 => Y = 2400.$$

p.    When Y = 2400, C = 400 + .75(2400) = 2200.

q.    When Y = 2400, S = –400 + .25(2400) = 200.

Check: Y = C + S, 2400 = 2200 + 200.

r.    I is unchanged at 200. Note that, in equilibrium, S = I.

s.    Saving has remained unchanged. In equilibrium, S = I, and I has remained unchanged.

2.   a.    some (probably most, in fact).

     b.    some.

If you answered "all" for (A) you should have answered "none" for (B). Such answers indicate you're not "typical"—most folks try to set some saving aside. Groups who don't are the young (who may have high initial expenses and low incomes) and the retired (who don't earn much).

     c.    You probably "agree" with all of these statements.

The "other things" in (i) and the logic behind (iv) will be developed in Chapter 14.

     d.    If I increase my personal spending by $1, my saving will *decrease* by exactly $1. If you missed this one, reread the first few pages of the chapter!

3.   a.    C + I exceeds C + S because I exceeds S.

     b.    aggregate expenditure.

     c.    No.

     d.    Firms will have to reduce their inventories unexpectedly.

     e.    Actual investment = planned investment + unplanned inventory change.

     f.      15        =       20      +      –5.

4.   a.    Zero. If consumption equals income, no income can be saved.

     b.    False. Because MPC equals .9, we can say that MPS equals .1.

     c.    is not; greater than.

     d.    10. Multiplier = 1 / (1 – MPC) = 1 / .1 = 10.

     e.    negative. Planned aggregate expenditure exceeds aggregate output.

     f.    rise; 1000; rise; 900; rise; 100. The "gap" between planned aggregate expenditure and aggregate output is 100. The multiplier is 10. Equilibrium income will fall by 1000. MPC is .9. Given the increase in income, consumption will increase by 1000 × .9. MPS is .1. Given the increase in income, saving will increase by 1000 × .1.

g.  100; −100. If income changes from zero to 1000, consumption increases by 900 to 1000 (because MPC is .9). We know, therefore, that consumption is (1000 − 900) when income is zero. Because income equals consumption plus saving, saving must equal −100.

h.  C = 100 + .9Y.

i.
$$
\begin{aligned}
Y &= C + I \\
&= 100 + .9Y + 100 \\
&= 200 + .9Y \\
Y - .9Y &= 200 \\
.1Y &= 200 \\
Y &= 2000.
\end{aligned}
$$

j.  See the diagram below.

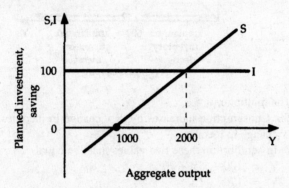

5.  a.  See the table below. When income rises by 100 (from 100 to 200), consumption rises by 80 (from 180 to 260). MPC, therefore, is .8. MPC + MPS = 1, therefore MPS = .2. Given MPC, the consumption column can be filled in. Given income and consumption, saving can be derived by subtraction. Investment is assumed to be constant at 20. The expenditure column is derived by adding consumption and investment.

| Income | Consumption | Saving | Investment | Expenditures |
|--------|-------------|--------|------------|--------------|
| 0 | 100 | −100 | 20 | 120 |
| 100 | 180 | −80 | 20 | 200 |
| 200 | 260 | −60 | 20 | 280 |
| 300 | 340 | −40 | 20 | 360 |
| 400 | 420 | −20 | 20 | 440 |
| 500 | 500 | 0 | 20 | 520 |
| 600 | 580 | 20 | 20 | 600 |
| 700 | 660 | 40 | 20 | 680 |
| MPC .8 | | MPS .2 | | |
| multiplier = 5 | | | | |

b.  600. Equilibrium occurs where planned expenditure equals income (and where saving equals investment).

c.  C = 100 + .8Y

d.
$$
\begin{aligned}
Y &= 100 + .8Y + 20 \\
.2Y &= 120 \\
Y &= 600.
\end{aligned}
$$

e.    reduction; increase
f.    See the diagram below (not drawn to scale).

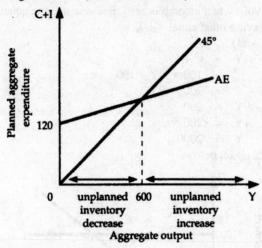

g.    250. The multiplier is 5.
h.    200; 50. Consumption increases by .8 x change in income. Saving increases by .2 x change in income.
i.    70; 70. In equilibrium these two values must be equal.
j.
$$Y = 100 + .8Y + 70$$
$$.2Y = 170$$
$$Y = 850$$
$$C = 100 + .8Y$$
$$= 100 + .8(850) = 780.$$
At $Y = 600$, C was 580 (See the table above.)
$$S = Y - C = 850 - 780 = 70.$$
At $Y = 600$, S was 20 (See the table above.)

k.    30. The economy's equilibrium income level is 850, 150 short of the goal. The multiplier is 5, so an autonomous 30-unit increase, multiplied by 5, will hit the target.

6.    The slope of the consumption function is MPC and the slope of the saving function is MPS. We know that MPC + MPS equals one. MPC decreases as the consumption function becomes flatter, so MPS must increase and the saving function must become steeper. The value of the multiplier is given by the formula: 1 / MPS. As MPS increases, the size of the multiplier will decrease as income increases. In fact, the effect of this weakened multiplier can be shown graphically. The same vertical increase in aggregate spending will push the economy's equilibrium income level less far when the slope of the AE curve is decreasing.

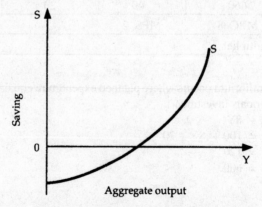

7.  The AE function is the total of the consumption function and the investment function. In the original model, the slope of AE is determined solely by the slope of the consumption function—i.e., MPC. However, the slope of the AE curve is properly interpreted as the change in spending (from both sources) that occurs as income changes. If investment also increases, as income increases, the AE curve will become steeper. The value of the multiplier will increase too; in the more complex model we'll be developing in later chapters, the multiplier formulas we have devised are incomplete. In fact, the effect of this strengthened multiplier can be shown graphically. The same vertical increase in aggregate spending will push the economy's equilibrium income level farther as the AE curve becomes steeper.

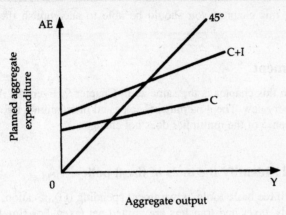

# 10 The Government and Fiscal Policy

## OBJECTIVES: POINT BY POINT

After completing this chapter, you should be able to accomplish the objectives listed below.

### General Comment

The basic logic in this chapter is the same as in Chapter 9. Even the Appendix material adds little that's very new. The government sector and international trade are added to the model but the essence of the multiplier does not change.

### OBJECTIVE 1: Identify the tools of fiscal policy.

Fiscal policy has three basic tools: government spending (G), taxation, and transfer payments. Collectively, taxes and transfers are termed net taxes. For simplification, the text model assumes (except in Appendix 10B) that net taxes are not related to income.

### Practice

1. Each of the following might be a specific fiscal policy action except
   A. reducing interest rates to stimulate consumer demand.
   B. increasing government spending on military helicopters.
   C. easing the eligibility requirements for Employment Insurance recipients.
   D. increasing personal income tax rates.

   **ANSWER:** A. Interest rate changes come under the category of monetary policy.

### OBJECTIVE 2: Describe how the inclusion of the government sector affects the aggregate expenditure model.

The chapter begins by adding the government sector to the simplified model of Chapter 9. Initially, the model remains a closed economy model (that is, exports and imports are both zero). Exports and imports are added later in the chapter. When the government sector is added to the simplified aggregate expenditure model, government spending is included directly in aggregate expenditure alongside consumption and investment. Consumption and saving are based on disposable (after-tax) income. The equilibrium condition is:

$$Y = C + I + G + EX - IM \text{ which implies}$$

$$Y = C + I + G$$

if exports and imports are both zero. (page 203)

## Practice

2. Disposable income is total income
   A. plus transfer payments.
   B. plus net taxes.
   C. minus net taxes.
   D. plus taxes.

   **ANSWER: C.** Be careful with the concept of net taxes. Net taxes are taxes less transfer payments.

3. Which of the following is the correct identity?
   A. $Y \equiv C + S + G$
   B. $Y \equiv C + S + I$
   C. $Y \equiv C + S + IM$
   D. $Y \equiv C + S + T$

   **ANSWER: D.** Aggregate income that has not been saved or consumed has gone to the government in the form of net taxes (T).

4. The government budget deficit is
   A. $G - T$.
   B. $T - G$.
   C. $EX - IM$.
   D. $C - S$.

   **ANSWER: A.** The government budget deficit is the excess of what government spends (G) less what it collects in net taxes (T).

5. When the government sector is added to the model, the consumption function formula is
   A. $C = a + b(Y + Y)$.
   B. $C = a + b(Y - T)$.
   C. $C = a - b(Y + T)$.
   D. $C = a - b(Y - T)$.

   **ANSWER: B.** See p. 203. $(Y - T)$ is disposable income.

6. In equilibrium
   A. planned aggregate expenditure equals consumption.
   B. unplanned inventory change equals saving.
   C. planned investment spending must be zero.
   D. planned investment spending equals actual investment spending.

   **ANSWER: D.** If planned investment spending equals actual investment spending, there is no unintended investment in inventories (unplanned inventory change is zero) and there is equilibrium. Option A is incorrect because planned aggregate expenditure contains investment, government expenditure, and (later in the chapter) net exports as well as consumption. For option B, in equilibrium unplanned inventory change equals zero and for option C, planned investment need not be zero in equilibrium. See p. 203.

Use the following table to answer the next four questions, assuming that exports and imports are zero. The abbreviations are those used in the textbook.

| Y | T | $Y_d$ | C | S | I | G | AE |
|---|---|---|---|---|---|---|---|
| 1000 | 200 | _____ | 1060 | _____ | 340 | 400 | 1800 |
| 2000 | 200 | _____ | 1860 | _____ | 340 | | |
| 3000 | 200 | _____ | 2660 | _____ | _____ | _____ | _____ |
| 4000 | _____ | _____ | _____ | _____ | _____ | _____ | _____ |
| 5000 | _____ | _____ | _____ | _____ | _____ | _____ | _____ |
| 6000 | _____ | 5800 | 5060 | _____ | 340 | 400 | 5800 |

7. Complete the table.

   **ANSWER:** See the *Answers and Solutions* section.

8. The marginal propensity to consume is
   A. .6.
   B. .75.
   C. .8.
   D. .85.

   **ANSWER:** C. As disposable income changes by 1000 (e.g., from 1800 to 2800), consumption changes by 800 (from 1860 to 2660).

9. Equilibrium income level is
   A. 3000.
   B. 4000.
   C. 5000.
   D. 6000.

   **ANSWER:** C. This is where AE = Y.

10. In equilibrium, the government has a
    A. deficit of 200.
    B. deficit of 240.
    C. surplus of 200.
    D. surplus of 240.

    **ANSWER:** A. The government's deficit is 200 because spending (G) is 400 and net tax revenues (T) are 200.

## OBJECTIVE 3: Derive the government spending multiplier, the tax multiplier, and the balanced-budget multiplier.

The *government spending multiplier* is identical to the investment multiplier developed in the previous chapter—if MPC is .75, a one dollar increase in government spending will cause the equilibrium income level to expand by $4. The multiplier is 4. The formula for the government spending multiplier in this model is 1 / MPS.          (page 206)

The *tax multiplier* is absolutely smaller than the government spending multiplier because, with a tax cut, not all of the resulting increase in disposable income will be spent—some will leak away into saving. The tax multiplier is negative—an *increase* in taxes leads to a *decrease* in production. If MPC is .75, a one dollar increase in tax collections will cause the equilibrium income level to decrease by $3. The tax multiplier is –3. The formula for the tax multiplier in this model is –MPC / MPS.          (page 208)

The *balanced-budget multiplier* is always equal to one in our model. An equal increase in government spending and net taxes will have a dollar-for-dollar expansionary effect on equilibrium income.          (page 209)

## OBJECTIVE 4: Analyze the effects of a change in government spending and/or a change in taxes on output.

An increase (decrease) in government spending will initially increase (decrease) planned aggregate expenditure, dollar for dollar. A decrease (increase) in net taxes will initially increase (decrease) planned aggregate expenditure—but *not* dollar for dollar. In each case there will be multiplier effects, but because the initial effect of the tax change on output is smaller, the tax multiplier will also be smaller. (page 210)

Consider cutting a government deficit by either reducing government expenditure or increasing taxes. In this model, reducing government expenditure will have the more powerful (negative) economic effect because the government spending multiplier is more powerful.

> **Caution:** When working out the effects of policy actions, take a moment to make sure the result looks sensible. It's easy to forget a negative sign or mess up the arithmetic. Have confidence in your own intuition. If your results don't look right, they probably aren't!

> **Graphing Pointer:** A one-dollar increase (decrease) in government spending or a one-dollar decrease (increase) in net taxes will shift the AE curve vertically upward (downward) but not by the same amount. The shift caused by the tax change will be smaller.

## Practice

Use the table you completed for Practice Question 7 to answer the next question.

11. In the table, the government spending multiplier is _____ and the tax multiplier is _____.
    A.  4, –3.
    B.  4, 3.
    C.  5, –4.
    D.  5, 4.

    **ANSWER: C.** As disposable income changes by 1000 (e.g., from 1800 to 2800), saving changes by 200 (from –60 to 140). MPS is .2. The formula for the government spending multiplier is 1 / MPS, and the formula for the tax multiplier is –MPC / MPS.

12. In the nation of Arbez, which has a government sector and can be modelled as in Chapter 10, an increase in investment spending of 100 will cause equilibrium income level to increase by 1000. The government spending multiplier is _____.
    A.  5.
    B.  6.
    C.  9.
    D.  10.

    **ANSWER: D.** If an increase in investment can be "multiplied" tenfold, then the multiplier must be 10. If so, MPC is .9 and MPS is .1. Note that, with taxes that do not depend on income, the MPC formulas in Chapter 9 and Chapter 10 are equivalent. The formula for the government spending multiplier is 1 / MPS, so, in this case, the multiplier is 10.

Use the table you completed for Practice Question 7 to answer the next four questions.

13. The equilibrium income level would be 6000 if government spending
    A. increased by 200.
    B. increased by 1000.
    C. decreased by 200.
    D. decreased by 1000.

    **ANSWER:** A. The multiplier is 5. The increase in equilibrium income ($\Delta Y$) = 1000 = $\Delta G \times 1$ / MPS = 200 × 5.

14. The equilibrium income level would be 4000 if net taxes
    A. increased by 200.
    B. increased by 250.
    C. decreased by 200.
    D. decreased by 250.

    **ANSWER:** B. The tax multiplier is –4. Decrease in equilibrium income ($\Delta Y$) = 1000 = $\Delta T \times$ –MPC / MPS = 250 × –4.

15. If government spending increased by 100 and taxes decreased by 100, equilibrium income level would
    A. increase by 100.
    B. increase by 900.
    C. decrease by 100.
    D. not change.

    **ANSWER:** B. Split this question into two parts—the effect of the spending change and the effect of the tax change.
    Spending change: $\Delta Y = \Delta G \times 1$ / MPS = 100 × 5 = +500.
    Tax change: $\Delta Y = \Delta T \times$ –MPC / MPS = –100 × –4 = +400.

16. If government spending decreased by 100 and taxes decreased by 100, equilibrium income level would
    A. increase by 100.
    B. decrease by 900.
    C. decrease by 100.
    D. not change.

    **ANSWER:** C. This is a "balanced-budget" change (i.e., $\Delta G = \Delta T$).

Refer to the following diagram to answer the next five questions.

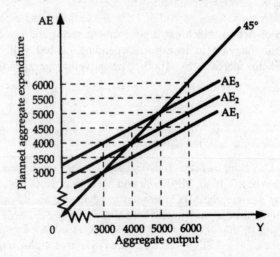

17. If expenditures are as shown by $AE_2$, the equilibrium income level is
    A. 3000.
    B. 4000.
    C. 5000.
    D. 6000.

    **ANSWER: B.** $AE_2$ crosses the 45° line at this income level.

18. Given $AE_2$, if the income level is at 3000, we know that
    A. government spending is greater than net taxes.
    B. government spending is less than net taxes.
    C. unplanned inventory investment is positive.
    D. unplanned inventory investment is negative.

    **ANSWER: D.** Expenditure exceeds production; inventory level will be decreasing.

For questions 19, 20, and 21, assume the basic model of Chapter 10 in which taxes do not depend on income.

19. The government spending multiplier is _____ and the tax multiplier is _____.
    A. 2, –1.
    B. 2, –3.
    C. 4, –3.
    D. 4, –5.

    **ANSWER: A.** As income level rises by 1000 (from 3000 to 4000), planned expenditure rises by 500 (from 3500 to 4000). MPC is .5 and MPS is .5.

20. To shift the AE curve from $AE_2$ to $AE_3$, we could
    A. increase government spending by 500.
    B. increase government spending by 1000.
    C. increase net taxes by 500.
    D. increase net taxes by 1000.

    **ANSWER: A.** Increasing taxes will reduce aggregate expenditure—consumers would have less after-tax income to spend. Increasing government spending by 500 will work. Note that the vertical distance between $AE_2$ and $AE_3$ is 500.

21. Given $AE_2$, each of the following policies except _____ would reduce the equilibrium output level to 3000.
    A. decreasing government spending by 1000 and decreasing taxes by 1000.
    B. decreasing government spending by 1000.
    C. increasing government spending by 500 and increasing taxes by 2000.
    D. increasing taxes by 1000.

    **ANSWER: B.** The government spending multiplier is 2. $\Delta G \times 1 / MPS = -1000 \times 2 = -2000$. Option A is the balanced-budget case. Option C is quite complex but works as follows: Government spending change = $\Delta G \times 1 / MPS = 500 \times 2 = 1000$. Tax change: $\Delta T \times -MPC / MPS = 2000 \times -1 = -2000$.

22. Given $AE_3$, suppose aggregate output is 4000 and planned investment is 500. Planned investment plus unplanned investment is
    A. 0.
    B. 500.
    C. 1000.
    D. 1500.

    **ANSWER: A.** Unplanned inventory change is output less planned aggregate expenditure or $4000 - 4500 = -500$. Planned investment plus unplanned inventory change = $500 + (-500) = 0$.

## OBJECTIVE 5: Explain how the inclusion of the international sector in the model affects the aggregate expenditure model and the multiplier.

When the closed economy model studied so far is changed to an open economy model, planned aggregate expenditure now must include exports (EX), as these are expenditures made by foreigners for goods and services produced in Canada. Components of consumption (C), investment (I), government expenditure (G), and exports that are produced elsewhere should not be counted in Canadian output. Thus we subtract imports (IM). The equilibrium condition becomes:

$$Y = C + I + G + EX - IM \qquad \text{(page 211)}$$

If net exports (exports minus imports or EX - IM) are zero, that does not change anything from the previous analysis. If net exports are not zero, this component must be included when solving for equilibrium, but it does not change the basic logic or the multiplier analysis. (See the examples below.) For example, if exports and imports do not depend on income (that is, they are "autonomous"), the multiplier will be exactly the same as for G, I, or autonomous consumption (the intercept "a" in the consumption function "a + bY"). Of course the multiplier for an increase in imports will be negative because imports are produced elsewhere.

If imports are not autonomous and instead depend on income, the multiplier will be reduced because, as income increases in the multiplier process, some of the spending will "leak" out of the economy as imports, as for example Canadian workers will use some of their increased earnings to buy imported goods. Details are provided in Appendix 10C.

## OBJECTIVE 6: Describe the leakages/injections approach to equilibrium.

In Chapter 9 it was shown in equilibrium of that simplified model that the "leakage" of spending to saving must equal the "injection" of spending from planned investment. In the more general model in Chapter 10, net taxes and imports are leakages from spending, and government spending and exports are injections of spending. Hence the leakages/injections equilibrium condition now becomes

$$S + T + IM = I + G + EX$$

> **TIP:** Remember this Keynesian model is a model of economic activity. Not all measures that increase economic activity will make Canadians better off. For example, a government policy designed to create economic activity by increasing exports and decreasing imports (sometimes called a "mercantilist" policy) can harm Canadians. For example, a government policy that banned fruit imports might conceivably create jobs in the Canadian fruit industry (as Canadian consumers switched to Canadian-produced fruits) but would also deny Canadians access to oranges and bananas and make other fruits more expensive. These issues are explored in Chapters 20 and 21.

> **TIP:** Sometimes economists will use X rather than EX to denote exports, M rather than IM to denote imports, and NX to denote net exports, EX – IM.

## Practice

Use this model of the economy for the following four questions:

$C = 20 + .8Y_d$      (Consumption spending; note $Y_d$ is disposable income)
$I = 100$      (Investment spending)
$G = 250$      (Government purchases)
$T = 200$      (Net taxes)
$EX = 50$      (Exports)
$IM = 80$      (Imports)

23. Given the model above, what is equilibrium output?
    A. 600.
    B. 700.
    C. 800.
    D. 900.

    **ANSWER: D.** Always begin with $Y = C + I + G + EX - IM$, then replace the components with their expressions and finally solve. Follow these steps:

$$\begin{aligned}
Y &= C + I + G + EX - IM \\
&= 20 + .8Yd + 100 + 250 + 50 - 80 \\
&= 340 + .8Y - 200) \text{ because } Y_d = Y - T \\
&= 180 + .8Y \\
\text{or } .2Y &= 180 \\
\text{or } Y &= (1 / .2) \times 180 = 900
\end{aligned}$$

It might be instructive to note that disposable income will be $Y_d = Y - T = 900 - 200 = 700$ so that consumption will be $C = 20 + .8Y_d = 20 + .8(700) = 580$. Saving will be $Y_d - C = 700 - 580 = 120$. So $S + T + IM = 120 + 200 + 80 = 400$ which should and does equal $I + G + EX = 100 + 250 + 50 = 400$.

24. If I or G increases by 1, how much will output increase?
    A. 2.
    B. 3.
    C. 4.
    D. 5.

    **ANSWER: D.** You can try increasing I to 101 or G to 251 and solving as above: You will find output is 905. You may also note that $(1 / .2) = 5$ is the multiplier.

25. If EX increases by 1, how much will output increase?
    A. 2.
    B. 3.
    C. 4.
    D. 5.

    **ANSWER: D.** Again, you can try increasing EX to 51 and solving as above: You will find output becomes 905. But again you may note that the multiplier is ($1 / .2 = 5$). Exports enter planned aggregate expenditure in exactly the same way as planned investment or governmental purchases, so it is not surprising that they will have the same multiplier.

26. If IM increases by 1, how much will output increase?
    A. 2.
    B. 4.
    C. 5.
    D. none of the above.

    **ANSWER: D.** An increase in imports will reduce planned aggregate expenditure on domestic goods and hence reduce output. Indeed, you can work out that an increase in imports of 1 will reduce output by 5 to 895 (that is, increase output by –5). Again, the multiplier effect is 5. It should not be surprising that imports here have an equal and opposite effect to exports.

Now use this model of the economy for the next seven questions:

$C = 10 + .6Y_d$      (Consumption spending; note $Y_d$ is disposable income)
$I = 20$      (Investment spending)
$G = 30$      (Government purchases)
$T = 50$      (Net taxes)
$EX = 60$      (Exports)
$IM = 40$      (Imports)

27. Given the model above, what is equilibrium output?
    A. 100.
    B. 125.
    C. 150.
    D. 175.

    **ANSWER: B.**
    $$\begin{aligned} Y &= C + I + G + EX - IM \\ &= 10 + .6Y_d + 20 + 30 + 60 - 40 \\ &= 80 + .6(Y - 50) \\ &= 50 + .6Y \\ \text{or } .4Y &= 50 \\ \text{or } Y &= (1 / .4) \times 50 = 125 \end{aligned}$$

    While not needed for the answer, note $Y_d = Y - T = 125 - 50 = 75$ so that consumption will be $C = 10 + .6Y_d = 10 + .6(75) = 55$. Saving will be $Yd - C = 75 - 55 = 20$. So $S + T + IM = 20 + 50 + 40 = 110$ which should and does equal $I + G + EX = 20 + 30 + 60 = 110$.

28. If I, G, or EX increases by 1, how much will output increase?
    A. 2.
    B. 2.5.
    C. 3.
    D. 4.

    **ANSWER: B.** You can try increasing I to 21, G to 31 or EX to 61 and solving as above: You will find output becomes 127.5. You may also note that $(1 / .4) = 2.5$ is the multiplier. While not necessary for this question, you can also confirm that an increase in imports by 1 will reduce output by 2.5.

29. If net taxes increase by 1, how much will output decrease?
    A.  1.
    B.  1.5.
    C.  2.
    D.  2.5.

    **ANSWER:  B.**   Again, you can try increasing T to 51 and solving as above: You will find output falls to 123.5. You may also recall from the text that for this simple model, the multiplier for an increase in taxes will be $-MPC / (1 - MPC)$ or $-.6 / (1 - .6) = -1.5$.

30. If government purchases increase by 10, how much will output increase?
    A.  20.
    B.  25.
    C.  30.
    D.  40.

    **ANSWER:  B.**   Again you can work it out, but it is quicker to note that the multiplier is 2.5 and that $2.5 \times 10 = 25$.

31. If government purchases decrease by 5, how much will output increase?
    A.  −20.
    B.  −12.5.
    C.  10.
    D.  12.5.

    **ANSWER:  B.**   Government purchases have increased by −5 and $2.5 \times -5 = -12.5$.

32. If government purchases are increased by 1 and net taxes also increase by 1, how much will output increase?
    A.  1.
    B.  −1.
    C.  −1.5.
    D.  −2.5.

    **ANSWER:  A.**   If you try increasing government purchases to 31 and increasing taxes to 51 and solving, you will find that output increases to 126. A shortcut is to add the multiplier effect of the increase in government spending (2.5) to the multiplier effect of the increase in taxes (−1.5) to get a total increase of $2.5 + (-1.5) = 1$. This is the so-called balanced-budget multiplier where, in the simple Keynes cross model, a balanced budget increase in government spending and taxes will increase output by the same amount.  Note that the balanced-budget multiplier does not require that the budget actually be balanced, just that the changes in government purchases and taxes are equal so that the budget balance *does not change*.

33. If government purchases and net taxes both decrease by 5, how much will output increase?
    A.  −5.
    B.  0.
    C.  5.
    D.  10.

    **ANSWER:  A.**   This again is the balanced budget multiplier effect, so that in the simple Keynes cross model, output will change by the same amount and in the same direction as the changes in government purchases and net taxes.

34. Compare two identical "Keynes cross" model economies of the kind studied in this chapter. In model A, the economy is closed. In model B, the economy is open but exports equal imports. Equilibrium output is:

A.   higher in economy A than in economy B.

B.   higher in economy B than in economy A.

C.   equal in both economies.

D.   equal in both economies even though net exports exceed zero in B.

**ANSWER:** C.  $Y = C + I + G + EX - IM$. It does not make any difference whether $EX = IM = 0$, as in model A, or $EX - IM = 0$, as in model B: In both cases net exports $EX - IM$ can be ignored. Answer D is not correct because net exports are zero in model B.

35. Continuing from question 34, now suppose that model A is unchanged but in model B, exports now exceed imports but neither exports nor imports depend on income. Equilibrium output is:

A.   higher in economy A than in economy B.

B.   higher in economy B than in economy A.

C.   equal in both economies.

D.   equal in both economies even though net exports exceed zero in B.

**ANSWER:** B.  Compared to question 34, the increase in net exports will increase output in B by a multiplier effect. Incidentally, because neither exports nor imports depend on income, the multiplier in these two otherwise identical economies will be the same.

36. Continuing from the previous two questions, now suppose that model A is unchanged but in model B, imports now increase when income increases. As compared to model A, for B the planned Aggregate Expenditure line is _____ and the multiplier is _____.

A.   flatter; smaller.

B.   steeper; smaller.

C.   flatter; greater.

D.   steeper; greater.

**ANSWER:** A.  The planned Aggregate Expenditure line slopes upwards because an increase in aggregate output (income) on the horizontal axis increases planned Aggregate Expenditure in our simple model solely because of the effect on consumption (C). However, if imports depend on income, the effect of the increase will be lessened because some of the additional expenditure stimulated by the increase in income will be on goods produced elsewhere. As always when the planned Aggregate Expenditure line is flatter, the multiplier is smaller. The model is studied in detail in Appendix 10C, but the basic idea is that multiplier effects will be smaller when some of any increase of spending "leaks" out into imports.

37. In an economy with a balanced government budget and a zero trade balance (i.e., net exports equal zero):

A.   Saving exceeds investment.

B.   Investment exceeds saving.

C.   Investment equals saving.

D.   Cannot be determined with the information given.

**ANSWER:** C.  Leakages equal injections, so $S + T + IM = I + G + EX$. If $T = G$ and $EX = IM$, $S = I$.

38. In an economy in which saving equals investment,
    A. the government budget surplus will equal net exports.
    B. net exports must be positive.
    C. the government budget must be in surplus.
    D. saving equals exports.

    **ANSWER:** A. S + T + IM = I + G + EX. If S = I, T + IM = G + EX. Subtracting G from both sides and IM from both sides, T – G = EX – IM, where the left hand side is the government surplus and the right-hand side is net exports. This kind of equation is sometimes used to show a link between government deficits and trade deficits.

39. National saving is sometimes defined as saving plus the government surplus (as the government surplus is saving by the government). An economy with national saving in excess of investment must
    A. have a trade deficit.
    B. have a trade surplus.
    C. have a government budget surplus.
    D. have a government budget deficit.

    **ANSWER:** B. S + T + IM = I + G + EX implies that S + T – G = I + EX – IM. The left-hand side of this equation is saving plus the government surplus or national saving, so it can only exceed I on the right hand side of the equation if EX – IM is positive, that is, there is a trade surplus.

## OBJECTIVE 7: Define full-employment budget, structural deficit, and cyclical deficit.

This year's government *budget balance* is the difference between government revenues this year and government spending this year i.e., T – G. A positive budget balance is called a *surplus*; a negative budget balance is called a *deficit*. The f*ederal debt* is the total amount owed by the federal government to the public (because of deficits of previous years). (page 215)

*Automatic stabilizers* (revenue or expenditure items in the federal budget that adjust in magnitude as the level of economic activity changes) operate as the economy moves through the business cycle. During a recession, for instance, when incomes are low, transfer payments increase and partly replace the lost income—spending doesn't fall so much as it otherwise would have. Tax liabilities decrease, too, in such a situation. Automatic stabilizers reduce the severity of fluctuations in the business cycle. (page 217)

*Fiscal drag* occurs because as the economy expands and/or inflation occurs, incomes rise, pushing taxpayers into higher tax brackets and increasing the average tax rate. Out of each dollar, less is available to spend or save than otherwise would have been the case. The tax structure slows the rate of economic expansion. (page 218)

The *full-employment budget* is an estimate of what the federal budget would be if the economy were producing at a full-employment level of output. A deficit that would remain if the economy were at full employment is called the *structural deficit*. A surplus would be a *structural surplus*. The *cyclical deficit* is the structural surplus less the actual surplus. As an example, if the economy were at full employment, the surplus with current tax and spending programs would be $12 billion, but in reality, because of high unemployment, the surplus is $2 billion. The structural surplus is $12 billion; the cyclical deficit is $12 billion – $2 billion = $10 billion. (page 218)

> **TIP:** It can be surprisingly tricky to remember that the deficit is the negative of the surplus and the surplus is the negative of the deficit. The government budget surplus is T – G; the deficit is G – T.

## Practice

40. Automatic stabilizers make the federal surplus _____ during recessions and _____ during expansions.
    A. larger, larger.
    B. larger, smaller.
    C. smaller, larger.
    D. smaller, smaller.

    **ANSWER:** C.  See p. 217.

41. If the economy were at full employment, it is estimated that the federal surplus would be $20 billion, but at the actual level of employment, the federal budget surplus is $5 billion. The structural deficit is _____ and the cyclical deficit is _____ .
    A. $20 billion; $5 billion.
    B. $20 billion; $15 billion.
    C. –$20 billion; $15 billion.
    D. –$20 billion; 0.

    **ANSWER:** C.  This is slightly tricky because the question asks for a structural *deficit* when there is in fact a structural *surplus* of $20 billion, and a surplus is a negative deficit just as a deficit is a negative surplus. The cyclical deficit is the reduction in the budget balance associated with the economy's position below full employment: that is the full-employment budget surplus less the actual budget surplus or $20 billion – $5 billion = $15 billion.

## OBJECTIVE 8 (APPENDIX 10A): Derive the fiscal policy multipliers algebraically.

Appendix A shows how to work with these models in algebraic form. A given model is solved so that aggregate output (income) (Y) is on the left-hand side while the right-hand side has "a multiplier" multiplied by the various "autonomous" items that do not depend on Y themselves but can induce changes in Y. For example in the model in Appendix A:

$$Y = (1 / (1 - b)) \times (a + I + G - bT + EX - IM)$$

the multiplier $1/(1-b)$ is multiplied by the sum of autonomous consumption (a, the intercept of the consumption function), planned investment spending (I), government spending (G), exports (EX) less imports (IM), and an adjustment for net taxes (T). Note the multiplier for T is different from the others because T is multiplied by negative b as well as by $1 / (1 - b)$ so that the tax multiplier is $-b / (1 - b)$.

> **TIP:** Different models may have different components which depend on Y and this will change the multiplier. (Examples are in Appendixes 10B and 10C). Also, if you happen to know calculus (not necessary to understand this material!), you will likely have noticed by now that "multipliers" are just derivatives, so that the government spending multiplier is the derivative of output with respect to government spending.

## Practice

42. The starting point for solving the Keynes cross model algebraically is the equilibrium condition:
    A.  $Y = C + I + G + EX + IM$.
    B.  $Y = C + I + G - T + EX - IM$.
    C.  $Y = C + I + G + EX - IM$.
    D.  $Y = C + I - S + G - T + EX - IM$.

    **ANSWER: C.** This is an easy question but if you get the first step wrong, everything that follows will be wrong as well.

## OBJECTIVE 9 (APPENDIX 10B): Show algebraically how the fiscal policy multipliers are reduced when tax revenues depend on income.

When a tax rate is introduced into the model, the formula for the expenditure multiplier must be adjusted—the multiplier's value is reduced (because the leakage of additional spending power is greater than before). Graphically, the consumption function and the AE function become flatter. As income increases, consumption still increases, but at a slower rate, because some of the increase goes to taxes rather than to disposable income.

## Practice

In the following four questions, assume that consumption is the only spending component that depends upon income and that net taxes $T = T_o + tY$, where t is the tax rate and $T_o$ is lump sum taxes (the component of taxes that does not depend on Y).

43. In Arboc, the tax rate is 20% and the MPC is .75. The government spending multiplier is
    A.  2.5.
    B.  3.0.
    C.  3.75.
    D.  4.0.

    **ANSWER: A.** The multiplier's formula is $1 / (1 - b + bt)$, where b is MPC and t is the tax rate. In this case, the value is $1 / (1 - .75 + .75(.2))$, or $1 / .4$, which gives a value of 2.5.

44. In Arboc, the tax rate is 20% and the MPC is .75. The tax multiplier for an increase in lump sum taxes is
    A.  –1.5.
    B.  –1.875.
    C.  –3.75.
    D.  –2.75.

    **ANSWER: B.** The multiplier's formula is $-b / (1 - b + bt)$, where b is MPC and t is the tax rate. In this case, the value is $-.75 / (1 - .75 + .75(2))$, or $-.75 / .4$, which gives a value of –1.875. The magnitude of the tax multiplier is less than it would be if taxes did not depend on income.

45. In Arboc, the tax rate is 20% and the MPC is .75. An increase of 1000 in government spending would cause equilibrium income to
    A.    increase by 2500.
    B.    increase by 1000.
    C.    decrease by 1000.
    D.    increase by 4000.

    **ANSWER:** A.   The government spending multiplier is 2.5.

46. In Arbez, the tax rate is 50% and the MPC is .80. To increase equilibrium income by 400, lump sum taxes should be
    A.    increased by 80.
    B.    increased by 300.
    C.    decreased by 80.
    D.    decreased by 300.

    **ANSWER:** D.   The lump-sum tax multiplier formula is $-b / (1 - b + bt)$, where b is MPC and t is the tax rate. In this case, the value is $-.80 / (1 - .80 + .80(.50))$, or $-.80 / .50$, which gives a value of $-1.333$. To increase output, taxes should decrease. $\Delta T \times (-1.333) = 400$; $\Delta T = -300$.


## OBJECTIVE 10 (APPENDIX 10C): Show algebraically how the fiscal multipliers are reduced when imports depend on income.

Allowing imports to depend upon income reduces the multiplier, because only part of any increase in income will be respent within the domestic economy: Some of the spending will "leak" into spending on imported goods made in other economies. This is explained in the text, but the appendix gives a numerical example in algebraic form.


## Practice

The following three questions use the following model. Note that it is the same model used for questions 27–33 above except that now imports depend on income. Because of this, you will find for questions 48 and 49 that the multipliers for this model are smaller in magnitude than those for the comparable questions 28 and 29.

$C = 10 + .6Y_d$       (Consumption spending; note $Y_d$ is disposable income)
$I = 20$           (Investment spending)
$G = 30$           (Government purchases)
$T = 50$           (Net taxes)
$EX = 60$          (Exports)
$IM = 40 + .1Y_d$      (Imports)

47.   What is equilibrium output?
      A.    110.
      B.    120.
      C.    130.
      D.    140.

      **ANSWER:** A.
$$\begin{aligned} Y &= C + I + G + EX - IM \\ &= 10 + .6Y_d + 20 + 30 + 60 - (40 + .1Y_d) \\ &= 80 + .5(Y - 50) \\ &= 55 + .5Y \\ \text{or } .5Y &= 55 \\ \text{or } Y &= (1 / .5) \times 55 = 110 \end{aligned}$$

48. If I, G, or EX increases by 1, how much will output increase?
   A.  2.
   B.  2.5.
   C.  3.
   D.  4.

   **ANSWER:**  A.   You can try increasing I to 21, G to 31, or EX to 61 and solving as above: You will find output becomes 112. You may also note that (1 / .5) = 2 is the multiplier.

49. If net taxes increase by 1, how much will output decrease?
   A.  1.
   B.  1.5
   C.  2.
   D.  2.5.

   **ANSWER:**  A.   Increase T to 51 and solve as above: You will find output falls to 109. The magnitude of the tax multiplier is smaller than it would be if imports did not depend on income.

## PRACTICE TEST

**I.**    **MULTIPLE CHOICE QUESTIONS.** Select the option that provides the single best answer. Unless it is otherwise specified, assume a standard Keynes cross model with taxes not dependent upon income, and consumption the only spending component that does depend upon income. Remember MPS is the marginal propensity to save.

_____ 1.    MPS is .1. An increase in lump-sum taxes of 100 will
   A.    shift the AE function up by 100.
   B.    shift the AE function down by 100.
   C.    shift the AE function down by 90.
   D.    shift the AE curve up by 10.

_____ 2.    If MPS is .2, a decrease in government spending of 100 will
   A.    increase income by 500.
   B.    increase output by 500.
   C.    decrease saving by 100.
   D     decrease output by 400.

_____ 3.    An increase in government spending of 100 causes the level of output to rise by 250. MPS is
   A.    .25.
   B.    .4.
   C.    .6.
   H     2.5.

_____ 4.    The government wants output to increase by 300. Also, it wants the change in the deficit caused by any policy action to be minimized, but government spending must rise by no more than 75. MPC is .75. Assuming you are using a Keynes cross model, you would recommend
   A.    increasing government spending by 75.
   B.    reducing net taxes by 100.
   C.    a balanced-budget increase of 300.
   D.    a balanced-budget increase of 75.

_____ 5. Government spending rises by a dollar. If taxes were _____, equilibrium production level could remain unchanged.
   A. raised by more than a dollar.
   B. raised by less than a dollar.
   C. cut by more than a dollar.
   D. cut by less than a dollar.

_____ 6. Saving rises from $150 to $190 as income rises from $600 to $800. The marginal propensity to
   A. consume is .8 and the government spending multiplier is 5.
   B. save is .4 and the government spending multiplier is 2.5.
   C. save is .25 and the balanced-budget multiplier is 1.0.
   D. save is .2 and the tax multiplier is –6.

_____ 7. Automatic stabilizers stabilize
   A. taxes.
   B. the deficit.
   C. income.
   D. investment.

_____ 8. The economy is experiencing widespread unemployment. A Keynesian economist might suggest that the government
   A. decrease taxes.
   B. decrease government spending.
   C. decrease the deficit.
   D. increase investment spending.

_____ 9. There is a sharp fall in investment spending. The government could maintain the economy at its current output level by _____ government spending or _____ taxes.
   A. raising, lowering.
   B. lowering, raising.
   C. raising, raising.
   D. lowering, lowering.

_____ 10. MPC = .8. The government wants to raise output by $100 million. It could achieve that goal by doing any of the following except
   A. simultaneously raising government spending by $40 million and cutting taxes by $50 million.
   B. cutting taxes by $25 million.
   C. simultaneously raising government spending by $100 million and raising taxes by $100 million.
   D. raising government spending by $20 million.

_____ 11. All of the following are true except
   A. during a recession, there is a cyclical deficit.
   B. during a recession, there must be a structural deficit.
   C. at full employment, there may be a structural deficit.
   D. at full employment, there is no cyclical deficit.

_____ 12. A budget deficit occurs when
   A. taxes exceed government spending.
   B. total tax receipts exceed total government debt.
   C. transfer payments exceed government spending.
   D. government spending exceeds net tax collections.

Use the following diagram for the next five questions.

The economy is in initial equilibrium at an output level of Y = 5000. Consumption is a + b(Y-T) where b is the marginal propensity to consume and T is taxes. Government spending is fixed at 500 and planned investment spending is fixed at 300. Net taxes are 200. Net exports are zero. The following figure is not drawn to scale.

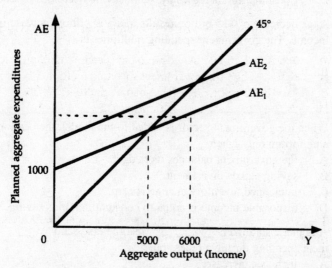

_____ 13. Calculate the marginal propensity to consume. (Hint: With government spending, planned investment spending, net exports and net taxes all fixed, only consumption depends on income (Y) and hence the slope of the AE line is the MPC.)
   A.   .60.
   B.   .75.
   C.   .80.
   D.   .85.

_____ 14. Derive the formula for the saving function.
   A.   S = –360 + .20(Y – T).
   B.   S = –360 – .20(Y – T).
   C.   S = –1000 + .20(Y – T).
   D.   S = –1000 – .20(Y – T).

_____ 15. Calculate the tax multiplier.
   A.   4.
   B.   5.
   C.   –4.
   D.   –5.

_____ 16. The government wishes to shift the AE1 function to AE2 by changing lump-sum taxes. Taxes should
   A.   increase by 200.
   B.   increase by 250.
   C.   decrease by 200.
   D.   decrease by 250.

_____ 17. Given the tax change in question 16, calculate how much consumption and saving, respectively, must change to attain the new equilibrium.
   A.   Consumption increases by 800, saving increases by 200.
   B.   Consumption increases by 1000, saving increases by 250.
   C.   Consumption increases by 1000, saving increases by zero.
   D.   Consumption increases by 1200, saving decreases by 200.

_____ 18. A tax decrease of $15 billion results in a $60 billion increase in equilibrium income. The government spending multiplier is
   A.   –5.
   B.   –4.
   C.   4.
   D.   5.

_____ 19. When the government sector is added to the model, the economy can be in equilibrium only when
   A.   the government balances its budget.
   B.   saving equals investment.
   C.   unplanned inventory change is zero.
   D.   disposable income is equal to consumption plus saving.

_____ 20. Automatic stabilizers _____ income taxes and _____ government spending during a recession.
   A.   increase, increase.
   B.   increase, decrease.
   C.   decrease, increase.
   D.   decrease, decrease.

## II.   APPLICATION QUESTIONS

1.   a.   Use the information below to fill in the gaps in the table. MPC is constant, and investment, government spending, and net exports are determined autonomously. Taxes are lump-sum at a level of 200.

| Real GDP Income | Consumption | Planned Investment | Government Spending | Net Exports | Aggregate Planned Expenditures |
|---|---|---|---|---|---|
| 0 | | | | | |
| 1000 | 1200 | | 400 | | |
| 2000 | 2000 | | | | |
| 3000 | | 300 | | | 3600 |
| 4000 | 3600 | | | 100 | |
| 5000 | 4400 | | | | |
| 6000 | | | | | |
| 7000 | | 300 | | | |

   b.   Calculate MPC and MPS.
   c.   Determine the equilibrium income level for this economy.
   d.   If real GDP is 3000, is unplanned inventory investment positive or negative? Predict how businesses will respond.
   e.   If real GDP is 7000, is unplanned inventory investment positive or negative?
   f.   At which output level is saving zero?

g.   If government spending fell by 200, would the equilibrium output level fall by more than 200, less than 200, or equal to 200? Use the table to confirm your answer. Describe the pressure that would cause the equilibrium output level to change.

2.   You have been called in by the Arbezani Minister of Finance. The full-employment level of output is 124 000 opeks. She tells you that an econometrician has provided the following model of the Arbezani economy. The currency is opeks.

(1)   Consumption function:   $C = 6000 + .75Y_d$
(2)   Investment function:   $I = 11\ 000$
(3)   Government spending:   $G = 20\ 000$
(4)   Net taxes:   $T = 16\ 000$
(5)   Disposable income:   $Y_d = Y - T$
(6)   Net exports:   $EX - IM = 0$
(7)   Equilibrium:   $Y = C + I + G + EX - IM$

a.   Calculate the current equilibrium income level.
b.   Determine the value of the government spending multiplier and the tax multiplier.

The Minister, who is extremely concerned about the level of the national debt, is considering two proposals:

Proposal I:   Maintain the current level of government spending and increase taxes until the budget is balanced.
Proposal II:   Maintain taxes at their present level and decrease federal spending until the budget is balanced.

c.   The policies are contractionary. Which proposal will have the smaller impact on output and employment?
d.   How large will the output reductions be under both proposals?

Due to rising protests about the level of unemployment, the Minister scraps both of the proposals above and turns her attention to expansionary policies.

e.   She is presented with several possible courses of action, listed below, and asks you to evaluate them. In each case, does the proposal restore full employment?

Proposal III:   Increase government spending on defence by 8000 opeks.
Proposal IV:   Increase welfare payments by 8000 opeks.
Proposal V:   Increase lump-sum taxes by 4000 opeks and increase spending on defence by 9000 opeks.
Proposal VI:   Increase welfare payments by 6000 opeks and reduce lump-sum taxes by 2000 opeks.

f.   Of the proposals that achieve the goal of establishing output at the full-employment level, which is preferred in terms of helping to balance the budget?
g.   Of the proposals that achieve the goal of establishing output at the full-employment level, which will increase consumption the most?

3. Use the following information to calculate the multipliers. Assume that taxes are lump-sum and that imports do not depend on income.
a.   $MPS = .2$. The government spending multiplier is _____.
b.   $MPC = .95$. The government spending multiplier is _____.
c.   $MPS = .4$. The government spending multiplier is _____.
d.   $MPC = .9$. The tax multiplier is _____.
e.   $MPS = .2$. The tax multiplier is _____.

f.  If the government spending multiplier is 8, then the tax multiplier is _____.

g.  If the tax multiplier is –5, then the government spending multiplier is _____.

h.  MPS = .2. The government spending multiplier is _____ and the tax multiplier is _____.

Using the information from (h), we know that a simultaneous decrease in G and T of $200 each would cause the following total changes in:

i.  Y _____.

j.  C _____.

k.  S _____.

l.  G _____.

m.  T _____.

4.  Use the information in the table to answer the following questions if net exports are zero.

| Output (Income) | Saving | Planned Investment | Government Spending | Net Taxes | Consumption |
|---|---|---|---|---|---|
| 1300 | 150 | 200 | 100 | 50 | |
| 1500 | 200 | 200 | 100 | 50 | |
| 1700 | 250 | 200 | 100 | 50 | |
| 1900 | 300 | 200 | 100 | 50 | |

a.  Fill in the "consumption" column.
b.  Calculate MPC _____ and equilibrium level of income _____.
c.  Calculate the level of unplanned inventory investment when Y is 1300.
d.  Would the equilibrium level of output (income) increase or decrease if the government were required to cut expenditures to balance its budget?
e.  What action could the government have taken to achieve the full employment level of production (2000)?
f.  Calculate the new equilibrium level of output (income) if G increases by 50 and T increases by 50.

5.  At the equilibrium output (income) level of 720, the following values occur:

$$G = 300 \qquad T = 250$$
$$I = 110 \qquad MPC = .75$$
$$C = 300 \qquad EX - IM = 10$$

a.  Calculate the equilibrium value of saving. _____
b.  Calculate the marginal propensity to save. _____
c.  Calculate the value of the expenditure multiplier. _____
d.  The government deficit now has a value of _____.

Pessimism occurs in the business community. Planned investment falls by 15. How much of an effect does this have on equilibrium GDP?

e.  GDP will _____ (rise/fall) by _____.
f.  At the original GDP level, unplanned inventories are now _____ (rising/falling).

The government attempts to restore the original production level by changing the tax level.

g.  Taxes should be _____ (raised/lowered) by _____.
h.  After the economy has reached its final equilibrium, the deficit is _____.
i.  The final value for consumption is _____.

6.  a. Fill in the blanks in the table. Assume I, G, EX, and IM are all fixed.

| Y | T | $Y_d$ | C | S | I | G | EX | IM | AE |
|---|---|---|---|---|---|---|---|---|---|
| 0 | 20 | | | | | | 20 | 20 | |
| 100 | 20 | | | | 30 | 10 | | | |
| 200 | 20 | | | | | 10 | | | |
| 300 | 20 | | | 0 | | 10 | | | |
| 400 | 20 | | | 20 | 30 | | | | |

    b. Find MPC _____, MPS _____, the government spending multiplier _____, and the tax multiplier _____.

    c. Express the consumption function algebraically. _____

    d. What is the equilibrium income level? _____

7.  Assume the following data for an economy which is in equilibrium at an output level of 480. This example is similar to the textbook's Appendix 10B.

$$G = 150 \qquad MPC = 5/7$$
$$T = -24 + .3Y \qquad MPS = 2/7$$
$$C = 280 \qquad EX - IM = -20$$
$$S = 80$$
$$I = 70$$

    a. Calculate the value of the government spending multiplier. _____

Currently the economy is in a recession. You, as economic adviser, have been asked by how much government spending must be raised to increase equilibrium Y to 550.

    b. Calculate the change in output necessary to achieve equilibrium at 550.

    c. Use the multiplier to deduce the change in G needed to bring about the above change in equilibrium income.

    d. Draw a 45° line picture representing the problem you've just solved.

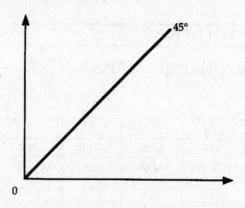

Now government spending has risen, as have taxes. The new level of government spending is the old level plus the policy recommendation you've calculated. The change in taxes can be derived using the tax rate.

    e. What was the deficit originally? _____

    f. How much have tax collections changed? _____

    g. The new deficit is _____.

8. Suppose Canada has full employment and a balanced budget. Suddenly, because of a drop in planned investment, there is a recession.
   a. What will happen to the deficit? Explain why.
   b. Has the structural deficit changed, or has the cyclical deficit changed?
   c. Suppose the government responds by increasing government spending and taxes by an equal amount. The tax increase is achieved by increasing tax rates. What will happen to the structural deficit and to the full-employment budget?

9. In this question remember that in a realistic model of the Canadian economy, imports will depend upon income.
   a. An early sign of improved growth in the Canadian economy is often an increase in imports. Why?
   b. Suppose as the Canadian economy became more open to international trade in the last half of the twentieth century, imports became a bigger component of consumption, such that a given increase in income led to a bigger increase in imports. To someone using a Keynesian model, what did this mean for the size of the multiplier?

10. Consider this simple economy, similar to the model in Appendix 10C:

   $C = 30 + .8Y_d$     (Consumption spending; note $Y_d$ is disposable income)
   $I = 100$     (Investment spending)
   $G = 250$     (Government purchases)
   $T = 200$     (Net taxes)
   $EX = 50$     (Exports)
   $IM = 80 + .4Y_d$     (Imports)

   a. Solve for equilibrium output.
   b. Calculate the change in G needed to increase equilibrium output to 510.
   c. What was the trade deficit originally?
   d. What is the trade deficit after the change in G?

## ANSWERS AND SOLUTIONS

## ANSWERS TO PRACTICE QUESTIONS

7.

| Y | T | $Y_d$ | C | S | I | G | AE |
|------|-----|------|------|------|-----|-----|------|
| 1000 | 200 | 800  | 1060 | −260 | 340 | 400 | 1800 |
| 2000 | 200 | 1800 | 1860 | −60  | 340 | 400 | 2600 |
| 3000 | 200 | 2800 | 2660 | 140  | 340 | 400 | 3400 |
| 4000 | 200 | 3800 | 3460 | 340  | 340 | 400 | 4200 |
| 5000 | 200 | 4800 | 4260 | 540  | 340 | 400 | 5000 |
| 6000 | 200 | 5800 | 5060 | 740  | 340 | 400 | 5800 |

Remember that exports and imports are both zero in this example.

# Practice Test

## I. SOLUTIONS TO MULTIPLE CHOICE QUESTIONS

1. C. An increase in lump-sum taxes will decrease consumption and, therefore, shift the AE function downward. If taxes rise by 100, disposable income will fall by 100. If MPC is .9, consumption (and AE) will decrease by 90.

2. C. If MPS is .2, the government spending multiplier is 5. Income will decrease by 500 (100 × 5). If income decreases by 500 and MPS is .2, saving will decrease by 100.

3. B. For an increase in government spending to make output rise by 250, the multiplier must be 2.5. If MPS is .4, the government spending multiplier is 2.5.

4. A. If MPC is .75, the government spending multiplier is 4 and the tax multiplier is −3. If government spending increases by 75, output would increase by 300. The deficit would rise by 75. Reducing taxes by 100 would achieve the required expansion in output, but the increase in the deficit is 100 (greater than with option A). Option C cannot be considered because the maximum increase in government spending allowable is 75. Option D will not work because output would expand by only 75.

5. A. Expenditure rises by a dollar. To neutralize this change, taxes would have to be increased. If taxes are raised by a dollar, consumption would fall, but by less than a dollar. To neutralize the increase in expenditures, taxes will have to increase by more than a dollar.

6. A. If saving increases by 40 as income increases by 200, MPS is .2. MPC, therefore, is .8. When MPS is .2, the government spending multiplier (1 / MPS) is 5.

7. C. See p. 217.

8. A. If expenditure increases, equilibrium output will increase. The government can increase government spending and/or cut taxes. Either action will increase the deficit. Investment decisions are made by the private sector.

9. A. To neutralize the effect on AE of the investment decrease, the government wants an action that will make AE increase.

10. A. When MPC is .8, the government spending multiplier is 5 and the tax multiplier is −4. If government spending increases by 20, output will increase by 100 (20 × 5). If taxes are cut by 25, output will increase by 100 (−25 × −4). Similarly, the balanced-budget change will achieve the objective. Option A won't. The government spending increase will raise output by 200 (40 × 5), while the tax cut will raise output by a further 200 (−50 × −4).

11. B. The presence or absence of a structural deficit depends on government policy.

12. D. See p. 202.

13. C. As income rises by 5000 (from zero to 5000), AE rises by 4000 (from 1000 to 5000). As consumption is the only component of AE to depend on income, this means consumption has increased by 4000. Hence the MPC is 4000/5000 = 0.8.

14. A. First, find the consumption function. It will be of the form $C = a + bY_d$ and from question 13, b = 0.8. To find a, autonomous consumption, find consumption when Y = 0.

   Note AE = C + I + G + EX − IM
   or   AE = $a + bY_d$ + 300 + 500 + 0
   or   AE = a + 0.8(Y − 200) + 800
   or   AE = a + 640 + 0.8Y

   From the graph when Y = 0, AE = 1000 so 1000 = a + 640 + 0.8(0) or a = 360. Therefore C = $a + bY_d$ = 360 + 0.8Yd. As $C + S = Y_d$, then $360 + 0.8Y_d + S = Y_d$ so $S = -360 + 0.2Y_d = -360 + 0.2(Y − T)$.

15. C. If MPC = .80, the tax multiplier is −4.

16. D. If MPC = .80, the tax multiplier is –4. The desired change in income is +1000.

17. B. When Y = 5000, C = 4200, because Y = C + I + G + EX – IM and I = 300, G = 500 and EX – IM = 0. So C = 5000 – 300 – 500 – 0 = 4200. Disposable income is $Y_d = Y - T = 5000 - 200 = 4800$. $S = Y_d - C = 4800 - 4200 = 600$. When Y = 6000, C = 6000 – 300 – 500 – 0 = 5200. $Y_d = 6000 - (-50) = 6050$ (note that net taxes are negative, meaning that transfers from the government exceed taxes). S = 6050 – 5200 = 850. Therefore C has increased by 1000. S has increased by 250.

18. D. If a tax decrease of $15 billion results in a $60 billion increase in equilibrium income, the tax multiplier is –4. In a model where only consumption depends on income, the tax multiplier formula is –MPC / MPS. MPC = .8 and MPS = .2. (MPC and MPS must add to one.) The government multiplier formula is 1 / MPS, so the value in this case is 5.

19. C. Option D is not an equilibrium condition—this identity holds whether or not equilibrium is established. Option B was an equilibrium condition in the previous chapter, but it is no longer when a government and international sector have been added to the model.

20. C. See p. 217.

## II. SOLUTIONS TO APPLICATION QUESTIONS

1. a. Refer to the table below.

| Real GDP Income | Consumption | Planned Investment | Government Spending | Net Exports | Aggregate Planned Expenditures |
|---|---|---|---|---|---|
| 0 | 400 | 300 | 400 | 100 | 1200 |
| 1000 | 1200 | 300 | 400 | 100 | 2000 |
| 2000 | 2000 | 300 | 400 | 100 | 2800 |
| 3000 | 2800 | 300 | 400 | 100 | 3600 |
| 4000 | 3600 | 300 | 400 | 100 | 4400 |
| 5000 | 4400 | 300 | 400 | 100 | 5200 |
| 6000 | 5200 | 300 | 400 | 100 | 6000 |
| 7000 | 6000 | 300 | 400 | 100 | 6800 |

   b. MPC = .8 and MPS = .2.
   c. Aggregate planned expenditures equal real GDP at 6000.
   d. When real GDP = 3000, aggregate planned expenditures exceed 3000 (3600), causing unplanned inventory decumulation. Businesses will respond by hiring more resources and increasing output.
   e. When real GDP = 7000, aggregate planned expenditures are less than 7000 (6800), causing unplanned inventory accumulation.
   f. Saving is zero when income is 3000.
   g. Equilibrium output would fall by 1000 to 5000. At an income level of 5000, C + I + G + NX equals 4400 plus 600. The decrease in expenditures will result in unplanned inventory accumulation. Firms will cut production, forcing the equilibrium output level to fall.

2. a. Y = C + I + G + EX – IM = 6000 + .75(Y – T) + 11 000 + 20 000 + 0 = 37 000 + .75Y – .75T. But T = 16 000, therefore, Y – .75Y = 37 000 – .75(16 000). .25Y = 25 000; therefore, Y = 100 000.
   b. MPC = .75; therefore the government spending multiplier is 4.0 and the tax multiplier is –3.0.

c. Proposal I is less contractionary.

d. Proposal I: The deficit is currently 20 000 – 16 000, or 4000 opeks. A 4000-opek increase in taxes will reduce output by 12 000 opeks.

Proposal II: A 4000-opek decrease in government spending will lead the economy to contract by $4000 \times 4$, or 16 000 opeks.

e. Proposal III is overkill! The multiplier is 4; therefore an autonomous increase in government spending of 8000 will push the economy past the full-employment output level.

Proposal IV will work. The tax multiplier is –3 and an increase in welfare payments operates in the same way as a reduction in taxes.

Proposal V will work. $\Delta T (4000) \times -3 = -12,000$. $\Delta G(9000) \times 4 = 36\,000$. The net change in income is +24 000, which is the amount required.

Proposal VI will work. Welfare is a form of negative tax. $\Delta T(-2000) \times -3 = 6000$. $\Delta$ welfare $(-6000) \times -3 = 18\,000$. The total change in income is +24 000, which is the amount required.

f. The deficit = G – T = 4000.

Proposal IV will reduce net taxes by 8000 and increase the deficit by 8000.

Proposal V will increase net taxes by 4000 but increase government spending by 9000. The deficit will increase by 5000 opeks.

Proposal VI will reduce net taxes by 6000 + 2000, or 8000 opeks. The deficit will increase by 8000 opeks.

Proposal IV and VI are equivalent, but Proposal V is better than either.

g. Proposal IV will reduce net taxes by 8000 and increase consumption autonomously by 6000 opeks. As income increases by 24 000, consumption will be induced to increase by an additional 18 000. Total increase in consumption is 24 000 opeks.

Proposal V will increase net taxes by 4000 and reduce consumption autonomously by 3000. As income increases by 24 000, consumption will be induced to increase by an additional 18 000. Total increase in consumption is 15 000 opeks.

Proposal VI will increase welfare payments by 6000 opeks and increase consumption autonomously by 4500 opeks. The reduction in lump-sum taxes will increase consumption autonomously by 1500 opeks. As income increases by 24 000, consumption will be induced to increase by an additional 18 000. Total increase in consumption is 24 000 opeks.

Proposal IV and VI have identical effects on consumption.

3. a. 5.    e. –4.    h. 5; –4.    k. –40.
   b. 20.    f. –7.    i. –200.    l. –200.
   c. 2.5.    g. 6.    j. –160.    m. –200.
   d. –9.

4. a. See the table below.

| Output (Income) | Saving | Planned Investment | Government Spending | Net Taxes | Consumption |
|---|---|---|---|---|---|
| 1300 | 150 | 200 | 100 | 50 | 1100 |
| 1500 | 200 | 200 | 100 | 50 | 1250 |
| 1700 | 250 | 200 | 100 | 50 | 1400 |
| 1900 | 300 | 200 | 100 | 50 | 1550 |

b. MPS is .25, so MPC is .75; Y = C + I + G + EX – IM at an income level of 1700, (recall that net exports EX – IM are zero).

c. $AE = C + I + G + EX - IM = 1400$. If output is 1300, inventory is falling by 100.

d. Decrease. If G is cut by 50, output will fall by 200.

e. Increase government spending by 75 (with a multiplier of 4), decrease net taxes by 100 (with a tax multiplier of –3), or undertake a balanced budget increase of 300.

f. This is a balanced-budget change and the balanced-budget multiplier is 1. Income level will increase by 50 to 1750.

5. a. In equilibrium, $S + T + IM = I + G + EX$, or $S + T = I + G + EX - IM$. Substituting in numerical values, we get $S + 250 = 110 + 300 + 10$. $S = 420 - 250 = 170$.

b. $MPS = 1 - MPC = 1 - .75 = .25$.

c. Multiplier = 1 / MPS = 1 / .25 = 4.

d. Deficit = G – T = 300 – 250 = 50.

e. Spending change: $\Delta Y = \Delta I \times 1 / MPS = -15 \times 4 = -60$.

f. Unplanned inventories are rising. Expenditure has fallen, so unsold stock is accumulating.

g. Lowered by 20. We want income to rise by 60. Tax change: $\Delta Y = 60 = \Delta T \times (-MPC / MPS) = -20 \times -3$.

h. Deficit = G – T = 300 – 230 = 70. Taxes were 250, then were cut by 20.

i. The equilibrium income level is unchanged, but disposable income has risen by 20 (because of the tax cut). As MPC is .75, consumption will increase by 15 ($20 \times .75$) to 315.

6. a. See the table below.    Saving rises by 20 as income rises by 100. MPS = .2, MPC = .8. This is enough information to complete the saving and consumption columns. Investment is constant at 30, government spending is constant at 10, and exports and imports are both always 20. Disposable income is $Y - T$.

| Y | T | $Y_d$ | C | S | I | G | EX | IM | AE |
|---|---|---|---|---|---|---|---|---|---|
| 0 | 20 | –20 | 40 | –60 | 30 | 10 | 20 | 20 | 80 |
| 100 | 20 | 80 | 120 | –40 | 30 | 10 | 20 | 20 | 160 |
| 200 | 20 | 180 | 200 | –20 | 30 | 10 | 20 | 20 | 240 |
| 300 | 20 | 280 | 280 | 0 | 30 | 10 | 20 | 20 | 320 |
| 400 | 20 | 380 | 360 | 20 | 30 | 10 | 20 | 20 | 400 |

b. MPC = .8; MPS = .2 (see answer a above); the government spending multiplier is 1 / MPS = 5; the tax multiplier is –MPC / MPS = –4.

c. $C = 56 + .8(Y - T)$.

d. Equilibrium occurs at 400, where $S + T + IM = I + G + EX$.

7. a. The government spending multiplier is $1 / (1 - b + bt)$, where b = MPC = 5 / 7 and t = .3. The multiplier value is 2.

b. Given that the economy is in equilibrium at 480, the government wishes output to increase by 70 (550 – 480).

c. Spending change: $\Delta Y = 70 = \Delta G \times 1 / MPS = 35 \times 2.0$. G must increase by 35.

d. See the diagram below, not drawn to scale.

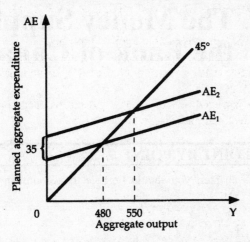

e. Originally, the deficit $(G - T) = 150 - 120 = 30$. $(T = -24 + .3(480) = 120)$

f. Income has risen by 70. The tax rate is .3. Increase in tax collections $= .3 \times 70 = 21$. $(T = -24 + .3(550) = 141)$.

g. Now the deficit $(G - T) = (150 + 35) - (120 + 21) = 44$.

8. a. A decrease in investment, consumption, or exports will reduce aggregate expenditure and output. As output falls, transfer payments will increase and tax revenues will decrease, opening up a deficit without any explicit government action.

b. This change has occurred because of the recession—it is a cyclical deficit.

c. The structural deficit will decrease. At the current level of output below full employment, the increase in tax revenues exactly matches the increase in government expenditure, so there is no change in the actual deficit. But the structural deficit is measured as if the economy were at full employment and, at that level of output, the new tax rates would generate additional revenue, lowering the deficit.

9. a. Imports increase as income starts to increase. (As it turns out, imports are measured with relatively little lag and hence changes in imports are often one of the first signs of overall changes in the economy.)

b. The higher marginal propensity to import flattens the planned aggregate expenditure line and lowers the multiplier. More of any increase in income now leaks out in terms of spending on import goods rather than being respent as part of the multiplier process.

10. a.
$$Y = C + I + G + EX - IM$$
$$= 30 + .8Y_d + 100 + 250 + 50 - (80 + .4Yd)$$
$$= 350 + .4(Y - 200) \text{ because } Y_d = Y - T$$
$$= 270 + .4Y$$
$$\text{or } .6Y = 270$$
$$\text{or } Y = (1 / .6) \times 270 = 450$$

b. From above, the multiplier is $1 / .6$. (Alternatively, for this model it is $1 / (MPS + MPM) = 1 / (.2 + .4) = 1 / .6$, where MPM is the marginal propensity to import.) To increase output by 60, $\Delta G \times (1 / .6) = 60$ or $\Delta G = 36$.

c. When $Y = 450$, $Yd = 450 - 200 = 250$ and $IM = 80 + .4(250) = 180$. Hence the trade balance is $EX - IM = 50 - 180 = -130$. (That is, the trade deficit is 130.)

d. When $Y = 510$, $Y_d = 510 - 200 = 310$ and $IM = 80 + .4(310) = 204$ and the trade deficit increases to 154.

# 11

# The Money Supply and the Bank of Canada

## OBJECTIVES: POINT BY POINT

After completing this chapter, you should be able to accomplish the objectives listed below.

### General Comment

This chapter begins the process of building a model of the financial market that is continued in Chapter 12, where the factors that determine the demand for money holdings and the establishment of money market equilibrium are considered. This model will then be combined with the aggregate expenditure model in Chapter 13. It is important that you develop a good understanding of financial markets at this point.

### OBJECTIVE 1: Distinguish among the medium of exchange, store of value, and unit of account roles of money.

The three functions of money are:
    a.   a medium of exchange (money used as a means of payment),
    b.   a store of value (money used as an asset), and
    c   a unit of account (money used as a consistent way of quoting prices).
(page 228)

### OBJECTIVE 2: Distinguish between commodity and fiat money.

Before money, there was barter. But because trading goods for goods relies on a double coincidence of wants, barter was inefficient. *Commodity money* (a good that has some value over and above its value as money) was an intermediate stage between barter and the *fiat money* of the modern economy. Gold and cigarettes are examples of commodity money. Paper currency (Bank of Canada notes) is fiat money—it derives its value from the willingness of individuals to accept it as payment. (page 229)

### Practice

1.   Money's prime function is as
    A.   the standard for credit transactions.
    B.   the medium of exchange.
    C.   a store of value.
    D.   a unit of account.

    **ANSWER:** B.   The main reason for having money is that it eases the process of exchange. See p. 228.

2. In a barter economy,
   A. money functions only as a medium of exchange.
   B. buyers cannot buy unless they have a commodity sellers want.
   C. money functions as a medium of exchange and as a store of value.
   D. saving cannot occur.

   **ANSWER:** B.   In a barter economy, there is no money, so Options A and C are incorrect. Saving can occur; saving, recall, is non-consumption. In a barter economy, trade will be in a variety of goods; in an economy with money, almost all trades will involve money.

Use the following information to answer the next two questions.

At a flea market, Mary spots some valuable Depression glassware valued at a ridiculously low price of 25¢. She hands over the quarter to secure the item.

3. The price tag on the glassware used money in its role as a
   A. medium of exchange.
   B. store of value.
   C. unit of account.
   D. means of payment.

   **ANSWER:** C.   Money serves as a way of establishing a consistent way of quoting prices.

4. As Mary hands over the quarter, she is using money in its role as a
   A. medium of exchange.
   B. store of value.
   C. unit of account.
   D. form of credit.

   **ANSWER:** A.   See p. 228.

5. Jack is saving money to buy a new VCR. Money is functioning as a
   A. medium of exchange.
   B. store of value.
   C. unit of account.
   D. standard of deferred payment.

   **ANSWER:** B.   See p. 228.

6. Each of the following is an example of commodity money except
   A. five-dollar bills.
   B. gold.
   C. cigarettes.
   D. salt.

   **ANSWER:** A.   Five-dollar bills have no value other than as five-dollar bills—they are fiat money. The three commodities have all been used as money. Salt, in fact, is the source of the term "salary."

## OBJECTIVE 3: Define the alternative money supply measures M1 and M2.

At the heart of the various measures of the money supply is the concept of *liquidity*. The more easily and cheaply an asset can be converted into spending power, the more liquid it is. The most liquid assets are included in M1, the narrowest definition of money. M1, or narrow money, includes notes and coins held by the public, plus demand deposits. M2 (broad money) includes everything in M1 plus *notice deposits* which include savings deposits.                                                              (page 230)

## Practice

7.  Which of the following is not included in M2?
    A.  Currency.
    B.  Excess reserves.
    C.  Demand deposits.
    D.  Savings accounts.

    **ANSWER:** B. Excess reserves are not money in any sense. Note that demand deposits and currency are included in M2 because they are included in M1. See p. 232.

8.  Near monies are
    A.  included in M1.
    B.  liquid assets such as term deposits that are close substitutes for narrow money.
    C.  stocks, bonds, and collectible artwork.
    D.  Bank of Canada notes.

    **ANSWER:** B. See p. 232.

## OBJECTIVE 4: List the four types of firms called the pillars of the Canadian financial system.

The Canadian financial system can be described as having four pillars: (1) chartered banks, (2) trust and mortgage loan companies, (3) insurance companies, and (4) securities firms.

9.  Chartered banks
    A.  are a type of financial intermediary because they take deposits and make loans.
    B.  have about two-thirds of the assets of all deposit-taking institutions in Canada.
    C.  in Canada typically have many branches.
    D.  all of the above.

    **ANSWER:** D. See p. 233.

## OBJECTIVE 5: Define desired reserve ratio. Explain how the banking system creates money through deposit creation. Apply the deposit multiplier in numerical problems.

Bankers have discovered that, because they need only keep a fraction of their total reserves available for withdrawal (*desired reserves*), the rest (*excess reserves*) can be lent out at a profit. Banks create money through these lending activities. When lent out, the funds advanced to the borrower increase her/his spending power and count as an addition to the money supply. Each bank, therefore, can expand the money supply by the value of its excess reserves. As a whole, the banking system, by recirculating deposits, can expand total deposits by a multiple (the *deposit multiplier*) of its reserves, the multiple being determined by the fraction of funds that is held as desired reserves (the *desired reserve ratio*). This determines the maximum size of the deposit multiplier, which is equal to 1 / (reserve ratio).                                                (page 238)

**TIP:** Remember that the balance sheet is looked at from the viewpoint of the bank—not that of the customer.

**TIP:** The best way to practise the case of money "destruction," which can effectively challenge your understanding, is by increasing the desired reserve ratio. Banks will have inadequate funds. They will have to reduce their lending activities and add to their reserves instead.

**Tip:** Remember that the difference between the deposit multiplier and the money multiplier is that the former corresponds only to bank deposits while the latter corresponds to the total money supply (deposits plus currency outside banks). Many examples in the text and in this guide are simplified by assuming that all money is held in the form of bank deposits and hence in those cases the deposit multiplier and the money multiplier are the same thing.

The following table will help to organize your thoughts on the money creation process. Suppose Alice takes $1000 from her mattress and deposits it in her bank (Bank A). Further suppose all banks set their desired reserve ratios to 20%. Reserves increase by $1000 (of which $200 are desired reserves, which won't be lent out) and $800 are excess reserves (which may be lent out). A loan to Jack is made and $800 worth of spending power is released. Jack writes an $800 cheque to Brenda, who deposits it in her bank (Bank B). Bank A's excess reserves fall to zero when the cheque is cleared, but it has the $1000 deposit, $200 in desired reserves, and $800 in loans.

Bank B has $800 in deposits, $160 in desired reserves, and $640 in excess reserves. The Bank lends $640 to Jill, who writes a cheque to Chris. Chris deposits the cheque in Bank C. When Jill's cheque is cleared, Bank B's excess reserves fall to zero, but it has the $800 deposit, $160 in desired reserves, and $640 in loans. And so on.

|  | New Demand Deposits = | Change in Reserves = | Change in Desired Reserves + | Change in Excess Reserves | Change in Loans |
|---|---|---|---|---|---|
| A. | 1000 | 1000 | 200 | 800/0 | 800 |
| B. | 800 | 800 | 160 | 640/0 | 640 |
| C. | 640 | 640 | 128 | 512/0 | 512 |
| D. | 512 | 512 | 102.4 | 409.6/0 | 409.6 |
| etc. | ... | ... | ... | ... | ... |
| Total | 5000 |  | 1000 | 0 | 4000 |

Points to note:

a. The "change in excess reserves" column contains two steps, the first indicating how much excess reserves increase, the second assuming that all excess reserves have been lent out and the borrower's cheque has been honoured.

b. It becomes clear, using the table, that the expansion process will continue until all of the original injection of new reserves ($1000) has been converted into desired reserves. At that point the process stops.

c. The expansion in demand deposit liabilities is balanced on the asset side of the balance sheet by $1000 of desired reserves and $4000 of loans. Total deposits have increased by $5000 but the money supply has increased by only $4000, because Alice's mattress money is now in bank vaults.

d. Another way of saying that a bank has no excess reserves is to say that the bank is fully loaned up.

e. In answering practice questions, try to distinguish whether the question is asking you what the *initial* effect is (for example, the initial effect of Alice's new deposit is no change in the money supply, an increase in bank reserves by $1000 and an increase in Bank A's excess reserves by $800) or what the *total* effect is after the deposit creation process has run its course (an increase in total deposits of $5000 and an increase in loans by $4000).

## Practice

10. The basic equation for a firm's balance sheet is
    A. Liabilities = Assets + Net Worth.
    B. Net Worth = Liabilities + Assets.
    C. Assets = Liabilities + Net Worth.
    D. Assets = Liabilities – Net Worth.

    **ANSWER:** C. See p. 235.

11. Assets are things that are _____; on a balance sheet they are entered on the _____.
    A. owned, right.
    B. owned, left.
    C. owed, right.
    D. owed, left.

    **ANSWER:** B. See p. 235.

Use the following balance sheet for Snow Bank to answer the next three questions. Snow Bank has a desired reserve ratio of 20%.

| Assets | | Liabilities | |
|---|---|---|---|
| Reserves | $2 500 000 | Chequing deposits | $6 000 000 |
| Loans outstanding | 5 500 000 | | |
| Other assets | 1 000 000 | Net worth | 3 000 000 |
| Total | $9 000 000 | Total | $9 000 000 |

12. Snow Bank has $2 500 000 in reserves, chequing deposits of $6 000 000, and a desired reserve ratio of 20%. At that moment, Snow Bank has _____ of desired reserves and _____ of excess reserves.
    A. $500 000, $2 000 000.
    B. $500 000, $5 500 000.
    C. $1 200 000, $1 300 000.
    D. $1 200 000, $4 800 000.

    **ANSWER:** C. The desired reserves are calculated relative to the bank's liabilities, therefore $6 000 000 × .2. Total reserves = desired reserves + excess reserves.

13. Assuming prudent management, Snow Bank can increase its loans by up to
    A. $1 300 000.
    B. $1 500 000.
    C. $2 000 000.
    D. $3 000 000.

    **ANSWER:** A. Snow Bank can immediately increase its loans by the extent of its excess reserves.

14. Assuming all banks have a desired reserve ratio of 20%, and that the other banks had no excess reserves initially, after the deposit creation process is finished the nation's money supply could expand by
    A. $1 300 000.
    B. $6 500 000.
    C. $12 500 000.
    D. $10 000 000.

    **ANSWER:** B. The money supply can expand by the extent of the excess reserves ($1 300 000) times the multiplier, which is 1 / .20 = 5.

Use the following balance sheet for Grand Bank to answer the next two questions.

| Assets | | Liabilities | |
|---|---|---|---|
| Reserves | $400 000 | Chequing deposits | $1 000 000 |
| Loans outstanding | 600 000 | | |
| Total | $1 000 000 | Total | $1 000 000 |

15. Grand Bank is fully loaned up. The reserve ratio is
    A. 2.5%.
    B. 40%.
    C. 60%.
    D. 250%.

    **ANSWER:** B. If there are no excess reserves, Grand Bank must desire to hold 40% of deposit liabilities.

16. Assume that Grand Bank is the only bank in the economy and the banking system is closed to foreign banks. The desired reserve ratio is 40%. Now an additional $100 000 is deposited. After the deposit creation process has finished, the bank will have expanded its loans up to the point where its total deposits are
    A. $1 100 000.
    B. $1 250 000.
    C. $1 400 000.
    D. $2 000 000.

    **ANSWER:** B. Total reserves will be $500 000. The money multiplier is 2.5.

## OBJECTIVE 6: List the main functions of the Bank of Canada.

The main macroeconomic role of the Bank of Canada is to control the money supply. As well, it functions as the bankers' bank; it is the government's bank, the lender of last resort to private banks, and issues currency. (page 239)

## OBJECTIVE 7: Identify the three main tools by which the Bank of Canada controls the money supply and explain how each tool works.

The Bank of Canada (or simply the Bank, with an upper case B) uses three main tools of monetary policy:

    a.    open market operations
    b.    transfers of government deposits (the most frequently used)
    c.    changes in the Bank rate (which largely have an announcement effect)

(page 241)

To expand the money supply, the Bank of Canada can buy government securities (which increases the reserves of the banking system), transfer government deposits from itself to private banks (again increasing the reserves in the banking system), or cut the Bank rate. In the last case, the Bank rate is the interest rate at which private banks borrow from the Bank of Canada if they need extra funds: A lower Bank rate may induce private banks to risk setting a somewhat lower desired reserve ratio, and a smaller desired reserve ratio translates into a larger money supply. But the real significance of changes in the Bank rate is that they announce changes in monetary policy, with decreases signalling a looser monetary policy and increases signalling a tighter monetary policy. (page 241)

> **TIP:** The following "trick" will help you remember how open market operations work: The Bank (B)uys securities to make the money supply (B)igger, and (S)ells them to make it (S)maller.

## Practice

17. The Bank wants to increase the money supply. The most likely monetary policy might include the _____ of bonds by the Bank and the _____ of the Bank rate.
    A.    purchase, lowering.
    B.    purchase, raising.
    C.    sale, lowering.
    D.    sale, raising.

    **ANSWER:** A. Buying securities from the private banks will increase their reserves; cutting the Bank rate announces a looser monetary policy and may encourage a reduction in the desired reserve ratio.

18. Which of the following instruments is not used by the Bank to change the money supply?
    A.    Open market operations.
    B.    The Bank rate.
    C.    The tax rate on interest earnings.
    D.    Transfers of government deposits between the Bank of Canada and private banks.

    **ANSWER:** C. Changes in tax rates are passed by Parliament and are part of fiscal policy.

19. Government securities are a(n) _____ of the Bank; currency notes are a(n) _____ of the Bank.
    A.  asset, asset.
    B.  asset, liability.
    C.  liability, asset.
    D.  liability, liability.

    **ANSWER:** B.  The securities are claims against the government and owned by the Bank. Currency notes are issued by the Bank and are liabilities.

20. Which of the following is not a responsibility of the Bank?
    A.  Banking for the government.
    B.  Acting as a clearinghouse for cheques.
    C.  Managing the money supply.
    D.  Issuing bonds to finance the federal debt.

    **ANSWER:** D.  The government issues bonds, although the Bank buys and sells them.

21. The preferred instrument of monetary policy is
    A.  the tax rate.
    B.  the desired reserve ratio.
    C.  open market operations.
    D.  transfers of government deposits.

    **ANSWER:** D.  See page 242.

22. *Ceteris paribus*, an open market sale of government securities to Snow Bank will _____ Snow Bank's assets and _____ Snow Bank's liabilities.
    A.  increase, increase.
    B.  increase, not change.
    C.  not change, increase.
    D.  not change, not change.

    **ANSWER:** D.  The composition, but not the level, of Snow Bank's assets will change.

Use the following information for the next two questions. The banking system has deposits of $60 million and it is fully loaned up. The desired reserve ratio is 25%. Assume no leakages from the banking system occur.

23. If the desired reserve ratio is reduced from 25% to 20%, the banking system may eventually
    A.  increase loans by $3 million.
    B.  increase loans by $12 million.
    C.  increase loans by $15 million.
    D.  increase loans by $20 million.

    **ANSWER:** C.  When the ratio is 25%, desired reserves are $60 million × .25, or $15 million. When the ratio is 20%, desired reserves are $60 million × .20, or $12 million. Because reserves have not changed, this means that the banking system has excess reserves of $3 million. The multiplier is 1 / .20, or 5.

24. The Bank wants deposits to increase to $90 million. This would occur (after the deposit creation process is finished) if the private banks changed the desired reserve ratio from 25% to
   A. 12%.
   B. 15%.
   C. 16.67%.
   D. 67%.

   **ANSWER:** C. When the ratio is 25%, required reserves are $60 million × .25, or $15 million. If the reserve ratio is 16.67, the money multiplier is 1 / .1667, or 6. $15 million × 6 = $90 million.

25. Which of the following is false? Open market operations
   A. involve Bank of Canada buying and selling of government securities.
   B. could involve purchases and sales of gold.
   C. could involve purchases and sales of foreign exchange.
   D. have no money multiplier effects.

   **ANSWER:** D. For example, an open market purchase puts additional funds in the hands of the seller, who may deposit some in a private bank, initiating the money multiplier process.

26. The desired reserve ratio is not a tool of monetary policy because
   A. only chartered banks have desired reserve ratios.
   B. it has no effect on the money supply.
   C. in practice, private banks have no idea what their reserve holdings are.
   D. unlike in some other countries such as the United States, in Canada the reserve ratio is not set by law, but is determined by each private bank independently.

   **ANSWER:** D. See p. 236. (Recall that the text's numerical examples are based upon the simplifying *assumption* that the desired reserve ratio is constant across banks.) Option A is incorrect because all deposit-taking institutions must decide how much to hold in reserves. Option B is incorrect because the desired reserve ratio affects the multiplier and with respect to option C, no one should hold deposits in a bank that cannot even account for its own holdings.

27. Which of the following is a problem with the Bank rate as a tool of monetary policy?
   A. In practice, the private banks do not borrow much from the Bank of Canada.
   B. The Bank rate cannot be adjusted quickly.
   C. The Bank rate has no relationship to the overnight rate that private banks actually use for short-term loans (from each other).
   D. Financial markets ignore the Bank rate.

   **ANSWER:** A. See p. 242. For option B, the Bank rate can be adjusted instantly. For option C, the Bank of Canada currently adjusts monetary policy to keep the overnight rate within an "operating band" just under the Bank rate. For option D, because of the point in option C and because the Bank rate is a signal of overall monetary policy, the Bank rate is watched closely.

## OBJECTIVE 8 (APPENDIX 11A): Derive the deposit and money multipliers algebraically.

Even if you do not study the appendix you should be able to understand that if a fraction of deposits is held as currency (sometimes called *cash drain*), (a) the deposit multiplier will be smaller the larger the cash drain (as money held as cash is not redeposited and re-lent through the banking system) and (b) the money multiplier is no longer the same as the deposit multiplier (as the money multiplier includes the total increase in the money supply including deposits but also including the increase in currency held outside banks). For a practice question, see Application Question 11.

# PRACTICE TEST

**I.**   **MULTIPLE CHOICE QUESTIONS.** Select the option that provides the single best answer.

_____ 1.   Each of the following is included in M1 except
   A.   paper currency held outside banks.
   B.   coins held outside banks.
   C.   demand deposit accounts.
   D.   credit card balances.

_____ 2.   Which of the following is not a function of money?
   A.   A form of speculation.
   B.   A medium of exchange.
   C.   A unit of account.
   D.   A store of value.

_____ 3.   Robin Hood borrows $100 in cash from Friar Tuck and deposits it at Sherwood Forest Bank. The desired reserve ratio is 25%. After the deposit creation process is completed, what is the maximum amount by which the banking system can expand total deposits?
   A.   $500.
   B.   $100.
   C.   $300.
   D.   $400.

_____ 4.   Excess reserves equal
   A.   demand deposits plus desired reserves.
   B.   actual reserves minus desired reserves.
   C.   total reserves minus actual reserves.
   D.   demand deposits minus desired reserves.

_____ 5.   If it is assumed the Bank of Canada can keep the money supply constant at all interest rate levels, the money supply curve is _____ and it _____ affected by changes in the interest rate.
   A.   horizontal, is.
   B.   vertical, is.
   C.   vertical, is not.
   D.   horizontal, is not.

_____ 6.   Chequing account deposits at Canada Trust are Canada Trust _____; money market accounts at Canada Trust are Canada Trust _____.
   A.   assets, assets.
   B.   assets, liabilities.
   C.   liabilities, assets.
   D.   liabilities, liabilities.

_____ 7. In a T account (balance sheet), liabilities go on the _____ side and net worth goes on the _____ side.
   A.   left, left.
   B.   left, right.
   C.   right, left.
   D.   right, right.

_____ 8. An increase in the desired reserve ratio will
   A.   be a consequence of a cut in the Bank rate.
   B.   reduce the money supply.
   C.   increase the value of the money multiplier.
   D.   increase the amount of excess reserves.

_____ 9. The reserve ratio is 20%. $200 is deposited into a demand deposit account in the banking system.
   A.   Initially, the money supply has changed its composition but not its size.
   B.   Eventually, the money supply will increase by $1000.
   C.   Initially, the money supply will increase by $200.
   D.   Initially, the money supply will increase by $40.
   (Be careful on this one! There is only one correct answer.)

_____ 10. The Bank of Canada does not
   A.   set the Bank rate.
   B.   establish a required reserve ratio for the private banks.
   C.   act as banker for the federal government.
   D.   buy government securities.

Use the following information to answer the next two questions.

The private banks are loaned up and have reserves of $500 billion. Now the desired reserve ratio is changed from 25% to 10%.

_____ 11. Initially, excess reserves will
   A.   increase by 15%.
   B.   decrease by $300 billion.
   C.   increase by $300 billion.
   D.   increase by $3000 billion.

_____ 12. Eventually, after the deposit creation process is complete, total deposits can
   A.   increase by 15%.
   B.   increase by a multiple of 10.
   C.   increase by $1250 billion.
   D.   increase by $3000 billion.

_____ 13. Which one of the following policy actions would definitely *not* increase the money supply?
   A.   Open market sales of securities.
   B.   Open market purchases of securities.
   C.   Transferring government deposits from the Bank of Canada to private banks.
   D.   Reducing the Bank rate.

_____ 14. The reserve ratio is 25%. First Bank makes an additional loan of $500 000. If the banking system is holding no excess reserves, then the eventual increase in total deposits will be
   A. zero.
   B. $500 000.
   C. $1 500 000.
   D. $2 000 000.

_____ 15. If Nazish deposits $5000 cash into her savings account, the immediate effect is that
   A. M1 goes down and M2 goes up.
   B. M1 goes up and M2 goes down.
   C. M1 goes down and M2 stays the same.
   D. M1 stays the same and M2 goes down.

_____ 16. The value of the money multiplier will be reduced when
   A. recipients of bank loans redeposit the proceeds of their loans into another bank.
   B. each bank holds zero excess reserves.
   C. recipients of bank loans do not keep any of the loan as cash.
   D. individuals increase the proportion of funds they hold as currency.

_____ 17. Transferring government deposits from the Bank of Canada to private banks
   A. reduces the money supply because it reduces bank reserves.
   B. reduces the money supply because it increases bank reserves.
   C. increases the money supply because it reduces bank reserves.
   D. increases the money supply because it increases bank reserves.

_____ 18. The Bank rate is the interest rate paid by
   A. the Bank of Canada to banks who deposit funds with it.
   B. banks when they borrow from the Bank of Canada.
   C. banks when they borrow from each other.
   D. government securities.

_____ 19. Most of the Bank of Canada's liabilities are
   A. currency.
   B. loans made to the private banks.
   C. government securities.
   D. bank reserves deposited by depository institutions.

_____ 20. The reserve ratio is 25%, and all banks, whose total reserves are valued at $200 million, are fully loaned up. If the desired reserve ratio falls to 20% and the deposit creation process runs its course, the banking system could support an additional
   A. $100 million in deposits.
   B. $200 million in deposits.
   C. $400 million in deposits.
   D. $500 million in deposits.

## II.   APPLICATION QUESTIONS

1. Suppose a certain percentage of deposits are held in foreign accounts. How does that affect the deposit multiplier in Canada?
2. The reserve ratio is 20% in a number of banks. All banks are "loaned up." Assume that banks lend their excess reserves.

a. Now First Bank discovers an additional $1000 in excess reserves. Make the final entries on the T account of each of the following banks after deposits have been received, loans made, spending undertaken, and cheques cleared. Assume that the loan from First Bank results in deposits at Second Bank, and so on.

| First Bank | | | |
|---|---|---|---|
| **Assets** | | **Liabilities** | |
| Reserves | _____ | Deposits | _____ |
| Loans | _____ | | |

| Second Bank | | | |
|---|---|---|---|
| **Assets** | | **Liabilities** | |
| Reserves | _____ | Deposits | _____ |
| Loans | _____ | | |

| Third Bank | | | |
|---|---|---|---|
| **Assets** | | **Liabilities** | |
| Reserves | _____ | Deposits | _____ |
| Loans | _____ | | |

| Fourth Bank | | | |
|---|---|---|---|
| **Assets** | | **Liabilities** | |
| Reserves | _____ | Deposits | _____ |
| Loans | _____ | | |

b. Calculate the extent of overall expansion in the money supply from the deposits at Second Bank, Third Bank, and Fourth Bank.

3. ArbeFed (the central bank of Arbez) has assets of 1000 opeks (in the form of government securities). ArbeFed's liabilities are 800 opeks of currency and 200 opeks of deposits by banks in the central bank. All banks are "loaned up" and will remain so and all currency is held by the public (i.e., not by banks). Assume that no leakages from the banking system occur.

a. Draw a balance sheet showing ArbeFed's financial position.

b. The required reserve ratio is 20%. (In Arbez, reserve ratios are set by law.) Determine the size of the Arbezani money supply, M1 (currency plus demand deposits).

c. ArbeFed wishes to increase the money supply to 2000 opeks by adjusting the reserve requirement.
  i. Would the reserve requirement have to increase or decrease?
  ii. What should the new reserve requirement be?

d. ArbeFed decides to reduce the money supply by 300, opting for an open market operation.
  i. Should ArbeFed buy bonds or sell bonds on the open market?
  ii. How big should this transaction be if ArbeFed sells to the banking system? Assume the reserve ratio is 20%.
  iii. How big should this transaction be if ArbeFed sells to the public which pays by cheque?

4. How would each of the following, *ceteris paribus*, affect the M1 and M2 measures of the money supply? (Consider initial effect only.)

a. Households move $10 billion of their liquid wealth from demand deposits to notice deposit accounts.

b. Households withdraw $10 billion worth of currency from their chequing accounts.

5. List the following assets in terms of their liquidity—i.e., ease and cheapness of conversion into spending power. Put the most liquid first, the least liquid last.

A house; a five-dollar bill; a car; some Seagram stock; a collector's edition plate; a passbook savings account.

1. _____     4. _____

2. _____     5. _____

3. _____     6. _____

6. Use the following information to calculate the total value of M1 (narrow money) and M2 (broad money) as defined in the text.

| | |
|---|---|
| Credit card balances | 403 |
| Stock market holdings | 1009 |
| Demand deposits | 240 |
| Currency notes held by public | 146 |
| Nonpersonal notice deposits | 246 |
| Treasury bills | 708 |
| Personal savings accounts | 300 |
| Government of Canada bonds | 513 |
| Coins held by the public | 10 |
| Gold | 73 |

M1 _____

M2 _____

7. The following table gives several possible desired reserve ratios.

| Desired Reserve Ratio | Money Multiplier | Max. Expansion (Single Bank) | Max. Expansion (Banking System) |
|---|---|---|---|
| 10% | | | |
| 12.5% | | | |
| 20% | | | |
| 25% | | | |

a. Calculate the money multipliers and enter the values in the table.

b. Suppose a "loaned up" bank receives a deposit of $100. Given the reserve ratio, calculate the maximum amount by which the bank could expand its *loans* in the initial round of the money multiplier process.

c. In each case, calculate the maximum amount by which the banking system will be able to expand its *deposits*.

8. Suppose that Ace deposits $1000 into his bank (Bank A), which is fully loaned up. Complete the following table, showing the maximum amount by which deposits, reserves, and loans can increase. Assume that the desired reserve ratio is 12.5% in all cases.

| | New Demand Deposits = | Change in Reserves = | Change in Desired Reserves + | Change in Excess Reserves | Change in Loans |
|---|---|---|---|---|---|
| A | | | | | |
| B | | | | | |
| C | | | | | |
| D | | | | | |
| etc. | | | | | |
| Total | | | | | |

9.  A private bank has deposits of $100 000 and total reserves amounting to $31 000. The desired reserve ratio is 15%. All other banks are loaned up.
    a.  What is the largest loan that this bank will make? _____
    b.  What is the value of the money multiplier? _____
    c.  If the initial loan is made, what is the maximum expansion that can occur in total deposits if other banks maintain the same reserve ratio? _____

10. Arboc's central bank (Arbobank) holds 2000 opeks in government securities. The private banks have deposited 200 opeks with Arbobank and hold 100 in vault cash. 700 opeks are held as currency by the public. The required reserve ratio is 20% (by law); banks are loaned up.
    a.  The deposit multiplier value is _____.
    b.  Calculate Arboc's money supply. _____

    It is felt that the money supply should be increased by 900 opeks. Either an open market operation or a change in the reserve ratio is possible.
    c.  If the reserve ratio is changed, what should be the new ratio? _____
    d.  If an open market operation is undertaken, it should be a purchase/sale of _____ opeks.

11. (Based on Appendix 11A) Suppose the desired reserve ratio is 1% and 4% of deposits are held as currency. What are the values of the deposit and money multipliers?

## ANSWERS AND SOLUTIONS

## PRACTICE TEST

## I.    SOLUTIONS TO MULTIPLE CHOICE QUESTIONS

1.  D.  From the economist's point of view, credit cards are a means of obtaining a loan, not a means of payment. Payment comes later, when you write a cheque to Visa or MasterCard.
2.  A.  See p. 228 for a discussion of the functions of money.
3.  D.  The deposit multiplier is 4 (1 / reserve ratio). Chequing accounts (demand deposits) will increase by 400 (100 × 4). See p. 239.
4.  B.  See p. 237. Typically, some of a bank's actual reserves will be excess reserves.
5.  C.  See p. 243.

6. D. Canada Trust owes depositors the value of their chequing accounts; Canada Trust also owes depositors the value of their money market accounts. Both are liabilities.

7. D. Assets to the left; liabilities to the right. Net worth is the value of the firm (the difference between assets and liabilities).

8. B. Given the reserves of the banking system, if more reserves are desired to be held back, the deposit multiplier (1 / reserve ratio) will decrease and the money supply will decrease. Excess reserves = total reserves – desired reserves. As desired reserves increase, excess reserves decrease.

9. A. On its own, the deposit has no effect on the money supply. The "currency held outside banks" category decreases by $200; the "demand deposits" category increases by $200. Eventually, because the deposit multiplier is 5, total deposits will increase by $1000, but currency held outside banks has decreased by $200. The net change in the money supply is $800.

10. B. The Bank of Canada does not set a required reserve ratio for private banks.

11. C. When the banking system is loaned up, all reserves are desired reserves. Excess reserves are zero. If the reserve ratio is 25%, the banking system's reserves must be supporting $2000 billion (500 billion × 4) in deposits. If the desired reserve ratio decreases to 10%, only $200 billion will be desired, liberating $300 billion as excess reserves.

12. D. If the reserve ratio is 10%, the banking system's reserves can support $5000 billion (500 billion × 10) in deposits—an increase of $3000 billion.

13. A. An open market sale of securities draws reserves away from the private banking system, reducing the money supply. Under options B, C, and D, the money supply would increase.

14. D. The money multiplier is 4. Each dollar lent out will be multiplied four times by the banking system as a whole.

15. C. M2 includes all components of M1, so the transfer has no effect on the total value of M2. M1 is reduced because savings accounts are a type of notice deposit and are not included in M1.

16. D. To the extent that at each stage of the money multiplier process, some of the currency lent by banks is held by individuals rather than being entirely redeposited, there are fewer new reserves at each stage and hence a smaller multiplier.

17. D. See p. 242.

18. B. See p. 242. Recall that the rate charged when banks borrow from each other for very short periods is the overnight rate.

19. A. See p. 241.

20. B. If the banking system is fully loaned up, all reserves are desired reserves. With a reserve ratio of 25%, total deposits must be $800 million ($200 million × 4). If the reserve ratio falls to 20%, the money multiplier will increase to 5, and the banking system will be able to support $1000 million of deposits ($200 million × 5)—an increase of $200 million.


## II.   SOLUTIONS TO APPLICATION QUESTIONS

1. The leakage of currency to foreign accounts reduces the deposit multiplier because some of the relending in the deposit creation process is done by foreign banks outside the Canadian system.

2.   a.   See the following T accounts.

| First Bank | | | | |
| --- | --- | --- | --- | --- |
| **Assets** | | | **Liabilities** | |
| Reserves | | −1000 | Deposits | _____ |
| Loans | | +1000 | | |

| Second Bank | | | | |
| --- | --- | --- | --- | --- |
| **Assets** | | | **Liabilities** | |
| Reserves | | +200 | Deposits | +1000 |
| Loans | | +800 | | |

| Third Bank | | | | |
| --- | --- | --- | --- | --- |
| **Assets** | | | **Liabilities** | |
| Reserves | | +160 | Deposits | +800 |
| Loans | | +640 | | |

| Fourth Bank | | | | |
| --- | --- | --- | --- | --- |
| **Assets** | | | **Liabilities** | |
| Reserves | | +128 | Deposits | +640 |
| Loans | | +512 | | |

   b.   The money supply has expanded so far by $1000 + $800 + $640 = $2440.

3.   a.   See the following balance sheet.

| ArbeFed | | | |
| --- | --- | --- | --- |
| **Assets** | | **Liabilities** | |
| Securities | 1000 | Currency | +800 |
| | | Deposit of banks | 200 |

   b.   Currency = 800. Because the banking system is fully loaned up, bank reserves are 200 opeks and the money multiplier is 5.00, demand deposits are 200 × 5, or 1000. M1 is 1800 opeks.

   c.   i.   The reserve requirement must be decreased to expand the money supply.
        ii.  The new reserve requirement should be 16.67%. The new money multiplier is 1 / .1667, or 6. Bank reserves are 200, therefore demand deposits will be 1200 opeks. Currency remains at 800 opeks, so the total is 2000.

   d.   i.   ArbeFed should sell bonds.
        ii.  If the central bank sells bonds worth 60 opeks to the banking system and the money multiplier is 5, the money supply will decrease by 300 opeks.
        iii. If the central bank sells bonds worth 60 opeks to the public and the public uses demand deposits from the banking system, banking system reserves will fall by 60. The banking system's reserves are 48 opeks too low (i.e., 60 × .80) so it must call in loans. Assuming the public repays all loans by cheque, deposits must fall. Deposits will shrink by an additional 240 opeks (i.e., 48 × 5). Total decrease is 300 opeks.

4.   a.   Moving funds from demand deposits to notice deposits: M1, which includes demand deposits but not notice deposits, would decrease by $10 billion; M2 would remain unchanged.

b. M1 and M2 both include both demand deposits and currency, so each would remain unchanged.

5. A five-dollar bill; a passbook savings account; some Seagram stock; a collector's edition plate; a car; a house.

6. M1 is 396—that is, the total of currency notes and coins held by the public, and demand deposits; M2 is 942—that is, M1 plus personal savings accounts and non-personal notice deposits.

7. a. See the table below.

| Desired Reserve Ratio | Money Multiplier | Max. Expansion (Single Bank) | Max. Expansion (Banking System) |
|---|---|---|---|
| 10% | 10 | $90.00 | $1000 |
| 12.5% | 8 | $87.50 | $ 800 |
| 20% | 5 | $80.00 | $ 500 |
| 25% | 4 | $75.00 | $ 400 |

b. See the table above.
c. See the table above.

8. See the table below.

| | New Demand Deposits = | Change in Reserves = | Change in Desired Reserves + | Change in Excess Reserves | Change in Loans |
|---|---|---|---|---|---|
| A | $1000.00 | $1000.00 | $ 125.00 | $ 875.00/0 | $ 875.00 |
| B | $ 875.00 | $ 875.00 | $ 109.38 | $ 765.62/0 | $ 765.62 |
| C | $ 765.62 | $ 765.82 | $ 95.70 | $ 669.92/0 | $ 669.92 |
| D | $ 669.92 | $ 669.92 | $ 83.74 | $ 586.18/0 | $ 586.18 |
| etc. | $4689.46 | | $ 586.18 | $4103.28/0 | $4103.28 |
| Total | $8000.00 | | $1000.00 | $7000.00/0 | $7000.00 |

9. a. Desired reserves are $15 000 and excess reserves are $16 000. The bank can lend out all of its excess reserves—that is, $16 000.
   b. The money multiplier = 1 / reserve ratio = 1 / .15 = 6.667
   c. $16 000 × 6.667 = $106 666.67.

10. a. The deposit multiplier = 1 / reserve ratio = 1 / 0.20 = 5.
    b. Bank reserves are vault cash (100) and deposits at the central bank (200). If the banks are loaned up and the multiplier is 5, demand deposits must be 1500 (300 × 5). The money supply includes currency (700) and demand deposits (1500) = 2200 opeks.
    c. To support a money supply of 3100, with 2400 opeks of demand deposits (1500 + 900), using the same quantity of reserves (300), the multiplier must be 8 (2400 / 300). To get a multiplier of 8, the required reserve ratio must be 12.5%.
    n If the multiplier is 5, a purchase of 180 opeks will increase the money supply by 900.

11. Using the formulas of Appendix 11A, the deposit multiplier is 1/(0.04+0.01) = 20. The money multiplier is (1+0.04)/(0.04+0.01) = 20.8.

# 12 Money Demand, Interest Rates, Exchange Rates, and Monetary Policy

## OBJECTIVES: POINT BY POINT

After completing this chapter, you should be able to accomplish the objectives listed below.

### OBJECTIVE 1: list the determinants of the "demand for money."

Individuals must decide how much of their financial assets to hold as money and how much to hold in other types of financial securities such as bonds. Individuals will increase their demand for money the greater their need is for money for transactions (and hence the greater are income and the price level). They will also increase their demand for money the lower the interest rate (that is, the lower the opportunity cost of holding money instead of an interest-bearing asset).

The *interest rate* is the annual interest payment expressed as a percentage of the total loan (as opposed to *interest*, which is the charge imposed by a lender on a borrower for the use of funds). (page 247)

For simplicity, the text assumes that there is only one interest rate and that money earns no interest. The assumption that money earns no interest is reasonably accurate—currency doesn't, and chequing accounts earn little or no interest.

Even as a student with (presumably) limited means, you face the tradeoff described above. Having amassed a bankroll from summer work, how do you allocate your assets? Typically, funds that are less liquid earn higher interest rates, but there may be a "penalty for early withdrawal." Holding all your funds as cash or in a chequing account results in an opportunity cost (the interest earnings not obtained). If you could visit the bank only once a month, you would be obliged to hold a fair portion of your assets in readily available form (cash, chequing account). With the convenience of the neighbourhood 24-hour ATM, you can cut back on idle cash or assets earning lower interest rates. But note the effects will be much stronger for wealthy individuals or companies (e.g., supermarkets) that can hold substantial cash. The higher the interest rates, the greater the incentive such companies/individuals have to minimize cash holdings.

Sometimes we describe the demand for money in terms of the *speculation motive* and the *transaction* motive.

The *speculation motive* for holding money focuses on the negative relationship between bond prices and the interest rate. In a two-asset world, expectations about future bond prices and the interest rate affect money demand. When the interest rate rises, bond prices fall; when the interest rate is expected to rise, bond prices are expected to fall. One reason to hold money is therefore "in speculation" that interest rates are about to increase. An investor who expects such an increase will want to hold money instead of bonds to avoid the capital loss when bond prices fall. (page 248)

The *transaction motive* shows that money is demanded to finance transactions, and that the demand for money increases when the dollar value of transactions increases. This may happen if prices rise, or it may happen if there is a greater amount of economic activity. An increase in aggregate output or an increase in the price level will shift the money demand curve to the right. (page 249)

## Practice

1.  Hansel borrows $50 from Gretel. The loan will last one year. At the end of the year, Hansel will pay Gretel $60. The interest received by Gretel is _____; the interest rate is _____.
    A.  $10, 10%.
    B.  $10, 20%.
    C.  $60, 10%.
    D.  $60, 20%.

    **ANSWER: B.** Interest is the fee charged by Gretel for the use of the $50. The interest rate is the annual interest payment ($10) expressed as a percentage of the loan amount ($50).

2.  In economics, when discussing Tessa's "demand for money," we mean
    A.  how much cash Tessa would like to have.
    B.  the income that Tessa would need, per time period, to satisfy her minimum living requirements.
    C.  how much wealth Tessa would like to have.
    D.  the quantity of Tessa's financial assets that she wishes to hold in non-interest-bearing form.

    **ANSWER: D.** The meaning of this phrase is quite specific in economics. See p. 248.

3.  The optimal money balance will certainly increase if the interest earned on bonds _____ and the costs of switching between bonds and money _____.
    A.  increases, increase.
    B.  increases, decrease.
    C.  decreases, increase.
    D.  decreases, decrease.

    **ANSWER: C.** The lower the interest rate, the lower the opportunity cost of holding money. If transaction costs are higher, it costs more to obtain extra cash if needed, so it is better to hold more money. See p. 250.

4.  When the interest rate falls,
    A.  bond prices fall.
    B.  bond prices rise.
    C.  the demand for bonds is higher than normal.
    D.  the yield on bonds is higher than normal.

    **ANSWER: B.** There is a negative relationship between the interest rate and bond prices.

5. Carlos expects a decline in interest rates. He will
   A. hold bonds instead of cash. An interest rate decrease will bring about a decrease in the price of bonds.
   B. hold bonds instead of cash. An interest rate decrease will bring about an increase in the price of bonds.
   C. hold cash instead of bonds. An interest rate decrease will bring about a decrease in the price of bonds.
   D. hold cash instead of bonds. An interest rate decrease will bring about an increase in the price of bonds.

   **ANSWER:** B. A decrease in the interest rate causes an increase in the price of bonds. If Carlos expects bond prices to rise, he should buy bonds now and sell them after the price increase.

6. Wulong bought a standard bond four years ago for $3000 and sold it yesterday for $2560. Such a result most likely has been caused by
   A. a decrease in interest rates.
   B. a decline in the level of activity in the economy.
   C. a decrease in the Bank rate.
   D. an increase in the level of interest rates.

   **ANSWER:** D. The price of the bond has fallen, implying an increase in the interest rate.

7. The demand for money curve will shift to the left when
   A. the interest rate increases.
   B. the price level increases.
   C. aggregate output decreases.
   D. the price of bonds is expected to decrease.

   **ANSWER:** C. Less money will be demanded if the dollar volume of transactions decreases because of a price level decrease or an output level decrease. Changes (Option A) or expected changes (Option D) in the interest rate don't cause a shift in the position of the demand curve; they correspond to a move along the demand curve.

8. Each of the following will cause the demand for money curve to shift rightwards except
   A. an increase in aggregate output.
   B. an increase in the price level.
   C. an increase in the transactions cost of switching between money and bonds.
   D. an increase in the money supply.

   **ANSWER:** D. An increase in the money supply will affect the interest rate and the quantity of money demanded, but the demand curve will not shift position. Option C will increase money demand: At each interest rate, more idle cash balances will be held.

9. If the price level falls, the money demand curve will
   A. shift to the right.
   B. shift to the left.
   C. become steeper.
   D. become flatter.

   **ANSWER:** B. See p. 251.

## OBJECTIVE 2: Explain how the equilibrium interest rate is determined by supply and demand in the money market.

The money market is modelled quite simply. The money demand curve shows the negative relationship between the quantity of money demanded and the interest rate. Money supply is fixed at a particular level at any point in time—the curve is vertical. The interaction of money supply and money demand establishes an equilibrium interest rate, where quantity demanded equals quantity supplied. If, for example, the demand for money increases, interest rates will rise. At the original interest rate, an excess demand for money occurs. To dissuade individuals from holding cash and to encourage bond purchases, the interest rate must increase. (page 255)

> **Graphing Pointer:** Keep in mind the factors that can shift the money demand curve: aggregate income level and the price level. An increase in either will shift the curve to the right. Changes in the interest rate will cause *a movement along the curve*.

## OBJECTIVE 3: Explain how the Bank of Canada can influence the interest rate.

One key player in the money market is the Bank of Canada, of course, because Bank actions can increase or decrease the money supply. (page 256)

> **Tip:** Review the material in Chapter 11 referring to the Bank's three main monetary policy instruments.

## Practice

10. If the supply of money increases as a result of an open market _____ of securities by the Bank of Canada, the interest rate will _____.
    A. purchase, increase.
    B. purchase, decrease.
    C. sale, increase.
    D. sale, decrease.

    **ANSWER: B.** The Bank buys bonds to increase the money supply. An increase in the money supply decreases the equilibrium interest rate.

11. If the supply of money decreases as a result of a(n) _____ in the Bank rate, the size of money balances will _____.
    A. increase, increase.
    B. increase, decrease.
    C. decrease, increase.
    D. decrease, decrease.

    **ANSWER: B.** The Bank raises the Bank rate when it is tightening the money supply. A decrease in the money supply increases the equilibrium interest rate and decreases the size of money balances.

12. If the demand for money decreases as a result of a(n) _____ in the price level, the interest rate will _____.
    A. increase, increase.
    B. increase, decrease.
    C. decrease, increase.
    D. decrease, decrease.

    **ANSWER:** D. As the price level falls, less cash is needed to finance a given level of transactions.

Use the following diagram to answer the next four questions.

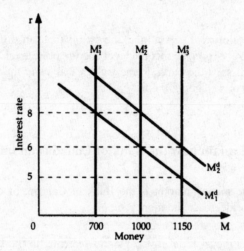

13. The money demand curve is $M_1^d$ and the money supply curve is $M_2^s$. At an interest rate of 5%, there is an excess
    A. demand of 150.
    B. demand of 300.
    C. supply of 150.
    D. supply of 300.

    **ANSWER:** A. At 5%, quantity demanded (1150) exceeds quantity supplied (1000).

14. The money demand curve might shift from $M_1^d$ to $M_2^d$ if
    A. the money supply increased.
    B. the interest rate decreased.
    C. The Bank bought bonds in the open market.
    D. the real output level increased.

    **ANSWER:** D. The real output level is a determinant of money demand. See p. 255.

15. The money supply curve might shift from $M_2^s$ to $M_3^s$ if
    A. the Bank undertook an easy monetary policy such as an open market purchase of securities.
    B. the Bank undertook an easy monetary policy such as an open market sale of securities.
    C. the Bank undertook a tight monetary policy such as an open market purchase of securities.
    D. the Bank undertook a tight monetary policy such as an open market sale of securities.

    **ANSWER:** A. The shift from $M_2^s$ to $M_3^s$ is an expansion, caused by an easy money policy. An open market purchase of securities could cause this.

16. The equilibrium interest rate will definitely increase if the money demand curve shifts from _____ and the money supply curve shifts from _____.
    A. $M_1^d$ to $M_2^d$, $M_1^s$ to $M_2^s$.
    B. $M_1^d$ to $M_2^d$, $M_2^s$ to $M_1^s$.
    C. $M_2^d$ to $M_1^d$, $M_1^s$ to $M_2^s$.
    D. $M_2^d$ to $M_1^d$, $M_2^s$ to $M_1^s$.

    **ANSWER:** B.  See the diagram.

17. Which of the following pairs of events will most likely result in a decrease in the equilibrium interest rate? A(n) _____ in the level of aggregate output and a(n) _____ in the Bank rate.
    A. increase, increase.
    B. increase, decrease.
    C. decrease, increase.
    D. decrease, decrease.

    **ANSWER:** D.  A decrease in money demand will accompany a decrease in output, while an increase in money supply will likely accompany a decrease in the Bank rate. Both factors should reduce interest rates.

18. Which of the following pairs of events will most likely result in an increase in the equilibrium interest rate? A(n) _____ in the price level and an open market _____ of securities.
    A. increase, purchase.
    B. increase, sale.
    C. decrease, purchase.
    D. decrease, sale.

    **ANSWER:** B.  An increase in money demand will accompany an increase in the price level. An open market sale of securities is a tight monetary policy. Both factors will increase interest rates.

19. Which of the following pairs of actions is the most certain to be a tight monetary policy? A transfer of government deposits _____ private banks and an open market _____ of securities.
    A. out of, purchase.
    B. out of, sale.
    C. into, purchase.
    D. into, sale.

    **ANSWER:** B.  Both actions will reduce the money supply.

## OBJECTIVE 4: Define fixed and flexible exchange rates. Explain how the distinction matters for monetary policy.

Under a fixed exchange rate, the Bank of Canada would be committed to buying and selling the Canadian dollar at a given price against another currency (almost surely the U.S. dollar). As no one would pay more or accept less than the Bank of Canada's price, this fixes the value of the Canadian dollar. Under a flexible exchange rate (sometimes called a "floating" exchange rate), the Bank of Canada does not commit to a given exchange rate. However, it may sometimes buy and sell in exchange rate markets or use its other monetary instruments with the goal of influencing the exchange rate (*a managed or dirty floating exchange rate*), or it could in principle ignore the exchange rate entirely in its policy decisions (*a freely or pure floating exchange rate*).

Under fixed exchange rates, the rate of interest in Canada will be essentially determined by world interest rates (in practice, U.S. interest rates). For example, if the exchange rate is fixed and expected to remain so and the U.S. interest rate is 7%, no one in Canada will accept a lower rate of interest because she/he could instead convert her/his Canadian dollars to U.S. dollars, lend in the United States at 7% and then convert her/his earnings back to Canadian dollars. Similarly, no one in Canada will borrow at an interest rate higher than that available in the U.S. (In practice, interest rates could still be a bit different because of the transactions costs of converting money back and forth, and because the perceived risk of lending may be different in the two countries.) But the main point is that under fixed exchange rates, the Bank of Canada must set the money supply to maintain the exchange rate and cannot use monetary policy to influence other economic variables.

To the extent that it allows freely floating exchange rates, the Bank of Canada can aim its monetary policy tools at interest rates. If Canadian interest rates are higher than U.S. interest rates, some holders of U.S. bonds will want to sell them and purchase Canadian dollars in order to buy higher-paying Canadian bonds. This increased demand for the Canadian dollar will lead to an increase in the value of the Canadian dollar (that is, the Canadian dollar will *appreciate*). If Canadian interest rates are lower than U.S. interest rates, some holders of Canadian bonds will want to sell them for Canadian dollars, then in turn sell the Canadian dollars for U.S. dollars in order to buy higher-paying U.S. bonds. This increased supply of the Canadian dollar will in turn lead to a decrease in the value of the Canadian dollar (that is, the Canadian dollar will *depreciate*).           (page 256)

> **TIP:** Canada has not had fixed exchange rates since 1970. But nonetheless, there are times when the Bank of Canada manages the exchange rate heavily: It buys and sells the Canadian dollar (that is, it contracts and expands the Canadian money supply) with the sole goal of maintaining the exchange rate (and hence it gives up its influence over interest rates). For example, in March 2001, the Canadian dollar was valued at an historic low of about 63 U.S. cents and interest rates were somewhat below U.S. interest rates. The main ongoing monetary policy issue was whether or not the Bank of Canada should strengthen the value of the dollar by increasing interest rates (i.e., devote monetary policy to the exchange rate).

> **TIP:** Remember that under flexible exchange rates, interest rates can be different in Canada than in the United States. If exchange rates are flexible and can change, interest rates are no longer perfectly comparable across countries. While a complete treatment of this point can be complex (and is covered in Chapter 22), as an example, note that you might decide to buy Canadian bonds paying only 4% even if U.S. bonds were paying an interest rate of 7% if you thought that the Canadian dollar would appreciate by more than 3% per year during the term of the bond: The 3% appreciation would act as a bonus to make up for the lower interest rate.

> **TIP:** The supply and demand diagrams in this chapter are all of the *money market* which determines the interest rate. Reference is made to the determination of the value of the Canadian dollar by supply and demand (in the *foreign exchange market* where Canadian dollars are bought and sold), but for simplicity, no diagrams are given. If you want to learn more about the foreign exchange market and see the relevant supply and demand diagrams, see Chapter 21.

## Practice

20. In fixing the exchange rate for one Canadian dollar at between 92 and 93 cents American (as was done in 1962), the Bank of Canada might do all of the following except
    A. offer to buy Canadian dollars at 92 cents American each.
    B. offer to sell Canadian dollars at 93 cents American each.
    C. tighten the money supply if the Canadian dollar appeared to be falling below 92 cents.
    D. legally prohibit selling the Canadian dollar for prices outside that range.

    **ANSWER:** D. Even if the Bank of Canada could enforce such a prohibition in Canada, it surely could not on foreign exchange markets in other countries. All the other options might represent part of the strategy for fixing the exchange rate in that range (see p. 256). Note: Buying Canadian dollars at 92 cents American is a method of reducing the Canadian money supply, so that options A and C are similar.

21. In fixing the exchange rate as in question 20 above, it may be more difficult for the central bank to maintain the floor price than the ceiling price because maintaining the
    A. ceiling price requires foreign exchange reserves.
    B. floor price requires foreign exchange reserves.
    C. ceiling price may require additional Canadian dollars.
    D. floor price may require additional Canadian dollars.

    **ANSWER:** B. To maintain the floor price of, say, 92 cents American, the Bank of Canada must always be prepared to buy Canadian dollars, and that requires foreign exchange reserves, such as U.S. dollars. To maintain a ceiling price of, say, 93 cents American, the Bank of Canada must be prepared to sell Canadian dollars, but the Bank of Canada can always issue more Canadian dollars if these are required. See p. 256.

22. If, during a period of floating exchange rates, the Bank of Canada suddenly and unexpectedly increases the Bank rate, the most likely result will be
    A. an exchange rate appreciation.
    B. an exchange rate depreciation.
    C. a sharp and rapid expansion in the money supply.
    D. in increase in net exports.

    **ANSWER:** A. A higher Bank rate signals a tighter monetary policy and higher interest rates, and this will lead to an appreciation of the Canadian dollar. See p. 259.

23. A fall in the differential of Canadian over U.S. interest rates during the early 1990s led to a
    A. fall in the value of the U.S. dollar relative to the Canadian dollar.
    B. decrease in the value of the Canadian dollar relative to the U.S. dollar.
    C. a fall in Canadian net exports.
    D. a sharp decline in the Canadian money supply.

    **ANSWER:** B. See p. 260. In practice, during the 1970s and 1980s, Canadian interest rates tended to exceed U.S. interest rates, presumably to compensate for greater perceived risk. When this differential shrunk in the early 1990s, the Canadian dollar depreciated.

## OBJECTIVE 5: Contrast "tight" and "expansionary" monetary policies and their implications for the interest rate and the exchange rate.

Under fixed exchange rates, the Bank of Canada cannot adjust the money supply to meet targets besides the exchange rate, so it only makes sense to consider expansionary (or easy) and tight monetary policy under a flexible exchange rate policy such as Canada now has. Easy monetary policy involves expanding the money supply, which reduces interest rates and in turn leads to an exchange rate depreciation. The lower interest rates stimulate investment spending; the depreciated exchange rate makes Canadian exports cheaper on world markets and imports to Canada more expensive, increasing net exports. Both of these effects tend to increase output. Tight monetary policy involves restricting the money supply, increasing interest rates, leading to an exchange rate appreciation. The higher interest rates reduce investment spending, while the higher value of the Canadian dollar tends to reduce net exports, and these effects tend to reduce output.

## Practice

24. Because the Canadian dollar value has fallen, Rosanna chooses to take her January vacation skiing in Banff, Alberta, rather than going to Florida. This is potentially an example of an easier monetary policy
    A.  stimulating investment spending.
    B.  increasing exports.
    C.  reducing imports.
    D.  reducing exports.

    **ANSWER: C.** Travel by Canadians to other countries is counted as Canada importing goods and services. Rosanna has shifted her spending towards Canadian produced services (tourist services in Banff) which stimulates Canadian output.

25. Suppose there is an increase in the Bank rate with the announced goal of "defending the dollar." This is an example of
    A.  a tight monetary policy directed towards reducing inflation.
    B.  a tight monetary policy directed towards managing the exchange rate.
    C.  an easy monetary policy directed towards stimulating output.
    D.  an easy monetary policy directed towards managing the exchange rate.

    **ANSWER: B.** Increasing the Bank rate is an example of a restrictive monetary policy, and as such will tend to lead to upward pressure (or at least reduced downward pressure) on the value of the dollar. As an example, during spring 1998, the Bank of Canada was frequently called upon to increase interest rates to increase the value of a falling Canadian dollar, even though many economists were worried that a tighter monetary policy would slow output growth.

## OBJECTIVE 6 (APPENDIX 12A): Distinguish the different types of interest rates and explain how monetary policy may affect them differently.

There is not one "interest rate," but rather a whole family of rates. The *expectations theory of the term structure of interest rates* links the behaviour of long-term rates to current short-term rates and expected short-term rates. Essentially, long-term rates are based on current short-term rates and expectations about how short-term rates will change in the future. The Bank of Canada has less control over long-term rates.

Because it is difficult to forecast future interest rates, a simple model that works reasonably well is that the long-term real rate of interest is fairly constant, say 5% as an example. Hence the long-term actual or nominal rate of interest would be equal to 5% plus the expected rate of inflation. Hence it is possible that a tight monetary policy will increase short-term interest rates (as described in the body of the chapter) but reduce long-term interest rates if it is expected that the tighter monetary policy might eventually reduce inflation, as will be discussed in later chapters. The most important point is that the interest rate in the models of Chapter 12 is a short-term interest rate. (page 267)

## Practice

26. Government securities that take longer than one year to mature are called
    A. Treasury bills.
    B. government bonds.
    C. certificates of deposit.
    D. Guaranteed Investment Certificates.

    **ANSWER:** B. See p. 268. Bills mature in less than a year, bonds in one or more years. Options C and D are issued by the private sector.

27. The current interest rate on a one-year bond is 4%. On a similar bond next year the rate is expected to be 6%. According to the expectations theory of the term structure of interest rates, the current rate on a two-year bond is about
    A. 2%.
    B. 4%.
    C. 5%.
    D. 10%.

    **ANSWER:** C. The two-year rate is about the average of the current one-year rate and the one-year rate expected in the future—i.e., (6 + 4) / 2. See p. 267.

28. The current interest rate on a one-year bond is 4%. The current rate on a two-year bond is 7%. According to the expectations theory of the term structure of interest rates, the expected rate on a similar one-year bond next year is about
    A. 3%.
    B. 5.5%.
    C. 7%.
    D. 10%.

    **ANSWER:** D. The two-year rate (7%) is the average of the current one-year rate (4%) and the one-year rate expected in the future (10%). See p. 267.

29. Suppose the rate of interest paid by one-year government bonds is 5% and the rate of inflation is 1%. The real (or inflation-adjusted) rate of interest is
    A. 1%.
    B. 2%.
    C. 3%.
    D. 4%.

    **ANSWER:** D. The real rate of interest is the actual (sometimes called nominal) rate of interest less the inflation rate. It gives the increase in purchasing power achieved by the holder of the bond.

30. If the Canadian dollar were expected to appreciate steadily by 4% relative to the U.S. dollar, and the rate of interest on secure Canadian bonds were 5% per year, we would expect the rate of interest paid by similar U.S. bonds to be approximately
   A.  9%.
   B.  5%.
   C.  4%.
   D.  1%.

**ANSWER:** A.  If the U.S. dollar is losing value to the Canadian dollar at a rate of 4% per year, we would expect that holders of U.S. dollar securities would have to be compensated for that with interest rates 4% higher. Otherwise, U.S. bondholders would want to switch to Canadian bonds.

# PRACTICE TEST

**I.    MULTIPLE CHOICE QUESTIONS.** Select the option that provides the single best answer.

_____ 1.  If during a period of flexible exchange rates, the Bank of Canada buys Canadian dollars on the foreign exchange market, which of the following statements is likely false?
   A.   The Bank's policy is not a pure floating exchange rate.
   B.   The Bank is reducing the money supply.
   C.   The Bank is acting to prevent exchange rate appreciation.
   D.   The Bank is putting upward pressure on short-term interest rates.

_____ 2.  If under fixed exchange rates the Bank of Canada attempts to lower interest rates relative to U.S. interest rates, the problem it most likely will face is
   A.   downward pressure on the value of the Canadian dollar.
   B.   upward pressure on the value of the Canadian dollar.
   C.   a need to increase the money supply continually.
   D.   counteraction by the U.S. Federal Reserve Bank.

_____ 3.  The money market is in equilibrium. Now the Bank of Canada buys securities. There will be an excess _____ money. This will cause the interest rate to _____.
   A.   demand for, fall.
   B.   supply of, rise.
   C.   demand for, rise.
   D.   supply of, fall.

_____ 4.  The quantity of money demanded is _____ related to the dollar volume of transactions and _____ related to the interest rate.
   A.   positively, positively.
   B.   positively, negatively.
   C.   negatively, positively.
   D.   negatively, negatively.

_____ 5.  A fall in the price level will _____ the demand for money, and a rise in the number of transactions will _____ the demand for money.
   A.   increase, increase.
   B.   increase, decrease.
   C.   decrease, increase.
   D.   decrease, decrease.

_____ 6. Each of the following will make the public wish to hold more money balances except
A. an increase in the price level.
B. a decrease in the interest rate.
C. an increase in the opportunity cost of holding money.
D. an increase in the dollar volume of transactions.

_____ 7. The money market is in equilibrium. Now there is an expansion in the money supply. This will cause the interest rate to _____ and the quantity of money demanded to _____.
A. increase, increase.
B. decrease, increase.
C. decrease, decrease.
D. increase, decrease.

_____ 8. The demand for money is a _____ measure, and the supply of money is a _____ measure.
A. flow, flow.
B. flow, stock.
C. stock, flow.
D. stock, stock.

_____ 9. Which summary statement is most accurate? A fixed exchange rate policy is a "complete" monetary policy because it
A. can never be changed.
B. devotes monetary policy instruments solely to the exchange rate.
C. precludes fiscal policy.
D. eliminates the possibility of open market operations by the Bank.

_____ 10. You read in the newspaper that "bond prices have rallied." If this situation persists, this is most likely very good news for all of the following except someone
A. currently seeking a mortgage to buy a house.
B. with a large bond portfolio.
C. with bonds with a term that ends tomorrow.
D. who has large loans at a market-varying interest rate.

_____ 11. Suppose interest rates are expected to stay constant at 5% for ten years. Suddenly there is a change, and interest rates are now expected to stay constant at 6% for ten years. The price of all existing bonds of term ten-years or shorter _____ and the price of long-term bonds changes _____ than the price of short-term bonds.
A. increases, more.
B. increases, less.
C. decreases, more.
D. decreases, less.

_____ 12. Under flexible exchange rates, an increase in output given constant money supply will likely cause a(n) _____ in interest rates and a(n) _____ in the exchange rate.
A. increase, appreciation.
B. increase, depreciation.
C. decrease, appreciation.
D. decrease, depreciation.

_____ 13. Stefan runs a catering business and is deciding both whether to borrow money to expand and whether to switch his standard "house" wine from a domestic to an imported brand. The Bank of Canada changes to an easier monetary policy. The results will likely make Stefan _____ likely to expand his business and _____ likely to switch wines.
   A. more, more.
   B. more, less.
   C. less, more.
   D. less, less.

_____ 14. The slope of the money demand curve illustrates the idea that there is
   A. a positive relationship between the interest rate and the quantity of money demanded.
   B. a positive relationship between the price level and the quantity of money demanded.
   C. a negative relationship between the interest rate and the quantity of money demanded.
   D. a negative relationship between the value of transactions and the quantity of money demanded.

_____ 15. The money demand curve will shift right in each of the following cases except when
   A. the price level increases.
   B. the interest rate increases.
   C. the nominal output level increases.
   D. the real output level increases.

_____ 16. Which of the following pairs of events will most likely result in an increase in the equilibrium interest rate? A(n) _____ in the level of aggregate output and a(n) _____ in the supply of money.
   A. increase, increase.
   B. increase, decrease.
   C. decrease, increase.
   D. decrease, decrease.

_____ 17. As the number of economic transactions increases,
   A. more money will be demanded.
   B. less money will be demanded.
   C. more money will be supplied.
   D. less money will be supplied.

_____ 18. The Bank of Canada conducts an open market sale of government securities. We would predict each of the following except
   A. a decrease in the money supply.
   B. an increase in the interest rate.
   C. an increase in the price of bonds.
   D. a decrease in the quantity of money demanded.

_____ 19. If the Bank of Canada were to announce that it would follow an "easy" monetary policy over the next few months, we would expect to see each of the following except
   A. an increasing money supply.
   B. open market purchases of securities by the Bank.
   C. falling interest rates.
   D. a rising value of the Canadian dollar.

_____ 20. A theory described later in this book argues that if the economy expands too quickly, it leads to inflation, and that sometimes the Bank of Canada may decide to dampen growth to reduce inflation. If this theory is accepted and the Bank of Canada pursues a tighter monetary policy, inflation may also be reduced by the effects of
A. exchange rate appreciation on import prices.
B. exchange rate depreciation on import prices.
C. exchange rate appreciation on export prices.
D. the effects of higher interest rates on increasing business costs.

## II. APPLICATION QUESTIONS

1. Explain what will happen to the price of bonds and to money holdings if the Bank of Canada changes the interest rate as a result of a decrease in the money supply.

2. Suppose a company issues two kinds of $1000 bonds, one type with a one-year term and one with a ten-year term. Both pay 5% per annum interest. Each bond is somewhat unusual in that all interest and principal are paid at the end of the term; that is, there are no coupons for interim interest.
   a. Calculate how much each bond will pay at the end of its term.
   b. Calculate the present value of each bond.
   c. Suppose the moment after the bonds are issued, interest rates (for both one-year and ten-year terms) increase from 5% to 6%. Calculate the new present values of each bond.
   d. Redo part c assuming instead interest rates decrease to 4%.

3. Suppose you borrow U.S. $1000 at a rate of interest of 5% per year with the intent of converting the money into Canadian dollars. When you borrow the dollars the Canadian dollar is worth 72 U.S. cents, but when you repay the loan in one year the Canadian dollar is worth only 68 U.S. cents.
   a. How many Canadian dollars have you borrowed?
   b. How many Canadian dollars must you repay?
   c. What is the effective rate of interest (in terms of Canadian dollars)?
   d. Redo the question assuming the Canadian dollar had not fallen to 68 cents American but had instead risen to 75 cents American.

4. Maureen buys a $1000 fixed rate perpetual bond at the going market interest rate of 10%. Note: A perpetual bond (or "consol") is a bond with no maturity date. The payment received on the bond is constant at $100 per year. To calculate the yield on the bond, use the formula:

$$(\text{Payment on bond} \times 100\%) / \text{Price of bond}$$

Initially, the yield on the bond is competitive with the interest rate to be earned elsewhere in the financial market. Suppose now that the market interest rate decreases to 5% (Situation A).

| | Price of Bond | Payment on Bond | Yield on Bond | Market Interest Rate |
|---|---|---|---|---|
| Initial Purchase | $1000 | $100 | 10% | 10% |
| Situation A | _____ | $100 | _____ | 5% |
| Situation B | _____ | $100 | _____ | 20% |

a. What yield must Maureen's bond have to be competitive with other financial assets?

b. In Situation A, is Maureen's bond attractive or unattractive to potential buyers?

c. If Maureen decides to sell the bond, which price is fair, relative to the rest of the market?

Suppose the interest rate increases from 10% to 20% (Situation B).

d. In Situation B, is Maureen's bond attractive or unattractive to potential buyers?

e. If Maureen decides to sell the bond, which price is fair, relative to the rest of the market?

5. The Arbezani money demand curve is given by the following equation:

$$M^d = 5000 - 10\ 000r + .5Y$$

$M^d$ is money demand, r is the real interest rate, and Y is aggregate income.

a. Suppose that aggregate income is 3000. Graph the money demand curve ($M^d_1$) below. (It's a straight line.)

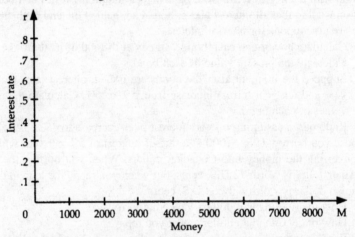

b. Why does the equation have a negative value for the second term and a positive value for the third term?

c. At an interest rate of 10% (r = .1), calculate money demand.

d. At an interest rate of 20% (r = .2), calculate money demand.

e. Suppose that the equilibrium interest rate is 30% (r = .3). Draw the money supply curve (Ms) on the diagram.

f. Income rises from Y = 3000 to Y = 5000. Draw the new money demand curve ($M^d_2$) on the diagram.

g. At the existing interest rate, there is an excess _____ (demand / supply) of money.

h. The new equilibrium interest rate will be _____.

i. How much must the money supply increase to restore the original interest rate?

j. The required reserve ratio (by law) in Arbez is 10%. How great an open market purchase or sale of securities should ArbeFed (the central bank) undertake to restore the original interest rate? Purchase / sale of _____.

6. Arlene, Charlene, and Darlene each earn and spend $24 000 each year. Spending is at a constant amount per day. What is the average money holding in each case?
   a. Arlene is paid yearly. _____
   b. Charlene is paid quarterly. _____
   c. Darlene is paid monthly. _____

   In each case, assume the earnings are paid at the beginning of each period and each woman keeps all unspent balances in her chequing account.

7. Will money demand increase (I) or decrease (D) in each of the following cases?
   a. _____ The aggregate price level rises.
   b. _____ New technology makes access to the stock market instantaneous using a home computer.
   c. _____ More credit cards are accepted.
   d. _____ It is arranged nationally that all bills and income will be received on the first day of each month.
   e. _____ The nominal GDP level increases.
   f. _____ Weakening of strict regulation of the financial sector makes buying bonds more risky.
   g. _____ Banks begin to require a $1000 minimum balance to be kept in chequing accounts at all times.

8. The reserve ratio is 20%. The Bank wants to reduce the money supply by $60 million. Describe an open market operation that will achieve this goal.

   Open market _____ (purchase/sale) in the amount of $_____.

9. Graphically, the supply curve for money is _____. The money supply does not depend on the _____ _____ or the level of _____ _____ (both factors that influence the demand for money). In the money market, the equilibrium interest rate is established such that the quantity of money supplied equals the quantity demanded. If the interest rate is "too high," the quantity supplied will be _____ (greater/less) than the quantity demanded. To reach equilibrium, the interest rate must _____ (rise/fall). This will happen because, with an _____ (excess demand for/excess supply of) money, households will try to _____ (increase/decrease) their money holdings by _____ (buying/selling) bonds. Those selling bonds will be able to do so at a _____ interest rate.

   If the interest rate is "too low," the quantity supplied will be _____ (greater/less) than the quantity demanded. To reach equilibrium, the interest rate must _____ (rise/fall). This will happen because, with an _____ (excess demand for/excess supply of) money, households will try to _____ (increase/decrease) their money holdings by _____ (buying/selling) bonds. Bond issuers will have to offer _____ (higher/lower) interest rates to attract buyers.

10. What happens to the amount of money demanded or supplied in each of the following cases? Draw a separate money demand and money supply graph for each part of this question, label the axes, and show how the change will shift the money demand and/or the money supply curve. Explain any curve shifts in each case. Show initial and final equilibrium interest rate and quantity of money. Assume pure floating exchange rates.

a. The Bank sells securities in the open market while the economy is experiencing high output growth.

b. The Bank increases the money supply during a recession.

c. During a deep recession, the Bank moves to hold the interest rate constant.

d. A rise in nominal GDP is accompanied by an increase in the Bank rate.

e. The Bank conducts an open market purchase of securities, and banks begin imposing a $50 charge on all returned cheques.

f. The economy moves into a downturn, and the private banks become more cautious in their lending policies.

# ANSWERS AND SOLUTIONS

## PRACTICE TEST

### I.    SOLUTIONS TO MULTIPLE CHOICE QUESTIONS

1.    C.   In buying Canadian dollars, the Bank of Canada is not allowing a freely float-ing exchange rate, but instead is trying to prevent exchange rate depreciation by reducing the money supply. This will put upward pressure on short-term interest rates. In practice, the Bank will sometimes maintain that it is not so much trying to prevent exchange rate movements but to slow them.

2.    A.   If interest rates are higher in the United States, Canadian bondholders will sell Canadian bonds and Canadian dollars to obtain U.S. interest-bearing assets, leading to downward pressure on the Canadian dollar. The Bank of Canada will have to buy up this excess supply of dollars, reducing the money supply, and as shown in the text in Figure 12.7, the end result will be that Canadian interest rates cannot be lowered.

3.    D.   When the Bank of Canada buys securities, the money supply increases. There will be an excess supply of money at the initial interest rate, causing the interest rate to decrease.

4.    B.    Individuals need more money as their level of transactions increases. The amount of money demanded decreases when the interest rate increases because the interest rate is the opportunity cost of holding money. See p. 253.

5.    C.   When goods can be bought for less, fewer dollars are needed. See p. 252.

6.    C.   An increase in the opportunity cost of holding money is another way of describ-ing an increase in the interest rate.

7.    B.   As the money supply increases, the interest rate will decrease, causing a move-ment down along the money demand curve (an increase in quantity demanded).

8.    D.   Both the demand for and the supply of money are measured at a point in time—clear evidence that they are stock variables. A flow is measured over a period of time.

9.    B.   Under fixed exchange rates, the central bank must set the money supply to main-tain the exchange rate and therefore cannot use monetary policy to influence other economic variables such as interest rates. See p. 258. Option A is incorrect: a gov-ernment can leave a fixed exchange rate, and Option D is wrong because such oper-ations can still be used as part of maintaining the exchange rate. For Option C, the government can still conduct fiscal policy, that is, change taxes and government spending.

10.   C.   An increase in bond prices is the same thing as a fall in interest rates, and dif-ferent types of interest rates tend to move together. But a bond due tomorrow is unlikely to increase very much with a general fall in interest rates because the increased yield will only apply for one day. For example, a $1000 dollar bond due tomorrow will be worth very close to $1000 today, and no reasonable change in interest rates will change that. If the individual in Option C intended to buy more bonds tomorrow when his/her current bonds expired, the change is actually bad news because the interest yield from those bonds will now be smaller.

11.   C.   Interest rate increases mean that bond prices fall. A given change in interest rates has more effect on bond price the longer the term over which the interest rate applies. See p. 249.

12.   A.   The increase in output will increase the demand for money, and that will tend to increase interest rates, in turn leading to an exchange rate appreciation.

13.   B.   An easier monetary policy should lower interest rates but lead to a depreciation of the Canadian dollar, making imported wine more expensive. (Both of these effects will tend to increase Canadian output.)

14.　C.　The downward slope shows that the quantity of money demanded decreases as the interest rate increases. Note that it is true that an increase in the price level will increase the demand for money, but this is depicted as a rightward shift of the money demand curve.

15.　B.　A change in the interest rate causes a movement along the demand curve. Note that nominal output is the price level times real output.

16.　B.　An increase in the level of aggregate output will increase the demand for money, while a decrease in the money supply will reinforce the upward pressure on interest rates.

17.　A.　The dollar volume of transactions has a positive relationship with money demand.

18.　C.　An open market sale will reduce the money supply—see Chapter 11. A decrease in the money supply will drive up the interest rate. When the interest rate increases, the price of bonds decreases.

19.　D.　Looser monetary policy tends to lower interest rates and lead to exchange rate depreciation.

20.　A.　The tighter monetary policy will tend to lead to an exchange rate appreciation, reducing the prices of imported goods used by Canadians. Incidentally, the effect described in Option D is one reason that tight monetary policy may not dampen inflation, although most economists believe the inflation-reducing effects in Option A and through slowing growth are usually more important.

## II.　SOLUTIONS TO APPLICATION QUESTIONS

1.　If the Bank decreases the money supply, perhaps through an open market sale of securities, the equilibrium interest rate will increase. At the initial equilibrium interest rate, say 5%, the quantity of money demanded will now exceed quantity supplied—individuals do not have enough funds available to finance their necessary transactions. As a result, individuals will attempt to increase their money holdings by selling off bonds. As the demand for bonds dwindles, bond sellers must increase the reward for holding bonds (the interest rate) to attract customers. This interest rate is the opportunity cost of holding money. As the interest rate rises, the quantity of money demanded falls. The process continues until equilibrium is achieved.

2.　a.　The short-term bond will pay $1000 \times 1.05 = $1050$. The long-term bond will pay $1000 \times 1.05^{10} = $1629$.

　　b.　The present value of the short-term bond is $1050 / 1.05$ and the present value of the long-term bond is $1629 / (1.05^{10})$, which (as should be no surprise) in each case is $1000.

　　c.　At the new prevailing rate of interest, the present value of the short-term bond is now $1050 / 1.06 = $991$ and the present value of the long-term bond is $1629 / (1.06^{10}) = $910$. As expected, the price of existing bonds falls when interest rates rise, and the effect of a given change in interest rates is larger on long-term bonds. Remember: A (standard) existing bond does not change its payment schedule when the interest rate changes, so these bonds are still going to pay $1050 and $1629 at the end of their respective terms. However, the change in interest rates does change the present values of these bonds.

　　d.　The present value of the short-term bond is now $1050 / 1.04 = $1010$ and the present value of the long-term bond is $1629 / (1.04^{10}) = $1100$. A fall in interest rates leads to an increase in the value of existing bonds, with a larger increase for longer-term bonds.

3.  a.  US$1000 / .72 = $1389 in Canadian funds.
    b.  You must repay US$1050 which will be 1050 / .68 = $1544 in Canadian funds.
    c.  $1544 / $1389 = 1.11 implying an 11% effective rate of interest. (The U.S. rate of interest of 5% has been increased by an approximate 6% depreciation of the Canadian dollar, from 72 U.S. cents to 68 U.S. cents. The Canadian dollar fell in value during the period of the loan, making it more difficult to repay a U.S. dollar loan.)
    d.  You still have borrowed $1389 in Canadian funds, but now the US$1050 you repay is worth 1050 / .75 = $1400. The effective rate of interest is $1400 / $1389 = 1.01, implying a 1% effective rate of interest. (The U.S. rate of interest of 5% has been offset by an approximate 4% appreciation of the Canadian dollar, making it easier to repay a U.S. dollar loan.)

4.  a.  5%.
    b.  Attractive. At the moment, it is yielding 10%, which is better than the market-wide 5%.
    c.  The yield should be comparable with the market interest rate, otherwise Maureen is selling too cheaply.
        Yield = Payment on bond × 100% / Price of bond
        $100 × 100% / Price of bond = 5%.
        The market price of the bond is $2000.
    d.  Unattractive. At the moment, Maureen's bond is yielding 10%, which is less than the market-wide 20%.
    e.  The yield should be comparable with the market interest rate, otherwise Maureen is asking too high a price.
        Yield = Payment on bond × 100% / Price of bond
        $100 × 100% / Price of bond = 20%.
        The market price of the bond is $500.

    As shown by the table, there is an inverse relationship between the market interest rate and the price of bonds.

|  | Price of Bond | Payment on Bond | Yield on Bond | Market Interest Rate |
|---|---|---|---|---|
| Initial Purchase | $1000 | $100 | 10% | 10% |
| Situation A | $2000 | $100 | 10% | 5% |
| Situation B | $ 500 | $100 | 10% | 20% |

5.  a.  See the diagram below. When the interest rate is zero, money demand is 6500. When money demand is zero, 10 000r = 5000 + 1500. r = 65, i.e., 65%.

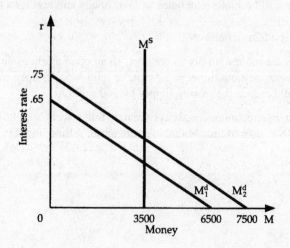

b.      All this means is that there is a negative relationship between the demand for money and the interest rate, and a positive relationship between the demand for money and the level of spending in the economy.

c.      Money demand = 5000 − 10 000(.1) + 1500 = 5500.

d.      Money demand = 5000 − 10 000(.2) + 1500 = 4500.

e.      Money demand = 5000 − 10 000(.3) + 1500 = 3500. In equilibrium, the money supply, which graphs as a vertical line, must also be 3500. See the diagram above.

f.      See the diagram above. When the interest rate is zero, money demand is 7500. When money demand is zero, 10 000r = 7500. r = .75, i.e., 75%.

g.      Excess demand. In fact, we can be precise. Money supply = 3500. Money demand = 5000 − 10 000(.3) + 2500 = 4500. There is an excess demand of 1000.

h.      Money supply = 3500. To restore equilibrium, money demand must be 3500. Money demand = 5000 − 10 000($r$) + 2500 = 3500. $r$ = .40. The equilibrium interest rate is 40%.

i.      $1000. See the answer to part g.

j.      The money multiplier = 1 / reserve ratio = 10. An open market purchase of $100 worth of securities would expand the money supply by $1000.

6.    a.      With smooth spending, Arlene will begin the year with $24 000 and end with zero. Therefore, on average she will have $12 000 money holdings.

     b.      Charlene will begin each quarter with $6000 and end each quarter with zero. On average she will have $3000 money holdings.

     c.      Darlene will begin each month with $2000 and end each month with zero. On average she will have $1000 money holdings.

(These examples illustrate why money holdings might vary with frequency of payment. However, as discussed in the text, money holdings also vary with the interest rate. These women could hold their assets in some form which generates more interest than a chequing account, but this aspect is not considered in this question.)

7.    a.      I.     Volume of transactions has a positive effect on money demand.

     b.      D.    The transactions cost of transferring funds has become less, so withdrawals of money will be more frequent but less sizable.

     c.      D.    As credit cards are used more, cash will be used less.

     d.      D.    Money holdings needed to pay the flow of bills will be reduced as income and bills arrive simultaneously.

     e.      I.     Volume of transactions has a positive effect on money demand. See p. 250.

     f.      I.     There will be more reluctance to hold bonds and less reluctance to hold money.

     g.      I.     This is a transactions cost.

8.    The Bank wants the money supply to contract, so an open market sale of securities is called for. The money multiplier = 1 / reserve ratio = 5. An open market sale of $12 million would reduce the money supply by $60 million.

9.    vertical; interest rate; economic activity; greater; fall; excess supply of; decrease; buying; lower; less; rise; excess demand for; increase; selling; higher.

10.  See the solutions below.

a.  The Bank sale reduces the money supply; the rising output level will increase money demand. The two changes will drive the interest rate higher.

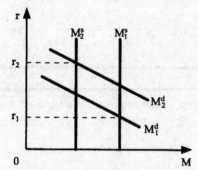

b.  Money demand will decrease during the recession. Together with the increase in the money supply, the changes will lower the interest rate.

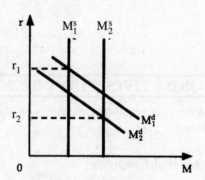

c.  During a deep recession, money demand will shift left (decrease). This will decrease the interest rate. The Bank must reduce the money supply to hold the interest rate constant.

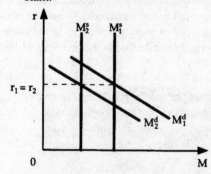

d.  A rise in nominal GDP will increase the demand for money. An increase in the Bank rate will decrease the money supply. Together, the changes will increase the interest rate.

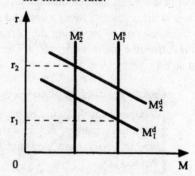

e.  The open market purchase of securities will increase the money supply. The $50 bank charge will either encourage individuals to use cash more or to keep more funds in their (M1) chequing accounts. The effect on the interest rate is ambiguous. It is drawn here as if the two effects on interest rates cancel each other out exactly.

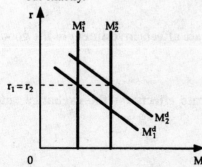

f.  The downturn in the economy will decrease the demand for money; the new caution in lending will increase excess reserves, decrease the money multiplier, and reduce the money supply. The effect on the interest rate is ambiguous. Again, it is drawn here as if the effects on interest rates cancel each other out.

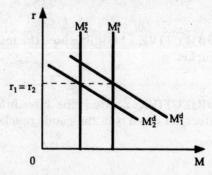

# 13 Money, the Interest Rate, and Output: Analysis and Policy

## OBJECTIVES: POINT BY POINT

After completing this chapter, you should be able to accomplish the objectives listed below.

### General Comment

There's not much in this chapter that is new—it combines material that has been built up independently. The best study tip is to review your notes before beginning this material. If you lose track of the discussion, refer to the earlier chapters.

The most common mistake is *not* recognizing how the goods and money markets influence each other. Think of it this way: If the demand for goods and services is to be met, then output in the goods market must match demand, and this affects the dollar volume of transactions in the economy. Money demand must adjust to this circumstance. The money market must respond by matching the demand and supply of money. Changes in the money market affect the interest rate which impacts on investment decisions in the goods market. And so on.

> **TIP:** The *Answers and Solutions* section in this guide offers more detail and carefully traces the relationships between the goods market and money market. Think of the "Answers" as additional practice—be sure to verify each step and to verify *why* each incorrect option is incorrect.

> **TIP:** The text is beginning to incorporate some "economic shorthand." It's very useful for you in note-taking, it shows the logical sequence of events, and it summarizes all the steps neatly. For some extra practice, work through each case in the textbook's Figure 13-6.

**Caution!** It is easy to forget that an economic notation like "—>" represents underlying behavioural relationships that you must understand (rather than just memorize). Take the time to think about each step in these very condensed sequences.

**OBJECTIVE 1: Outline how the interest rate affects investment in the goods market.**

**OBJECTIVE 2: Describe how interest rate effects on the exchange rate affect net exports in the goods market.**

## OBJECTIVE 3: Explain how aggregate output (income) affects the interest rate in the money market.

There are two links between the goods market and the money market.

a. Goods market to money market link: Money demand is affected by the price level and the level of real output. A change in the interest rate changes the quantity of money demanded. If planned expenditure increases (decreases) in the goods market, the demand for money will increase (decrease), pushing up (down) the equilibrium interest rate leading in turn to an appreciation (depreciation) of the Canadian dollar. Because the demand for money depends on the level of economic activity, equilibrium in the money market depends on circumstances in the goods market. (page 274)

b. Money market to goods market link: If the interest rate rises, planned investment falls—higher borrowing costs make fewer investment projects profitable—and equilibrium output level falls. An appreciated Canadian dollar encourages imports and discourages exports, reducing net exports. Because the level of planned aggregate expenditure (which includes planned investment and net exports) depends on the interest rate, equilibrium in the goods market depends on circumstances in the money market. (page 274)

There must be a unique combination of output level and interest rate that will give simultaneous equilibrium in both markets.

> **TIP:** There are two main points to note here. First, the two markets are interlinked—the movement to equilibrium in one affects equilibrium in the other. Second, it's a two-way street—changes in the goods market affect the money market, and changes in the money market affect the goods market.

**Comment:** The text says that there is only one unique combination of r and Y that will equilibrate both markets simultaneously. Don't get this wrong! It doesn't mean that the economy can be in equilibrium only if the interest rate is 8% and output is $1025 billion, for example. As "given" variables—G, T, or $M^s$ for example—change, so will the specific r and Y values that will ensure equilibrium.

> **TIP:** Follow through the *feedback effects* between the two markets, and you will see that neither the AE nor the money demand curve will settle down to its final equilibrium immediately. As each one adjusts, so the other will adjust a little more. Eventually, they will reach final equilibrium. The diagrams have been drawn to depict the final equilibrium.

## Practice

1. The equilibrium interest rate is determined in the _____ market and the equilibrium output level is determined in the _____ market.
   A. goods, goods.
   B. goods, money.
   C. money, goods.
   D. money, money.

   **ANSWER:** C. See p. 273. In this chapter, we discover that the two markets do not operate in isolation.

2.  Which of the following statements is false? *Ceteris paribus*,
    A.  an increase in income will reduce the equilibrium interest rate.
    B.  an increase in the interest rate will reduce planned investment.
    C.  a decrease in money supply will decrease equilibrium output.
    D.  when the economy slips into a recession, the interest rate will decrease.

    **ANSWER:** A.  An increase in income will increase the demand for money, and this will increase the equilibrium interest rate.

3.  When the interest rate decreases, the cost of financing investments _____ and _____ investments projects will be undertaken.
    A.  increases, more.
    B.  increases, fewer.
    C.  decreases, more.
    D.  decreases, fewer.

    **ANSWER:** C.  Lower interest rates mean lower borrowing costs for firms. As costs decrease, more projects become viable. See p. 275.

4.  A decrease in the interest rate will cause
    A.  the money supply curve to shift left.
    B.  the money supply curve to shift right.
    C.  the planned aggregate expenditure curve to shift up.
    D.  the planned aggregate expenditure curve to shift down.

    **ANSWER:** C.  A decrease in the interest rate will stimulate investment. As investment rises, the AE curve will shift up.

5.  Which of the following statements is true? *Ceteris paribus*,
    A.  r (up) —> Y (up) —> I (up) and EX – IM (up) —> AE (up).
    B.  r (up) —> Y (down) —> I (down) and EX – IM (down) —> AE (down).
    C.  r (up) —> AE (down) —> Y (down) —> I (down) and EX – IM (down).
    D.  r (up) —> I (down) and EX – IM (down) —> AE (down) —> Y (down).

    **ANSWER:** D.  See p. 275.

6.  Which of the following statements is true? *Ceteris paribus*,
    A.  Y (up) —> $M^s$ (up) —> r (up).
    B.  Y (up) —> $M^s$ (down) —> r (up).
    C.  Y (up) —> $M^d$ (up) —> r (up).
    D.  Y (up) —> $M^d$ (down) —> r (up).

    **ANSWER:** C.  See p. 278.

# OBJECTIVE 4: Distinguish between fiscal and monetary policy and expansionary and contractionary policy.

Expansionary (contractionary) policy is intended to expand (reduce) the equilibrium output level. Expansionary fiscal policy manipulates the economy through increases in the level of government spending and decreases in net taxes—contractionary fiscal policy reverses these changes. Expansionary monetary policy manipulates the economy through increases in the money supply. Tools of expansionary monetary policy include open market purchases and transfers of government deposits to private banks.        (page 279)

## Practice

7.    The main goal of an expansionary fiscal policy is to _____; the main goal of an expansionary monetary policy is to _____.
A.    increase output, increase output.
B.    increase output, decrease the interest rate.
C.    decrease the interest rate, increase output.
D.    decrease the interest rate, decrease the interest rate.

**ANSWER:  A.**   Any expansionary policy is designed to make the economy grow. As a stepping-stone to achieving this goal, the interest rate may be decreased.

8.    A decrease in net taxes intended to change output in a particular direction is best described as a(n)
A.    expansionary fiscal policy.
B.    contractionary fiscal policy.
C.    expansionary monetary policy.
D.    contractionary monetary policy.

**ANSWER:  A.**   A reduction in taxes will increase disposable income, consumption, and spending.

Use the diagram to answer the following question. $AE_1$ is the initial planned expenditure level, $AE_2$ is an intermediate level, and $AE_3$ is the final planned expenditure level. $r_1$ is the initial interest rate.

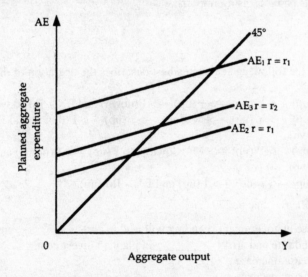

9.    Which policy action would produce the changes seen in the diagram?
A.    An open market purchase.
B.    A decrease in net taxes.
C.    An increase in the Bank rate.
D.    A decrease in government spending.

**ANSWER:  D.**   Cutting government spending will cut AE, given the interest rate. As output falls, money demand will fall, the interest rate will decrease, and investment spending will increase. Option C is also a contractionary policy, but the interest rate would increase as the economy moved from $AE_1$ to $AE_2$. (The increase in the Bank rate may lead to a reduction in the money supply.) In the diagram it is shown as being constant.

## OBJECTIVE 5: Describe crowding out.

Expansionary fiscal policy, while raising expenditures, also raises money demand and the interest rate—and the higher interest rate (the cost of borrowing funds) *discourages* planned investment. The policy *crowds out* planned investment spending. The more sensitive investment plans are to changes in the interest rate, the greater the crowding out. The presence of the crowding-out effect reduces the potency of fiscal policy and the size of the government spending multiplier. The Bank of Canada can restore the potency of fiscal policy by increasing the money supply to prevent the interest rate increase.      (page 280)

> **TIP:** Notice an interesting point with the crowding-out effect—it occurs whether it's government spending or some other variable that's boosting the interest rate. If consumption were suddenly to increase, the extra aggregate expenditure would increase money demand and the interest rate, and investment would be reduced. In the real world, the crowding-out effect reduces not only the government spending multiplier, but the other expenditure multipliers too, even the balanced-budget multiplier.

> **Tip:** For simplicity the text emphasizes crowding out of planned investment spending. But it also notes net exports may be crowded out if higher interest rates lead to exchange rate appreciation, cutting exports and increasing imports.

## Practice

10.   Which of the following statements best describes the operation of the crowding-out effect?
   A.   G (up) —> Y (up) —> r (up) —> I (down) and EX – IM (down).
   B.   G (up) —> Y (up) —> $M^d$ (up) —> r (up) —> I (down) and EX – IM (down).
   C.   G (up) —> Y (up) —> $M^d$ (down) —> r (up) —> I (down) and EX – IM (down).
   D.   G (up) —> r (up) —> I (up) and EX – IM (up).

**ANSWER:** B.   See p. 279.

11.   An increase in government spending will lead to a(n) _____ in planned aggregate expenditure and a(n) _____ in planned investment.
   A.   increase, increase.
   B.   increase, decrease.
   C.   decrease, increase.
   D.   decrease, decrease.

**ANSWER:** B.   The government spending increase crowds out investment spending because of a higher interest rate, but, despite this, the expansionary fiscal policy will still cause planned expenditure to increase.

12.   The crowding-out effect depends on all of the following except
   A.   the interest sensitivity of investment.
   B.   how much money demand increases as spending increases.
   C.   the slope of the planned investment schedule.
   D.   how much the money supply decreases as spending increases.

**ANSWER:** D.   Money supply doesn't decrease as spending increases. Note that Options A and C are saying the same thing.

13. An open market sale of securities will be more _____, the _____ the interest sensitivity of investment.
    A. expansionary, greater.
    B. expansionary, less.
    C. contractionary, greater.
    D. contractionary, less.

    **ANSWER:** C. An open market sale is a contractionary policy that will increase the interest rate. The effect on planned investment (and aggregate expenditure) will be greater the more interest-sensitive investors are.

14. The more sensitive investment demand is to the interest rate, the _____ effective fiscal policy is and the _____ effective monetary policy is.
    A. more, more.
    B. more, less.
    C. less, more.
    D. less, less.

    **ANSWER:** C. If investment is very sensitive to interest-rate changes, fiscal policy effectiveness is reduced because of the crowding-out effect. Monetary policy, whose influence on spending is through changes in the interest rate, is made more powerful.

Use the following diagrams to answer the next question.

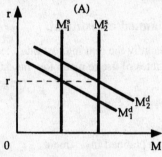

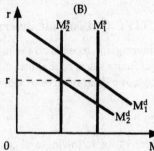

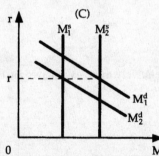

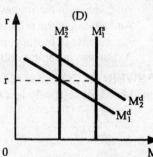

15. An expansionary policy mix which causes no change in interest rates is best depicted in money market diagram
    A. A.
    B. B.
    C. C.
    D. D.

    **ANSWER:** A. An expansionary fiscal policy increases money demand, and an expansionary monetary policy increases money supply to prevent an interest rate increase. See p. 283.

16. The government is running a deficit. A new balanced-budget requirement is passed that will take effect next year. This change will make the AE curve shift _____. To maintain the same level of output next year, the central bank should adopt a(n) _____ monetary policy.
    A. up, expansionary.
    B. up, contractionary.
    C. down, expansionary.
    D. down, contractionary.

**ANSWER: C.** To balance the budget, either G must decrease or T must increase—a contractionary fiscal policy. To counteract this, the central bank will have to adopt an expansionary policy.

17. Arboc is in a deep recession, with 35% of its capital not being used. A(n) _____ _____ policy is most likely to be effective in increasing output.
    A. expansionary fiscal.
    B. expansionary monetary.
    C. contractionary fiscal.
    D. contractionary monetary.

**ANSWER: A.** This economy needs an expansionary policy. Investment, with such high underutilization of capital, is unlikely to be responsive to interest rate reductions—the crowding-out effect will be slight. Also, if investment is not responsive to interest rate changes, monetary policy is unlikely to have much effect.

## OBJECTIVE 6: List four determinants of planned investment.

Planned investment depends on the interest rate (especially the real interest rate), expectations about future sales, capital utilization rates (low rates of usage mean low investment), and the cost of capital relative to labour. (page 285)

## Practice

18. Which of the following will cause an increase in planned investment?
    A. An increase in the interest rate.
    B. An increase in the relative cost of labour.
    C. An increase in business pessimism.
    D. A decrease in capital utilization rates.

**ANSWER: B.** If the cost of labour becomes relatively more expensive, the cost of capital becomes relatively less expensive.

## PRACTICE TEST

### I. MULTIPLE CHOICE QUESTIONS. Select the option that provides the single best answer.

_____ 1. In each of the following cases we would expect the interest rate to decrease, except when
    A. there is an open market purchase.
    B. the government increases tax collections.
    C. government spending is increased.
    D. there is a reduction in the level of economic activity.

_____ 2. The feedback effect between the goods market and money market is best illustrated by the situation when, for example,
   A. contractionary monetary policy leads to a reduction in the money supply.
   B. consumption suddenly rises, causing a fall in investment due to a rising interest rate.
   C. contractionary fiscal policy leads to a reduction in the money supply.
   D. the value of the money multiplier is reduced due to an increasing reserve ratio.

_____ 3. If the Bank of Canada simultaneously lowered the Bank rate and sold government securities, which one of the following would not be a possible consequence?
   A. An increase in money supply and an increase in money demand.
   B. An increase in money supply and a decrease in money demand.
   C. A decrease in money supply and a decrease in money demand.
   D. A rise in the interest rate.
   (Be careful on this one!)

_____ 4. Which of the following would not accompany a fall in the Bank rate?
   A. An expansion in the money supply.
   B. A rise in planned investment.
   C. An unplanned rise in inventories.
   D. An increase in aggregate output (income).

_____ 5. The money and goods markets are in equilibrium. Now there is an expansion in the money supply. This will _____ investment and cause the demand for money to _____.
   A. reduce, increase.
   B. stimulate, increase.
   C. stimulate, decrease.
   D. reduce, decrease.

_____ 6. An increase in planned aggregate expenditure will make the interest rate _____ while an increase in the money supply will make planned expenditure _____.
   A. increase, increase.
   B. increase, decrease.
   C. decrease, increase.
   D. decrease, decrease.

_____ 7. An increase in money supply will result in _____ output and a _____ interest rate.
   A. higher, lower.
   B. higher, higher.
   C. lower, lower.
   D. lower, higher.

_____ 8. MPC is .8. Which of the following might achieve the goal of increasing output by $200 billion? Assume that some crowding out occurs.
   A. An increase in government spending of $40 billion.
   B. A decrease in taxes of $50 billion.
   C. An increase in government spending of $50 billion.
   D. An increase in government spending and in taxes, each of $50 billion.

_____ 9. An open market purchase of securities by the Bank of Canada will cause
A. the interest rate to fall.
B. a decrease in the quantity of money demanded.
C. a shortage of money at the original equilibrium interest rate.
D. the AE curve to shift down (to the right).

_____ 10. A simultaneous increase in net taxes and an open market sale of securities by the Bank of Canada will _____ equilibrium output and _____ the interest rate.
A. increase, decrease.
B. decrease, have an indeterminate effect on.
C. decrease, increase.
D. have an indeterminate effect on, increase.

_____ 11. Planned investment certainly will increase when the interest rate _____ and the cost of labour _____ (relative to the cost of capital).
A. increases, increases.
B. increases, decreases.
C. decreases, increases.
D. decreases, decreases.

_____ 12. Which of the following statements is false? _Ceteris paribus,_
A. the lower the level of aggregate output, the lower the interest rate.
B. when the interest rate falls, planned aggregate expenditure increases.
C. as real output increases, money demand increases.
D. as money demand increases, real output increases.

_____ 13. An open market sale of government securities is a(n) _____ monetary policy. The AE curve will shift _____.
A. expansionary, up.
B. expansionary, down.
C. contractionary, up.
D. contractionary, down.

_____ 14. The intended goal of an expansionary policy
A. is an increase in the level of aggregate output.
B. is an increase in the interest rate.
C. is a decrease in the interest rate.
D. depends on whether a fiscal policy or a monetary policy is used.

Use the diagram to answer the following question. $AE_1$ is the initial planned expenditure level, $AE_2$ is an intermediate level, and $AE_3$ is the final planned expenditure level. $r_1$ is the initial interest rate.

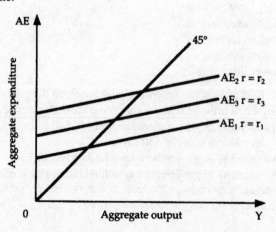

_____ 15. Which policy action would produce the changes seen in the diagram?
  A.  An open market purchase.
  B.  A decrease in net taxes.
  C.  An increase in the reserve ratio.
  D.  An increase in government spending.

_____ 16. An increase in government spending will cause a decrease in planned investment, most directly as a result of an increase in
  A.  aggregate output.
  B.  the interest rate.
  C.  the money supply.
  D.  the price level.

_____ 17. Which circumstances will not strengthen the crowding-out effect?
  A.  A higher interest-sensitivity of investment.
  B.  A higher money demand as spending increases.
  C.  A steeper slope of the AE curve.
  D.  A greater money multiplier.

_____ 18. Which of the following statements best describes an expansionary monetary policy?
  A.  $M^s$ (up) —> r (up) —> I (down), EX – IM (down) —> Y (up).
  B.  $M^s$ (up) —> r (down) —> I (down), EX – IM (down) —> Y (down).
  C.  $M^s$ (up) —> r (down) —> I (up), EX – IM (down) —> Y (up).
  D.  $M^s$ (up) —> r (down) —> I (up), EX – IM (up) —> Y (up).

_____ 19. In the presence of a crowding-out effect, a contractionary fiscal policy will result in a _____ in output than if there were no crowding-out effect.
  A.  larger increase.
  B.  smaller increase.
  C.  larger decrease.
  D.  smaller decrease.

_____ 20. There is a negative relationship between planned investment and the interest rate described by the equation $I = 120 - 10r$. Planned investment will decrease by moving along the curve if
  A.  the Bank of Canada buys bonds in the open market.
  B.  the government increases welfare payments.
  C.  entrepreneurs expect sales to decline in the future.
  D.  the government cuts back in government spending.

_____ 21. If the Bank of Canada buys bonds in the open market at the same time as the government increases government spending, the crowding-out effect will be _____. The _____ interest-sensitive planned investment is, the smaller the crowding-out effect will be.
  A.  heightened, more.
  B.  heightened, less.
  C.  diminished, more.
  D.  diminished, less.

## II.  APPLICATION QUESTIONS

1.  A businesswoman hires you as an economic consultant to assist her in her investment decisions.
  a.  The government has announced a reduction in income taxes and an increase in welfare benefits. Interpret these policy actions.

      i.   Are they expansionary or contractionary?

      ii.  How will they affect the interest rate?

      iii. Importantly, how will they affect planned business investment?

b.    Ignore the policy actions in part a. The Bank of Canada announces an immediate increase in its sales of bonds on the open market and a decrease in the Bank rate. Interpret these policy actions.

      i.   Are they expansionary or contractionary?

      ii.  How will they affect the interest rate?

      iii. Importantly, how will they affect planned business investment?

c.    Ignore the policy actions in parts a and b. The government initiates an aggressive program of highway construction and inner-city development, effective immediately. Simultaneously, the Bank of Canada announces an immediate increase in its purchases of bonds on the open market. Interpret these policy actions.

      i.   Are they expansionary or contractionary?

      ii.  Is the Bank of Canada action accommodating? Why?

      iii. How will the policy actions affect the interest rate?

      iv. Importantly, how will they affect planned business investment?

      v.   Her business sells to the consumer sector. What other factor(s) ought she to include in determining her investment plans?

2.    The Arbocali Minister of Finance (a confirmed believer in the multiplier) notes that the marginal propensity to consume out of income is .8. Because Arboc is presently in a recession, he predicts that a 5-million-opek increase in government spending will boost output by 25 million opeks. Although a quite junior official in the Ministry, you believe that he is incorrect. Indicate as many assumptions as you can that he has made to arrive at his prediction.

3.    Farview, an economic forecasting firm, has hired you as a promising addition to the staff. Your assignment is to predict the effect of a given economic change on a number of variables, where "+" represents increase, "–" represents decrease, "0" represents no change, and "?" represents an ambiguous result. Assume that there are progressive federal income taxes and that the initial change in a variable is the dominant one.

a.    The Bank of Canada purchases bonds in the open market. Predict the effect on:

| Y | R | C | S | I | $M^s$ | $M^d$ | Federal Deficit |
|---|---|---|---|---|---|---|---|
| ___ | ___ | ___ | ___ | ___ | ___ | ___ | ___ |

b.    The government cuts personal income taxes. Predict the effect on:

| Y | R | C | S | I | $M^s$ | $M^d$ | Federal Deficit |
|---|---|---|---|---|---|---|---|
| ___ | ___ | ___ | ___ | ___ | ___ | ___ | ___ |

c.    The capital utilization rate is 70% and firms believe that it should be 85%. Predict the effect on:

| Y | R | C | S | I | $M^s$ | $M^d$ | Federal Deficit |
|---|---|---|---|---|---|---|---|
| ___ | ___ | ___ | ___ | ___ | ___ | ___ | ___ |

d. There is heightened expectation of an interest rate decrease. Predict the effect on:

| Y | R | C | S | I | $M^s$ | $M^d$ | Federal Deficit |
|---|---|---|---|---|-------|-------|-----------------|
| ___ | ___ | ___ | ___ | ___ | ___ | ___ | ___ |

4. Determine the effect of each policy and other actions on the following five given variables. Label it (I) if the variable will increase, (D) if it will decrease, (U) if it will remain unchanged, and (?) if the result is ambiguous.

| Policy | r | Y | $M^s$ | $M^d$ | I |
|--------|---|---|-------|-------|---|
| Increase $M^s$ | | | | | |
| Increase T | | | | | |
| Increase G | | | | | |
| An increase in optimism by entrepreneurs | | | | | |

5. Refer to the following diagram to answer this question.

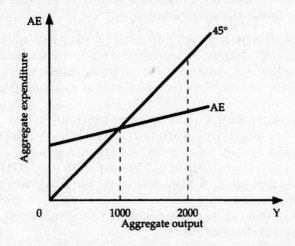

MPC is .8 and the full-employment level of production is 2000. The diagram is not to scale.

a. Draw the money market in equilibrium. Label the curves $M_1^d$ and $M_1^s$.

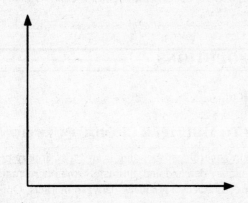

b. Using the *simple* goods market model, by how much would government spending have to change to move the economy to the full-employment equilibrium? Increase/decrease by _____. The government spending multiplier is _____.

c. Similarly, by how much would the tax level have to change to move the economy to full-employment equilibrium? Increase/decrease by _____. The tax multiplier is _____.

d. Similarly, by how much would government spending and tax levels have to increase (balanced-budget change) to move the economy to full-employment equilibrium? Increase by _____. The balanced-budget multiplier is _____.

*Suppose we adopt the balanced-budget policy from part d.*

e. How much will the AE function shift vertically? Increase/decrease by _____. Show this on the diagram as AE′.

f. Unplanned inventory levels will _____ and output will _____.

g. Show the changes that occur in the money market. Label any new curves clearly.

h. Depict the new AE curve as AE″ on the diagram. What has caused the change you've drawn?

i. Is the balanced-budget multiplier still equal to the value given in (d) above?

j. Suppose the Bank of Canada acts to prevent the crowding out. Amend your money market picture accordingly.

6. The text provides several examples of "economic shorthand" while tracing through the effects of given changes. Without referring back to the text, test your knowledge by indicating how each variable will change in the examples below. Write "U" if the variable goes up and "D" if the variable does down as a consequence of the previous step.

a. Expansionary fiscal policy involving a $100 change in G.
$G$ (U/D) —> $Y$ (U/D) —> $M^d$ (U/D) —> $r$ (U/D) —> $I$ (U/D) —> $Y$ (U/D)

b. Expansionary fiscal policy involving a $100 change in T.
$T$ (U/D) —> $Y$ (U/D) —> $M^d$ (U/D) —> $r$ (U/D) —> $I$ (U/D) —> $Y$ (U/D)

c. Will the total change in Y be greater in (a) than in (b)? Why or why not?

d. Expansionary monetary policy:
Begin by selecting the correct option for each monetary policy tool.
Open market sale/purchase:                                    }
Bank rate increase/ decrease:                                 } $M^s$ (U/D)
Transfers of government deposits to/from the private banks:    }
—> $r$ (U/D) —> $I$ (U/D) —> $Y$ (U/D) —> $M^d$ (U/D) —> $r$ (U/D)

e. The effects go in the opposite direction for contractionary policies.

## ANSWERS AND SOLUTIONS

## PRACTICE TEST

## I.   SOLUTIONS TO MULTIPLE CHOICE QUESTIONS

1. C. The increase in government spending is an expansionary policy. Expansionary policies increase money demand and, ultimately, the interest rate.

2. B. Option B correctly traces a feedback between markets. Options A and D are confined to the money market only. Option C is just wrong—the money supply is affected only by monetary policy variables.

3.	B.	Lowering the Bank rate is an expansionary monetary policy; selling securities is a contractionary monetary policy. The net effect on the money supply, therefore, is uncertain. If the money supply increases, the interest rate decreases, and the economy expands. This will increase money demand (Option A). If the money supply decreases, the interest rate increases (Option D), and the economy contracts. This will decrease money demand (Option C).

4.	C.	The Bank rate reduction is an expansionary policy, causing the money supply to increase (Option A) and the interest rate to decrease. An interest rate decrease will stimulate investment (Option B) and aggregate output (Option D). As spending increases, there will be an unplanned decrease in inventory levels.

5.	B.	The increase in the money supply will decrease the interest rate and stimulate investment. Planned aggregate expenditure will increase, prompting an increased transaction demand for money.

6.	A.	If planned aggregate expenditure increases, the demand for money will increase, as will the interest rate. An expansion in the money supply, which pushes down the interest rate, will stimulate investment and, therefore, planned aggregate expenditure.

7.	A.	This expansionary monetary policy will reduce the interest rate and raise output.

8.	C.	If MPC is .8, the expenditure multiplier is 5, and the tax multiplier is –4. (Check Chapter 10 if you can't verify these values.) As noted on p. 279, the feedback effect from the money market reduces the size of these multipliers. Options A and B will fall short of $200 billion. The balanced budget action (Option D) has a maximum increase of $50 billion. Option C may be overkill (we can't tell), but it has the possibility of hitting the $200 billion target.

9.	A.	An open market purchase will increase the money supply, causing an excess supply at the original interest rate (not Option C) and making the interest rate decrease (Option A). The interest rate decrease will increase the quantity of money demanded (not Option B). This interest rate decrease will stimulate investment and planned aggregate expenditure (not Option D). As planned expenditure increases, there will be an increased transaction demand for money.

10.	B.	An increase in net taxes is a contractionary policy and a sale of securities is also a contractionary policy. Equilibrium output will decrease. The sale of securities will decrease the money supply, forcing up the interest rate. However, the contraction in output will reduce the transaction demand for money. A decrease in the demand for money will pull down the interest rate. The effect on the interest rate is ambiguous.

11.	C.	As the interest rate decreases, the cost of new investments decreases and their profitability increases. As the cost of labour increases, employers will use less labour-intensive and more capital-intensive methods of production.

12.	D.	As real output level increases, more money is demanded to finance the increased volume of transactions (Option C). However, as money demand increases, the interest rate rises, and this depresses investment and real output (so Option D is false). As output decreases, money demand and the interest rate decrease (Option A). Decreases in the interest rate stimulate investment and expenditure (Option B).

13.	D.	An open market sale reduces the money supply, increases the interest rate, discourages investment, and pushes down the AE curve.

14.	A.	All expansionary policies are intended to expand equilibrium output.

15.	A.	An open market purchase will reduce the interest rate (from $r_1$ to $r_2$) and stimulate planned aggregate expenditure through higher investment. As spending increases, money demand increases, pushing up the interest rate (to $r_3$). Planned expenditure will decrease. Options B and D would result in the same shifts in the AE curve, but $r_2$ would be the same as $r_1$.

16. B. An increase in government spending will increase aggregate output (Option A), but the most direct reason for the "crowding out" of investment is the interest rate increase. See p. 281.

17. D. The size of the money multiplier is irrelevant. As government spending increases, the steeper the AE curve, the greater the initial expansion in spending. Given the spending increase, the more money demand increases, the more the interest rate will increase. The more sensitive entrepreneurs are to interest-rate increases, the greater the decrease in investment.

18. D. See p. 281. The higher money supply reduces the interest rate, which stimulates planned investment, increasing spending and output.

19. D. The crowding-out effect reduces fiscal policy effectiveness. See p. 279.

20. B. A movement along the curve is caused by a change in the interest rate. If the interest rate increases, investment will decrease. Option A indicates an increase in the money supply and, therefore, a decrease in the interest rate. Option C would shift the curve. Option D is a contractionary policy, reducing income. Option B will expand spending, increasing the demand for money and the interest rate.

21. D. If the Bank of Canada increases the money supply, the interest rate will decrease. If the government increases government spending, money demand will increase and the interest rate will increase. The effects counteract each other, leading to a lesser crowding-out effect. Given the interest rate change, the impact on planned investment will be lower the less influenced entrepreneurs are by the interest rate.

## II. SOLUTIONS TO APPLICATION QUESTIONS

1. a. Both actions will stimulate private sector spending—they are similar to an increase in government spending. As the economy expands, money demand will increase, causing an increase in the interest rate. A higher interest rate will reduce planned investment.

   b. The first action is contractionary, while the second is expansionary. The effect on the interest rate is uncertain; therefore the effect on planned investment is uncertain.

   c. Both actions are expansionary. The Bank of Canada action is accommodating—the spending initiative will drive up interest rates while the Bank of Canada action will reduce them. The effect on the interest rate is uncertain; therefore the effect on planned investment is uncertain. As these policies are expansionary, you should predict higher levels of consumer spending. Even if the interest rate is unchanged, her planned investment might rise in expectation of increased sales, higher capital utilization rates, and more optimism about the future.

2. He has assumed that:

   i. the marginal propensity to consume will remain constant as the economy expands;

   ii. the bond-financed expansion in government spending will not provoke an increase in interest rates;

   iii. aggregate supply is horizontal, i.e., that, as aggregate demand increases, no price level increases will occur. (This is discussed in Chapter 14.)

3. a. If the Bank of Canada purchases bonds in the open market, the money supply will increase and the interest rate will decrease. Investment will be stimulated, and aggregate output will increase. Consumption and saving will rise. Higher spending will provoke a higher money demand (which will partially offset the

interest rate decrease). A higher level of activity will increase tax collections, reducing the federal deficit.

| Y | R | C | S | I | M$^s$ | M$^d$ | Federal Deficit |
|---|---|---|---|---|---|---|---|
| + | − | + | + | + | + | + | − |

    b.    If the government cuts personal income taxes, consumption and saving will increase, and aggregate output will rise. Higher spending will increase the demand for money and push up the interest rate, which causes an offsetting decrease in the demand for money. As spending increases, tax collections will rise again somewhat.

| Y | R | C | S | I | M$^s$ | M$^d$ | Federal Deficit |
|---|---|---|---|---|---|---|---|
| + | + | + | + | − | 0 | + and − | + |

    c.    If the capital utilization rate is too low, firms will reduce investment. As investment falls, output will decrease. Consumption, saving, and tax collections will fall. The deficit will increase. There is no effect on money supply, but money demand will be reduced. This will result in an offsetting decrease in the interest rate and a partially offsetting increase in investment.

| Y | R | C | S | I | M$^s$ | M$^d$ | Federal Deficit |
|---|---|---|---|---|---|---|---|
| − | − | − | − | − | 0 | − and + | + |

    d.    A heightened expectation of an interest rate decrease implies a heightened expectation of a bond price increase. Asset holders will reduce the demand for money and increase the demand for bonds. As there is no change in the money supply, the interest rate will decrease. A decrease in the interest rate will stimulate additional planned investment and raise aggregate output. As output (income) increases, consumption and saving will rise, as will tax collections. The increase in expenditures will cause a partially offsetting increase in money demand and in the interest rate.

| Y | R | C | S | I | M$^s$ | M$^d$ | Federal Deficit |
|---|---|---|---|---|---|---|---|
| + | − | + | + | + | 0 | − and + | − |

4.    See the table below.

| Policy | r | Y | M$^s$ | M$^d$ | I |
|---|---|---|---|---|---|
| Increase M$^s$ | D | I | I | I | I |
| Increase T | D | D | U | D and I | I* |
| Increase G | I | I | U | I and D | D |
| An increase in optimism by entrepreneurs | I | I | U | I and D | I |

Examples:

*An increase in net taxes* is a contractionary fiscal policy. Output (Y) will decrease because consumers' disposable income is reduced. As output decreases, money demand will decrease. Because there is no monetary policy change, the money supply is unchanged and the interest rate is decreased, causing an increase in money demand to offset the initial decrease. As the interest rate decreases, planned investment is increased.

\* Note the unusual result on investment in this model when net taxes are increased.

*An increase in optimism* will stimulate planned investment, which will lead spending (and output) to increase. As spending increases, money demand increases and, given the unchanged money supply, the interest rate will increase. This will limit the increase in planned investment.

5.  a.  See the money market diagram below (also for 5g and 5i).

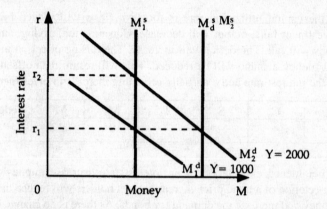

   b.  MPC is .8, therefore the government expenditure multiplier is 5. To move the economy to the full-employment output level, government spending would have to increase by 200.

   c.  MPC is .8; therefore the tax multiplier is –4. To move the economy to the full-employment output level, taxes would have to decrease by 250.

   d.  The balanced-budget multiplier is 1. Increase G and T by 1000.

   e.  AE will increase by 200. See the diagram below.

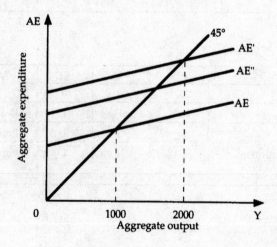

f. Inventory levels will fall and output will rise.

g. See the money market diagram above, notably the shift in $M^d$ to $M^d_2$.

h. See the goods market diagram above. Investment, part of AE, has been driven down somewhat (presumably not by as much as 200!) because of the higher interest rate which has discouraged some investment projects.

i. No. The investment fall has reduced the power of the balanced budget multiplier. (You would get the same sort of result if you had used a straight increase in G or reduction in T.)

j. See the money market diagram in part a above, notably the shift in $M^s$ to $M^s_2$, which lowers r to its original value.

6. a. $G\ (U) \longrightarrow Y\ (U) \longrightarrow M^d\ (U) \longrightarrow r\ (U) \longrightarrow I\ (D) \longrightarrow Y\ (D)$

b. $T\ (D) \longrightarrow Y\ (U) \longrightarrow M^d\ (U) \longrightarrow r\ (U) \longrightarrow I\ (D) \longrightarrow Y\ (D)$

c. The change will be greater in (a) because the government-spending multiplier is greater than the tax multiplier.

d. Open market purchase:                            }

Bank rate decrease:                                  } $M^s\ (U)$

Transfers of government deposits to the private banks:   }

$\longrightarrow r\ (D) \longrightarrow I\ (U) \longrightarrow Y\ (U) \longrightarrow M^d\ (U) \longrightarrow r\ (U).$

# 14 Aggregate Demand, Aggregate Supply, and Inflation

## OBJECTIVES: POINT BY POINT

After completing this chapter, you should be able to accomplish the objectives listed below.

### OBJECTIVE 1: Define aggregate demand curve. Explain why it slopes downward.

If the overall price level is allowed to increase, it will raise the interest rate through the increase in the demand for money. Higher interest rates will reduce planned investment spending and will also lead to an appreciated Canadian dollar, cutting net exports. Because planned investment spending and net exports are components of output, equilibrium output falls. There is a negative relationship between the price level and the level of aggregate demand. The *aggregate demand* (AD) curve depicts the negative relationship between the price level and aggregate output. Each point on the curve is a point of equilibrium in both the money market and the goods market. (page 291)

> **TIP:** AS/AD analysis is a powerful, but simple, tool. Remember that the AD curve is *not* a market demand curve in any sense. It relates equilibrium *aggregate* output (income) to the *overall* price level.

> **Graphing Pointer:** When you shift the aggregate demand curve, it is easier to think of the curve as moving right or left, rather than up or down. Ask yourself, if you hold the price level constant, how the equilibrium level of aggregate output will respond to changes in the policy variables (G, T, M$^s$) or changes in the determinants of consumption and planned investment.

**Nominal vs. Real Values:** When the price level changes, the distinction between real and nominal values takes on some importance. Nominal variables are affected by price level changes; real variables are not. Aggregate output (Y) on the horizontal axis of the aggregate demand/aggregate supply diagram is *real* output.

## Practice

1.  The level of aggregate output demanded decreases as the price level increases because
    A.  higher prices make the interest rate fall.
    B.  as prices increase, producers will sell more output.
    C.  some goods become relatively more expensive.
    D.  the demand for money increases, making the interest rate increase.

    **ANSWER: D.**  A higher price level means that more money will be demanded, forcing up the interest rate (the cost of borrowing).

2.  The best description of the operation of the real wealth effect is that as the price level increases,
    A.  the interest rate decreases, making interest earnings decrease. This makes consumption decrease.
    B.  the interest rate increases. This makes the cost of investment increase and results in a decrease in planned investment.
    C.  profitability increases, encouraging investors to increase planned investment.
    D.  the purchasing power of household assets decreases, discouraging consumption.

    **ANSWER: D.**  See p. 293.

3.  When the price level decreases, the resulting _____ in the interest rate will _____ investment.
    A.  increase, increase.
    B.  increase, decrease.
    C.  decrease, increase.
    D.  decrease, decrease.

    **ANSWER: C.**  Lower interest rates mean lower borrowing costs for firms.

## OBJECTIVE 2: Identify how the aggregate demand curve shifts as monetary and fiscal policy changes.

The AD curve will shift to the right (increase) if there is an increase in government spending or in the money supply, or a decrease in net taxes.          (page 294)

> **TIP:** Anything that would increase aggregate output (income) in the Keynes cross model of Chapters 9 and 10 will shift the aggregate demand curve to the right.

## Practice

4.  A cut in government spending will cause a(n) _____ in aggregate demand, and an increase in the money supply will cause a(n) _____ in aggregate demand.
    A.  increase, increase.
    B.  increase, decrease.
    C.  decrease, increase.
    D.  decrease, decrease.

    **ANSWER: C.**  At each price level, a decrease in government spending shifts the AE curve downward—AD will decrease. An increase in the money supply lowers the interest rate—AD will increase.

Refer to the following diagram to answer the next question.

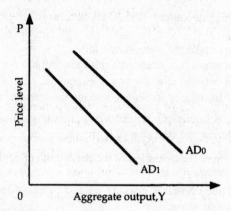

5. The aggregate demand curve would shift from $AD_0$ to $AD_1$ if
   A. the government increased welfare payments.
   B. the Bank of Canada sells government securities.
   C. the government cut taxes.
   D. the demand for money decreased.

   **ANSWER: B.** A decrease in aggregate demand could be caused by a contractionary monetary policy.

6. The Arbocali Finance Ministry increases both government spending and net taxes by one million opeks. Aggregate demand will
   A. shift to the right.
   B. shift to the left.
   C. remain unchanged, but the price level will increase.
   D. remain unchanged, but the price level will decrease.

   **ANSWER: A.** This is a balanced-budget expansionary policy. At the given price level, AE and, therefore AD, will increase.

## OBJECTIVE 3: Define short-run aggregate supply curve. Explain why it slopes upward and what factors will shift it.

The *aggregate supply* (AS) curve shows how the aggregate output supplied by the economy's productive sector responds to changes in the price level.

In the short run, as prices rise (but input prices do not or rise by less), producers increase output. The *short-run AS curve* grows steeper at higher output levels because, as the economy approaches full employment, the additional cost incurred in producing more output increases more rapidly. Eventually, when the economy reaches its full productive capacity, the short-run AS curve becomes vertical.                                                                 (page 296)

> **Graphing Pointer:** Get into the habit now of drawing the short-run AS curve as a curve rather than as a straight line. The economics of the situation requires this and your ability to analyze the effects of policy actions depends upon it.

The short-run AS curve can shift if there are changes in any of the factors affecting the supply decisions of individual firms. These factors include "cost shocks" (such as an increase in energy prices), economic growth or stagnation, shifts in public policy, and natural events, such as weather. (page 298)

## Practice

7.  The aggregate supply curve plots the relationship between
    A.  the overall price level and wages—as wages increase, prices increase.
    B.  output and supply. As supply increases, more output is available.
    C.  the overall price level and the aggregate quantity of output supplied.
    D.  equilibrium output and the rate of inflation.

    **ANSWER:** C.  See p. 295.

8.  If the economy is in a deep recession, a modest increase in aggregate demand is likely to cause _____ in price and _____ in output level.
    A.  an increase, an increase.
    B.  an increase, little or no increase.
    C.  little or no change, an increase.
    D.  little or no change, little or no increase.

    **ANSWER:** C.  When the economy is in a recession, the short-run AS curve may be horizontal. An increase in demand will increase output with little or no increase in price level. See p. 297.

9.  The economy is operating at full capacity. The short-run AS curve is _____. An increase in the price level will _____ output.
    A.  horizontal, increase.
    B.  horizontal, not change.
    C.  vertical, increase.
    D.  vertical, not change.

    **ANSWER:** D.  The short-run AS curve is vertical at full capacity—additional price inducement can stimulate no further production. See p. 297.

10. The short-run aggregate supply curve tends to be flat when there is _____ unemployment and _____capacity.
    A.  high; excess.
    B.  high; a shortage of.
    C.  low; excess.
    D.  low; a shortage of.

    **ANSWER:** A.  See p. 297.

11. For the short-run aggregate supply curve to have a positive slope
    A.  changes in the overall price level must be fully anticipated.
    B.  input price changes must be fully anticipated.
    C.  changes in the overall price level must lag behind input price changes.
    D.  input price changes must lag behind changes in the overall price level.

    **ANSWER:** D.  See p. 296.

12. The aggregate supply curve will be positively sloped in each of the following cases except when input prices change _____ output price changes.
    A. at the same rate as.
    B. more slowly than.
    C. in the opposite direction to.
    D. not at all in response to.

    **ANSWER:** A. See p. 296. If input prices change at the same rate as output prices, the changes neutralize each other—relatively, inputs become neither more nor less expensive.

13. Short-run aggregate supply would increase in each of the following cases except
    A. an increase in the female labour-participation rate.
    B. the imposition of an energy tax.
    C. an increase in the stock of capital.
    D. an improvement in the health and nutrition of the labour force.

    **ANSWER:** B. An energy tax would raise production costs.

14. The effect of an increase in the proportion of Canadian workers who negotiate automatic cost-of-living adjustments (COLAs) in their wage contracts would be to make the short-run aggregate supply curve
    A. vertical.
    B. horizontal.
    C. steeper.
    D. flatter.

    **ANSWER:** C. The more rapidly input costs can respond to price changes, the less the impact of a price change on output. See p. 296.

Refer to the following diagram to answer the next question.

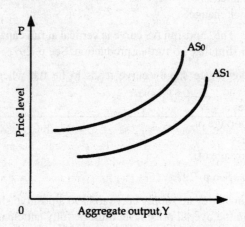

15. Which of the following would shift the short-run aggregate supply curve from $AS_0$ to $AS_1$?
    A. A fall in the number of migrant workers from other countries.
    B. An increase in income taxes.
    C. An increase in welfare benefits.
    D. A loosening of the restrictions on child labour.

    **ANSWER:** D. For AS to shift right (an increase in supply), either more resources must be made available or existing resources must become more productive.

**OBJECTIVE 4:** Explain the distinction between the short-run aggregate supply and long-run aggregate supply curve and the implications for macroeconomic policy.

**OBJECTIVE 5:** Outline the short-run and long-run effects on output and the price level of an expansionary or contractionary monetary or fiscal policy.

Absolute maximum capacity for the economy is the point where the short-run aggregate supply curve becomes vertical. However it is doubtful that such a high level of output, with every factory working full-out and so many workers working overtime, can be sustained. Instead we define *potential output* as the output level that can be sustained in the long run with no inflation.

Suppose output initially equals potential output but then the aggregate demand curve shifts outward, so that it intersects the short-run aggregate supply curve at a point where output exceeds potential output. It is assumed that at this higher level of output, labour and other input markets will be tight and the result will be cost increases. Such cost increases shift the short-run aggregate supply curve up until potential output is restored. (See Figure 14.10 in text.) Similarly if from the initial position the aggregate demand curve shifts downward, it is assumed there will be input cost decreases and downward shifts of the short-run aggregate supply curve until potential output is restored. (See Figure 14.11 in text). Hence regardless of the price level, in the long run, output will always be at potential output. On the aggregate demand/aggregate supply diagram we draw a vertical line upward from potential output and call it the long-run aggregate supply curve.

> **TIP:** The short-run aggregate supply curve is not vertical because in the short run, when the price level increases, not all input prices increase by the same amount, so it is profitable for firms to expand beyond potential output. On the long-run aggregate supply curve, all prices and input prices fully adjust and increase by the same amount: It is not profitable for firms to change their output level.

The main implication for policy is that in the long run the economy will always return to potential output. Expansionary monetary and fiscal policy will increase output and the price level in the short run, but in the long run potential output will be restored and the only result will be an increase in the price level. Contractionary monetary and fiscal policy will decrease output and the price level in the short run, but in the long run potential output will be restored and the only result will be a decrease in the price level. A major argument among economists is how long the long run is. Some economists think adjustment to the long-run position is rapid and hence using expansionary or contractionary policy to speed adjustment makes little sense. Other economists argue that, particularly when the economy is in a slump, adjustment to potential output is too slow and expansionary policy is necessary.

> **TIP:** It is simplest to think of potential output as being consistent with zero inflation. However, one can use the model to consider the case in which there is a steady level of inflation to which the economy has adjusted. In this case potential output is thought of as consistent with constant inflation: If output exceeds potential output, inflation will *increase* over this steady level and if output is less than potential output, inflation will *decrease*. Similarly, rather than thinking of potential output as a constant, we can think of it as something that increases over time because of increases in resources and technology. The aggregate demand/ aggregate supply model can then be interpreted as describing situations where it grows faster than usual or more slowly than usual.

Comment: The answer to many economic questions is "it depends." A policy that might be the correct one in one circumstance (for example, a recession) might be the wrong one in another. The multipliers of Chapters 9 and 10 were derived assuming a fixed price level. In the aggregate demand/aggregate supply model, the price level can change. Hence the multiplier varies depending upon whether the economy is in a slump (in which the expansionary effect may be largely on output with little effect on prices) or in a boom (in which case any expansionary effect will likely be dissipated by increasing inflation with little effect on output).

> **Graphing Pointer:** Remember that, graphically, long-run equilibrium is shown by the intersection of three curves (AD, SRAS, LRAS). See the diagram for Questions 19–21. If you shift AD or SRAS and end up at points A, B, C, or D, those points only represent short-run equilibrium. In the long run, additional adjustments will have to be made.

## Practice

16.  Currently, output is substantially less than potential output. Now the Bank of Canada buys securities. In the short run we would expect
     A.  an unanticipated decrease in business inventories.
     B.  an increase in the interest rate because the demand for money has decreased.
     C.  a decrease in planned investment because securities are scarcer.
     D.  a decrease in production as inflation erodes spending power.

     **ANSWER:** A.  The Bank of Canada action is an expansionary policy. Check Chapter 11 if you missed this point. Interest rates fall, planned investment increases, aggregate expenditure and aggregate demand increase, and inventories unexpectedly decrease.

17.  An expansionary fiscal policy is most effective when aggregate demand is _____ initially and when the Bank of Canada simultaneously _____ the money supply.
     A.  high, increases.
     B.  high, decreases.
     C.  low, increases.
     D.  low, decreases.

     **ANSWER:** C.  The flatter the short-run AS curve, the smaller the increase in price level that will be caused by the fiscal policy (and the smaller reductions in consumption and investment). A simultaneous increase in the money supply would help to keep interest rates low, to prevent the crowding out of investment. (Such a monetary policy is called "accommodating.")

18. Suppose the economy is initially at potential output and the MPC is .8. In the long run, the most accurate value for the government spending multiplier is _____, and for the tax multiplier the most accurate value is _____.
   A.   5, –4.
   B.   more than 5, less than –4.
   C.   less than 5, more than –4.
   D.   zero, zero.

   **ANSWER: D.** In the long run, output will return to potential output and hence fiscal policy actions will have no long-run effect on output. See p. 306.

Use the following diagram to answer the next three questions. The economy is initially at point E.

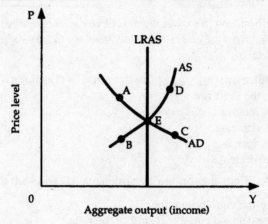

19. In the short run, an increase in energy prices would move the economy to a point such as _____.
   A.   A.
   B.   B.
   C.   C.
   D.   D.

   **ANSWER: A.** An increase in energy prices is a "cost shock" that will shift the short-run AS curve to the left. See p. 298.

20. In the short run, an increase in net taxes would move the economy to a point such as

   _____.
   A.   A.
   B.   B.
   C.   C.
   D.   D.

   **ANSWER: B.** This is a contractionary fiscal policy. Aggregate demand would decrease.

21. In the long run, an increase in the money supply initially would make aggregate demand _____ and later cause the short-run aggregate supply to _____.
   A.   increase, increase.
   B.   increase, decrease.
   C.   decrease, increase.
   D.   decrease, decrease.

   **ANSWER: B.** A money supply increase is an expansionary monetary policy, designed to shift the aggregate demand curve (to a new equilibrium such as point D). Aggregate supply will then shift left, and continue to shift until potential GDP is restored. See p. 302.

22. In the long run, an increase in the money supply would make aggregate supply shift left because
    A. eventually, all the additional money would be spent.
    B. eventually, input prices would increase because the economy would be working beyond its capacity in the short run.
    C. interest rates would decrease, discouraging investment in factories and infrastructure.
    D. higher prices discourage consumers, and producers cut production when there is a lack of customers.

    **ANSWER:** B. With high demand, the economy has been pushed past the potential level of output. There is an upward pressure on costs, which causes the short-run AS curve to shift left.

Use the following information to answer the next three questions. Arbez is in long-run (and short-run) equilibrium. Now the central bank increases the money supply. Simultaneously, the government cuts taxes.

23. We would predict a(n) _____ in the price level and a(n) _____ in the output level in the short run.
    A. increase, increase.
    B. increase, decrease.
    C. decrease, increase.
    D. decrease, decrease.

    **ANSWER:** A. Both changes are expansionary. AD will shift to the right.

24. To restore long-run equilibrium, the
    A. aggregate demand curve will shift to the right.
    B. aggregate demand curve will shift to the left.
    C. short-run aggregate supply curve will shift to the right.
    D. short-run aggregate supply curve will shift to the left.

    **ANSWER:** D. See p. 302.

25. Relative to the initial situation, we would predict a(n) _____ in the price level and _____ in the output level in the long run.
    A. increase, an increase.
    B. increase, no change.
    C. decrease, an increase.
    D. decrease, no change.

    **ANSWER:** B. The long-run aggregate supply is vertical. Therefore, although the price level will change, the initial equilibrium output level will be restored.

## OBJECTIVE 6: Distinguish demand-pull and cost-push inflation. Explain why sustained inflation is believed to be a purely monetary phenomenon.

Inflation, a rise in the overall price level, may be caused by a shift to the right in aggregate demand (*demand-pull inflation*) or by a shift to the left in aggregate supply (*cost-push inflation*). Cost-push inflation results in higher prices and lower production—*stagflation*. Inflation may be fuelled by inflationary expectations. If higher prices are expected, suppliers may continue to raise prices even if demand is not increasing. Sustained inflation cannot occur unless the Bank of Canada releases additional money into the economy to keep moving the AD curve upwards—long-run inflation is a monetary phenomenon. (page 307)

## Practice

26. Demand-pull inflation occurs when the aggregate _____ curve shifts _____.
    A. demand, right.
    B. demand, left.
    C. supply, right.
    D. supply, left.

    **ANSWER:** A. An increase in demand will increase the price level. See p. 307.

27. If the government undertakes an expansionary fiscal policy, the result will be _____ in the long run than in the short run, and it will be _____ if the Bank of Canada increases the money supply.
    A. more inflationary, more inflationary.
    B. more inflationary, less inflationary.
    C. less inflationary, more inflationary.
    D. less inflationary, less inflationary.

    **ANSWER:** A. In the long run, output doesn't change—all demand increases result in higher prices.

28. Which statement is false? An expansionary fiscal policy will be more inflationary
    A. in the long run than in the short run.
    B. if monetary policy is also expansionary.
    C. in the short run, if the short-run aggregate supply curve simultaneously shifts to the right.
    D. the closer the economy is to full employment.

    **ANSWER:** C. If the short-run AS curve shifts to the right, the increase in production will absorb some of the increased demand with less of a price-level increase.

29. If there is an increase in inflationary expectations by firms that causes them to raise their prices, then we would expect the aggregate
    A. demand curve to shift right.
    B. demand curve to shift left.
    C. supply curve to shift right.
    D. supply curve to shift left.

    **ANSWER:** D. At each output level, firms will require higher prices than before. See p. 308.

30. In the mainly agricultural economy of Arbez there has been an extremely poor harvest because of heavy rains. The central bank initiates an open market purchase of securities. As a result of the policy, we would expect to see the output level _____ and the price level _____.
    A. decrease more than otherwise, increase more than otherwise.
    B. decrease more than otherwise, increase less than otherwise.
    C. decrease less than otherwise, increase more than otherwise.
    D. decrease less than otherwise, increase less than otherwise.

    **ANSWER:** C. Aggregate supply is decreasing, reducing output and raising the price level (stagflation). The policy increases aggregate demand. This will stimulate output somewhat by increasing the price level still further.

## PRACTICE TEST

**I.    MULTIPLE CHOICE QUESTIONS.** Select the option that provides the single best answer.

_____ 1.    One inflation-fighting policy is to shift AD to the _____ by _____.
  A.    right, increasing net taxes.
  B.    left, decreasing net taxes.
  C.    right, increasing government purchases.
  D.    left, decreasing government purchases.

_____ 2.    Each of the following will make the AD curve shift to the right except
  A.    a tax cut.
  B.    an open market sale of securities by the Bank of Canada.
  C.    a decrease in the reserve ratio.
  D.    an increase in government spending.

_____ 3.    *Ceteris paribus,* an increase in the price level will cause
  A.    the interest rate to fall.
  B.    an increase in the quantity of money supplied.
  C.    an excess demand for money at the original equilibrium interest rate.
  D.    the aggregate demand curve to shift to the left.

_____ 4.    Government spending increases and the price of raw materials falls. In an economy initially below potential output, we would predict that, in the short run,
  A.    prices would rise and output would fall.
  B.    prices would fall and output would rise.
  C.    prices would rise but the effect on output would be uncertain.
  D.    the effect on prices would be uncertain but output would increase.

_____ 5.    The Federal government abolishes all production subsidies to corporations. At the same time it cuts taxes so that there are no net effects on aggregate demand. In the short run, this will cause the price level to _____ and output to _____.
  A.    increase, increase.
  B.    increase, decrease.
  C.    decrease, increase.
  D.    decrease, decrease.

_____ 6.    An increase in the price level will certainly cause the AE curve to shift _____ as the interest rate _____.
  A.    upward, increases.
  B.    upward, decreases.
  C.    downward, increases.
  D.    downward, decreases.

_____ 7.    During an expansionary fiscal policy action, the interest rate _____; during an expansionary monetary policy action, the interest rate _____.
  A.    increases, increases.
  B.    increases, decreases.
  C.    decreases, increases.
  D.    decreases, decreases.

_____ 8. An increase in government spending will cause
   A. the aggregate demand curve to shift to the right.
   B. the money demand curve to shift to the left.
   C. the AE curve to shift downward.
   D. planned investment to increase.

_____ 9. The _____ curve will shift to the _____ if the Bank of Canada
   buys securities.
   A. AD, right.
   B. AD, left.
   C. AS, right.
   D. AS, left.

_____ 10. A decrease in the price level will _____ money demand and
   _____ the interest rate.
   A. increase, increase.
   B. increase, decrease.
   C. decrease, increase.
   D. decrease, decrease.

Use the following money market diagram to answer the next two questions.

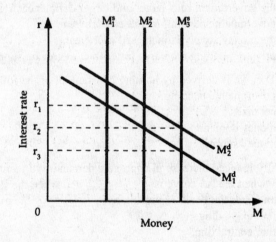

_____ 11. The government undertakes an expansionary fiscal policy such as a(n)
   _____. The Bank of Canada can prevent this from affecting interest
   rates by, for example, _____.
   A. increase in net taxes, buying securities.
   B. increase in net taxes, selling securities.
   C. decrease in net taxes, buying securities.
   D. decrease in net taxes, selling securities.

_____ 12. Given the policies described in the previous question, which of the follow-
   ing outcomes is possible? Money demand moves from _____ and
   money supply moves from _____.
   A. $M_1^d$ to $M_2^d$, $M_1^s$ to $M_2^s$.
   B. $M_1^d$ to $M_2^d$, $M_2^s$ to $M_1^s$.
   C. $M_2^d$ to $M_1^d$, $M_3^s$ to $M_2^s$.
   D. $M_2^d$ to $M_1^d$, $M_2^s$ to $M_3^s$.

_____ 13. The short-run aggregate supply curve is not vertical because
A. input prices are fixed.
B. output prices are fixed.
C. input prices respond fully to changes in the overall price level.
D. input prices do not respond fully to changes in the overall price level.

_____ 14. In the short run, the aggregate supply curve would shift inward in each of the following cases except
A. a decrease in the labour force participation rate.
B. a deterioration in the nation's infrastructure.
C. an increase in emigration.
D. a decrease in the tax rate on production.

_____ 15. The economy is currently at the potential output level. An increase in government spending will result in a _____ in planned investment spending and/or a _____ in net exports.
A. increase; increase.
B. increase; reduction.
C. reduction; reduction.
D. reduction; increase.

_____ 16. Ultimately, inflation can be sustained from year to year only if
A. the government runs larger and larger deficits each year.
B. government spending increases each year.
C. the money supply is increased each year.
D. private spending increases faster than aggregate supply.

_____ 17. The AD curve is derived by holding constant all of the following except
A. government spending.
B. net taxes.
C. money demand.
D. money supply

_____ 18. A fiscally-induced increase in aggregate demand will increase prices most sharply when the AS curve is _____ and when the Bank of Canada accommodates the fiscal expansion by _____ the money supply.
A. flat, expanding.
B. flat, contracting.
C. steep, expanding.
D. steep, contracting.

_____ 19. Suppose potential output is consistent with a "natural" rate of unemployment of 6%. The present unemployment rate is 5%. As time passes, in this model we would expect the
A. long-run aggregate supply curve to shift to the right.
B. long-run aggregate supply curve to shift to the left.
C. short-run aggregate supply curve to shift to the right.
D. short-run aggregate supply curve to shift to the left.

Use the following diagram to answer the next three questions. The economy is in initial long-run equilibrium at point A.

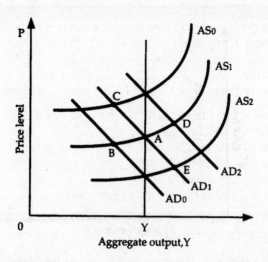

0       Y

**Aggregate output,Y**

_____ 20. Demand-pull inflation is best represented by the move from
        A.    A to B.
        B.    A to C.
        C.    A to D.
        D.    A to E.

_____ 21. The price of oil increases. Initially, this will shift the aggregate
        A.    demand curve to $AD_0$.
        B.    demand curve to $AD_2$.
        C.    supply curve to $AS_0$.
        D.    supply curve to $AS_2$.

_____ 22. The price of oil increases. The government initiates a contractionary fiscal
policy to offset the inflationary effects of the rising energy prices. This will
shift the aggregate demand curve to
        A.    $AD_0$ and intensify the decline in output.
        B.    $AD_0$ and offset the decline in output.
        C.    $AD_2$ and intensify the decline in output.
        D.    $AD_2$ and offset the decline in output.

_____ 23. The price of oil has increased. The government has initiated a contractionary fiscal policy to offset the inflationary effects of the rising energy
prices. Given that information, the long-run equilibrium will be restored by
        A.    aggregate demand curve shifting to the right.
        B.    aggregate demand curve shifting to the left.
        C.    short-run aggregate supply curve shifting to the right.
        D.    short-run aggregate supply curve shifting to the left.

## II.    APPLICATION QUESTIONS

1.    The Arbocali economy is initially in long-run equilibrium.
      a.    Draw the aggregate demand curve ($AD_0$), short-run aggregate supply curve
          ($AS_0$), and the long-run aggregate supply curve (LRAS). Label equilibrium
          output and overall price level $Y_0$ and $P_0$, respectively.

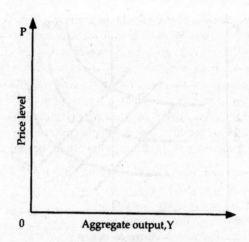

b. There is a slump in consumer confidence and consumption level falls. Show how the diagram will change. Subscript any new curves "1."

c. Now the government decreases taxes by an amount equal to the initial decrease in consumption. What will happen to aggregate demand, output, and the price level? Is there an inflationary gap?

d. Aggregate demand will not shift far enough to the right to restore full employment. Why?

e. Because the tax cut did not achieve full employment, the government hikes spending by an amount equal to the initial decrease in consumption. Show any curve shifts on the diagram and subscript any new curves "2." How will output and the overall price level change? Show these new levels, with "2" subscripts.

The following diagram shows the money market in original equilibrium (before the slump in consumer confidence). The central bank is committed to maintaining the interest rate at 6%.

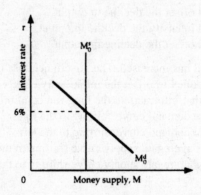

f. Given the changes in parts a through e above, show how the money market diagram will stand at the end of part e. Subscript any new curves "2." Describe what will happen to the interest rate and to bond prices.

g. Given the central bank's commitment, what policy action should it choose? How might it implement this policy? Show how the money market diagram will stand immediately after the policy action. Subscript any new curves "3."

h. What will happen to the AS/AD diagram? Subscript any new curves "3." How will output and the overall price level change? Show these new levels, with "3" subscripts.

i.   Given the changes in the AS/AD diagram, will there be any further change in the money market diagram? If so, what? Subscript any new curves "4."

j.   Describe the central bank's policy response. Is it inflationary?

k.   If the central bank had undertaken no expansionary monetary policy, (i.e., the money supply curve remained at $M_0^s$), show on the AS/AD diagram where the economy will reach equilibrium in the long run (point B).

l.   Assuming that the central bank makes no further changes to the money supply, (i.e., $M_3^s$ is the final money supply curve), show on the AS/AD diagram where the economy will reach equilibrium in the long run (point C).

2.   For each "event," indicate the specific "result" that will occur.
*Result A*: increase in aggregate demand.
*Result B*: decrease in aggregate demand.
*Result C*: increase in aggregate supply.
*Result D*: decrease in aggregate supply.

| Result | Event |
|--------|-------|
| a. _____ | The government cuts personal income taxes. |
| b. _____ | The price of intermediate goods falls. |
| c. _____ | The interest rate rises. |
| d. _____ | Inflationary expectations of firms increase. |
| e. _____ | New, stringent standards for the construction of residential dwellings are enacted. |
| f. _____ | Employers' payroll taxes are decreased. |

3.   Short-run aggregate supply suddenly shifts to the left.

a.   What might have caused this?

b.   Predict how price and output levels will change.

c.   What name is used to describe this phenomenon?

d.   How might the government respond to this supply-side change?

e.   Describe what will happen to the price level and output level if AS shifts to the left and the government pursues an expansionary fiscal policy.

4.   a.   Draw a goods market diagram and a money market diagram in the space below. Show the equilibrium interest rate ($r_0$) and output level ($Y_0$).

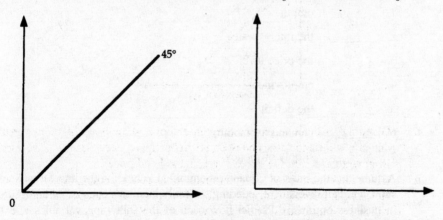

b.   Suppose the price level falls from $P_0$ to $P_1$. Show all the curves that shift.

c. On the diagram below, sketch in the aggregate demand curve. Make your labelling consistent!

d. Explain why the AD curve has a negative slope.
e. Now suppose that the money supply increases. Show how this will affect all the diagrams.

5. In each of the following cases, indicate if the variable will increase (I), decrease (D), or remain unchanged (U).

a. Assume that the Bank of Canada is committed to holding the interest rate constant, and the government undertakes a contractionary fiscal policy (increasing taxes). Predict how each of the following variables will be affected.

1. _____ output

2. _____ the price level

3. _____ employment

4. _____ the deficit (government spending – net taxes)

5. _____ the demand for labour

6. _____ supply of money

b. Assume that the Bank of Canada has no interest rate commitment and the government increases government purchases. Predict how each of the following variables will be affected.

1. _____ output

2. _____ the interest rate

3. _____ the price level

4. _____ employment

5. _____ the deficit

6. _____ demand for labour

7. _____ supply of money

c. Assume that the Bank of Canada is committed to holding the interest rate constant, and that investment spending suddenly increases because of an upsurge in business optimism. Predict how each of the following variables will be affected.

1. _____ planned expenditure (initial change)

2. _____ demand for money (initial change)

3. _____ the interest rate (initial change)

4. _____ the price level

5. _____ the deficit (assuming tax revenues increase with output)

6. _____ demand for labour

7. _____ supply of money

6. Explain what will happen as a result of the following events. In each case, draw an aggregate demand and short-run aggregate supply diagram showing the initial equilibrium output level ($Y_0$) and price level ($P_0$). Show any changes and indicate the final equilibrium output level and price level.

a. The economy is in a recession. Now a reduction in foreign consumption of Canadian products occurs.

b. The economy is operating near potential output. Now very bad weather increases all firms' costs.

_____
_____
_____

c. The economy is in a recession. An increase in government purchases occurs. The Bank of Canada tries to maintain the interest rate.

d. The economy is operating near potential output. An import tax (tariff) is imposed on foreign consumer goods while the Bank of Canada tries to maintain the interest rate.

_____
_____
_____

e. The economy is in a recession. Household confidence about the future is reduced. New information makes firms expect greater inflation in the future.

f. The economy is operating near full capacity. Now there is an increase in the price of oil. The Bank of Canada attempts to maintain the output level.

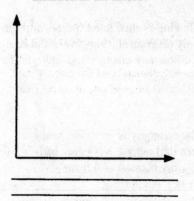

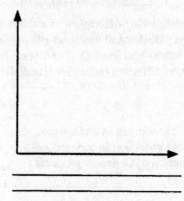

## ANSWERS AND SOLUTIONS

## PRACTICE TEST

### I.    SOLUTIONS TO MULTIPLE CHOICE QUESTIONS

1.    D.   Shifting the AD curve to the left helps to reduce inflation. This may be done by enacting a contractionary policy such as a decrease in government spending or a reduction in the money supply.

2.    B.   An open market sale of securities is a contractionary policy. A decrease in the money supply will increase the interest rate. This, in turn, will reduce planned investment (and net exports through an appreciating exchange rate) and cause a lower equilibrium in the goods market.

3.    C.   As the price level increases, money demand will shift to the right. At the original interest rate, an excess demand will now exist and the interest rate will increase. A change in the price level leads to a movement along the AD curve, not a shift.

4.    D.   The fiscal policy action will increase aggregate demand, which will promote increasing prices and increasing output. The price decrease for raw materials will make the short-run aggregate supply curve shift to the right, prompting a decrease in prices and an increase in output. Together, the changes will certainly raise output, but the effect on the price level is ambiguous.

5.    B.   Removing the subsidies increases production costs—the aggregate supply curve will shift left. As supply contracts, price will increase and output will decrease.

6.    C.   Higher prices reduce consumption and investment because of a higher interest rate and the real wealth effect. Reductions in consumption and investment shift the AE curve downward.

7.    B.   Higher government spending (or lower net taxes) increase(s) aggregate demand and money demand, and therefore, the interest rate. An increased money supply reduces the interest rate.

8.    A.   See p. 294.

9.  A.  If the Bank of Canada buys securities then, *at the same price level*, the money supply will increase, the interest rate will decrease and the exchange rate will depreciate. Planned investment and net exports will increase, shifting the AD curve to the right.

10. D.  One of the factors affecting money demand is the price level. This is one step in explaining why the AD curve slopes down. See p. 290.

11. C.  Cutting taxes is an expansionary policy. It will push up the interest rate. To prevent this, the Bank of Canada must expand the money supply, for example by buying securities.

12. A.  An expansionary fiscal policy will cause money demand and the interest rate to increase. If the Bank of Canada acts to maintain the interest rate at its original level, it must increase the money supply.

13. D.  See p. 296.

14. D.  The tax rate cut will increase the incentive to produce.

15. C.  The increase in government expenditure will push up interest rates and in turn the exchange rate will appreciate. Planned investment spending and net exports will fall, fully offsetting the increase in government expenditure.

16. C.  To have sustained inflation, the money supply must expand. Option A is only possible, ultimately, if the Bank of Canada creates money to cover the government's debts. See p. 309.

17. C.  When the price level changes, government spending, net taxes, and the money supply need not change. Money demand, however, will, forcing changes in the interest rate and planned investment.

18. C.  A given expansionary fiscal policy will be augmented if the Bank of Canada expands the money supply. The closer to capacity the economy is (the steeper the AS curve), the more inflationary the result.

19. D.  The production level is higher than the full employment level. To compensate, the short-run aggregate supply curve will shift to the left.

20. C.  The moves from A to B and from A to E represent decreases in the price level. The move from A to C is caused by a shift in the position of the short-run aggregate supply curve.

21. C.  Oil is an input. Production costs rise, affecting the supply side of the economy.

22. A.  A contractionary policy will shift the aggregate demand curve to the left.

23. C.  The economy is in short-run equilibrium below potential GDP. Input prices will fall.

## II.   SOLUTIONS TO APPLICATION QUESTIONS

1.  a.   See the diagram below.

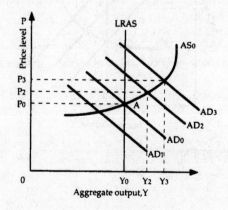

b. See the diagram above. Aggregate demand will shift to $AD_1$.

c. Aggregate demand will increase as consumers' disposable income increases and therefore, output and the overall price level will increase. Output is less than full-employment output; therefore there is no inflationary gap.

d. The tax multiplier is less than the multiplier for consumption.

e. See the diagram above. Aggregate demand will shift to $AD_2$. Recall that the demand curve shift reflects both the government spending increase and the tax cut. Output and overall price level will both increase.

f. Money demand, $M_0^d$, is based on the initial (full-employment) level of expenditures. When the consumption decrease, tax decrease, and government spending increase have taken place, aggregate demand will be at $AD_2$. Money demand will increase to $M_2^d$. The interest rate will rise; bond prices will fall. Check Chapter 12 if you're unsure about this.

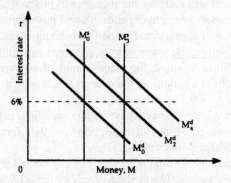

g. The Bank should increase the money supply by buying bonds, decreasing the Bank rate, or transferring government deposits to private banks. Money supply will shift to $M_3^s$. See the diagram above.

h. AD will shift further to the right to $AD_3$. See the diagram above. The price level will increase.

i. Higher expenditures will result in higher money demand ($M_4^d$). See the diagram above. The interest rate will increase.

j. If the central bank wishes to maintain its target interest rate of 6%, it will be obliged to increase the money supply once more. Central bank actions are inflationary.

k. See the diagram below.

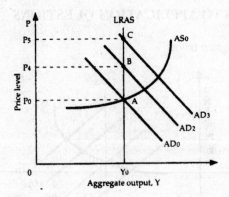

l. See the diagram above.

2.  a.  A      c.  B      e.  D
    b.  C      d.  D      f.  C

Note: Some of these "shocks" may affect both AD and AS curves. The above answers are for the single strongest change.

3.  a.  Many possible factors could be given. Increases in oil prices have been one major factor. Increased government red tape, poor weather, emigration, or war are other factors.

    b.  As the short-run AS curve shifts left, the economy will experience a rising price level and decreasing output.

    c.  Stagflation. See p. 305.

    d.  The traditional response has been to increase demand (through increased government spending, reductions in taxes, or an expansionary monetary policy). A more recent approach, which is discussed in Chapter 19, has been to expand supply (by reducing tax rates to encourage greater work effort).

    e.  The price level will certainly increase, while output might fall, rise, or remain unchanged, depending on the relative strengths of the shifts.

4.  a.  See the diagrams below.

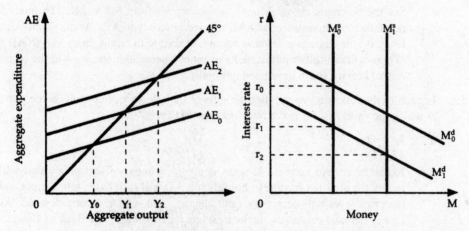

    b.  See the diagrams above. Money demand will shift to the left ($M_1^d$). The interest rate will fall to $r_1$. The interest rate decrease will boost planned investment, and in addition the falling interest rates will lead to a depreciation in the Canadian dollar and a fall in net exports. AE will increase to $AE_1$. Note that this feedback process between the goods and money markets could continue for a while—the money demand curve ($M_1^d$), for instance, is based on an equilibrium income level that changes as planned investment changes.

    c.  See the diagram below. The AD curve is $AD_1$1. At $P_0$, income level was $Y_0$. At the new, lower, price level $P_1$, the level of demand that provides equilibrium in goods and money markets simultaneously is $Y_1$.

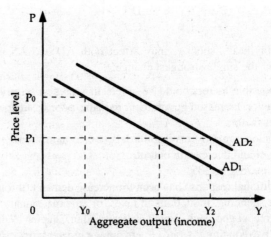

d.  A fall in the price level means that less money will be demanded to purchase planned expenditures. The interest rate will fall from $r_0$ to $r_1$. At a lower interest rate more investment will occur, increasing AE from $AE_0$ to $AE_1$. The real level of output rises in response to a fall in price level.

e.  See the diagrams above. Money supply moves from $M_0^s$ to $M_2^s$. The interest rate falls to $r_2$. Investment and AE will increase, say to $AE_2$. At the given price level, $P_1$, the aggregate demand curve will shift to the right, from $AD_1$ to $AD_2$. (There will be further adjustments as money demand increases—in the interests of brevity, these have been ignored.)

5.  In each of the following cases, the strengths of the effects will depend on the point at which the short-run AS curve intersects the AD curve.

a.  1.  D        2.  D        3.  D
    4.  D        5.  D        6.  D

    Explanation:  An increase in taxes is a contractionary fiscal policy that will reduce the after-tax income of households. AD will shift to the left. Output and the price level will decrease—both changes will reduce money demand. As money demand decreases, the interest rate will decrease. The Bank of Canda's policy will be to reduce the money supply so that the interest rate will be unchanged. Note that this is an additional contractionary policy. As output decreases, the demand for labour by firms will decrease and there will be cyclical unemployment. Government spending has not changed, but taxes have risen, so the deficit will decrease. Note that if we have tax rates and transfer payments in our economy, rising unemployment will make the increase in net taxes somewhat smaller than it would otherwise be.

b.  1.  I        2.  I        3.  I        4.  I
    5.  I        6.  I        7.  U

    Explanation:  An increase in government spending is an expansionary fiscal policy that will make AD shift to the right. Output and the price level will increase—both changes will increase money demand. As money demand increases, the interest rate will increase. The Bank of Canada has no specific policy commitment, so assume the money supply will be unchanged. As output increases, the demand for labour by firms will increase and there will be more employment. Government spending has increased, so the deficit will increase.

c.  1.  I        2.  I        3.  I        4.  I
    5.  D        6.  I        7.  I

Explanation: An increase in optimism will lead to greater planned investment and the AE curve will shift upward. This will make AD shift to the right. Short-run AS (which is based on existing capital) will not shift. Output and the price level will increase—both changes will increase money demand. Initially, as money demand increases, the interest rate will increase. The Bank of Canada's policy will be to increase the money supply so that the interest rate will be unchanged ultimately. Note that this is an additional expansionary policy. As output increases, the demand for labour by firms will increase and there will be more employment. Government spending has not changed, but net taxes will increase, so the deficit will decrease.

6.   Note: Some of these "shocks" may affect both AD and AS curves. The following answers are for the single strongest change.

    a.   The decrease in foreign con-          b.   With the higher costs, the AS
         sumption will shift the AD                  curve will shift to the left, rais-
         curve to the left. In a recession,          ing price and reducing output.
         the fall in price level will be             Stagflation results.
         small; the main contraction will
         be in output.

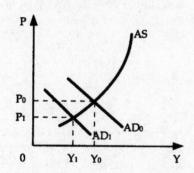          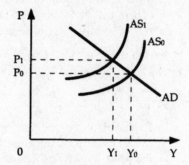

    c.   The increase in government pur-        d.   A tariff makes foreign consumer
         chases will shift AD to the right           goods more expensive—
         and raise the interest rate. The            demand for domestic goods will
         Bank of Canada will have to                 rise, moving AD rightward and
         increase the money supply,                  raising the interest rate. The
         which will increase AD even                 Bank of Canada will expand the
         more. In a recession, the price             money supply, which will
         level increase will be small; the           increase AD even more. The
         main expansion will be in out-              main effect will be to raise the
         put.                                        price level.

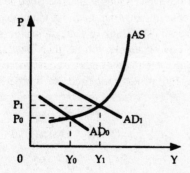          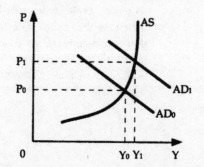

e. Low consumer confidence will cause reduced consumption and a decreasing AD curve. If firms expected greater inflation, AS will shift left. Both effects reduce output; the effect on the price level is ambiguous. Basically, a bad situation has become worse.

f. If oil (which is an input) rises in price, AS will shift to the left. To maintain the output level, the Bank of Canada would have to expand the money supply and shift the AD curve to the right. Both effects are inflationary.

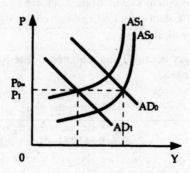

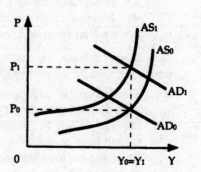

# 15 The Labour Market, Unemployment, and Inflation

## OBJECTIVES: POINT BY POINT

After completing this chapter, you should be able to accomplish the objectives listed below.

### General Comment

The textbook has addressed the issue of unemployment before. This chapter, however, isn't simply a re-run of previous material. Make a list of the theories relevant to unemployment. In most cases, this is new material. Note that the theories are not mutually exclusive.

### OBJECTIVE 1: Explain the classical view of the labour market and its implications for the aggregate supply curve.

Classical economists argued that wages adjust freely to clear the labour market. During economic upswings, workers accept higher wages and, in downturns, accept lower wages. Unemployment shouldn't persist—the wage rate should adjust until equilibrium is restored. Price level changes would cause rapid changes in wages, implying a vertical aggregate supply curve. The classical economists saw little role for active fiscal or monetary policy. Persistent (involuntary) unemployment is not possible in such a model; hence events during the Depression are difficult to interpret with this model.        (page 314)

> **Tip:** Keep in mind that the critical assumption of the classical economists is that wages are perfectly flexible. Keynesians, on the other hand, believe in the presence of "stickiness" in wages.

### Practice

1. _____ unemployment is the type that increases during recessions.
   A. Frictional.
   B. Structural.
   C. Cyclical.
   D. Natural.
   ANSWER: C. Cyclical unemployment varies with the business cycle. See p. 314.

Use the following diagram of the classical labour market to answer the next three questions.

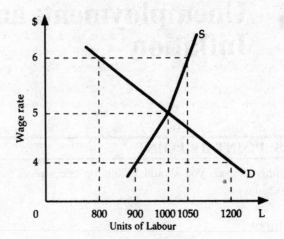

2.  At a wage rate of _____ there is an excess _____ labour of 300.
    A.  $4, demand for.
    B.  $4, supply of.
    C.  $6, demand for.
    D.  $6, supply of.

    **ANSWER:** A.  When the wage rate is low, firms increase quantity demanded and workers reduce quantity supplied. At $4, the excess demand is 300 (1200 – 900).

3.  If workers increase the value that they place on nonmarket activities, then the labour _____ curve will shift to the _____.
    A.  demand, right.
    B.  demand, left.
    C.  supply, right.
    D.  supply, left.

    **ANSWER:** D.  Changes in workers' preferences will affect the labour supply curve. In this case, at each wage rate, less labour would be supplied.

4.  In the diagram above, the equilibrium wage is _____. If workers increase the value that they place on nonmarket activities, then the equilibrium wage will _____.
    A.  $4, increase.
    B.  $5, increase.
    C.  $5, decrease.
    D.  $6, decrease.

    **ANSWER:** B.  Equilibrium occurs at the wage rate where quantity demanded equals quantity supplied. The change in preferences will shift the supply curve to the left.

5.  If the price of goods in the economy decreases, the labour demand curve will shift _____ while the labour supply curve will shift _____.
    A.  left; left.
    B.  left; right.
    C.  right; left.
    D   right; right.

    **ANSWER:** B.  Because the output of workers is worth less, firms will demand fewer workers at each wage rate. But because workers can purchase more with a dollar of wages, the labour supply curve shifts right.

6. The government introduces a "guaranteed living standard" program, a plan whereby all individuals, whether they work or not, receive a cheque equal to twice the poverty line. We would predict that the
A.    labour demand curve will shift right and the wage will increase.
B.    labour demand curve will shift left and the wage will decrease.
C.    labour supply curve will shift right and the wage will decrease.
D.    labour supply surve will shift left and the wage will increase.

**ANSWER:** D.   The opportunity cost of leisure has decreased—fewer people will seek jobs, at least for wages comparable to the government benefit.

7.    In Arboc, most workers have labour contracts that lock in the wage rate for a period of 3 years. In Arbez, however, wages are renegotiated every month. Fiscal policy will have more effect on output in _____; monetary policy will have more effect on output _____.
A.    Arboc, Arboc.
B.    Arboc, Arbez.
C.    Arbez, Arboc.
D.    Arbez, Arbez.

**ANSWER:** A.   Policy actions are most effective when the short-run aggregate supply curve is relatively flat. The more responsive input prices are to changes in economic conditions, the less impact policy actions will have.


# OBJECTIVE 2: Explain how implicit or explicit contracts might prevent labour market clearing.

> **TIP:** To help yourself organize the material in this and the next objective, note that there are four broad explanations of unemployment:
> a.    Sticky wage theories,
> b.    Efficiency wage theories,
> c.    Imperfect information, and
> d.    Minimum wage laws.

Some theories suggest that wages may be "sticky."
a.    The *implicit contract* explanation suggests that workers and employers share an unspoken "understanding" that cutting wages is not one of the rules of the game.                                                              (page 318)
b.    *Explicit contracts* attempt to insulate both workers and employers from short-term changes in the economy. Workers (at least the senior workers who may command the bulk of the workers' bargaining power) may prefer layoffs to wage cuts. Cuts in wages and prices are far more difficult to monitor.
                                                              (page 318)

> **TIP:** One fairly obvious reason why workers and employers sign contracts is so that they can avoid the costs of renegotiation. After all, would you like to haggle over your wage every morning before work?

**Practice**

8.  The _____ explanation is not included among the "sticky wage" theories of unemployment.
    A.  social contract.
    B.  efficiency wage.
    C.  relative-wage.
    D.  explicit contract.

    **ANSWER:** B.  See p. 317.

9.  During a recession, workers in the construction industry are laid off because of an unspoken agreement between employers and workers. This is consistent with the _____ explanation of unemployment.
    A.  social contract.
    B.  efficiency wage.
    C.  relative-wage.
    D.  explicit contract.

    **ANSWER:** A.  See p. 317.

10. During a recession, gold miners in Timmins, Ontario are laid off because gold prices have fallen while their contracted wage is fixed. This is consistent with the _____ explanation of unemployment.
    A.  social contract.
    B.  efficiency wage.
    C.  relative-wage.
    D.  explicit contract.

    **ANSWER:** D.  See p. 318.

## OBJECTIVE 3: Outline efficiency wage theory and the possible effects of a minimum wage law.

The following theories suggest that an above-equilibrium wage may be set. Persistent unemployment is a consequence.

The *efficiency wage theory* argues that worker productivity rises as the wage rate rises. Employers may choose to set the wage rate above the equilibrium to increase morale and productivity, to reduce turnover and retraining, and to establish and retain an experienced pool of workers.                                                        (page 318)

*Minimum wage* legislation may cause unemployment for inexperienced or less productive workers whom it isn't profitable to hire at the minimum wage. But the amount of unemployment such laws cause is probably small.                                        (page 319)

> **Tip:** With the profusion of theories, it's easy to miss the point of this section. The point is that economists are trying to explain why unemployment persists in the real world.

# Practice

11. Marley and Scrooge find that the costs of screening, hiring, and training workers is substantial. To reduce labour turnover, they pay higher-than-average wages. Their behaviour is consistent with the _____ explanation of unemployment.
    A. minimum wage.
    B. efficiency wage.
    C. imperfect information.
    D. cost effectiveness.

    **ANSWER:** B. See p. 318.

12. Refer to the diagram used in question 2 above. If the government imposed a minimum wage of $4,
    A. unemployment would be zero.
    B. unemployment would be 100 (1000 – 900).
    C. unemployment would be 250 (1050 – 800).
    D. unemployment would be 300 (1200 – 900).

    **ANSWER:** A. The equilibrium wage is $5. Setting a minimum wage that is less than $5 will have no impact on the labour market.

## OBJECTIVE 4: Use the aggregate demand/aggregate supply model to explain the Phillips Curve and its shifts.

The AS/AD diagram shows that an increase in aggregate demand leads to higher output (and employment). The unemployment rate would fall and inflation would occur. There would be an apparent trade-off between the unemployment rate and the inflation rate that is reflected in the *Phillips Curve*. In the 1960s, this relationship seemed so stable that many believed that unemployment and inflation were affected by the same single factor—the level of demand. The analysis rested on the fact that the AS curve had been fairly stable. In the 1970s and 1980s, supply-side factors (particularly the price of oil and higher inflationary expectations) became more important and the stable inflation-unemployment relationship collapsed. (page 322)

## Practice

13. Which factors led to the breakdown of the Phillips Curve in the 1970s?
    A. Supply-side policymakers reduced business taxes, which made the aggregate supply curve shift to the left.
    B. Adverse "supply shocks" such as the oil price increase of 1973–1974 made the aggregate supply curve shift to the left.
    C. Government spending resulted in large deficits and high inflation.
    D. The aggregate demand curve shifted to the left following the end of high exports to the U.S. associated with the war in Vietnam.

    **ANSWER:** B. As the AS curve shifted to the left, stagflation (rising inflation and rising unemployment) occurred. Reduced business taxes (Option A) would make the aggregate supply curve shift to the right.

14. If the AS curve is stable, there will be a _____ relationship between the inflation rate and the unemployment rate when the AD curve shifts to the right and a _____ relationship when the AD curve shifts to the left.
    A. positive, positive.
    B. positive, negative.
    C. negative, positive.
    D. negative, negative.

    **ANSWER:** D. Higher (lower) demand increases (decreases) the inflation rate and decreases (increases) the unemployment rate.

15. Evidence from 1970 to 2000 suggests that there is _____ relationship between inflation and unemployment.
    A. no simple.
    B. a weak negative.
    C. a strong negative.
    D. a weak positive.

    **ANSWER:** A. See p. 324.

16. In the 1970s, increasing inflation became a fact of life. Higher expected inflation may have shifted the AS curve to the _____ and shifted the Phillips Curve to the _____.
    A. right, right.
    B. right, left.
    C. left, right.
    D. left, left.

    **ANSWER:** C. As we saw in the previous chapter, the AS curve will shift to the left as firms expect increased inflation. The Phillips Curve will shift right. See p. 326.

17. The Bank of Canada increases the money supply. Assuming no changes in expectations, this policy would result in a(n) _____ in the unemployment rate and a(n) _____ in the inflation rate.
    A. increase, increase.
    B. increase, decrease.
    C. decrease, increase.
    D. decrease, decrease.

    **ANSWER:** C. The policy will shift AD to the right, increasing output and employment which decreases the unemployment rate and increases inflation.

## OBJECTIVE 5: Explain why a vertical long-run Phillips Curve implies a vertical long-run aggregate supply curve and describe the implications for monetary and fiscal policy.

If the long-run AS curve is vertical, then the long-run Phillips Curve is also vertical. Changes in fiscal or monetary policy will have no long-run impact on the output level or unemployment rate. Expansionary fiscal and monetary policies will have no long-run effect except to fuel inflation—in the long run, unemployment will gravitate to the *natural rate of unemployment* and output will remain at the potential GDP level. The *natural rate of unemployment* is the sum of frictional and structural unemployment. (page 326)

## Practice

18. The natural rate of unemployment is the sum of
    A. frictional and cyclical unemployment.
    B. frictional and structural unemployment.
    C. cyclical and structural unemployment.
    D. frictional, cyclical, and structural unemployment.

    **ANSWER:** B.  See p. 327.

19. If the Phillips Curve is vertical in the long run, then an increase in the money supply will _____ the natural unemployment rate and will _____ the inflation rate.
    A. increase, increase.
    B. increase, not change.
    C. not change, increase.
    D. not change, not change.

    **ANSWER:** C.  Fiscal or, in this case, monetary policies will not affect the natural rate of employment or the unemployment rate in the long run. However, as we saw in the previous chapter, persistent increases in the money supply fuel inflation.

20. Currently, the unemployment rate is greater than the natural rate of unemployment. In the long run, the natural rate will be attained if policymakers
    A. increase the money supply.
    B. decrease the money supply.
    C. do nothing.
    D. do any of the above.

    **ANSWER:** D.  This is a trick(y) question! In the long run it doesn't make any difference what policymakers do (or don't do). The natural rate of unemployment will prevail in the long run in any and all circumstances.

## Comment

In this chapter and the previous one you've been given a number of theories concerning the causes of unemployment and inflation. Notice that the list of causes isn't the same for both. Unemployment and inflation aren't opposite sides of the same problem (as the Phillips Curve might suggest), but rather, different problems. If you need proof, think about stagflation, where both problems occur simultaneously. This new view, that the two problems need to be addressed separately, is an important development in the thinking of economists and policymakers.

## PRACTICE TEST

**I.  MULTIPLE CHOICE QUESTIONS.** Select the option that provides the single best answer.

\_\_\_\_\_ 1.  In the classical model, it is always true that there will be full employment (no involuntary unemployment) because
    A. workers will bid wages downward if necessary.
    B. wages are sticky.
    C. employers set wages.
    D. unions and employers have equal bargaining strength.

_____ 2.   The existence of sticky wages suggests that
           A.   workers hold most of the bargaining power in wage negotiations.
           B.   wages will be constant over the business cycle.
           C.   some unemployment is caused by workers' and firms' unwillingness
                to negotiate wage cuts.
           D.   nominal wages are eroded during a period of inflation.

_____ 3.   If firms expect higher prices next quarter, the labour _____ curve
           will shift to the _____.
           A.   supply, right.
           B.   supply, left.
           C.   demand, right.
           D    demand, left.

_____ 4.   Which of the following reasons is given as an explanation for the fact that
           labour markets do not always clear?
           A.   Workers have better price information than employers.
           B.   The total demand for labour has fallen.
           C.   Workers are reluctant to accept a lower wage when they cannot be
                sure of the true financial position of the firm.
           D.   The supply of labour has fallen.

_____ 5.   The explicit contract explanation of sticky wages is based on the assump-
           tion that
           A.   the cost of negotiation is virtually zero.
           B.   firms are not willing to cut wages even when there is a recession.
           C.   search costs are virtually zero.
           D.   it is difficult to write contracts that will accommodate unforeseen
                events.

_____ 6.   Which of the following will lead to an increase in inflation?
           A.   a price hike by foreign oil producers.
           B.   an open market sale of securities by the Bank of Canada.
           C.   a cut in government spending.
           D.   an increase in the demand for money.

Use the following diagram, showing the demand for and supply of teenage labour in the
1980s, to answer the following question.

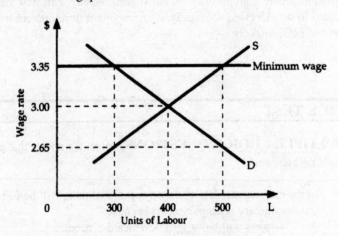

_____ 7. The government has imposed a minimum wage of $3.35 per hour. Unemployment would be
A. 500.
B. 300.
C. 200.
D. 400.

_____ 8. Which of the following is most likely to cause stagflation?
A. Falling prices on imported oil.
B. An increase in the money supply.
C. A decrease in the money supply.
D. Rising prices on imported oil.

_____ 9. The Phillips Curve has broken down since the early 1970s because of all of the following except
A. inflationary expectations became variable.
B. rising import prices became a significant feature of the economy.
C. aggregate demand was more variable than before.
D. the *ceteris paribus* assumptions, under which the analysis was made, were infringed.

_____ 10. The Phillips Curve in the 1960s showed that
A. the inflation rate and the price level were positively related.
B. increases in wages and unemployment were positively related.
C. the unemployment rate and the inflation rate were negatively related.
D. the money supply and the interest rate were negatively related.

_____ 11. When the economy is at the natural rate of unemployment there is
A. no structural unemployment.
B. no frictional unemployment.
C. some cyclical unemployment.
D. some frictional and structural unemployment.

_____ 12. The classical economists' model of the labour market is consistent with a
A. horizontal aggregate demand curve.
B. horizontal aggregate supply curve.
C. vertical aggregate demand curve.
D. vertical aggregate supply curve.

_____ 13. Many economists today believe that the Phillips Curve is _____ in the short run and _____ in the long run.
A. downward-sloping, vertical.
B. vertical, downward-sloping.
C. upward-sloping, vertical.
D. vertical, upward-sloping.

_____ 14. If the AD curve is stable, there will be a _____ relationship between the inflation rate and the unemployment rate when the AS curve shifts to the right, and a _____ relationship when the AS curve shifts to the left.
A. positive, positive.
B. positive, negative.
C. negative, positive.
D. negative, negative.

_____ 15. One of the main factors causing the large shifts to the left of the AS curve in the 1970s was
A. increasing government deficits.
B. substantial increases in the money supply.
C. increases in the price of imported raw materials.
D. aggressive labour union activity during 1973–1977.

Use the following diagram to answer the next five questions. The economy is initially at point E. Point E represents the rate of unemployment that is the natural rate.

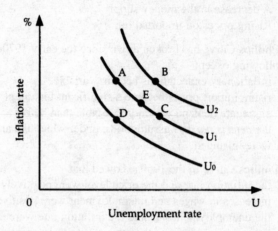

_____ 16. An increase in government spending would move the economy to point
A. A.
B. B.
C. C.
D. D.

_____ 17. A move from point E to point D is most likely to be caused by
A. a decrease in the inflationary expectations of firms.
B. a decrease in the money supply.
C. an increase in the price of imported oil.
D. an adverse supply shock, such as bad harvests.

_____ 18. An increase in the price of imported raw materials would move the economy to point
A. A.
B. B.
C. C.
D. D.

_____ 19. If point E represents the rate of unemployment that is the natural rate, then at point A, actual output _____ potential output, and structural and frictional unemployment rates are _____.
A. exceeds, positive.
B. exceeds, negative.
C. is less than, positive.
D. is less than, negative.

_____ 20. In the long run, the Phillips Curve will pass through
A. points A, E, and C.
B. points D, E, and B.
C. point E only.
D. none of these points because the long-run Phillips Curve is vertical.

## II. APPLICATION QUESTIONS

1.  The small nation of Arboc is at point A on its Phillips Curve. Inflation is expected to be 0%. The natural rate of unemployment is 6.0%.

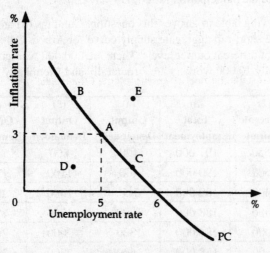

a.  If the natural rate of unemployment is 6% and the expected inflation rate is 0%, what sort of macroeconomic action could have moved the economy to point A?

What will happen to the price level and output in each of the following cases? In each case, will the factor in question affect the inflation rate and unemployment rate as a simple Phillips Curve would predict? Using point A as a reference, how would the economy move in the short run?

b.  A severe hurricane destroys the sugar cane crop, the main agricultural crop in this predominantly rural economy.
c.  The Arbocali government passes a new environmental protection law that requires producers to decrease emissions of atmospheric pollutants.
d.  In anticipation of a war with neighbouring states, the Arbocali government increases its military spending by 50%.
e.  Legislation is passed making it more difficult to unionize and making union activity such as picketting illegal.
f.  Consumer confidence in the economy is undermined because of a change in government.

Now suppose that none of the changes above took place. The economy will not remain at point A in the long run.

g.  Explain why the economy will not remain at point A.
h.  Suppose actual inflation remains at 3%. Explain how the economy will adjust in the long run.
i.  Sketch in the long-run Phillips Curve.

2.  Macrovia has a population of 160 000 citizens. Because of a highly sophisticated computerized job placement program, frictional and structural unemployment runs at a constant 10 000. The nation's labour demand and supply curves are $Q_D = 120 - W$ and $Q_S = 5W$, respectively. Q is the quantity of labour supplied or demanded in thousands of workers, W is the wage in sponduliks, the local currency.

a.  Calculate the equilibrium wage, the level of employment, and the unemployment rate in Macrovia.
b.  Calculate the size of the labour force and the participation rate.

c. The Secretary of Labour is under pressure to introduce a minimum wage. If the minimum wage is set at 22 sponduliks (a 10% increase), calculate the effect on employment, unemployment, the labour force, the unemployment rate, and the participation rate.

3. Use the following table to answer this question. Columns (1) and (2) give information about the short-run aggregate supply curve for Arboc. Column (3) shows total employment at different output levels. There are 200 000 workers in the total labour force. Normally 10 000 workers are structurally and frictionally unemployed.

| (1) Price Level | (2) Aggregate Output | (3) Total Employment | (4) Output Demanded | (5) Output Demanded | (6) Output Demanded | (7) Output Demanded |
|---|---|---|---|---|---|---|
| 4.60 opeks | 2550 | 191 000 | 100 | 800 | 1400 | 2200 |
| 4.50 opeks | 2500 | 190 000 | 400 | 1100 | 1700 | 2500 |
| 4.40 opeks | 2400 | 189 000 | 700 | 1400 | 2000 | 2800 |
| 4.30 opeks | 2300 | 188 000 | 1000 | 1700 | 2300 | 3100 |
| 4.20 opeks | 2000 | 184 000 | 1300 | 2000 | 2600 | 3400 |
| 4.10 opeks | 1600 | 178 000 | 1600 | 2300 | 2900 | 3700 |
| 4.00 opeks | 1000 | 168 000 | 1900 | 2600 | 3200 | 4000 |

a. Based on the behaviour of the aggregate supply curve, potential GDP is _____ and the natural rate of unemployment is _____%.

b. Draw the short-run aggregate supply (SRAS) curve below.

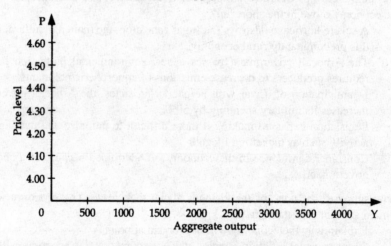

c. Currently, aggregate demand is shown by columns (1) and (4). Graph this AD curve (AD1). The equilibrium price level is _____ and equilibrium output is _____. The unemployment rate is _____%.

d. The central bank, Arbobank, undertakes an expansionary monetary policy, an open market _____ (purchase/sale) of securities. The aggregate demand curve will shift to the _____ (right/left). The new curve is described by columns (1) and (5). Graph this AD curve (AD2). The equilibrium price level is _____ and equilibrium output is _____. Employment has increased by _____. The unemployment rate is _____%. Cyclical unemployment is _____%.

e. If the central bank had undertaken a more expansionary monetary policy, AD would have shifted further, as described by columns (1) and (6). Graph this AD curve (AD3). The equilibrium price level is _____ and equilibrium output is _____. Employment has increased by _____. The unemployment rate is _____%.

f. If the central bank had undertaken a still more expansionary monetary policy, AD would have shifted further, as described by columns (1) and (7). Graph this AD curve (AD4). The equilibrium price level is _____ and equilibrium output is _____. Employment has increased by _____. The unemployment rate is _____%.

4. For each "event" affecting equilibrium, the inflation rate and unemployment rate, indicate the specific "result" that will occur.

*Result A:* inflation increases, unemployment increases.

*Result B:* inflation decreases, unemployment decreases.

*Result C:* inflation decreases, unemployment increases.

*Result D:* inflation increases, unemployment decreases.

| Result | Event |
|---|---|
| a. _____ | The government raises personal income taxes. |
| b. _____ | The price of imported final goods falls. |
| c. _____ | The interest rate rises. |
| d. _____ | The price of imported intermediate goods rises. |
| e. _____ | New, stringent standards for the construction of residential dwellings are enacted. |
| f. _____ | Environmental pollution standards are tightened substantially. |
| g. _____ | A reduction in foreign consumption of Canadian products occurs. |
| h. _____ | Payroll taxes are decreased. |
| i. _____ | The imposition of an import tax (tariff) on foreign consumer goods. |
| j. _____ | An increase in government purchases occurs. |
| k. _____ | There is an increase in the price of foreign oil. |
| l. _____ | Households prefer to save more. |
| m. _____ | An increased demand for new machinery or construction. |
| n. _____ | Inflationary expectations increase. |

5. For each pair of events, work out what will happen to aggregate demand and/or aggregate supply, and then predict the impact on the inflation rate and unemployment rate. Assume that each given change (there are two changes in each case) will affect only aggregate demand or aggregate supply, but not both curves. Note: As you saw in Chapter 4, if both demand and supply curves shift, the effect on at least one variable must be uncertain.

*Result A:* inflation change uncertain, unemployment increases.

*Result B:* inflation change uncertain, unemployment decreases.

*Result C:* inflation decreases, unemployment change uncertain.

*Result D:* inflation increases, unemployment change uncertain.

| Result | Event |
|---|---|
| a. _____ | The government raises business taxes and the Bank of Canada conducts open market purchases of securities. |
| b. _____ | Inflationary expectations of firms are reduced and government spending is increased. |
| c. _____ | The Bank of Canada raises the Bank rate and foreign oil becomes much more expensive. |
| d. _____ | The government increases income tax rates and decreases payroll taxes. |
| e. _____ | The government trims back on defence spending and gives more generous depreciation allowances for industrial firms. |

# ANSWERS AND SOLUTIONS

## PRACTICE TEST

### I. SOLUTIONS TO MULTIPLE CHOICE QUESTIONS

1. A. If there is an excess supply of workers—i.e., unemployment—workers will accept lower wages. See p. 314.
2. C. See p. 317.
3. C. Employers will demand more labour if it is thought that the value of workers' output will increase. See p. 315.
4. C. See p. 318.
5. D. See p. 318. From the discussion in this section of the chapter it is clear contracts may be based upon incorrect expectations.
6. A. The oil price hike will affect production costs and push the AS curve to the left, raising the price level. Options B and C are contractionary policies. In Option D, the demand for money will increase as a consequence of a price increase; it will not cause a price increase.
7. C. At the minimum wage level, quantity supplied is 500 and quantity demanded is only 300.
8. D. Oil price increases of the 1970s are sometimes cited as an example.
9. C. If aggregate demand became more (or less) variable, the Phillips Curve would not break down. The relationship developed as a result of aggregate demand changes.
10. C. The Phillips Curve revealed a negative relationship between the inflation rate and the unemployment rate.
11. D. The natural rate includes both structural and frictional unemployment.
12. D. See p. 316. As prices rise, wages rise to keep pace, and the level of employment is stable.
13. A. There is a trade-off between inflation and unemployment in the short run but, as wages adjust to catch up with rising prices, the natural rate of unemployment will be restored.
14. A. Higher (lower) supply decreases (increases) the inflation rate and decreases (increases) the unemployment rate.
15. C. The major raw material to show price increases was oil. Options A and B would shift aggregate demand. Option D is a fiction.
16. A. The spending increase is an expansionary fiscal policy that will shift the AD curve to the right. The unemployment rate will decrease and the inflation rate will increase—a move along the Phillips Curve.

17. A. The move from E to D represents a decrease in inflation and unemployment. This will occur if the AS curve shifts to the right, as will happen when firms expect less inflation.

18. B. The rise in the price of raw materials (imported or otherwise) will shift the AS curve to the left.

19. A. Point A represents unemployment that is lower than the natural rate, indicating that production is extremely high. Structural and frictional unemployment, although low, can't be negative!

20. C. The long-run Phillips Curve is vertical. However, because point E is the only point located at the natural rate, the long-run Phillips Curve will pass through this point only.

## II.    SOLUTIONS TO APPLICATION QUESTIONS

1. a. An increase in aggregate demand would decrease unemployment and increase inflation in the short run.

   b. Aggregate supply will shift left. The price level will increase and output will decrease. The negative relationship between the inflation rate and the unemployment rate will be absent. There would be a move off the existing Phillips Curve to point E.

   c. Aggregate supply will shift left. The price level will increase and output will decrease. The negative relationship between the inflation rate and the unemployment rate will be absent. There would be a move off the existing Phillips Curve to point E.

   d. Aggregate demand will increase, causing the price level to increase and output to increase. There would be a move along the existing Phillips Curve to point B.

   e. Aggregate supply will increase, causing the price level to decrease and output to increase. The inflation rate will decrease and the unemployment rate will decrease. There would be a move off the existing Phillips Curve to point D.

   f. Aggregate demand will decrease, causing the price level to decrease and output to decrease. The inflation rate will decrease and the unemployment rate will increase—a movement along the Phillips Curve to point C.

   g. There is a mismatch between the actual inflation rate (3%) and the expected inflation rate (0%). The Phillips Curve is based on a particular level of inflationary expectations. In the long run, the actual inflation rate and the expected inflation rate must be equal. Either expectations must increase, which would shift the Phillips Curve to the right, or the actual inflation rate must decrease.

   h. If actual inflation remains at 3%, the Phillips Curve will shift to the right (as expectations change). This shift will continue until expectations equal reality. When the expected inflation rate exceeds the actual future inflation rate, real wages will rise, unemployment will increase, and output will decrease. The short-run aggregate supply curve will shift to the left.

   i. The long-run Phillips Curve is vertical at an unemployment rate of 6%.

2. a. In equilibrium, $Q_D = Q_S$. $300 - W = 5W$. $120 = 6W$; therefore $W = 20$. When $W = 20$, employment is 100, i.e., 100 000. Frictional and structural unemployment run at a constant 10 000. There is no cyclical unemployment. The unemployment rate = 10 / 110 = 9.09%.

   b. Labour force = 100 000 employed + 10 000 unemployed = 110 000. Participation rate = labour force × 100% / population) = 110 000 / 160 000 = 68.75%.

c. If $W = 20$, $Q_D = 120 - (22) = 98$ and $Q_S = 5(22) = 110$.

Employment will decrease from 100 000 to 98 000.

Frictional and structural unemployment remain at 10 000, but an additional 12 000 individuals will be seeking work. Total unemployed is 22 000.

The labour force has increased by 10 000 to 120 000.

The unemployment rate, which is unemployed × 100% / labour force, will be 22 000 × 100% / 120 000, or 18.33%.

Participation rate = labour force × 100% / population = 120 000 × 100% / 160 000 = 75%.

3. a. Structural and frictional unemployment run at 10 000. The natural rate of unemployment is 10 000 / 200 000 or 5%. When 190 000 workers are employed, the output level is 2500, so potential GDP is 2500. Note that output from the short-run AS curve can be greater than the potential output level.

   b. See the diagram below.

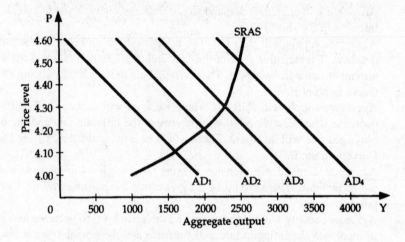

   c. The equilibrium price level (where AD = AS) is 4.10 opeks and equilibrium output is 1600. The unemployment rate is 11%.

   d. purchase; right. The price level is 4.20 opeks, and the output level is 2000. Employment has risen by 6000 workers. 8% of workers remain unemployed. Because structural and frictional unemployment are at 5%, cyclical unemployment must be 3%.

   e. The price level is 4.30 opeks, and output is 2300. Employment has risen by 4000 workers. 6% of workers remain unemployed.

   f. The price level is 4.50 opeks, and output is 2500. Employment has risen by 2000 workers. 5% of workers remain unemployed.

4. a. C    e. A    i. D    m. D
   b. C    f. A    j. D    n. A
   c. C    g. C    k. A
   d. A    h. B    l. C

Compare these results with those obtained in Application questions 2 and 6 in the preceding chapter.

Note: Some of these "shocks" may affect both aggregate demand and aggregate supply. The above answers are for the single strongest change.

5. a. D. An increase in business taxes will shift the AS curve to the left, while the open market purchase will increase the money supply and shift the AD curve to the right. Both shifts are inflationary, but the effect on output (and on the unemployment rate) is ambiguous.

b. B. As firms come to expect less inflation, they will be willing to produce more at any given price level—AS will shift to the right. The increase in government spending is expansionary and will shift the AD curve to the right. Both shifts will expand output and reduce unemployment, but the effect on the inflation rate is ambiguous.

c. A. As oil increases in price, the AS curve will shift to the left. The Bank of Canada action is contractionary and will shift the AD curve to the left. Both shifts will reduce output and increase unemployment, but the effect on the inflation rate is ambiguous.

d. C. The higher income tax will reduce consumption, and the AD curve will shift to the left. The reduction in payroll taxes will reduce the costs of production—AS will shift to the right. Both shifts will reduce inflation, but the effect on output (and on the unemployment rate) is ambiguous.

e. C. The cutback in defence spending will reduce aggregate demand. The increased depreciation allowances will increase the profitability of firms and encourage more production. In fact, this is a typical "supply-side" policy. See Chapter 18. AS will shift to the right. Both shifts will reduce inflation, but the effect on output (and on the unemployment rate) is ambiguous.

# 16 The Debt and Stabilization Policy

## OBJECTIVES: POINT BY POINT

After completing this chapter, you should be able to accomplish the objectives listed below.

### General Comment

This chapter contains an assortment of topics, none of which is worth a chapter on its own, but each of which is interesting. It gives you a good opportunity to review your understanding of the macroeconomic model and to analyze the economics behind your own political beliefs.

### OBJECTIVE 1: Explain the difference between the government deficit and the government debt.

A *federal deficit* $(G - T)$ is the difference between government tax receipts and expenditures. The federal government budget balance or *federal surplus* is the negative of the deficit or $T - G$. The Canadian federal government budget was in surplus in 2001. The *federal debt* is the accumulation of all previous deficits (minus surpluses). Just like a household, when the government incurs debt it must borrow and pay interest on the loans. Unlike a household, though, the government can refinance loans by issuing new bonds— this process could continue indefinitely. (page 332)

> **TIP:** Increases in government spending (G) and decreases in net taxes (T) will reduce the surplus (increase the deficit). Expansionary fiscal policies, therefore, reduce the surplus (increase the deficit). However, expansionary monetary policies increase the surplus (reduce the deficit). Why? Lower interest rates stimulate output, boost aggregate income, and increase tax receipts.

Note that recessions make the surplus smaller (deficit larger), given no change in government policy. Lower incomes mean lower income tax receipts, and longer unemployment lines mean larger unemployment benefit payouts.

### Practice

1. Which of the following statements about the deficit and debt is true?
   A. The federal debt is the total of all previous federal budget deficits not counting surpluses.
   B. About three-quarters of the federal debt is held by foreigners.
   C. A decrease in the deficit will result in a decrease in the debt.
   D. Much of the federal debt is an asset of Canadian bondholders.

   **ANSWER:** D. See p. 333. Note that the government has to run a surplus, not just reduce the deficit, to decrease the debt (Option C). Option A is incorrect—the debt is the net total of all previous deficits minus previous surpluses.

2. In 2000, interest payments were approximately what percentage of federal government expenditures?
   A. 5%.
   B. 18%.
   C. 26%.
   D. 53%.

   **ANSWER:** C.  See p. 336, Fast Facts.

3. About what percentage of Canadian government securities outstanding are Canada Savings Bonds?
   A. 7%.
   B. 17%.
   C. 37%.
   D. 70%.

   **ANSWER:** A.  See p. 334, Fast Facts.

## OBJECTIVE 2: Describe the impact of government debt on subsequent generations.

An increase in government debt represents spending that must "come from," or crowd out, some other component of aggregate expenditure. It could be crowding out, or reducing, private investment. This causes a lower level of capital stock in the future, and lower productivity, than would otherwise have occurred. It could crowd out net exports, which increases the amount of foreign ownership and/or foreign indebtedness of Canadians. This increases the fraction of future income that gets transferred to nonresidents.   (page 333)

Increases in government borrowing may be appropriate if the costs outlined in the above paragraph are less than the benefits. This borrowing may be necessary to enable spending on physical infrastructure or other initiatives giving a large enough future payoff to warrant these costs.                                                  (page 334)

## Practice

4. The prediction that there is complete long-run crowding out of government spending is a consequence of which assumption?
   A. Tight monetary policy and low inflation rates.
   B. The economy is at potential output and a vertical long-run aggregate supply curve.
   C. The government finances its spending through issuing securities (e.g., bonds).
   D. Net exports equal zero and investment is sensitive to interest rates.

   **ANSWER:** B.  See p. 333.

## OBJECTIVE 3: Explain how a commitment to a balanced government budget could destabilize output.

The sharp rise in government debt in Canada during the 1980s and early 1990s has been attributed in large part to two periods of high interest rates, one in the early 1980s and another around 1990. These resulted from tight monetary policy in order to reduce the inflation rate. This increased the deficit for two reasons: First, the higher interest rates increased government spending on interest on its existing debt, and second, to the extent that the high interest rates contributed to recessions during these two periods, the government had lower tax revenues than it would have had otherwise.                (page 335)

Problems of government debt have led to proposals of legislation to prevent future deficits, forcing long-term budgetary considerations onto the political agenda. The disadvantage of such legislation is that it would inhibit the "automatic stabilizer" effect of fiscal policy. Recessions would force governments to increase taxes and cut spending, which would reinforce the contraction. (page 336)

## Practice

5.  What two economic events were directly responsible for much of the growth in Canada's debt?
    A.  Low investment and high interest rates.
    B.  High inflation and high interest rates.
    C.  Recession and high interest rates.
    D.  Recession and high inflation.

    **ANSWER:** C.  See p. 335.

6.  Each of the following is a partial explanation for the fact that the federal deficit increases during a recession except
    A.  a decrease in output results in more government transfer payments to households.
    B.  a decrease in output causes personal income tax revenues to decrease (because taxable income decreases during an economic slowdown).
    C.  a decrease in output necessarily results in expansionary fiscal policy.
    D.  a decrease in output causes decreases in tax revenues collected from corporations.

    **ANSWER:** C.  The government may not choose to enact expansionary fiscal policies during a recession.

7.  A balanced-budget amendment would be destabilizing because, if the economy dips into a recession, the legislation would require _____ in government spending and/or _____ in net taxes.
    A.  increases, increases.
    B.  increases, decreases.
    C.  decreases, increases.
    D.  decreases, decreases.

    **ANSWER:** C.  See p 336.

8.  Deficit targeting is in effect when the economy is hit by a negative demand shock. The deficit will _____. By acting to balance the budget, government policy will make aggregate demand decrease _____.
    A.  increase, more.
    B.  increase, less.
    C.  decrease, more.
    D.  decrease, less.

    **ANSWER:** A.  See Figure 16.2.

## OBJECTIVE 4: Explain why inflation targeting by the Bank of Canada may or may not stabilize output in the AS/AD model.

As of writing, the announced goal of the Bank of Canada is to maintain inflation in the 1% to 3% range. If inflation is near the bottom (top) of this range, the Bank of Canada will undertake expansionary (contractionary) monetary policy. This will be stabilizing if low (high) inflation coincides with output levels below (above) potential GDP. It could be destabilizing, however. For example, a leftward shift in aggregate supply could result in high inflation and low output. The Bank of Canada would reduce the money supply to lower inflation, but in this case it would also drive output further away from potential GDP. (page 338)

## Practice

Use the following information to answer the next two questions. Arboc's central bank, Arbobank, is committed to maintaining inflation close to zero, a situation that currently exists. Suddenly, Arboc experiences sharply higher prices for steel (an important input).

9.   The shock experienced by Arboc is best described as a
     A.   positive demand shock.
     B.   positive supply shock.
     C.   negative demand shock.
     D.   negative supply shock.

     **ANSWER:** D.   Negative shocks reduce output. If the price of an input increases, it will have an adverse effect on supply—this is *stagflation.*

10.  Given the shock experienced by Arboc, Arbobank will _____ the money supply. Aggregate demand will _____.
     A.   increase, increase.
     B.   increase, decrease.
     C.   decrease, increase.
     D.   decrease, decrease.

     **ANSWER:** D.   To lower inflation, Arbobank will decrease the money supply, shifting AD to the left.

## OBJECTIVE 5: Outline the time lags of stabilization policy.

Fiscal and monetary *stabilization* policies are intended to smooth out fluctuations in output, employment, and prices, but policy actions do not operate immediately. There are *time lags*. Economists distinguish three:
   a.   The *recognition lag* is the time between the development of a problem and its recognition.
   b.   The *implementation lag* is the time necessary to hammer out and enact a policy following the recognition of the problem. Implementation lags tend to be shorter for monetary policy than for fiscal policy.
   c.   The *response lag* is the time it takes for the economy to react to the policy action. Response lags tend to be longer for monetary policy than for fiscal policy. (page 341)

A case ("the fool in the shower") can be made that stabilization policies actually destabilize the economy because, by the time a policy takes effect, the problem it is designed to address (rising unemployment, for example) may have been replaced by another (inflation, for example) for which the policy is completely inappropriate. (page 339)

> **Comment:** The main differences in terms of time lags between fiscal and monetary policy are at the implementation stage (where monetary policy can be almost instantaneous and fiscal policy lumberingly slow) and the response stage (where fiscal policy tends to work more quickly).
>
> The problems of policy effectiveness have led some economists to call for the complete abandonment of stabilization policy.

## Practice

11. Stabilization policy attempts to
    A. stabilize the federal budget.
    B. minimize changes in the money supply and interest rates.
    C. minimize changes in the levels of output and prices.
    D. increase the size of automatic stabilizers.

    **ANSWER:** C. See p. 339.

12. The response lag is shorter for
    A. fiscal policy, because changes in, say, government spending have an immediate impact on aggregate demand.
    B. fiscal policy, because monetary policy requires approval by a minimum of 75% of the Board of Governors of the Bank of Canada.
    C. monetary policy, because open market operations are very easy to perform.
    D. monetary policy, because money (currency, demand deposits) must be used in almost all transactions.

    **ANSWER:** A. See p. 343.

13. Implementation lags tend to be _____ for monetary policy than for fiscal policy; response lags tend to be _____ for monetary policy than for fiscal policy.
    A. shorter, shorter.
    B. shorter, longer.
    C. longer, shorter.
    D. longer, longer.

    **ANSWER:** B. See pp. 341-343.

14. The "fool in the shower" analogy argues that
    A. we should leave the economy to adjust on its own to cure fluctuations.
    B. the government and the Bank of Canada should coordinate policy actions throughout the business cycle.
    C. policymakers must provide alternating periods of stimulus and restraint to keep the economy from stagnating.
    D. given time lags, expansionary policies are required to stabilize the economy.

    **ANSWER:** A. See p. 339.

## Policy Problems

This chapter is excellent in pointing out the problems faced by policymakers. It's easy to think that we should be able to "fine tune" the economy, efficiently curing inflation, unemployment, output, the deficit, and so on. (Economists used to believe so, too.) But time lags, lack of coordination between the government and the Bank of Canada, political considerations, slippages in the economy, and the ticklish problem of expectations conspire to make policy much more like a blunt instrument than a surgeon's scalpel.

## PRACTICE TEST

**I.** **MULTIPLE CHOICE QUESTIONS.** Select the option that provides the single best answer.

_____ 1.  The response lag is the length of time between _____ and _____.
   A.  the recognition of a problem, the resolution of the problem.
   B.  the recognition of a problem, the implementation of a remedy.
   C.  the implementation of remedy, the resolution of the problem.
   D.  the development of a problem, the implementation of a remedy.

_____ 2.  Roughly _____ of the Canadian federal government debt comes to maturity in three years or less, and _____ of its debt is held by non-residents.
   A.  one quarter, one quarter.
   B.  one half, one quarter.
   C.  one quarter, one half.
   D.  one half, one half.

_____ 3.  An increase in government debt may crowd out
   A.  neither investment nor net exports.
   B.  investment, but not net exports.
   C.  net exports, but not investment.
   D.  both investment and net exports.

_____ 4.  In 1970, the federal government paid $1.9 billion in interest payments on its debt. By contrast, in 2000 it paid about
   A.  $0.3 billion.
   B.  $10 billion.
   C.  $42 billion.
   D.  $600 billion.

_____ 5.  Critics of the Bank of Canada argue that it contributed to the increase in the federal debt during the 1980s and early 1990s because its policies caused
   A.  high interest rates.
   B.  high inflation.
   C.  stagflation.
   D   dangerously low unemployment rates.

_____ 6.  Expansionary monetary policies _____ the deficit and expansionary fiscal policies _____ the deficit.
   A.  increase, increase.
   B.  increase, decrease.
   C.  decrease, increase.
   D.  decrease, decrease.

_____ 7.  Government spending decreases. If the Bank of Canada acts to reduce the effect of this policy on the output level, then interest rates will be _____ than otherwise and the deficit will be _____ than otherwise.
   A.  higher, greater.
   B.  higher, smaller.
   C.  lower, greater.
   D.  lower, smaller.

_____ 8. The implementation lag is the length of time between _____ and
_____.
   A. the recognition of a problem, the resolution of a problem.
   B. the recognition of a problem, the development and enactment of a
      remedy.
   C. the development of a problem, its ultimate resolution.
   D. the development of a problem, the development and enactment of a
      remedy.

_____ 9. Because the change occurs directly in aggregate demand, the _____
   lag for fiscal policy is _____ than that for monetary policy.
   A. implementation, shorter.
   B. implementation, longer.
   C. response, shorter.
   D. response, longer.

_____ 10. Legislation requiring balanced budgets is viewed as an automatic destabi-
   lizer because
   A. during a recession, it requires tax cuts if the deficit target has not
      been met.
   B. during a boom, it requires spending increases if the deficit target has
      not been met.
   C. during a recession, it requires contractionary fiscal measures if the
      deficit target has not been met.
   D. during a recession, it requires expansionary fiscal measures if the
      deficit target has not been met.

_____ 11. The government implements a tax cut. If the Bank of Canada acts to reduce
   the effect of this policy on the output level, then it will undertake
   A. an expansionary monetary policy to increase interest rates.
   B. an expansionary monetary policy to decrease interest rates.
   C. a contractionary monetary policy to increase interest rates.
   D. a contractionary monetary policy to decrease interest rates.

_____ 12. A federal deficit is a _____; the federal debt is a _____.
   A. flow, flow.
   B. flow, stock.
   C. stock, flow.
   D. stock, stock.

## II. APPLICATION QUESTIONS

1. a. Balanced budget legislation would operate as an additional automatic stabiliz-
      er. True or false? Explain.
   b. "If the Bank of Canada expands the money supply during a period of substan-
      tial excess capacity, the government deficit will be reduced." True or false?
      Explain.

2. The "insider-outsider theory" has been developed to explain the persistently high
   unemployment rates in Europe. Union members are insiders—they control wage
   negotiations and get the first choice of jobs. Nonunion members are outsiders—they
   receive any additional jobs. Any worker who is unemployed for a specified period
   of time is no longer eligible to be a union member. Following is a simple model to
   explain how long-term unemployment might occur.

The demand for labour ($Q_D$) is given by $Q_D = 600\ 000 - 20W$, where W is the wage. As a simplifying assumption, the total supply of labour ($Q_S$) is assumed to be fixed at 500 000. We will ignore frictional and structural unemployment.

a.  Determine the equilibrium wage and the unemployment rate.
b.  Now suppose that 400 000 workers unionize and negotiate a wage contract that will give them the highest possible wage without any unemployment of their members. Determine the equilibrium wage.
c.  Determine the unemployment rate.

Now suppose that contractionary monetary policies produce a recession (as happened in Europe in the early 1980s) and that 40 000 workers lose their jobs. These workers are no longer eligible to be union members.

d.  Calculate the number of union members and the number of outsiders.
e.  The "insiders" negotiate a new wage contract that will give them the highest possible wage without any unemployment of their members. Determine the equilibrium wage.
f.  Determine the unemployment rate.

Now the economy begins to expand, causing the demand for labour to increase. The new demand for labour ($Q_D$) is given by $Q_D = 700\ 000 - 20W$. (Graph this to verify that this is a rightward shift of the labour demand curve.)

g.  Given the new labour market environment, the "insiders" negotiate a new wage contract that, again, will give them the highest possible wage without any unemployment of their members. Determine the equilibrium wage.
h.  Determine the unemployment rate.
i.  Analyze the plausibility of the "insider-outsider" model.

3.  Suppose the economy is described by the following model:

    (1)  C  =  $280 + .8Y_d$
    (2)  I  =  400
    (3)  G  =  800
    (4)  T  =  $-400 + .2Y$
    (5)  $Y_d$  =  $Y - T$

    a.  Calculate the equilibrium income level (where $Y = C + I + G$).
    b.  Calculate the government deficit (D) where deficit = G – T.
    c.  The expenditure multiplier is _____.
    d.  Given the initial model, suppose that, suddenly, investment falls by 50. Calculate the change in the equilibrium income level.
    e.  How will this investment change affect the deficit?
    f.  Given the initial model, to achieve a balanced budget through a cut in government spending, GDP would have to fall by _____.
    g.  To achieve this GDP cut with a reduction in government spending, G must fall by _____.
    h.  Given the initial model, suppose that this year's deficit target is 200. Suddenly, as we saw above, investment falls by $50. To restore the deficit target of 200, government spending would have to _____ (rise/fall) by _____.
    i.  The investment change and the government spending change together would make income _____ (rise/fall) by _____.

4.  Suppose that the budget is required by law to be balanced.
    a.  What will happen to production and output if investment spending falls?
    b.  What will happen to tax receipts?
    c.  What will happen to public transfer payments?
    d.  Bearing these factors in mind, what must now be happening to the budget?
    e.  What would you recommend, given the balanced budget requirement that demands equality between government spending and net tax receipts.

f. What would your obligatory policy recommendation do to an economy already experiencing recession and growing unemployment?

5. The federal government cuts spending by 50 to reduce the deficit. If the spending multiplier has a value of 2, aggregate output will _____ (rise/fall) by _____. If the tax rate is .1, taxes will _____ (rise/fall) by _____ and the deficit will _____ (increase/decrease) by _____. If the multiplier has a value of 1.4, however, aggregate output would _____ (rise/fall) by _____. If the tax rate is still .1, taxes will _____ (rise/fall) by _____ and the deficit will _____ (increase/decrease) by _____. We can conclude that a given cut in government spending will be more effective in reducing the deficit the _____ (larger/smaller) the value of the spending multiplier.

# ANSWERS AND SOLUTIONS

## PRACTICE TEST

### I. SOLUTIONS TO MULTIPLE CHOICE QUESTIONS

1. C. See p. 341.
2. B. See p. 333 and Fast Facts on p. 334.
3. D. See p. 334.
4. C. See Fast Facts on p. 333.
5. A. See p. 335.
6. C. An expansionary monetary policy increases spending and income—net taxes increase and the deficit decreases. An increase in government spending or a decrease in net taxes results in an immediate increase in the deficit.
7. D. A cut in government spending (which is contractionary) will provoke a compensating increase in the money supply. The interest rate will decrease as a result. Output and net taxes will decrease less than otherwise.
8. B. See p. 341.
9. C. See p. 342.
10. C. A recession will lower tax revenues, requiring either spending cuts or tax rate increases to maintain a balanced budget.
11. C. A tax cut will increase disposable income and encourage higher consumption spending. A contractionary monetary policy will reduce the money supply and increase interest rates, reducing the increase in aggregate demand.
12. B. A flow is measured over a period of time—the deficit is for a particular year. A stock is measured at a point in time—the debt is measured, say, on December 31st.

### II. SOLUTIONS TO APPLICATION QUESTIONS

1. a. False. Balanced budget legislation would be destabilizing, calling, for example, for cuts in government spending during a recession. See p. 336.
   b. True. An expansionary monetary policy will increase output and employment. Net taxes will be increased, reducing the deficit.

2.  a.  In equilibrium, $Q_D = Q_S$, therefore 600 000 – 20W = 500 000. W = 5000. All workers have a job, therefore the unemployment rate is zero. Note that we are ignoring frictional and structural unemployment.

    b.  In equilibrium, $Q_D = Q_S$, therefore 600 000 – 20W = 400 000. W = 10 000. Note that employers may go along with this arrangement in order to avoid costly strikes.

    c.  The unemployment rate = 100 000 × 100% / 500 000 = 20%.

    d.  There are now 360 000 union members and 140 000 nonunion workers.

    e.  In equilibrium, $Q_D = Q_S$; therefore 600 000 – 20W = 360 000. W = 12 000.

    f.  The unemployment rate is 140 000 × 100% / 500 000 = 28%. Note that contractions in the economy raise wages and increase unemployment.

    g.  In equilibrium, $Q_D = Q_S$; therefore 700 000 – 20W = 360 000. W = 17 000.

    h.  The unemployment rate remains at 28% even when the economy is expanding.

    i.  Some of our simplifying assumptions are too simple. Total labour supply and union labour supply are unlikely to be perfectly vertical. However, the arrangement specified is clearly in the best interests of union members. Employers may benefit through fewer disruptions and the development of a skilled, motivated (union) labour force. Outsiders lose of course but, with Europe's generous unemployment benefits, may be compensated sufficiently not to protest.

3.  a.  
$$\begin{aligned}
Y &= C + I + G \\
&= 280 + .8(Y - T) + 400 + 800 \\
&= 1480 + .8(Y + 400 - .2Y) \\
&= 1480 + .8Y + 320 - .16Y \\
.36Y &= 1800 \\
Y &= 5000.
\end{aligned}$$

    b.  G – T = 800 + 400 – .2(5000) = 200.

    c.  multiplier = 1 / (1 – MPC) = 1 / (1 – .64) = 2.7778.
    Note: A simple way to get MPC is to conduct the following "thought experiment." If income (Y) increases by 100, taxes will increase by 20 (.2Y). Disposable income will increase by 80. Consumption increases by 64 (.8$Y_d$). As income changes by 100, consumption changes by 64.

    d.  
$$\begin{aligned}
Y &= C + I + G \\
&= 280 + .8(Y - T) + 350 + 800 \\
&= 1430 + .8(Y + 400 - .2Y) \\
&= 1430 + .8Y + 320 - .16Y \\
.36Y &= 1750 \\
Y &= 4861.11, \text{ so income decreases by } 138.89.
\end{aligned}$$
    Alternatively, ΔY = ΔI × multiplier = –50 × 2.7778 = –138.89.

    e.  G – T = 800 + 400 – .2(4861.11) = 227.78. The deficit increases by 27.78.

    f.  GDP must decrease by 1250.
    Thought experiment: A 100-dollar cut in spending will reduce income by 277.78. Taxes will fall by 55.56 (277.78 × .2). The deficit will be decreased by 44.44. To reduce the deficit by 200, income must decrease by 277.78 × (200 / 44.44) = 1250.

    g.  To achieve this change in income, government spending must decrease by 450. (ΔY = ΔG × multiplier = –1250 = –450 × 2.778).
    Check:  G = 350(800 – 450)
    $\qquad\qquad$ T = –400 + .2(3750) = 350.

h. When I decreases by 50, Y equals 4861.11, so income decreases by 138.89.
The deficit increases by .2 × 138.89 = 27.78.
We want the deficit to decrease by 27.78.
A 100-dollar cut in spending will reduce the deficit by 44.44. A 62.5 decrease in spending will achieve a 27.78 decrease in the deficit. (Get 62.5 from 100 × (27.78 / 44.44).

i.
$$Y = C + I + G$$
$$= 280 + .8(Y - T) + 350 + 737.5$$
$$= 1367.5 + .8(Y + 400 - .2Y)$$
$$= 1480 + .8Y + 320 - .16Y$$
$$.36Y = 1687.5$$
$$Y = 4687.5. \text{ Income will decrease by } 312.5.$$

Check: G = 737.5 (800 – 62.5)

$$T = -400 + .2(4687.5) = 537.5$$
$$G - T = 737.5 - 537.5 = 200.$$

4. a. Less demand, rising inventories, cutbacks in production and employment.
   b. Personal and corporate income tax revenues will fall, as will sales tax revenues.
   c. Welfare payments and unemployment compensation will be rising.
   d. It will be experiencing a deficit.
   e. Cut spending or increase taxes.
   f. Make the situation worse.

5. fall; 100; fall; 10; decrease; 40; fall; 70; fall; 7; decrease; 43; smaller.

# 17 Household and Firm Behaviour in the Macroeconomy

## OBJECTIVES: POINT BY POINT

After completing this chapter, you should be able to accomplish the objectives listed below.

### OBJECTIVE 1: Explain the life-cycle theory of consumption.

The life-cycle theory argues that current disposable income is not the only determinant of consumption, as in the simple Keynesian consumption function we have used up to now. Permanent income—i.e., current and expected future income—is important, as is wealth. The household's long-range goal is to maintain a fairly stable level of consumption over the life cycle. It accomplishes this goal by dissaving in low-income periods of the life cycle (young and old) and accumulating a "nest egg" during the prime earning years. The more permanent a change in income is perceived to be, the more consumption/saving behaviour will adjust. Temporary "blips" in income will have little effect on consumption. Note that, if it is permanent income that affects consumption, we get a conclusion that, at first glance, seems unusual. If Jill's income unexpectedly increases (she finds $100), the theory suggests that her consumption pattern will not change—she will save the money rather than spend it. (page 347)

Jack and Jill, who have identical current income levels, should have identical consumption levels according to the simple Keynesian view. But, according to the life-cycle theory, if Jack's permanent income is higher than Jill's, Jack will spend more of his current income, perhaps even borrowing against expected future income.

## Practice

1. _____ is the proportion of income households spend on consumption.
   A. Average propensity to consume.
   B. Marginal propensity to consume.
   C. The consumption ratio.
   D. The standard of living.

   **ANSWER: A.** See p. 347.

2. Keynes said that consumption _____ as current income increases, and that APC _____ as income increases.
   A. increases, increases.
   B. increase, decreases.
   C. decreases, increases.
   D. decreases, decreases.

   **ANSWER: B.** Households with more income spend more, but they save a larger percentage of their income. If so, APC must decrease as income increases. See p. 347.

3.    Permanent income is
      A.    the total income earned during one's lifetime.
      B.    after-tax income.
      C.    the income left after all unavoidable bills have been paid.
      D.    the average level of one's expected future income stream.

      **ANSWER:** D.   See p. 348.

4.    The _____ theory states that consumption and saving decisions are based on
      _____.
      A.    Keynesian, permanent income only.
      B.    Keynesian, current and expected future income.
      C.    life-cycle, current income only.
      D.    life-cycle, current and expected future income.

      **ANSWER:** D.   Keynesian consumption theory singles out current income; the life-cycle theory focuses on income expected throughout the life cycle.

## OBJECTIVE 2: Explain how current and expected future real wage rates, employment constraints, and nonlabour income affect households' consumption and labour supply decisions.

The Keynesian model emphasizes the effect of households' spending decisions on aggregate demand. A closely related decision, which we cannot ignore, is how much to work, or how much labour to supply. This of course determines how much income a household has to spend and save. The main factors affecting labour supply are:

*Wages:* Higher wages increase the opportunity cost of not working (referred to in macroeconomics as leisure), and so individuals and households will supply more labour (and earn and consume more money) when wages are higher.

*Prices:* What really matters to a worker when evaluating her wage is the amount of goods and services that can be purchased per hour spent working, more than the simple dollar amount. The former is the real wage, and depends on the latter, which is the nominal wage, and on prices. Higher prices, for example, without higher nominal wages, result in lower real wages, reduced labour supply, and lower (real) consumption.

*Expectations:* If individuals do some planning over their lifetime, their expectations of future wages, prices, and other variables matter for current decisions. If individuals expect higher wages in the future, for example, they are more likely to borrow to consume now.

*Employment Constraints:* If the economy is fully employed, the supply of labour is not constrained—workers seeking jobs will find them. In an economy suffering from unemployment, workers are restricted in the hours they actually work because they are on short-time or have been laid off. The actual number of hours worked depends less on the number of hours that households want to supply and more on how many they can get. Because the number of hours worked is no longer a variable households control, it is reasonable to argue that, if current income increased, so would current consumption. This was the original Keynesian position.

*Wealth and Nonlabour Income:* If a household is wealthy and/or has a large income stream from nonlabour sources (e.g., inheritances, interest income) then it does not have to provide as much labour as a less wealthy household that has the same labour supply options (jobs, wages). The wealthier household can also afford to consume more.

(page 350)

**OBJECTIVE 3: Describe how changes in taxes and government transfer programs may affect consumption and labour supply.**

*Taxes and Transfers:* Income taxes and transfers affect consumption through their effects on disposable income, and affect labour supply through their effects on after-tax wages and nonlabour income. The life-cycle theory predicts that income tax changes that are expected to be permanent will have a bigger impact on household behaviour than those thought to be temporary. (pages 350-351)

**OBJECTIVE 4: Identify how interest rate and stock market changes may affect consumption spending.**

*Interest Rates:* Interest rates have two opposing effects on consumption. Higher interest rates may reduce the consumption levels of some households, since purchases financed by borrowing become more costly. However, higher interest rates may increase the consumption of other households, since their wealth will generate more interest income than before. Most economists believe that the first effect is bigger. It is probably the real interest rate, which is the difference between the nominal interest rate and the inflation rate, that matters most, since it measures the annual cost (benefit) of borrowing (lending) money in terms of goods and services. (page 352)

High stock prices will increase wealth and hence consumption of stockholding households. (page 350)

> **TIP:** You might find exceptions to each of the cases mentioned. Exceptions do not prove the theory wrong. What is being described are the general relationships that apply most of the time for most households.

## Practice

5. The wage rate in current dollars is increasing, but prices are increasing at a faster rate. The overall effect is to _____ labour supply and _____ consumption.
   A. decrease, decrease.
   B. decrease, increase.
   C. increase, decrease.
   D. increase, increase.

   **ANSWER:** A. Labour supply depends on the purchasing power of wages, or real wages. Real wages are decreasing because prices rise faster than nominal wages. The opportunity cost of leisure falls, labour supply decreases, disposable income and consumption also decrease.

6. Mr. Micawber is in debt. The interest rate and his real wage do not change, but the inflation rate decreases. The real interest rate _____ and his consumption level will _____.
   A. decreases, decrease.
   B. decreases, increase.
   C. increases, decrease.
   D. increases, increase.

   **ANSWER:** C. The (nominal) interest rate minus the inflation rate is the real interest rate, which increases. Since Mr. Micawber is in debt, this causes his consumption to decrease. Since the costs of financing his existing debt will rise, and the cost of borrowing to finance further consumption will also rise.

7. Ebenezer Scrooge receives unexpected wealth. As a result, his consumption will _____ and his labour supply will _____.
   A. increase, increase.
   B. increase, decrease.
   C. decrease, increase.
   D. decrease, decrease.

   **ANSWER:** B.   Scrooge is richer; richer individuals consume more. Richer individuals also are able to have more leisure time. See p. 348, p. 350.

8. The government cuts unemployment benefits. As a result, consumption will _____ and labour supply will _____.
   A. increase, increase.
   B. increase, decrease.
   C. decrease, increase.
   D. decrease, decrease.

   **ANSWER:** C.   See p. 351.

9. Increased tax rates reduce after-tax income. If the tax rate increases and the change is thought to be permanent, the effect on current consumption will be _____ and the effect on labour supply will be _____ than if the tax rate increase is thought to be temporary.
   A. greater, greater.
   B. greater, smaller.
   C. smaller, greater.
   D. smaller, smaller.

   **ANSWER:** A.   A temporary change in circumstances can be ridden out without changing behaviour very much. In the face of a permanent change, behaviour will be affected more. See p. 351.

10. If Canada Pension Plan benefits are cut, and this is seen as a permanent reduction, personal saving for retirement will _____ and current consumption will _____.
    A. increase, increase.
    B. increase, decrease.
    C. decrease, increase.
    D. decrease, decrease.

    **ANSWER:** B.   The cut reduces the expected lifetime (permanent) income of households. Households consume less today and need greater private saving for use during retirement. See p. 351.

11. Of the following, the most effective way of increasing the supply of labour is
    A. an increase in personal tax rates.
    B. a decrease in personal tax rates.
    C. an increase in personal taxes by a lump-sum amount.
    D. a decrease in personal taxes by a lump-sum amount.

    **ANSWER:** C.   The lump-sum tax change affects income, but not the trade-off between work and leisure. A lump-sum decrease would increase household after-tax income—richer households would reduce their labour supply. A lump-sum increase, on the other hand, would unambiguously increase the supply of labour. With tax rate changes, there are two conflicting effects. See p. 351.

Use this information to answer the next two questions. The Finelli household needs to spend $2000 a month to maintain an adequate standard of living, but it is severely constrained (by part-time employment) to spending only $1200. They have no savings.

12. The consumption of the Finellis will likely be primarily determined by
    A. their expected future income.
    B. their current income.
    C. the interest rate.
    D. the stock market.

    **ANSWER: B.** See p. 349. The consumption of the Finellis is constrained by their lack of full-time employment.

13. The Finellis' part-time hours are cut back still more. We should expect each of the following except that
    A. saving will decrease.
    B. the average propensity to consume will decrease.
    C. the Finellis' income will decrease.
    D. the Finellis will consume less.

    **ANSWER: B.** APC will rise as income level decreases.

## OBJECTIVE 5: Explain why expectations and adjustment costs are important for firms' employment and investment decisions.

Firms must make decisions about their usage of capital and labour. When it buys new plant and equipment, the firm is making a commitment that may affect its production capacity for many years. The firm must choose whether to increase output by adopting a relatively capital-intensive or labour-intensive method of production. The relative costs of the inputs will clearly be an important factor in the choice of technology. (page 354)

Expectations about sales and profits also play a major role in investment choices. Keynes named the entrepreneur's feelings about the firm's prospects "animal spirits." Because expectations are subject to much uncertainty, rapid changes in investment are likely, making this a particularly volatile component of GDP. The *accelerator effect* is the name given to the tendency to postpone investment during slumps and to expand it rapidly during upturns. As a buffer against fluctuations in production (caused by fluctuations in sales), firms may hold excess labour and/or capital. Sharp shifts in the levels of capital stock and employment cause adjustment costs—in some cases, it may be cheaper to maintain excess inputs. (page 355)

Firms sometimes choose to hold excess labour or excess capital, that is more inputs than required to produce the current level of output, because there are adjustment costs to reducing and increasing capital stock and to laying off and hiring workers. Firms may hold excess labour and excess capital in expectation of an upturn in business. If firms are holding excess labour, measured productivity (output per worker) will be lower and when output increases by 1%, the number of new jobs will not rise by as much as 1%. Okun's Law is the hypothesis that unemployment will decrease by 1% if real GDP increases by 2.5% relative to potential GDP, but it is not a stable relationship in Canada. (page 355)

> **TIP:** Underpinning the discussion of the behaviour of the firm is the assumption of profit maximization. If you've done the microeconomics course, take some time to review your notes. If you've never heard of profit maximization, a (very brief) outline is given here.

> The goal of firms is assumed to be profit maximization. To achieve this goal, firms make decisions at the margin. Will this additional unit of output draw in more revenue than it costs to produce? If not, it shouldn't be produced. Will this extra unit of an input (a machine or worker) pay its way? If not, it shouldn't be hired. By hiring inputs until the final unit of each input just breaks even, and by producing until the final unit of output just pays its way, the firm will maximize profits.

## Practice

14. The firm can add to its capital stock by
    A. purchasing additional raw materials.
    B. reducing its inventory levels.
    C. investing in plant and equipment.
    D. hiring additional labour capacity.

    **ANSWER: C.** Investment is the addition to the capital stock. The capital stock can be increased by buying more plant and equipment or by accumulating additional inventory. See p. 353.

15. Technology X uses 10 units of capital and 20 units of labour. If Technology Y is relatively more capital-intensive, it might use
    A. 5 units of capital and 5 units of labour.
    B. 5 units of capital and 10 units of labour.
    C. 20 units of capital and 40 units of labour.
    D. 40 units of capital and 100 units of labour.

    **ANSWER: A.** A method of production is relatively more capital-intensive the greater the ratio of capital to labour. Options B and C have the same level of capital intensity as Technology X (1:2). Option D is less capital-intensive.

16. An auto plant exclusively uses a robotic, capital-intensive process: many machines and few workers. An expansion in output is likely to _____ the demand for labour and _____ the demand for capital.
    A. increase, increase.
    B. increase, decrease.
    C. decrease, increase.
    D. decrease, decrease.

    **ANSWER: A.** The demand for workers should increase modestly; the demand for machines should increase substantially. See p. 354.

17. An entrepreneur who is feeling very confident about the future is likely to
    A. invest in more capital-intensive methods of production.
    B. invest in more labour-intensive methods of production.
    C. hold excess supplies of labour and capital.
    D. reduce excess capacity.

    **ANSWER: C.** In anticipation of good times (and high production) ahead, the entrepreneur will be reluctant to reduce capacity.

18. Which of the following statements is true?
    A. Employment fluctuates more than output over the business cycle, causing high productivity during periods of high output and low productivity during periods of low output.
    B. Employment fluctuates more than output over the business cycle, causing high productivity during periods of low output and low productivity during periods of high output.
    C. Employment fluctuates less than output over the business cycle, causing high productivity during periods of high output and low productivity during periods of low output.
    D. Employment fluctuates less than output over the business cycle, causing high productivity during periods of low output and low productivity during periods of high output.

    **ANSWER:** C. By holding onto excess labour during downturns and by having existing employees work more during upswings, employment remains fairly stable. When output is high, therefore, productivity is high.

19. "Output per worker falls in recessions simply because firms hold excess labour during slumps." This statement implies that productivity figures are
    A. misleading, both in the short run and long run.
    B. misleading in the short run but not in the long run.
    C. not misleading in the short run, but misleading in the long run.
    D. not misleading in the short run nor in the long run.

    **ANSWER:** B. See p. 356.

20. When production increases, discouraged workers may _____ the ranks of the officially unemployed. This will _____ the unemployment rate.
    A. enter, increase.
    B. enter, decrease.
    C. leave, increase.
    D. leave, decrease.

    **ANSWER:** A. Higher production offers the prospect of jobs where none was before.

21. As output increases by 1%, the number of jobs tends to increase by less than 1%. In part, this is because
    A. firms expand output by expanding the number of hours worked by workers who are already on the payroll.
    B. discouraged workers enter the labour force.
    C. discouraged workers leave the labour force.
    D. firms reduce the quantity of excess capital.

    **ANSWER:** A. See p. 356. The presence or absence of discouraged workers (Options B and C) has no effect on the number of jobs created.

22. Although Okun's Law has been proved incorrect, it is true to state that there is a _____ relationship between the changes in GDP and the unemployment rate.
    A. positive and stable.
    B. positive but unstable.
    C. negative and stable.
    D. negative but unstable.

    **ANSWER:** D. As output increases, the unemployment rate decreases, but the trade-off depends on so many factors that it is unstable.

## OBJECTIVE 6: Discuss the role of inventories in the output decision.

*Inventory* is unsold production. Inventory investment occurs when production exceeds sales. Holding inventories involves both a cost and a benefit for the firm. Too low an inventory might mean lost sales, but too high an inventory involves storage costs and the tying up of funds that could be earning interest. The *optimal level of inventories* is at the point of balance between these two concerns. Sales tend to be more variable than production, and inventories can be used to smooth out the mismatch between the two, resulting in lower adjustment costs. (page 357)

An example of the smoothing function of inventories might be fireworks manufacturing. Typically, sales have large peaks—just before Victoria Day in Canada and July 4 in the U.S.—but production may occur for many months before. Inventories accumulate to prevent a rush of production at the last moment. Inventories, though, represent payments to inputs that have already been made, and there are risks and storage costs. These may be high in the case of fireworks.

> *Tip:* Think of the two types of investment as different kinds of activities. Firms often use inventory investment in response to short-term fluctuations in demand, as a buffer between production and sales. This may occur almost "accidentally," i.e., without conscious planning. Investment in plant and equipment is different in nature, representing reflections on the long-term trends in the firm's operations.

> TIP: In a way, saving operates for the household in the same way that inventories operate for the firm. Inventories allow the firm to smooth its production in the face of fluctuating sales; saving (and dissaving) permits the household to smooth consumption and maintain a stable standard of living in the face of fluctuating income.

## Practice

23. Stock of inventories (end of period) equals stock of inventories (beginning of period)
    A. plus production plus sales.
    B. plus production minus sales.
    C. minus production plus sales.
    D. minus production minus sales.

    **ANSWER:** B. See p. 357.

24. If the sales of the Caledonian Curling Stone Company are less than expected, inventories will be
    A. higher than expected and future production will increase.
    B. higher than expected and future production will decrease.
    C. lower than expected and future production will increase.
    D. lower than expected and future production will decrease.

    **ANSWER:** B. Unsold production will be greater than expected. This is a signal that the firm's production level is too high. See p. 358.

25. The desired, or optimal, level of inventories is the level at which the extra cost in lost sales from _____ inventories by a small amount is just equal to the extra gain (in interest revenue and _____ storage costs).
A.  increasing, increased.
B.  increasing, decreased.
C.  decreasing, increased.
D.  decreasing, decreased.

**ANSWER:** D.  See the discussion on p. 357.

---

# PRACTICE TEST

**I.     MULTIPLE CHOICE QUESTIONS.** Select the option that provides the single best answer.

_____ 1.    According to the life-cycle theory, Jill's APC will be less than one
A.    when Jill is young.
B.    when Jill is in her prime earning years.
C.    when Jill is old.
D.    both when Jill is young and when she is old.

_____ 2.    Which of the following likely will make labour supply increase?
A.    A decrease in nonlabour income.
B.    An increase in wealth.
C.    An increase in tax rates.
D.    A decrease in the nominal wage rate.

_____ 3.    Three major and interlinked economic decisions of households are
A.    how much to work, how much to invest, and how much to save.
B.    how much to consume, how much to invest, and how much to work.
C.    how much to work, how much to consume, and how much to save.
D.    how much to produce, how much to invest, and how much to borrow.

_____ 4.    According to the permanent income view, the household's estimate of its permanent income will be substantially affected by all of the following except
A.    a tax hike viewed as temporary.
B.    an annual merit raise.
C.    institutional changes, for example in the Canada Pension Plan.
D.    a tax hike viewed as permanent.

_____ 5.    During a slump, labour productivity will _____ and the amount of excess labour held by a firm will _____.
A.    increase, increase.
B.    increase, decrease.
C.    decrease, increase.
D.    decrease, decrease.

_____ 6. The nominal wage stays constant and the price level increases. Then work-ers' opportunity cost of each hour of leisure has _____ and they will wish to work _____ hours.
   A.   decreased, fewer.
   B.   decreased, more.
   C.   increased, fewer.
   D.   increased, more.

_____ 7. An increase in nonlabour income (such as transfer payments) will _____ consumption and _____ the labour supply.
   A.   increase, increase.
   B.   increase, decrease.
   C.   decrease, increase.
   D.   decrease, decrease.

_____ 8. Because of the ability of firms to _____ the number of hours worked per worker, employment _____ increase as rapidly as does output during an upswing.
   A.   increase, does.
   B.   increase, does not.
   C.   decrease, does.
   D.   decrease, does not.

_____ 9. A "temporary" lump-sum income tax increase will _____ output by _____ than a "permanent" tax increase of an equal amount.
   A.   increase, more.
   B.   increase, less.
   C.   decrease, more.
   D.   decrease, less.

_____ 10. Holding inventory allows the firm to
   A.   reduce storage costs.
   B.   lower its productive capacity.
   C.   increase its ability to meet unexpected demand.
   D.   smooth its sales pattern.

_____ 11. An increase in expected future sales will have a _____ effect on investment, and an increase in the cost of labour will have a _____ effect.
   A.   positive, positive.
   B.   positive, negative.
   C.   negative, positive.
   D.   negative, negative.

_____ 12. From the firm's perspective, an increase in expected future sales will have a _____ effect on employment, and an increase in the cost of labour will have a _____ effect.
   A.   positive, positive.
   B.   positive, negative.
   C.   negative, positive.
   D.   negative, negative.

_____ 13. The _____ the duration of the expected decline in sales and the _____ the adjustment cost, the greater the amount of excess labour that will be held.
A. shorter, smaller.
B. shorter, greater.
C. longer, greater.
D. longer, smaller.

_____ 14. Investment depends on each of the following except
A. expected future sales.
B. Okun's Law.
C. the cost of capital.
D. the cost of labour.

_____ 15. According to the life-cycle theory, the main determinants of consumption include all of the following except
A. current disposable income.
B. expected future income.
C. nominal wages.
D. wealth.

_____ 16. Lower income tax rates will _____ consumption and _____ labour supply.
A. increase, increase.
B. increase, decrease.
C. decrease, increase.
D. decrease, decrease.

_____ 17. Although Okun's Law is flawed, it is roughly true that the unemployment rate
A. increases by more than 1 percentage point for every 1% increase in GDP.
B. increases by less than 1 percentage point for every 1% increase in GDP.
C. decreases by more than 1 percentage point for every 1% increase in GDP.
D. decreases by less than 1 percentage point for every 1% increase in GDP.

Use the following diagram to answer the next two questions. "Income" refers to disposable (after-tax) income.

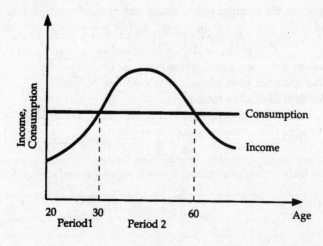

_____ 18. In the diagram above, average propensity to consume is _____ in Period 1, and the household is _____.
   A. high, saving.
   B. high, borrowing.
   C. low, saving.
   D. low, borrowing.

_____ 19. In the diagram above, average propensity to consume is _____ in Period 2, and the average propensity to save is _____.
   A. greater than 1, positive.
   B. greater than 1, negative.
   C. less than 1, positive.
   D. less than 1, negative.

## II.    APPLICATION QUESTIONS

1.  As the "baby boomers" age, what will happen to the national saving rate, according to the life-cycle model?

2.  Suppose that there is an increase in the hourly cost of child care for Jan's toddler, Teddy. How might this affect Jan's labour-supply decision?

3.  Forty-year-old Simon Simple is a life-long resident of Alberta—he has frequently observed that nothing could induce him to leave his home province. Simon is a high-ly skilled lathe operator employed in the furniture industry. He has some wealth and no debts. Indicate how each of the following circumstances will affect Simon's cur-rent consumption and saving.
    a.  Simon is told that a long-lost relative has left him a large bequest. The bequest, however, is to be kept in a trust, and Simon will not be able to with-draw funds from it until he is 50 years old.
    b.  Simon's doctor tells him that Simon has an amazingly healthy constitution and should easily expect to live until he is in his nineties. This prediction, which adds an additional 20 years to Simon's expected life span, does not influence Simon's plan to retire at age 60 in order to perfect his fishing skills.
    c.  Simon, who is a taxpayer, reads a reliable newspaper report that the Alberta government's budget deficit is much worse than had previously been thought. A substantial tax increase next year and in subsequent years now seems inevitable.
    d.  Because of foreign competition, which is thought likely to become increas-ingly intense in future years, Simon's employer has announced that, after the end of this year, no overtime work will be allowed and that, indeed, workers must anticipate reduced work weeks.

4.  Arbez has the following consumption function: C = 400 + .8Y.
    a.  What is the marginal propensity to consume in Arbez? _____
    b.  Calculate APC when income is:

| 1000 _____ | 2000 _____ | 3000 _____ |
|---|---|---|

    c.  At which of the three income levels from part b will saving be:

| zero _____ | positive _____ | negative _____ |
|---|---|---|

d. Based on (c), formulate a rule relating saving and the value of APC.

e. When APC is greater than 1.0, suggest two ways that a household might finance its consumption.

5. Arboc and Arbez are neighbouring nations with similarly sized economies. In each of the following cases, in which economy would we expect to see higher levels of inventory investment? Why?

a. Aggregate demand in Arbez is very stable, but aggregate demand in Arboc is highly variable and unpredictable.

b. The interest rate is historically lower in Arboc than in Arbez.

c. Arboc has begun to move away from manufacturing toward an economy that is more oriented to production of services. Arbez remains based in manufacturing.

6. Jack and Jill both earn $30 000 this year. Jack expects his income to increase by $2000 every year over the next 5 years. Jill expects her income to decrease by $2000 every year for the same period. Who should have the higher APC? Why?

7. Bill and Ben have identical current incomes.

a. Bill has more wealth than Ben. Who should have the higher level of consumption? _____ Who will tend to work more? _____

b. Bill receives dividend payments, but Ben doesn't. Who will have the higher level of consumption? _____ Who will tend to work more? _____

c. Personal income tax rates are cut in the province where Bill lives, but not in the province where Ben lives. Who should have the higher level of consumption? _____ Who will tend to work more? _____

d. As a new member of a credit union, Bill is eligible for a lower interest rate on loans. Who should have the higher level of consumption? _____

e. The Prime Minister pledges "no new taxes." Bill believes him; Ben doesn't. Who should have the higher level of consumption? _____

f. Bill spends more of his current income than Ben does (but not all of it). Now interest rates increase. Who is more likely to increase his savings? _____

g. Bill and Ben return to school. Bill attends a business school, while Ben embarks on a degree in theology. Who should have the higher consumption level today? _____

8. Here are two production functions for the Caledonian Curling Stones Company, "Mix 1" and "Mix 2."

| Output | Mix 1 | | Mix 2 | |
|--------|-------|-----|-------|-----|
|        | K     | L   | K     | L   |
| 11     | 6     | 1   | 2     | 7   |
| 12     | 7     | 3   | 3     | 10  |
| 13     | 9     | 5   | 4     | 14  |
| 14     | 12    | 7   | 5     | 20  |
| 15     | 15    | 9   | 6     | 26  |
| 16     | 21    | 11  | 7     | 32  |

a. The firm wishes to produce 14 units of output. Capital costs $4/unit and labour costs $2/unit. Which input mix will be chosen?

b.  At this output level, will this still be the cheaper method if the input prices change to $2 and $4, respectively?

c.  As the rental cost of capital falls from $4 to $2 and labour costs rise from $2 to $4, investment _____ (increases/decreases), and there is a _____ (positive/ negative) effect on employment.

9.  a.  Use the following table to calculate APC and MPC.

| Income | Consumption | APC | MPC |
|--------|-------------|-----|-----|
| 1000 | 1500 | | |
| 2000 | 2200 | | |
| 3000 | 2900 | | |
| 4000 | 3600 | | |
| 5000 | 4300 | | |

b.  Will APC ever be less than MPC in this model? Why?

# ANSWERS AND SOLUTIONS

## PRACTICE TEST

### I.  SOLUTIONS TO MULTIPLE CHOICE QUESTIONS

1.  B.  During the prime earning years, Jill's earnings (Y) will be more than her consumption (C). APC is C / Y. See p. 348.

2.  A.  As workers' nonlabour income decreases, they will wish to work more. See p. 350.

3.  C.  See p. 349. Note that, when deciding how much of current income will be consumed, the household is simultaneously determining how much will be saved.

4.  A.  A temporary change will have little permanent effect. See p. 351.

5.  C.  Although output has fallen, firms tend to retain extra workers during a slump to avoid the costs of rehiring them during a recovery. Each worker is producing less, so productivity decreases. See p. 356.

6.  A.  Real wages decrease, and so does the opportunity cost of leisure. This makes leisure more attractive relative to labour, reducing labour supply. (Note: It is theoretically possible that workers would wish to work more hours to try to make up for the lower real wages, but studies suggest that the first effect dominates.) (See p. 349.)

7.  B.  As household wealth increases, consumption increases. The desire to work will decrease. See p. 350.

8.  B.  Part-time workers can be made full-time, and full-time workers can be offered overtime. The firm does not need to increase the number of workers it employs—only the number of hours that they are employed.

9.  D.  A temporary tax increase will reduce aftertax income temporarily. As a result, households will reduce consumption less than if the tax increase had been permanent. The decrease in consumption will cause a decrease in output.

10.  C.  The firm does not have to match production to sales as closely when inventory is present. Production levels can be smoother.

11. A. If sales are expected to increase, the firm will wish to expand production capacity. As labour costs rise, machinery becomes relatively less expensive (and more attractive).

12. B. If sales are expected to increase, the firm will wish to expand its productive capacity, including its labour force. The more expensive workers are, the fewer the firm will wish to employ.

13. B. If a decline in sales is expected to last a long time, the relative cost involved in laying off workers becomes less. The smaller the cost of hiring and firing workers, the less excess labour will be held.

14. B. Okun's Law relates unemployment and real GDP growth.

15. C. The wage is an important part of income, but the nominal wage is less of a consideration than the real wage and is, in any case, included in the more general term "income."

16. A. As the tax rate decreases, after-tax income increases, increasing consumption. As after-tax income increases, the opportunity cost of not working increases, leading us to work more. Note that economic theory allows for labour supply to decrease, but studies suggest that it would increase. (See pp. 349-351.)

17. D. See p. 356.

18. B. Consumption exceeds income; therefore this household must be borrowing.

19. C. APC is consumption divided by income. In Period 2, consumption is less than income; the remaining income is saved. Note that average propensity to consume plus the average propensity to save equals one. See p. 348.

## II. SOLUTIONS TO APPLICATION QUESTIONS

1. The "baby boomers" are presently in their prime earning years. They should be saving for retirement. Current consumption, therefore, should be low relative to current income—i.e., APC is less than 1 and the national saving rate is comparatively high. As the baby boomers age and begin to retire, their income will decrease more sharply than their consumption levels—they will be dissaving—and the national saving rate will decrease.

2. In effect, Jan's hourly real wage rate has decreased, since an important price has risen. The opportunity cost of not working (staying home and caring for Teddy) has decreased—Jan may supply less labour. However, the increase in the cost of child care (and the effective wage decrease) has made Jan poorer. The poorer one is, the greater the need to work. Jan, therefore, is driven to supply more labour. Whether Jan works longer hours or chooses to stay home more will depend on the relative strengths of the two effects. Studies indicate the first effect tends to be stronger, and Jan would supply less labour.

3. a. Consumption will increase (saving will decrease). Although he cannot access the funds, Simon's permanent income has increased.

   b. Consumption will decrease (saving will increase). Simon must make his lifetime earnings last over a longer period.

   c. Consumption will decrease (saving will increase). Simon's expectation is that his after-tax income will be decreased in future years. This news reduces his lifetime income.

   d. Consumption will decrease (saving will increase). Simon's expectation is that his income will be decreased in future years. This news reduces his lifetime income.

4.  a.  .8. MPC is the rate at which consumption changes as income changes. If income increases by 1000, consumption will change by 800.

    b.  1.2; 1.0; .933. See the table below.

| Income | Consumption | APC |
|--------|-------------|-------|
| 0 | 400 | — |
| 1000 | 1200 | 1.200 |
| 2000 | 2000 | 1.000 |
| 3000 | 2800 | .933 |

    c.  2000; 3000; 1000. Saving = income – consumption.

    d.  When APC is greater than 1.0, saving is negative (dissaving occurs). When APC is less than 1.0, saving will occur.

    e.  The household could borrow, reduce accumulated savings, or receive wealth transfers (from parents, for example).

5.  a.  Arboc will hold higher stocks of inventories because the danger of inadequate stock is greater there.

    b.  Arboc. The interest rate is a major cost of holding inventories.

    c.  Arbez. It is impossible to hold inventories of services.

6.  Jack should have the higher APC because his consumption will be higher. It will be higher because his expected future income is greater. Jill will be saving more today, in anticipation of bad times to come.

7.  a.  Bill; Ben. Bill will be able to finance more consumption out of his wealth.

    b.  Bill; Ben. Dividend payments are nonlabour income. The higher one's income, the less one tends to work.

    c.  Bill; Bill. Bill's after-tax income has increased; Ben's has not. With more income, Bill will consume more and will work extra hours. Ben has no incentive to work extra hours because his tax rate did not change.

    d.  Bill. The cost of borrowing has decreased for Bill.

    e.  Bill will have the higher level of consumption. Bill's expectations about his future real income are more optimistic than Ben's. Ben is likely to work more now.

    f.  Bill is more likely to increase savings. Higher future interest income will encourage Ben to indulge in greater current consumption. Because this effect is smaller for Bill, his savings are more likely to increase.

    g.  The business school graduate (Bill) should expect a higher future income stream, and so his current consumption level should be higher than that of the theology student (Ben).

8.  a.  Mix 2 will be chosen; it will cost $60 [(5 × $4) + (20 × $2)] instead of Mix 1's $62 [(12 × $4) + (7 × $2)].

    b.  Mix 1 will have a total cost of $52 [(12 × $2) + (7 × $4)], while Mix 2 costs $90 [(5 × $2) + (20 × $4)].

    c.  As the input costs change, investment increases due to the higher desired level of capital stock, and there is a negative effect on employment (as the firm substitutes away from the relatively expensive input, labour).

9.  a. See the table.

| Income | Consumption | APC | MPC |
|--------|-------------|------|-----|
| 1000 | 1500 | 1.50 | — |
| 2000 | 2200 | 1.10 | .7 |
| 3000 | 2900 | 0.97 | .7 |
| 4000 | 3600 | 0.90 | .7 |
| 5000 | 4300 | 0.86 | .7 |

b.  No. APC will become closer to MPC, but it can never be less than MPC. As long as the marginal value is less than the average, the average will decrease.

# 18 Issues in Macroeconomic Policy: Monetarism, New Classical Theory, and Supply-Side Economics

## OBJECTIVES: POINT BY POINT

After completing this chapter, you should be able to accomplish the objectives listed below.

### General Comment

This chapter exposes some of the controversies that have boiled up within macroeconomics. It should remind you of the fact that no single model is accepted by all economists. Economics, unlike the physical sciences, is not governed by a set of undeniable laws. The model that is preferred often has as much to do with the prevailing philosophical attitude as it does with tested theories. A political dimension may be detected too. The activist "demand-side" Keynesian view is fairly liberal; the supply-side theory was a major plank of many conservatives in the 1980s; Milton Friedman, the most famous monetarist, influenced many central bankers; and the new classical economics advocates a "hands-off" approach to government intervention in the economy.

### OBJECTIVE 1: Outline the quantity theory of money.

### OBJECTIVE 2: Discuss the difference between monetarists and Keynesians in terms of policy recommendations.

The AS/AD model is essentially *Keynesian*: Keynesians believe that the money market and goods market are linked; it is possible for cyclical unemployment to persist; and government policy can influence economic activity. More recently, "Keynesianism" has come to be associated with "activist" fiscal and monetary policy. (page 365)

The *quantity theory (monetarist)* view of the economy relates the money supply (M) to nominal GDP (PY). On average, each dollar must be used a given number of times to buy all the goods produced; this given number is the velocity of money (V) and it is assumed to be (practically) constant. The central idea of the quantity theory is captured in the equation of exchange:

$$MV = PY$$

Given V, any change in M must cause a change in PY. If the economy tends to remain close to full employment (another part of the monetarist view), then sustained changes in M must show up as changes in the price level rather than as changes in output—inflation is caused solely by excessive growth in the money supply. To the extent that velocity is not constant—and there is, in fact, a positive relationship between velocity and the interest rate—the monetarist view is weakened. (page 369)

Keynesians support coordinated fiscal and monetary policy actions to stabilize the economy; monetarists argue for a "money growth rule"—the money supply should grow at a steady rate, equal to the long-term growth rate of the economy. If this is done, inflation is avoided. (page 369)

> **Tip:** As you study monetarism, focus on the "MV = PY" formula, which is sometimes called the "equation of exchange."

> **Tip:** In equilibrium, money demand ($M^d$) must equal money supply (M), therefore, in equilibrium, $M^d = M = PY/V$. One can think of an increase in velocity as being the equivalent of a decrease in money demand, and *vice versa*.

> **Tip:** Much of the difference between the Keynesian and monetarist schools of thought can be seen as a difference in time horizons. Keynesians function in the short run—sticky wages and cyclical unemployment are to be expected. Monetarists take a longer view—the AS curve is vertical and changes in aggregate demand have no effect on output (Y), changing only the price level (P).

## Practice

1. In 2000, Canada's nominal GDP was about $1000 billion. The money supply (M1) was about $100 billion. Velocity was approximately
   A.  1.
   B.  5.
   C.  10.
   D.  20.

   **ANSWER:** C.   V = nominal GDP / M.  Nominal GDP = PY.

2. In a hypothetical economy, the money stock is $400 million, the price level is 2, and velocity is 5.
   A.  Real GDP is $2000 million.
   B.  Real GDP is $1000 million.
   C.  Nominal GDP is $160 million.
   D.  Nominal GDP is $1000 million.

   **ANSWER:** B.   In the equation MV = PY, Y stands for real GDP.

3. Monetarists advocate
   A.  a coordinated fiscal and monetary policy.
   B.  a coordinated demand-side and supply-side policy.
   C.  a policy of steady, slow growth in the money supply.
   D.  an activist stabilization policy to control inflation and a passive stabilization policy to control unemployment.

   **ANSWER:** C.   See p. 369.

4. Which of the following statements is false?
   A. Velocity can be affected by institutional factors, such as the frequency of payments to workers.
   B. Velocity can be affected by the development of new methods of payment of bills.
   C. The quantity theory is strengthened if the demand for money is dependent on the interest rate.
   D. A 10% increase in M, coupled with a reduction in V, will result in a less than 10% increase in nominal GDP.

   **ANSWER:** C. The quantity theory is weakened if V is not constant. V will vary if the demand for money is interest-sensitive. See p. 367.

5. Which of the following is unlikely?
   A. Velocity increases as the interest rate increases.
   B. Velocity will change if there is a change in the frequency with which workers are paid.
   C. Velocity increases as the supply of money increases.
   D. Velocity will change if the banking system becomes more efficient.

   **ANSWER:** C. As the money supply increases, the interest rates decreases. The opportunity cost of holding money decreases, and there is an increase in the quantity of money demanded. For the same level of transactions, velocity will decrease. Note that institutional factors affect the demand for money (Options B and D).

6. "Strict" monetarists claim that most of the inflation experienced in the Canadian economy over the past 25 years could have been avoided if
   A. the federal government deficit had been reduced.
   B. the Bank of Canada had not expanded the money supply so rapidly.
   C. income taxes had not been reduced to stimulate labour supply.
   D. the banking industry had not been deregulated, because deregulation has increased velocity.

   **ANSWER:** B. For monetarists, inflation is purely a monetary phenomenon.

7. Monetarists believe that the demand for money depends primarily on
   A. the interest rate.
   B. the level of nominal GDP.
   C. consumption expenditures.
   D. the overall price level.

   **ANSWER:** B. Nominal GDP is PY. Option D is covered by the more general Option B.

8. In general, evidence since 1960 suggests that velocity
   A. has been fairly constant.
   B. has been increasing up to 1990 and decreasing after 1990.
   C. has been decreasing up to 1990 and increasing after 1990.
   D. decreased in the first part of the period, up to about 1977, and increased after that.

   **ANSWER:** B. See the diagram on p. 368.

# OBJECTIVE 3: Define rational expectations.

## OBJECTIVE 4: Describe the policy implications of the Lucas supply function.

The *new classical macroeconomics* has combined the assumption of *rational expectations* (a hypothesis that states that the individual forms expectations by incorporating all available information into a "true model" of the economy) with the *Lucas supply function*. Having rational expectations doesn't mean that one will be perfectly correct in one's predictions—the Lucas supply function tells us that price "surprises" (mismatches between the actual price level and the expected price level) can occur that will affect output—but it does mean that individuals will adjust for expected changes. The conclusion is that anticipated changes in government policy won't be a surprise, won't affect output, and won't affect employment. The issue boils down to one question—do individuals have a true model of the economy and are they well informed?                                    (page 370)

## Practice

9.  According to the Lucas supply function, when the _____ price level is greater than the expected price level, production will _____.
    A.  actual, increase.
    B.  actual, decrease.
    C.  previous, increase.
    D.  previous, decrease.

    **ANSWER:** A.  Firms and workers find their own price (or wage) to be higher than expected and produce more. See p. 373.

10. When there is a mismatch between the expected price level and the actual price level, the difference is called a(n)
    A.  rational expection.
    B.  irrational expection.
    C.  price surprise.
    D.  untrue model.

    **ANSWER:** C.  See p. 373.

11. According to the new classical economists, which of the following will affect output?
    A.  An expansionary and anticipated fiscal policy.
    B.  An expansionary and anticipated monetary policy.
    C.  A contractionary and unanticipated fiscal policy.
    D.  A contractionary and anticipated monetary policy.

    **ANSWER:** C.  Only unanticipated policy actions will be effective.

12. The Lucas supply function states that real output depends on the difference between
    A.  the actual output level and the potential output level.
    B.  the actual price level and the expected price level.
    C.  the actual price level and the equilibrium price level.
    D.  the actual output level and the expected output level.

    **ANSWER:** B.  See p. 373 for a discussion of the Lucas supply function.

13. According to the Lucas supply function, unemployment is due to
    A.  announced expansionary policies, whether fiscal or monetary.
    B.  announced contractionary policies, whether fiscal or monetary.
    C.  deficient aggregate demand within the private sector.
    D.  unpredictable shocks.

    **ANSWER:** D.  See p. 373.

14. Which of the following statements about expectations is false?
    A.  The traditional treatment of expectations is flawed in that it is inconsistent with the microeconomic assumption that individuals are forward-looking.
    B.  The traditional treatment of expectations is flawed in that it is inconsistent with the microeconomic assumption that individuals are rational.
    C.  The rational-expectations hypothesis assumes that errors in forecasting future inflation are systematic.
    D.  The rational-expectations hypothesis assumes that errors in forecasting future inflation are random.

    **ANSWER:** C.  If individuals use all available information with the true model, forecast errors will be randomly distributed, sometimes too large, sometimes too small.

15. The major argument against the rational-expectations hypothesis is that
    A.  it requires households and firms to know too much.
    B.  it is inconsistent with the assumptions of microeconomics.
    C.  it assumes that expectations are formed rather naively.
    D.  it assumes that information collection is costly.

    **ANSWER:** A.  See p. 374.

## OBJECTIVE 5: Describe supply-side economics and the Laffer Curve.

The market-clearing assumptions of real business cycle theory lead to a vertical AS curve, even in the short run; therefore, fluctuations in output must be caused only by shifts of the AS curve (supply shocks).

*Supply-side economics* came to prominence in the early 1980s and, in opposition to the traditional Keynesian "demand-side" policies, advocated policies designed to affect aggregate supply. Policies were intended to increase the incentives to supply labour, to save, and to invest. These policies were particularly popular in the United States. They include personal income tax reductions, investment tax credits, and lessened government regulation of the private sector. The goal of these policies is to shift the aggregate supply curve to the right, which would lower inflation and unemployment simultaneously. (See p. 375.)

The *Laffer Curve*, which relates tax rates and tax revenues, was a key part of this strategy. Its shape suggests that, if taxes are prohibitive, cuts in tax rates will increase tax collections as well as *increase* incentives to work. Studies have found little evidence to support the supply-side theory.                                                        (page 376)

> **Comment:** Changes in taxes are acceptable policy options for the demand-side Keynesians and for the supply-siders. The effect of the tax cut is viewed differently. A Keynesian economist would see the tax cut boosting consumption and, thus, aggregate demand, while a supply-side economist would emphasize the effect on labour supply.
>
> An investment tax credit should increase investment (demand-side) and productive capacity (supply-side)—again, the difference between the two views is one of emphasis. The Keynesian would believe that the stronger and more immediate effect would be felt through a change in aggregate demand, while the supply-side economist would argue that the most immediate effect would be felt in aggregate supply.

## Practice

16. According to the real business cycle theory, which of the following does not cause business cycles?
    A. A change in labour productivity.
    B. A change in the money supply.
    C. A change in the size of the labour force.
    D. A change in the real quantity of the capital stock.

    **ANSWER: B.** A change in money supply will affect aggregate demand; the other options will affect the supply side of the economy.

17. Supply-side economists argue that the government should focus on policies designed
    A. to stimulate demand.
    B. to stimulate supply.
    C. to discourage demand.
    D. to discourage supply.

    **ANSWER: B.** See p. 376.

18. According to the Laffer Curve, as tax rates increase, tax revenues will
    A. increase.
    B. decrease.
    C. increase and then decrease.
    D. decrease and then increase.

    **ANSWER: C.** See p. 376.

19. Which of the following is a potential supply-side policy?
    A. An increase in government spending.
    B. An increase in depreciation allowances for businesses intended to encourage investment.
    C. Increases in the employer contributions to the social security program.
    D. Increases in welfare benefits.

    **ANSWER: B.** Greater depreciation allowances will stimulate additional investment and greater aggregate supply. Note that the increase in planned investment will also increase aggregate demand.

20. Supply-side cuts in personal tax rates and increases in investment incentives would
    A. increase aggregate demand only.
    B. increase aggregate supply only.
    C. increase aggregate demand and aggregate supply.
    D. decrease aggregate demand and increase aggregate supply.

    **ANSWER: C.** Cutting tax rates and providing investment incentives would increase labour supply and the capital stock, but would also increase consumption and planned investment spending.

## Endpoint: Comparisons of the Keynesian, Monetarist, New Classical, and Supply-Side Models

Here are a few of the differences between the models that you've seen. Use these generalizations to help you sort out the different views and, perhaps, to find the one you feel is most accurate.

| Factor | Keynesian | Monetarist | New Classical | Supply-Side |
|---|---|---|---|---|
| Prices | rigid | flexible | flexible | flexible |
| Do markets clear? | no | yes | yes | yes |
| Policy preferences | demand-side fiscal and monetary policy | demand-side monetary policy | "hands-off"— no anticipated policy will work | supply-side fiscal policy |

The models in this chapter can all be interpreted in terms of the AD/AS diagram. Keynesianism focuses on the short-run diagram and manipulation of aggregate demand. Monetarism also focuses on movement of aggregate demand (ultimately through changes in the money supply), but the long run arrives more quickly. Supply-side economics also claims that policy actions can shift the economy—by moving the aggregate supply curve. Again, markets are competitive and responsive, and the long run arrives rapidly. New classical economists argue that government aggregate demand policy is destabilizing. With rational expectations, the economy achieves potential output rapidly.

Keynesian: shift AD
(monetary and fiscal policy)

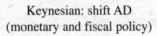

Monetarist: shift AD
(monetary policy)

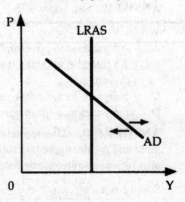

Supply-Side: shift AS
(fiscal policy)

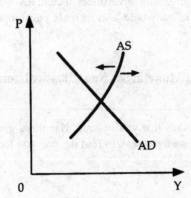

New Classical
(non-intervention)

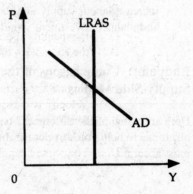

The debate about price surprises and employment can be quite difficult to follow. The table below will help you to grasp the main ideas.

| Price level | Inflation | | wage/hour | hrs worked | Reward/hour | |
| | expected | actual | | | expected | actual |
| --- | --- | --- | --- | --- | --- | --- |
| 1.00 | 0% | 0% | 10.00 | 8 | 10 | 10 |
| 1.00 | 0% | 0% | 11.00 | 9 | 11 | 11 |
| 1.10 | 0% | 10% | 11.00 | 9 | 11 | 10 |
| 1.10 | 10% | 10% | 11.00 | 8 | 10 | 10 |

Suppose an economy has no inflation and expects none. The price level is $1.00.

The first two rows of numbers represent the supply of labour that will occur at two different wage levels. Given the price level, the worker will work 8 hours for a nominal wage of $10.00 per hour and 9 hours for $11.00 per hour. What is the real wage in each case?

The next row shows that, unexpectedly, prices have jumped 10%. Employers can now offer higher (nominal) wages. Employment increases because workers are "fooled" into thinking that their real wage has risen to 11 units/hour. Eventually, when workers discover that their real reward is only 10 units/hour, the quantity of labour supplied will decrease.

Conclusion: A price surprise can cause production and employment levels to change.

# PRACTICE TEST

**I.    MULTIPLE CHOICE QUESTIONS.** Select the option that provides the single best answer.

_____ 1.    The velocity of money is
   A.    constant in the real world.
   B.    the number of times an average dollar is used to purchase GDP goods and services per year.
   C.    equal to nominal GDP divided by the value of goods and services traded in a year.
   D.    equal to nominal GDP divided by real GDP.

_____ 2.    The macroeconomic viewpoint that believes velocity is constant and that a direct relationship exists between growth of the money stock and the rate of inflation is
   A.    new classical economics.
   B.    classical economics.
   C.    the quantity theory.
   D.    the Keynesian theory.

_____ 3.    Under which of the following assumptions could we state that inflation is a purely monetary phenomenon?
   A.    Velocity is constant.
   B.    Real output is constant.
   C.    Both velocity and real output are constant.
   D.    The money supply is constant.

_____ 4. The rational expectations hypothesis assumes that
A. full employment always occurs because rational individuals always realize that they should adjust to wage changes.
B. there is no unanticipated inflation.
C. decision-makers have a theoretical model of how the economy works.
D. individuals are able to predict future inflation rates accurately.

_____ 5. According to the supply-side economic theory, the most important effect of a cut in personal income tax rates would be
A. increased consumption spending.
B. increased personal saving.
C. increased number of hours worked.
D. decreased tax revenues.

_____ 6. The Laffer Curve shows the relationship between tax rates and
A. inflation.
B. tax revenues.
C. the federal deficit.
D. national income.

_____ 7. Lucas hypothesized that aggregate _____ is reduced when the expected price level is _____ the actual price level.
A. demand, greater than.
B. demand, less than.
C. supply, greater than.
D. supply, less than.

_____ 8. According to monetarists, inflation has persisted because
A. the Bank of Canada has accommodated the federal deficit by cutting the rate of growth of the money supply.
B. aggregate supply has failed to expand adequately because of regulation and tax laws.
C. aggregate supply has risen quite sharply despite government regulation and tax laws.
D. the Bank of Canada has accommodated the federal deficit through expansionary monetary policy actions.

_____ 9. Rational expectations models
A. assume that individuals have perfect knowledge of the future.
B. assume that individuals form expectations in sophisticated ways.
C. assume that individuals do not value economic information.
D. assume that consumers have less information than producers.

_____ 10. According to the Lucas supply function,
A. anticipated expansionary fiscal policy actions can increase production.
B. unanticipated expansionary fiscal policy actions can increase production.
C. anticipated expansionary monetary policy actions can increase production.
D. anticipated contractionary fiscal policy actions can increase production.

_____ 11. The Bank of Canada increases the money supply. If velocity is constant then either output _____ or the price level _____.
A. increases, increases.
B. increases, decreases.
C. decreases, increases.
D. decreases, decreases.

_____ 12. The Bank of Canada increases the money supply by 10%; the interest rate decreases. Because velocity decreases, the _____ in nominal GDP will be _____.
A. increase, more than 10%.
B. increase, less than 10%.
C. decrease, more than 10%.
D. decrease, less than 10%.

_____ 13. M2 is _____ than M1; the measure of velocity based on M2 will be _____ than the measure of velocity based on M1.
A. larger, larger.
B. larger, smaller.
C. smaller, larger.
D. smaller, smaller.

_____ 14. Which of the following schools of thought is not directly opposed to the use of fiscal policy to manipulate the macroeconomy?
A. Keynesian.
B. Monetarist.
C. Rational expectations.
D. New classical.

_____ 15. The velocity of money is the ratio of
A. nominal GDP to the stock of money.
B. real GDP to the stock of money.
C. stock of money to real GDP.
D. the stock of money to nominal GDP.

_____ 16. When inflation is increasing and expectations are formed rationally, individuals will
A. consistently overestimate inflation.
B. consistently underestimate inflation.
C. estimate inflation correctly every time.
D. estimate inflation correctly on average, with randomly distributed errors.

_____ 17. Supply-siders argued that if, initially, tax rates were very high, then a cut in tax rates would _____ the amount of taxable income and _____ tax revenues.
A. increase, increase.
B. increase, decrease.
C. decrease, increase.
D. decrease, decrease.

_____ 18. According to the real business cycle theory, a beneficial productivity shock would _____ the unemployment rate and _____ the price level.
A. increase, increase.
B. increase, decrease.
C. decrease, increase.
D. decrease, decrease.

## II.    APPLICATION QUESTIONS

1.    In Arbez a simple proportional tax is imposed on wages. Tax revenues (T) are:

$$T = t \times W \times L$$

where t is the tax rate, W is the gross hourly wage rate, and L is the total supply of labour in hours.

The after-tax wage is        $Wn = (1 - t)W$

Suppose that W = $6, L = 10 000, and t = .3.
a.    Calculate tax revenues.
b.    What is the net hourly wage?
c.    Now suppose that the tax rate is reduced to .25. Calculate the new net hourly wage.
d.    For tax revenues to remain unchanged, how much must the labour supply increase (assuming that the gross hourly wage rate doesn't change)?

2.    a.    The values of P and Y in the table below give a short-run aggregate supply schedule. Calculate the values for PY and write them in the table.

| P | Y | PY | MV30 | MV45 |
|---|---|----|------|------|
| $0.50 | 50 | | | |
| $1.00 | 60 | | | |
| $2.00 | 70 | | | |
| $3.00 | 80 | | | |
| $4.00 | 90 | | | |
| $5.00 | 100 | | | |
| $6.00 | 110 | | | |

b.    Suppose that velocity (V) is constant and equal to 8, and that the money supply is equal to $30. Complete the MV30 column of the table, which represents M times V.
c.    In equilibrium, calculate the nominal GDP level, the price level, and the real output level.
d.    Now the Bank of Canada increases the money supply to $45 (a 50% increase). Velocity remains constant. Complete the MV45 column of the table.
e.    In equilibrium, calculate the nominal GDP level, the price level, and the real output level when the money supply is $45.

Can you see that the MV30 and MV45 columns represent the dollar value of expenditures at different levels of the money supply? For a monetarist, this is the same thing as an aggregate demand curve!

Our supply schedule is short-run—monetary policy actions have an effect on output. In the long run, however, a monetarist would claim that a ten percent increase in money supply would result in a ten percent increase in prices and in wages; real wage and output would be unaffected by price changes. Aggregate supply is vertical in the long run!

3.    Rational expectations theorists claim that the traditional (Keynesian) view of the formation of expectations about inflation leads to systematic mistakes. If formed rationally, these mistakes will not be systematic. (For example, they will tend not to be too large or too small in a predictable way.)

| | | | | | | | | | |
|---|---|---|---|---|---|---|---|---|---|
| Let $EP_t$ | = | Expected price level (this time period) |
| $P_t$ | = | Price level (this time period) |
| $EP_{t+1}$ | = | Expected price level (next time period) |

Suppose that individuals are backward-looking, following the formula $EP_{t+1} = EP_t + .5(EP_t - P_t)$ when they form their expectations.

Calculate the expected price level in the table below.

| Year | 0 | 1 | 2 | 3 | 4 | 5 | 6 | 7 | 8 | 9 |
|---|---|---|---|---|---|---|---|---|---|---|
| Price Level | 100 | 100 | 110 | 121 | 131 | 142 | 126 | 115 | 107 | 100 |
| Expected Price Level | 100 | __ | __ | __ | __ | __ | __ | __ | __ | __ |

Graph the values for the expected price level and the price level on the graph.

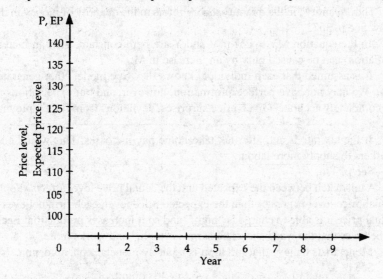

4.  a.  In the diagram below, why are tax collections zero at point A?

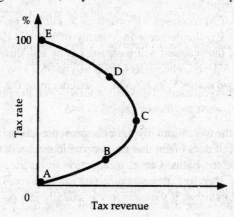

   b.  Why are tax collections zero at point E?
   c.  At which point on the curve did Laffer believe the U.S. economy was in the early 1980s?
   d.  What policy action would be called for if Laffer was correct?
   e.  Assuming spending programs remained unchanged, what effect would this policy have on the budget deficit?

f.  What effect did Laffer believe this sort of move would have on the supply of labour?

g.  If the tax rate was at point B, and the same policy were pursued, what would have happened to the deficit and the supply of labour?

# ANSWERS AND SOLUTIONS

## PRACTICE TEST

### I.  SOLUTIONS TO MULTIPLE CHOICE QUESTIONS

1.  B.  This is a good, easy-to-understand definition of velocity. Note that it does not require velocity to be constant.

2.  C.  The "quantity" in the quantity theory refers to the quantity of money in the economy. See p. 367.

3.  C.  In the equation MV = PY, if V and Y are both constant, then an increase in P (inflation) can be caused only by an increase in M.

4.  C.  It is assumed that each individual knows the "true model" that generates inflation. We may not have perfect information, however, and our expectations may not be completely accurate. Given price surprises, deviations from full employment will occur.

5.  C.  If the tax rate is cut, after-tax take-home pay increases. This would encourage workers to supply more labour.

6.  B.  See p. 376.

7.  C.  A mismatch between the expected and the actual price level affects supply. If the actual price level is greater than the expected price level, each firm believes that the actual price it is able to charge is "high," and so it increases production. Each worker believes that the wage she or he earns is "high," and works more.

8.  D.  Monetarists believe that inflation is a purely monetary phenomenon.

9.  B.  See p. 371.

10. B.  Anticipated changes will have no effect on the economy, according to the rational-expectations hypothesis.

11. A.  MV = PY so if M increases with constant V, either P or Y must increase.

12. B.  Given MV = PY, the decrease in V partly offsets the 10% increase in M. The right-hand side of the equation will increase, but by less than the full 10%.

13. B.  M2 includes M1 and other assets, such as personal savings deposits. Given the value of GDP, if we define V as PY / M, V will decrease the larger the value of M.

14. A.  See p. 370.

15. A.  See p. 367.

16. D.  The rational-expectations hypothesis does not claim that expectations will always be correct. It does claim that no systematic error will be made.

17. A.  According to the Laffer Curve, a reduction in tax rates will encourage more labour supply and, therefore, more income that can be taxed. Despite lower tax rates, tax revenues will increase, if the economy is initially at a point such as A in Figure 18.2 on p. 376.

18. D.  The AS curve will shift right.

### II.  SOLUTIONS TO APPLICATION QUESTIONS

1.  a.  Tax revenue = t × W × L = .3 × $6 × 10 000 = $18 000.
    b.  The net wage (after tax) = (1 – t)W = .7 × $6 = $4.20.
    c.  The net wage (after tax) = (1 – t)W = .75 × $6 = $4.50.

d.   It must change from 10 000 to 12 000. Tax revenue = t × W × L = .25 × $6 × 12 000 = $18 000.

2.   a.  See the table below.

| P | Y | PY | MV30 | MV45 |
|---|---|---|---|---|
| $0.50 | 50 | $ 25 | $240 | $360 |
| $1.00 | 60 | $ 60 | $240 | $360 |
| $2.00 | 70 | $140 | $240 | $360 |
| $3.00 | 80 | $240 | $240 | $360 |
| $4.00 | 90 | $360 | $240 | $360 |
| $5.00 | 100 | $500 | $240 | $360 |
| $6.00 | 110 | $660 | $240 | $360 |

b.   See the table above. In each case, M × V = 30 × 8 = 240.
c.   Nominal GDP = $240, price level = $3.00, output = 80. Recall that, in equilibrium, MV = PY.
d.   See the table above. In each case, M × V = 45 × 8 = 360.
e.   Nominal GDP = $360, price level = $4.00, output = 90.

3.   Example of calculations
Year 2: $EP_{t+1} = EP_t + .5(P_t - EP_t) = 100 + .5(100 - 100) = 100$
Year 3: $EP_{t+1} = EP_t + .5(P_t - EP_t) = 100 + .5(110 - 100) = 105$
Year 4: $EP_{t+1} = EP_t + .5(P_t - EP_t) = 105 + .5(121 - 105) = 113$
Year 5: $EP_{t+1} = EP_t + .5(P_t - EP_t) = 113 + .5(131 - 113) = 122$
Year 6: $EP_{t+1} = EP_t + .5(P_t - EP_t) = 122 + .5(142 - 122) = 132$
Year 7: $EP_{t+1} = EP_t + .5(P_t - EP_t) = 132 + .5(126 - 132) = 129$

| Year | 0 | 1 | 2 | 3 | 4 | 5 | 6 | 7 | 8 | 9 |
|---|---|---|---|---|---|---|---|---|---|---|
| Price Level | 100 | 100 | 110 | 121 | 131 | 142 | 126 | 115 | 107 | 100 |
| Expected Price Level | 100 | 100 | 100 | 105 | 113 | 122 | 132 | 129 | 122 | 114.5 |

In the graph below, note that at first individuals systematically underestimate increases in the price level and then overestimate them when the price level decreases.

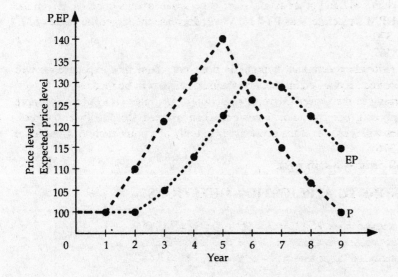

4.  a.  Tax collections are zero because the tax rate is zero.

    b.  If all income were taxed away, there would be no incentive to earn income. Income (and tax collections) would fall to zero.

    c.  Point D. Laffer felt that tax rates were acting as a significant disincentive to work.

    d.  Reduce tax rates, moving from point D toward point C.

    e.  The deficit would have fallen because tax revenues would have increased.

    f.  Because after-tax pay was rising, labour supply would have risen, according to Laffer.

    g.  If the tax rate were reduced from point B, the supply of labour should still have risen, but, because of shrinking tax revenues, the deficit would have increased.

# 19 Economic Growth and Productivity

## OBJECTIVES: POINT BY POINT

After completing this chapter, you should be able to accomplish the objectives listed below.

### OBJECTIVE 1: Define economic growth.

### OBJECTIVE 2: Identify the sources of economic growth.

*Economic growth* is an increase in real per capital GDP resulting in improved standards of living. This chapter is concerned with what causes the upward trend. Production is limited by the resources and technology that the economy possesses. Growth occurs when more resources become available or when current resources are used more efficiently. In terms of the production possibility frontier, the maximum levels of production shift to the right as the resource base expands and/or technology improves. (page 381)

Growth can take place in two ways: Either the economy discovers new resources or it uses its given resources more efficiently. Growth occurs, then, through:

a. an increase in resources,
   i. labour supply
   ii. physical capital
   iii. human capital;

b. the discovery of new ways to combine resources more efficiently—to increase their productivity,
   i. technological change
   ii. other advances in knowledge
   iii. economies of scale.

## Practice

1. Economic growth is defined as an increase in
   A. real output.
   B. consumption per household.
   C. economic well-being.
   D. the rate at which inventions occur.

   **ANSWER:** A. Growth is difficult to measure—the accepted yardstick is real GDP (or real GDP per capita).

2. When we draw a production possibility frontier (ppf), we assume that
   A. the quantity of capital available increases as we move along the ppf.
   B. the quantity of capital available increases and the quantity of labour decreases as we move along the ppf.
   C. the quantity of labour available increases as we move along the ppf.
   D. the quantity of capital and labour is fixed.

   **ANSWER:** D. It is assumed that the resource base and technology are fixed. Changes in any one of these constraints will cause the ppf to shift position.

3. Graphically, economic growth can be represented by a
   A. rightward shift of the aggregate demand curve.
   B. leftward shift of the aggregate demand curve.
   C. rightward shift of the production possibility frontier.
   D. leftward shift of the production possibility frontier.

   **ANSWER:** C.  Economic growth is an expansion in an economy's possible levels of production. See p. 382.

4. A production possibility frontier shows
   A. how much of a good will be produced as the price of the good changes.
   B. all the combinations of two goods that can be produced when all resources are being used efficiently.
   C. all the combinations of two resources that can be produced efficiently.
   D. how much of a product can be produced as additional units of input are added to the production mix.

   **ANSWER:** B.  See the diagram on p. 382.

5. Which of the following is an incorrect statement about the term "capital"?
   A. Capital has no effect on the productivity of labour.
   B. Capital yields services to people over a period of time.
   C. The act of producing capital goods may involve a sacrifice in terms of current consumption.
   D. The addition to the stock of capital is called investment.

   **ANSWER:** A.  Capital can be combined with labour to make workers more productive.

6. Colleen and Bill construct a net out of vines so that they can trap fish. Having never done this before, they find out that they are "learning by doing." Collleen and Bill are
   A. acquiring physical capital only.
   B. acquiring human capital only.
   C. acquiring physical capital and human capital.
   D. acquiring a consumption good.

   **ANSWER:** C.  The net is a tool that should increase their ability to catch fish—it is physical capital. By learning as they work, Colleen and Bill are increasing their human capital.

## OBJECTIVE 3: Define aggregate production function and explain the importance of diminishing returns.

A production function relates combinations of inputs to the maximum level of output of a good; an *aggregate production function* does the same thing for national output in the entire economy. Increases in the quantity and quality of resources and increases in productivity cause the output level to rise. (page 383)

As additional units of a resource (e.g., labour) are added to a fixed quantity of other resources, after some point their productivity will begin to decline. When capacity constraints begin to make themselves felt, diminishing returns result. This phenomenon was the reason for the gloomy predictions of Malthus and Ricardo.

> **Tip:** Each additional unit of a resource will experience diminishing returns when added to a fixed quantity of other resources. Also, note that diminishing returns apply to any resource, not just labour.

But growth still occurs even with diminishing returns because of increases in resource inputs and/or the introduction of new ways to use these resources more efficiently.

Although, since Confederation, Canada has achieved a record of growth that would be the envy of most nations, there has been some concern since the 1970s that the growth rate has fallen. Proposed public policies to correct sagging growth have included policies intended to:

    a.    stimulate investment in machinery and equipment,
    b.    improve education,
    c.    increase openness to trade and investment,
    d.    increase the saving rate, and
    e.    increase research and development.                    (pages 391-392)

**Tip:** Notice that monetary growth is not one of the variables listed as affecting long-term economic growth. The point is that changes in the quantity of money might influence production in the short term, but that monetary expansions, boosting aggregate demand, will ultimately run up against the supply-side constraint. Pumping up the money supply might enhance short-term growth, but also might breed inflation. Unanticipated inflation, which heightens risk and lessens the willingness of individuals to make long-term commitments, might have an adverse effect on investment. (Remember, too, that during rapid inflation, individuals may prefer to buy goods rather than save in a currency that is losing its spending power.)

**Comment:** Society can accumulate capital only through net investment, and investment in future production can occur only if current consumption is given up. Saving then has an important influence on growth. This key point can be applied both to the accumulation of physical capital and also to investment in human capital.

## Practice

7.    Malthus and Ricardo were concerned that the fixed supply of _____ would lead to diminishing returns.
    A.    capital.
    B.    technology.
    C.    labour.
    D.    land.

    **ANSWER:** D.   See p. 384.

8.    In Arbez, the capital stock is fixed. Because of immigration, the supply of labour increases. As diminishing returns set in, we would expect output to _____ and average labour productivity to _____.
    A.    increase, increase.
    B.    increase, decrease.
    C.    decrease, increase.
    D.    decrease, decrease.

    **ANSWER:** B.   As additional resources are added, output should increase, but more slowly. As diminishing returns set in, average productivity will decline. See p. 384.

9. Malthus and Ricardo believed that, in order to provide enough food for a rapidly growing population, farmers would have to cultivate _____ productive land _____ intensively.
   A. more, more.
   B. more, less.
   C. less, more.
   D. less, less.

   **ANSWER:** C. Presumably, the best land was already under cultivation, with less good land left unexploited. This land would have to be pressed into service and farmed intensively.

10. Diminishing returns to labour will occur if
    A. capital accumulation takes place, given the supply of labour.
    B. there is technological change, given the supply of labour.
    C. the labour supply grows more rapidly than the capital stock.
    D. the labour supply gains additional skills.

    **ANSWER:** C. See p. 384.

11. An increase in human capital will _____ labour productivity and _____ output.
    A. increase, increase.
    B. increase, decrease.
    C. decrease, increase.
    D. decrease, decrease.

    **ANSWER:** A. See p. 386.

12. As industries increase in size, they derive cost savings called
    A. innovations.
    B. inventions.
    C. external economies of scale.
    D. cost depreciations.

    **ANSWER:** C. As industries expand, "overheads" might be reduced—for example, by training or educational programs for employees—or the creation of a pool of skilled labour in a region.

13. Arboc has experienced growth, although the quantity of its inputs has remained unchanged. This growth must have been caused by
    A. random shocks to the economic system.
    B. an increase in the productivity of inputs.
    C. an increase in imports.
    D. a decrease in imports.

    **ANSWER:** B. If the quantity of resources is unchanged but more output is produced, productivity must have increased. Labour productivity is defined as output/labour. Changes in imports are irrelevant given that the quantity of inputs is unchanged. If Arboc had imported extra machinery, for example, the quantity of capital in Arboc would have changed.

14. An industrial consultant enters a car factory and reorganizes the layout of the assembly line. Without changing the amount of capital or the number of workers, car production can be increased by 10%. This change is
    A. both labour-saving and capital-saving.
    B. labour-saving but not capital-saving.
    C. capital-saving but not labour-saving.
    D. neither labour-saving nor capital-saving.

    **ANSWER:** A. Each worker and each unit of capital is more productive than before.

15. "New growth theory" emphasizes
    A. monetary policy.
    B. diminishing returns.
    C. the determinants of technological progress.
    D. population growth.

    **ANSWER:** C. See p. 387.

16. Which statement is true concerning the slower GDP growth Canada has experienced since 1973?
    A. This growth reduction is unique to Canada among the OECD countries.
    B. While the growth rate was lower in 1973, it increased in the early 1990s back to its 1960s' level.
    C. The slow growth is despite a high saving rate.
    D. One explanation that has been offered for lower growth is that it is increasingly difficult to measure output in today's advanced economies.

    **ANSWER:** D. Lower growth was experienced by virtually all OECD countries. See p. 389.

17. Which of the following has not been advanced as a way of increasing the rate of growth in Canada?
    A. Increasing the rate of consumption spending.
    B. Cutting government regulation of industry.
    C. Encouraging additional research and development.
    D. Implementing an industrial policy.

    **ANSWER:** A. Increasing the rate of consumption spending requires that the saving rate be decreased. One of the key determinants of growth is the economy's willingness to forgo current consumption.

## OBJECTIVE 4: Summarize the arguments for and against continued economic growth.

Growth is not a universally accepted goal; there are costs and benefits. The benefits are obvious—more leisure and material possessions—but costs are present too. Growth may be accompanied by pollution and other "bads" that adversely affect the quality of life and alienate the worker. Big business may induce demand for its products rather than respond to market demands. Rapid growth may deplete the world's resources while widening the gap between the "haves" and the "have-nots." As is usually the case in economics, the decision to encourage or discourage growth involves trade-offs.

(page 394)

### Practice

18. Supporters of growth claim all of the following except that
    A.   growth gives more choices.
    B.   growth saves time.
    C.   growth improves the standard of living.
    D.   growth reduces income inequalities.

    **ANSWER:** D.   In fact, it is one of the anti-growth arguments that growth increases income inequality.

19. Which of the following arguments is not made by opponents of economic growth?
    A.   Growth requires an unfair distribution of income.
    B.   Growth rapidly depletes the world's finite resources.
    C.   The net impact of growth on the quality of life is beneficial.
    D.   Growth encourages the creation of artificial needs.

    **ANSWER:** C.   Opponents of growth argue that increased growth removes many beneficial, if unmeasurable, aspects of life.

20. Which statement is true?
    A.   For poor nations, redistribution of existing income is a fast track to growth.
    B.   For poor nations, growth is the main hope for improvement in the standard of living in the long run.
    C.   Growth benefits all groups of society equally.
    D.   Advocates of economic growth argue that growth equals progress.

    **ANSWER:** B.   See p. 394.

## PRACTICE TEST

**I.   MULTIPLE CHOICE QUESTIONS.** Select the option that provides the single best answer.

_____ 1.   Economic growth refers to growth in
    A.   nominal GDP.
    B.   per capita real GDP.
    C.   nominal per capita GDP.
    D    real GDP.

_____ 2.   The law of diminishing returns suggests that increases in the _____, *ceteris paribus*, may not lead to increased _____.
    A.   stock of capital, employment.
    B.   number of workers, output per capita.
    C.   number of workers, efficiency of capital.
    D.   stock of capital, money supply.

_____ 3.   Which of the following is not one of the areas of government investment in human capital?
    A.   health care.
    B.   transportation infrastructure.
    C.   education.
    D.   job training.

_____ 4.  _____ generally enhances labour productivity. An increase in _____ can increase _____.
  - A.   Competition, output, income.
  - B.   Competition, population, output.
  - C.   Training, capital, income.
  - D.   Capital, capital, output.

_____ 5.  The amount of capital accumulation is limited ultimately by
  - A.   the interest rate.
  - B.   marginal tax rates.
  - C.   disposable (after-tax) income.
  - D.   the saving rate.

_____ 6.  In general, economic growth will occur when there are additions to
  - A.   the labour force.
  - B.   per capita nominal income.
  - C.   the stock of money.
  - D.   import purchases.

_____ 7.  A public policy strategy designed to increase productivity might include which one of the following?
  - A.   Increased regulations on industrial pollution.
  - B.   Tax breaks on interest income.
  - C.   Tax incentives to increase consumption spending.
  - D.   Increases in college tuition.

_____ 8.  Each of the following has been suggested as a likely reason for the decline in the growth rate of labour productivity in the 1970s except
  - A.   relatively low saving rates.
  - B.   government regulations.
  - C.   inadequate research and development spending.
  - D.   low energy costs.

_____ 9.  Each of the following has been proposed as a major anti-growth argument except
  - A.   the increased creation of "needs."
  - B.   the reduction in the quality of life.
  - C.   the increased choices available to the economy.
  - D.   the uneven distribution of benefits across the community.

_____ 10.  Long-term economic growth will occur except through
  - A.   an increase in the quantity of labour.
  - B.   an increase in the quality of labour.
  - C.   an increase in the quantity of money.
  - D.   an increase in the quantity of physical capital.

_____ 11.  Pro-growth supporters argue that growth allows a society to allocate resources
  - A.   to only those industries that produce goods without pollution.
  - B.   to compete against unfair foreign imports.
  - C.   to produce goods that households want.
  - D.   to increase government regulation.

_____ 12.  The introduction of computer catalogues in a library is a
  - A.   labour-saving invention.
  - B.   labour-saving innovation.
  - C.   capital-saving invention.
  - D.   capital-saving innovation.

_____ 13. Malthus and Ricardo were concerned that there would be insufficient food because of the fixed supply of land. They failed to foresee the effect of _____ on agricultural production.
A. additional labour supply.
B. technological improvements.
C. diminishing returns.
D. erosion.

_____ 14. An increase in the capital/labour ratio will
A. increase the productivity of capital.
B. increase the productivity of labour.
C. increase the productivity of labour and capital.
D. decrease the productivity of labour and capital.

_____ 15. A hallmark of economies experiencing modern economic growth is
A. a stable capital to labour (K / L) ratio.
B. an increasing capital to labour (K / L) ratio.
C. a decrease in public capital.
D. a decreasing capital to labour (K / L) ratio.

## II.   APPLICATION QUESTIONS

1. The following tables present data on three economies: Arbez, Arboc, and Aneyh. Complete the tables. What do the data tell you about the causes of growth?

| Arbez Period | L | K | Y | Y/L | Growth Rate of Output |
|---|---|---|---|---|---|
| 1 | 100 | 300 | 520.00 | | |
| 2 | 110 | 304 | 546.00 | | |
| 3 | 119 | 307 | 578.76 | | |
| 4 | 123 | 312 | 596.12 | | |

| Arboc Period | L | K | Y | Y/L | Growth Rate of Output |
|---|---|---|---|---|---|
| 1 | 100 | 300 | 520.00 | | |
| 2 | 105 | 309 | 551.20 | | |
| 3 | 111 | 317 | 589.78 | | |
| 4 | 114 | 327 | 619.27 | | |

| Aneyh Period | L | K | Y | Y/L | Growth Rate of Output |
|---|---|---|---|---|---|
| 1 | 100 | 300 | 520.00 | | |
| 2 | 105 | 304 | 540.90 | | |
| 3 | 111 | 307 | 567.84 | | |
| 4 | 114 | 312 | 579.20 | | |

2. How will each of the following affect the long-run measured growth rate in the nation of Noil?
   a. Noil's Ministry of the Environment imposes more stringent environmental regulations on business.
   b. The government increases spending on education. The additional spending is financed by a tax on consumers.
   c. The government pledges to trim the deficit by reducing the size of the Noilian army.
   d. The government pledges to trim the deficit by cutting expenditures on education.
   e. Noil opens its borders to migrant workers from Regit.

3. There are two neighbouring economies—Formica and Klorofill. Each economy has an identical production possibility frontier (ppf), as shown below. Currently at F1, Formica prefers to produce investment goods, while Klorofill, currently at K1, prefers a relatively high rate of consumption.
   Note: The ppfs are drawn as straight lines merely for simplicity.

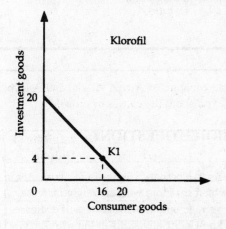 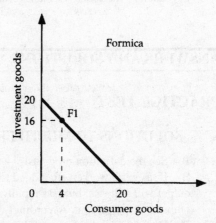

   Suppose that each economy was in a recession last time period. In fact, each economy produced 4 units of consumer goods and 4 units of investment goods.
   a. In Klorofill's case, the economy has moved to K1. How would you represent this change on an AS/AD diagram? In Formica's case, the economy has moved to F1. How would you represent this change on an AS/AD diagram?

   Let us assume that the depreciation rate in each economy is 4 machines per year, where one "machine" is one unit of the investment good.
   b. What is happening to the capital stock in Klorofill this year? In Formica?
   c. Describe the effect on the Klorofillian ppf. Describe the effect on the Formican ppf.
   d. Describe how Klorofill's AS/AD diagram will differ from that of Formica, as time passes.

   Let us assume that the depreciation rate in each economy is 5 machines per year.
   e. What is happening to the capital stock in Klorofill this year? In Formica?
   f. Describe the effect on the Klorofillian ppf. Describe the effect on the Formican ppf.
   g. Describe the differences in choices faced by Klorofillians and Formicans as time passes.

4. Write down the six factors that cause growth in the table below, and match each with one of the following examples.

| Letter | Factor |
|--------|--------|
|        |        |
|        |        |
|        |        |
|        |        |
|        |        |
|        |        |

Examples:

A. the construction of a new, larger factory  B. improvements in health  C. the implementation of a newly discovered production process  D. decreasing production costs as plant size increases  E. managerial skills  F. immigration

# ANSWERS AND SOLUTIONS

## PRACTICE TEST

### I.    SOLUTIONS TO MULTIPLE CHOICE QUESTIONS

1.    B.   See the definition on p. 381.
2.    B.   If, as extra workers are added to productive activity, diminishing returns set in, output will still rise, but less rapidly. Five percent more workers might increase output by four percent. Accordingly, the average output of workers will decrease.
3.    B.   Human capital refers to the stock of knowledge and skills in the workforce, and depends on things such as education, health, and on-the-job training. One could argue that investing in transportation would increase human capital through reduced injuries in traffic accidents, improved access to educational institutions, etc., but it affects output mainly through a more direct impact on the physical stock of public infrastructure. See p. 386.
4.    D.   Capital is usually a complement for labour. Additional capital increases the productivity of each worker.
5.    D.   See p. 391.
6.    A.   Growth occurs when inputs increase or improve, or technology changes.
7.    B.   If the rate of saving (non-consumption) is the ultimate constraint on growth, measures to encourage saving will encourage growth. Option C clearly moves in the opposite direction. Option A makes production more difficult while Option D reduces inputs in the future (i.e., human capital).
8.    D.   High energy costs as a reason for slower growth, as they led to investment designed to save energy rather than to enhance productivity. See p. 389.
9.    C.   See the list of arguments on p. 394.
10.   C.   Money, by itself, is not a productive resource. Robinson Crusoe, on his island, would have had little use for paper currency except, perhaps, to kindle a fire.
11.   C.   The ultimate goal of growth is to give people the things they want.
12.   B.   See p. 387.
13.   B.   Improved technology (better planting and harvesting techniques, improved fertilizers, hardier and better-yielding hybrids) has allowed farmers to increase production while reducing the amount of land under cultivation.

14.  B.   An increase in the capital/labour ratio means that each worker has more equipment with which to work. Labour productivity will increase. The productivity of capital will decrease because additional capital is being added to a given stock of labour.

15.  B.   See p. 386.

## II.   SOLUTIONS TO APPLICATION QUESTIONS

1.   See the tables below.

| Arbez Period | L | K | Y | Y/L | Growth Rate of Output |
|---|---|---|---|---|---|
| 1 | 100 | 300 | 520.00 | 5.20 | |
| 2 | 110 | 304 | 546.00 | 4.96 | 5.00% |
| 3 | 119 | 307 | 578.76 | 4.86 | 6.00% |
| 4 | 123 | 312 | 596.12 | 4.85 | 3.00% |

| Arboc Period | L | K | Y | Y/L | Growth Rate of Output |
|---|---|---|---|---|---|
| 1 | 100 | 300 | 520.00 | 5.20 | |
| 2 | 105 | 309 | 551.20 | 5.25 | 6.00% |
| 3 | 111 | 317 | 589.78 | 5.31 | 7.00% |
| 4 | 114 | 327 | 619.27 | 5.43 | 5.00% |

| Aneyh Period | L | K | Y | Y/L | Growth Rate of Output |
|---|---|---|---|---|---|
| 1 | 100 | 300 | 520.00 | 5.20 | |
| 2 | 105 | 304 | 540.80 | 5.15 | 4.00% |
| 3 | 111 | 307 | 567.84 | 5.12 | 5.00% |
| 4 | 114 | 312 | 579.20 | 5.08 | 2.00% |

The growth rate is greatest in Arboc. Compared with Aneyh, whose rate of growth in labour resources is identical, Arboc is superior in output/labour ratio. Compared with Arbez, Arboc's Y/L ratio is increasing, while that of Arbez is decreasing. However, Arbez is growing more rapidly than Aneyh because Arbez's labour force is expanding more rapidly.

2.   a   More stringent environmental regulations on businesses will reduce the measured growth rate. Profits will be reduced and less investment will occur.

   b.   The growth rate will rise because of additional investment in human capital and because the tax on consumption will encourage households to save more.

   c.   The growth rate will increase in the long run, because, with a reduced deficit, national saving will be greater and interest rates will be lower. Private investment will be encouraged. (In the short run, the government spending reduction will reduce GDP and its growth rate.)

   d.   The effect on the growth rate is uncertain. A reduced deficit will encourage investment (see part c, above), but lower educational expenditure represents a reduction in human capital investment (see part b, above). The growth rate will increase if there is a greater return on private investment or on education.

e.     Immigration increases the labour force and may reduce the capital to labour ratio. If so, productivity will decrease. However, the Regitani workers may be highly skilled and/or more highly motivated to succeed. If so, productivity would increase and Noil would benefit from the influx.

3.     a.     The AD curve has moved to the right by the same amount in each case. Total output has increased by the same amount in each country.

     b.     The capital stock in Klorofill is stationary, with 4 new machines being produced and 4 existing machines wearing out. In Formica, the capital stock is increasing by 12 (i.e., 16 – 4).

     c.     Klorofill's ppf is stationary; Formica's ppf is shifting outward as its productive resources increase through the increase in its capital stock.

     d.     Klorofill's AD curve will remain stationary with consumption at 16 units and investment at 4 units. Productive capacity is not increasing; therefore the aggregate supply curve will not shift. In Formica, aggregate supply will increase to match expansions in aggregate demand because of the expanding resource base.

     e.     The capital stock in Klorofill is declining, with 4 new machines being produced and 5 existing machines wearing out. In Formica, the capital stock is increasing by 11 (i.e., 16 – 5).

     f.     Klorofill's ppf is shifting inward; Formica's ppf is shifting outward as its productive resources increase.

     g.     As time passes, the Klorofillians will be forced to cut back their standard of living. Currently, their resource base is shrinking. To prevent this, they will have to increase investment good production at the expense of consumer good production. The Formicans face no such hard choice—their ppf is shifting outward, so they can increase consumption and investment levels.

4.     A.     an increase in physical capital.

     B.     an increase in human capital.

     C.     technological change.

     D.     economies of scale.

     E.     an advance in knowledge.

     F.     an increase in the supply of labour.

# 20 International Trade, Comparative Advantage, and Protectionism

## OBJECTIVES: POINT BY POINT

After completing this chapter, you should be able to accomplish the objectives listed below.

### OBJECTIVE 1: Define trade surplus and trade deficit.

In open economies such as Canada's, aggregate expenditures are affected by the presence of exports and imports. We have seen international trade steadily increase in importance throughout the last several decades. If exports exceed imports, the country runs a *trade surplus*. If imports exceed exports, the country runs a *trade deficit*.          (page 402)

> **Tip:** Learn the difference between exports and imports. Imports are foreign-produced goods consumed here. Exports are domestically-produced goods sold to customers overseas. Imports and exports are not opposites; they are determined by different factors.

**Comment:** The two terms, "balance of payments" and "balance of trade," are not synonymous. The balance of trade refers only to exports and imports of goods and services, while the balance of payments (discussed in Chapter 21 of *Principles of Macroeconomics*) includes all international transactions.

## Practice

1.  Canada's balance of trade for goods is typically a _____ while its balance of trade for services is typically a _____.
    A.  surplus, peak.
    B.  surplus, minimum.
    C.  surplus, deficit.
    D.  deficit, surplus.

    **ANSWER:** C.  See page 402 or Table 20.2 on p. 403 (where it is clear that the balance of trade on goods and services is usually less than the balance of trade on goods alone).

### OBJECTIVE 2: Distinguish between absolute advantage and comparative advantage.

### OBJECTIVE 3: Explain how both countries in a trading relationship can gain from trade with appropriate terms of trade. Explain how with fixed money prices, exchange rates affect the terms of trade.

The *theory of comparative advantage* provides the rationale for free trade. Given a two-country, two-good world, and assuming that the countries have advantages in the production of different goods, Ricardo showed that both trading partners could benefit from specialization in the production of the good in which they have the comparative advantage. Each country should specialize in the production of that good in which it has a comparative advantage and trade its surplus. Production and welfare will be maximized. Country A is said to have an *absolute advantage* if it can produce a unit of output with fewer resources than Country B. Comparative advantage, though, is a relative concept. Country A will have a *comparative advantage* in whichever good it can produce comparatively cheaper. Specialization and trade allow a country to consume more than it can produce of a good. (page 407)

**Tip:** If you're like most individuals, you'll need several numerical examples to strengthen your grasp of pure trade theory. The Applications below take you through all the steps included in the text. Review Application questions 2, 7, and 10 in Chapter 2 of this manual. They will lead you through the opportunity cost concept that underlies the theory of comparative advantage.

**Tip:** Comparative advantage hinges on the concept of opportunity cost. (Take a little time to go back and review the material you learned in Chapters 1 and 2.) The producer (person, firm, or country) with the lowest *opportunity cost* will hold the comparative advantage in that product.

**Graphing Pointer:** Using the production possibility frontier (ppf) diagram, trade will be advantageous if the ppf's have differing slopes. Differing slopes mean that a comparative advantage exists—i.e., that the relative costs of production differ. Even though Country A may be more efficient in producing both goods—an absolute advantage—it is the *comparative* advantage of Country A that will establish the preferred pattern of specialization and trade. The country with the flatter curve has an advantage in the good on the horizontal axis.

Given that specialization occurs, *the terms of trade* (the "price" of the traded commodities) must be negotiated. For trade to be beneficial, the "price" of the exported good (in terms of the imported good) must be greater than its cost of production. A range of terms of trade will exist. The deal cut within this range will depend on the relative negotiating strengths of the two partners. (page 408)

Many trade examples are discussed without reference to currency (e.g., one country trades wheat directly for cloth) but in real life, most international trade involves currencies. Trade flows are affected by prices in each country and by the exchange rate (the "price" of the domestic currency in terms of a foreign currency). There will be a range of exchange rates that will permit mutually beneficial specialization and trade. (page 410)

To buy foreign goods, there must be a purchase of foreign currency, which is bought and sold in the foreign exchange market. If the value of the dollar changes, the relative attractiveness of the foreign goods will be affected. The strengthening yen will increase the price tag of a Toyota for a Canadian buyer, but the price tag of the domestically-produced Chrysler will not change—the relative attractiveness of the Toyota will decline. Tourists watch exchange rates keenly—a stronger dollar is good news because each dollar will buy more foreign currency and, therefore, more foreign goods and services (which have, in that sense, become cheaper). Note that when we discuss the effects of exchange rate changes, we are assuming that domestic prices do not change. This seems reasonable as exchange rates can change every minute, but many goods prices change less frequently.

> **Tip:** Remember that an increase in the value of the dollar means that foreign goods cost Canadians less (imports increase), but Canadian goods cost foreigners more (exports fall).

## Practice

Refer to the following table to answer the next four questions. The table shows the possible output levels from one day of labour input.

|  | **Arbez** | **Arboc** |
|---|---|---|
| Wheat | 12 cubic metres | 6 cubic metres |
| Cloth | 12 metres | 12 metres |

2.  Arbez
    A.  has an absolute advantage in the production of cloth.
    B.  has an absolute advantage in the production of wheat.
    C.  has a comparative advantage in the production of cloth.
    D.  should export cloth to Arboc.

    **ANSWER: B.** Arbez can produce absolutely more wheat per worker than Arboc can.

3.  The opportunity cost of one cubic metre of wheat in Arboc is
    A.  1/2 metre of cloth.
    B.  2 metres of cloth.
    C.  6 metres of cloth.
    D.  12 metres of cloth.

    **ANSWER: B.** 6 cubic metres would cost 12 metres of cloth; therefore 1 cubic metre costs 2 metres of cloth.

4.  Which of the following statements is false?
    A.  Arboc has an absolute advantage in the production of wheat.
    B.  Arbez should export wheat to Arboc and import cloth from Arboc.
    C.  The opportunity cost of wheat is twice as high in Arboc as in Arbez.
    D.  The opportunity cost of a metre of cloth in Arbez is one cubic metre of wheat.

    **ANSWER: A.** Arboc is half as productive per worker as Arbez in wheat production.

5.  Arboc and Arbez decide to specialize according to the law of comparative advantage and trade with one another. We would expect that
    A.  the trade agreement will be somewhere between 1 cubic metre of wheat for 1 metre of cloth and 1 cubic metre of wheat for 2 metres of cloth.
    B.  the trade agreement will be somewhere between 1/2 cubic metre of wheat for 1 metre of cloth and 2 cubic metres of wheat for 1 metre of cloth.
    C.  Arboc will benefit from trading with Arbez, but Arbez will not benefit from trading with Arboc.
    D.  Arboc will specialize in the production of wheat and Arbez will specialize in the production of cloth.

    **ANSWER:** A.  The Arbezani opportunity cost of 1 cubic metre of wheat is 1 metre of cloth. Arboc's opportunity cost of 1 cubic metre of wheat is 2 metres of cloth.

6.  The ratio at which exports are traded for imports is known as
    A.  the exchange rate.
    B.  the trade balance.
    C.  the balance of exchange.
    D.  the terms of trade.

    **ANSWER:** D.  See p. 408.

Use the following diagrams, which show hypothetical production possibility frontiers (ppf's) for Malaysia and Sri Lanka, to answer the next nine questions.

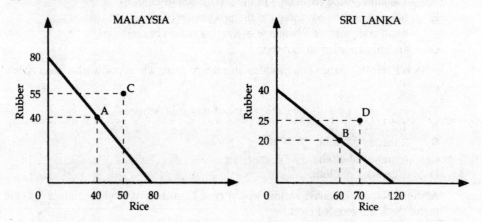

7.  Which of the following statements is true?
    A.  Malaysia has an absolute advantage in the production of rubber; Sri Lanka has an absolute advantage in the production of rice.
    B.  Sri Lanka has an absolute advantage in the production of rubber; Malaysia has an absolute advantage in the production of rice.
    C.  Malaysia has an absolute advantage in the production of both goods.
    D.  Sri Lanka has an absolute advantage in the production of both goods.

    **ANSWER:** A.  See p. 407.

8.  Which statement is false?
    A.  In Malaysia, the opportunity cost of one unit of rubber is one unit of rice.
    B.  In Malaysia, the opportunity cost of one unit of rice is one unit of rubber.
    C.  In Sri Lanka, the opportunity cost of one unit of rubber is three units of rice.
    D.  In Sri Lanka, the opportunity cost of one unit of rice is three units of rubber.

    **ANSWER:** D.  The Sri Lankan opportunity cost of one unit of rice is a third of a unit of rubber.

9. Which of the following statements is true?
    A. Malaysia has a comparative advantage in the production of rubber; Sri Lanka has a comparative advantage in the production of rice.
    B. Sri Lanka has a comparative advantage in the production of rubber; Malaysia has a comparative advantage in the production of rice.
    C. Malaysia has a comparative advantage in both goods.
    D. Sri Lanka has a comparative advantage in both goods.

    **ANSWER:** A.  See p. 407.

10. Given that Malaysia and Sri Lanka decide to trade,
    A. Malaysia should specialize in the production of rubber; Sri Lanka should specialize in the production of rice.
    B. Malaysia should specialize in the production of rice; Sri Lanka should specialize in the production of rubber.
    C. Malaysia and Sri Lanka should each devote half their resources to the production of each commodity.
    D. Malaysia should specialize in the production of rubber; Sri Lanka should produce some rice but continue to produce some rubber.

    **ANSWER:** A.  Malaysia's comparative advantage lies in rubber production; Sri Lanka's lies in rice.

11. Before trade, Malaysia produced at Point A on its ppf and Sri Lanka produced at Point B. Given complete specialization based on comparative advantage, total rubber production has risen by _____ and total rice production has risen by _____.
    A. 80, 120.
    B. 120, 80.
    C. 40, 60.
    D. 20, 20.

    **ANSWER:** D.  Total rubber production was 60 (40 + 20); now it is 80. Total rice production was 100 (40 + 60); now it is 120.

12. After trade, suppose Malaysia is consuming at Point C and Sri Lanka is consuming at Point D. Malaysia is exporting _____ units of rubber and Sri Lanka is exporting _____ units of rice.
    A. 80, 100.
    B. 55, 70.
    C. 25, 50.
    D. 15, 10.

    **ANSWER:** C.  Malaysian rubber production is 80, and domestic consumption is 55, leaving 25 for export. Sri Lankan rice production is 120, and domestic consumption is 70, leaving 50 for export.

13. After trade, suppose Malaysia is consuming at Point C and Sri Lanka is consuming at Point D. Malaysia is importing _____ units of rice and Sri Lanka is importing _____ units of rubber.
    A. 80, 100.
    B. 50, 25.
    C. 25, 50.
    D. 15, 10.

    **ANSWER:** B.  See the answer to the previous question. In a two-country world, Country A's exports are Country B's imports.

14. Which statement is true?
    A. Only Sri Lanka will benefit if the terms of trade are set at 1 : 2, rubber to rice.
    B. Only Malaysia will benefit if the terms of trade are set at 1 : 2, rubber to rice.
    C. Both countries will gain if the terms of trade lie between 3 : 1 and 1 : 1, rubber to rice.
    D. Both countries will gain if the terms of trade lie between 1 : 1 and 1 : 3, rubber to rice.

    **ANSWER: D.** Check these values against the opportunity cost values you calculated in question 8. Also note the assumed value of the rubber : Rice ratio in question 12 is between 1 : 1 and 1 : 3.

15. Which statement is false? If the terms of trade are set at
    A. 1 : 1, rubber to rice, only Sri Lanka will gain.
    B. 1 : 2, rubber to rice, both countries will gain.
    C. 1 : 3, rubber to rice, only Malaysia will gain.
    D. 1 : 4, rubber to rice, both countries will wish to produce rice.

    **ANSWER: D.** If the terms of trade are set at 1 : 4, rubber to rice, rubber is relatively valuable and can cover its opportunity cost in both countries. Both will wish to produce rubber.

16. Suppose the exchange rate is one British pound equals $1.75. If the exchange rate changes to one British pound equals $1.50 (with constant prices), we can conclude that, for a British buyer, Canadian lumber has become _____ expensive and, for a Canadian buyer, a British cashmere sweater has become _____ expensive.
    A. more, more.
    B. more, less.
    C. less, more.
    D. less, less.

    **ANSWER: B.** Each pound is worth less Canadian currency—British buyers are becoming poorer. The opposite is true for Canadian buyers of British goods.

17. Given constant prices, if the exchange rate changes from one British pound equals $1.50 to one British pound equals $2.00, British traders will gain _____ from trade with Canada, and Canadian traders will gain _____ from trade with the United Kingdom.
    A. more, more.
    B. more, less.
    C. less, more.
    D. less, less.

    **ANSWER: B.** Each pound is worth more Canadian currency. British producers, selling the same amount of exports, will be able to claim more Canadian goods than before.

Use the following table, which shows hypothetical domestic prices per unit of steel and corn in Slovakia and Slovenia, to answer the next three questions.

18. If the exchange rate is 1 koruna = 1 tolar, then

|  | Slovakia | Slovenia |
|---|---|---|
| Steel | 20 koruna | 48 tolars |
| Corn | 30 koruna | 87 tolars |

A. Slovakia will import both steel and corn.
B. Slovenia will import both steel and corn.
C. Slovakia will import steel and Slovenia will import corn.
D. Slovakia will import corn and Slovenia will import steel.

**ANSWER: B.** In Slovenia, the domestic prices of steel and corn are 48 tolars and 87 tolars, respectively. The imported prices are 20 tolars and 30 tolars, respectively.

19. If the exchange rate is 1 koruna = 3 tolars, then
A. Slovakia will import both steel and corn.
B. Slovenia will import both steel and corn.
C. Slovakia will import steel and Slovenia will import corn.
D. Slovakia will import corn and Slovenia will import steel.

**ANSWER: A.** In Slovakia, the domestic prices of steel and corn are 20 koruna and 30 koruna, respectively. The imported prices are 16 koruna and 29 koruna, respectively.

20. Two-way trade will occur only if the price of the koruna is between
A. 1.0 tolars and 3.0 tolars.
B. 1.5 tolars and 2.4 tolars.
C. 2.4 tolars and 2.9 tolars.
D. 1.5 tolars and 3.0 tolars.

**ANSWER: C.** If the exchange rate is 1 koruna = 2.4 tolars, no trade in steel will occur. If the exchange rate is 1 koruna = 2.9 tolars, no trade in corn will occur. Between these rates, Slovakia will import steel and Slovenia will import corn.

## OBJECTIVE 4: Outline the Heckscher-Ohlin theorem.

The *Heckscher-Ohlin theorem* builds on the theory of comparative advantage by focusing on the different factor endowments of countries. Some countries seem more labour-abundant (India, China), while others are more capital-abundant (United States, Canada, Japan). The Heckscher-Ohlin theorem states that a country will specialize in and export that good whose production calls for a relatively intensive use of the input that the country has in abundance; India should export labour-intensive goods and import capital-intensive goods, for example. (page 412)

The assembly of audiocassettes requires a large stock of semi-skilled cheap labour with little capital. This favours Mexico. The production of timber requires an abundant stock of forest land—a requirement that Canada meets.

## Practice

21. We observe that Arbez produces wooden ornaments (a labour-intensive activity), and that Arboc produces plastic containers (a capital-intensive activity). Which of the following statements is true?
A. Arbez has more labour than Arboc; Arboc has more capital than Arbez.
B. Arboc has more labour than Arbez; Arbez has more capital than Arboc.
C. Labour is relatively abundant in Arbez.
D. Labour is relatively abundant in Arboc.

**ANSWER: C.** Assuming that the two countries are being rational, Arbez is producing the good in which it has a comparative advantage.

**OBJECTIVE 5: Describe how economies of scale in production can lead to international trade.**

Another possible explanation for trade is that countries specialize in certain goods because of economies of scale. For example, perhaps a plant that just served the Canadian television market would be inefficiently small so instead Canadians buy televisions made in the United States or Japan. However, Canada might have an efficiently-sized fibre optics plant, much too big for the Canadian market alone, which thrives by exporting to markets in other countries. (page 412)

## Practice

22. Switzerland is famous for watches, which it exports. This specialization is best explained by
    A. the large population of Switzerland, which provides many potential watch-makers.
    B. Swiss steel refineries which produce steel used in watch parts.
    C. Swiss diamond mines, as diamonds are used in watch mechanisms.
    D. economies of scale in the watch industry.

    **ANSWER:** D. As the watch industry became established, an input supply network developed within Switzerland. Also, existing watchmakers could teach their techniques to new workers. Both developments lowered the cost of firm expansion or the cost to new firms.

**OBJECTIVE 6: Define tariff, export subsidy, and quota. Show how a tariff reduces the gains from trade and how the loss can be measured.**

Tariffs, export subsidies, and quotas are examples of trade barriers. *Tariffs* are taxes on imports, designed to force up their price; *export subsidies* are government payments to domestic exporters, intended to make them more competitive overseas; *quotas* are limits on the quantity of imports. *Dumping* is meant to price competitors out of the market; having achieved market domination, the firm can then raise prices. (page 413)

## Practice

23. A tariff imposed on imported French wine will cause the Canadian price of French wine to _____ and Canadian production of wine to _____.
    A. increase, increase.
    B. increase, decrease.
    C. decrease, increase.
    D. decrease, decrease.

    **ANSWER:** A. The tax will push up the price of the import. This will increase the demand for substitutes.

Use the following diagram to answer the next three questions. The diagram shows the hypothetical Canadian demand for and supply of T-shirts. The world price is $4 per shirt.

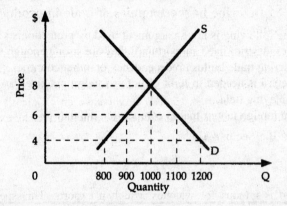

24. In an unrestricted open market, Canada will
    A. export 400 T-shirts.
    B. export 200 T-shirts.
    C. import 400 T-shirts.
    D. import 200 T-shirts.

    **ANSWER:** C. At a price of $4, there is an excess Canadian demand of 400.

25. The garment industry successfully lobbies the federal government to impose a $2 per shirt tax on imports. Now Canada will
    A. export 400 T-shirts.
    B. export 200 T-shirts.
    C. import 400 T-shirts.
    D. import 200 T-shirts.

    **ANSWER:** D. An excess demand remains that must be met from overseas.

26. The government will collect _____ in tariff revenues.
    A. $100.
    B. $200.
    C. $400.
    D. $800.

    **ANSWER:** C. The government collects $2 per shirt on each of the 200 imported shirts.

## OBJECTIVE 7: List the pros and cons of trade protection.

Free trade may improve competition within an economy, forestall retaliatory trade restrictions by other countries, and help domestic industries that depend on foreign inputs. The case for free trade is also based on the theory of comparative advantage. Trade benefits the participants. Welfare increases if trade flows are allowed to follow their "natural" pattern; obstacles, such as tariffs and quotas, reduce that welfare. Trade restrictions increase consumer prices.                                                                                      (page 415)

The argument in favour of protection is based on the observation that efficient foreign competition will result in job loss for domestic workers and lost production. (The counterargument is that inefficient industries should be closed so that workers and capital move to more competitive sectors, painful as that process can be.) Individual arguments for protection from foreign competition may include claims that cheap foreign labour is "unfair," that national security must be protected, that trade encourages dependency on foreigners, and that we need to let infant industries develop.                                           (page 418)

**Practice**

27. Which of the following is not an argument used by protectionists?
    A.  Infant industries need support until they are strong enough to complete.
    B.  Restricting trade builds up dependency on other countries.
    C.  Protection is needed in light of unfair foreign practices, in order to ensure a level playing field.
    D.  Cheap foreign labour makes competition unfair.

    **ANSWER:** B.  See p. 420.

---

# PRACTICE TEST

**I.     MULTIPLE CHOICE QUESTIONS.** Select the option that provides the single best answer.

_____ 1.  According to the textbook, which of the following is not a major export of Canada?
          A.  Automobiles, trucks, and motor vehicle parts.
          B.  Cocoa, coffee, and tea.
          C.  Forest products.
          D   Natural gas.

_____ 2.  A country imports less than it exports. It has
          A.  an export subsidy.
          B.  a tariff quota.
          C.  a trade surplus.
          D.  a trade deficit.

_____ 3.  Relative to Arboc, Arbez has a comparative advantage in the production of goat milk. We can say that Arbez
          A.  uses fewer resources to produce goat milk than does Arboc.
          B.  must also have an absolute advantage in the production of goat milk.
          C.  is the producer with the lower opportunity cost of producing goat milk.
          D.  should diversify into other products rather than trade with the high-cost, inefficient Arbocalis.

_____ 4.  In Arbez/Arboc trade, an increase in the value of the Arbezani currency (the bandu) relative to that of the Arbocali currency (the opek) means that
          A.  Arbezani goods will appear to be relatively cheaper to the Arbocalis.
          B.  Arbocali goods will appear to be relatively cheaper to the Arbezanis.
          C.  Arbez will lose any comparative advantage that it had.
          D.  Arbez will experience a decreasing trade deficit.

_____ 5.  The Heckscher-Ohlin theorem states that Arbez will have a(n) _____ advantage in the production of a good that uses its relatively _____.
          A.  absolute, scarce input intensively.
          B.  absolute, abundant input intensively.
          C.  comparative, abundant input intensively.
          D.  comparative, scarce input intensively.

_____ 6.  Two goods are produced, pins and needles. Jill has a comparative advantage in the production of pins. Relative to Jack,
    A.  Jill is better at producing pins than at producing needles.
    B.  Jill is better at producing both pins and needles.
    C.  Jill can produce more pins per hour.
    D.  Jill can produce more needles per hour.

_____ 7.  Jill chooses to trade pins for needles with Jack. It is likely that
    A.  Jill's gains equal Jack's losses.
    B.  pins are more expensive than needles.
    C.  each trader receives goods that he or she values more highly than those he or she gives up.
    D.  neither trader can gain more than the other.

For questions 8–10, assume that Arbez and Arboc have the same amount of resources and similar preferences for both goat milk and bananas. The table shows the number of labour hours needed to produce 1 litre of goat milk and 1 kilo of bananas.

|           | Arbez | Arboc |
|-----------|-------|-------|
| Goat milk | .3    | .6    |
| Bananas   | .5    | .2    |

_____ 8.  According to the table above,
    A.  Arbez has a comparative advantage in the production of both goods.
    B.  Arbez has a comparative advantage in the production of bananas, and Arboc has a comparative advantage in the production of goat milk.
    C.  Arbez has a comparative advantage in the production of goat milk, and Arboc has a comparative advantage in the production of bananas.
    D.  Arboc has a comparative advantage in the production of both goods.

_____ 9.  According to the table, one hour of labour produces
    A.  3 litres of goat milk in Arbez and 6 litres in Arboc.
    B.  5 kilos of bananas in Arbez and 2 kilos in Arboc.
    C.  2 kilos of bananas in Arbez and 5 kilos in Arboc.
    D.  6 litres of goat milk in Arboc and 2 kilos of bananas in Arboc.

_____ 10.  For trade to occur, the terms of trade might be
    A.  2 litres of goat milk for 1 kilo of bananas.
    B.  1 litre of goat milk for 4 kilos of bananas.
    C.  1 litre of goat milk for .7 kilo of bananas.
    D.  3 litres of goat milk for 1 kilo of bananas.

_____ 11.  Tariffs and quotas are economically inefficient because
    A.  the government does not collect any revenues under a tariff.
    B.  imports rise and this reduces the welfare of consumers.
    C.  producers are saved from the pressure of foreign competition.
    D.  domestic prices must be reduced.

_____ 12.  Which of the following is a common argument in favour of increased protection?
    A.  Canadian consumers have become too dependent on foreign countries for their luxury goods.
    B.  Political independence can be jeopardized if too many strategic supplies are produced by foreigners.
    C.  Protection promotes competition in domestic markets.
    D.  Higher tariffs increase the welfare of consumers.

_____ 13. Each of the following can be a trade barrier except a(n)
   A.   flexible exchange rate.
   B.   quota.
   C.   export subsidy.
   D.   tariff.

_____ 14. Statement 1:  A country with an absolute advantage in the production of a good must also have a comparative advantage.
   Statement 2:  A country with a comparative advantage in the production of a good must also have an absolute advantage.
   Statement 1 is _____; Statement 2 is _____.
   A.   true, true.
   B.   true, false.
   C.   false, true.
   D.   false, false.

_____ 15. A tariff _____ increase the government's tax receipts; a quota _____ increase the government's tax receipt.
   A.  does, does.
   B.  does, does not.
   C.  does not, does.
   D.  does not, does not.

_____ 16. In Tokyo, suppose a Big Mac sells for 500 yen. The dollar : yen exchange rate is one dollar per 125 yen. The price of the Big Mac in dollars is
   A.   500.
   B.   .25.
   C.   4.
   D.   5.

_____ 17. In Tokyo, suppose a Big Mac sells for 500 yen. The exchange rate changes from one dollar for 125 yen, to one dollar for 250 yen. The price of the Big Mac in dollars
   A.   has increased.
   B.   has decreased.
   C.   has not changed.
   D.   has doubled.

_____ 18. The Heckscher-Ohlin theorem explains the pattern of trade by focusing on
   A.   comparative advantage.
   B.   absolute advantage.
   C.   relative factor endowments.
   D.   exchange rate variations.

_____ 19. As the exchange rate changes from one British pound equals $2.50 to one British pound equals $2.00, the terms of trade shift _____ Canada. Canadian traders will gain _____ from trade with the United Kingdom.
   A.   in favour of, more.
   B.   in favour of, less.
   C.   against, more.
   D.   against, less.

20. We would expect a tariff imposed on an import to _____ the price of the import and to _____ the price of domestic substitutes for the import.
   A. increase, increase.
   B. increase, not affect.
   C. decrease, decrease.
   D. decrease, not affect.

## II. APPLICATION QUESTIONS

1. The Arbezani Minister of Trade asks your advice regarding some recent changes within the Arbezani economy. Arbez has established a free-trade region with its sole trading partner, Arboc. Previously it did not trade at all. What will be the impact of the following changes on the flow of trade, assuming the Heckscher-Ohlin theorem?
   a. Arbezani unions in a substantial number of industries lobby successfully for increased restrictions on movement between industries, e.g., longer apprenticeships, work permits, drug testing of new entrants into an industry.
   b. It has been discovered that Arbez and its trading partner, Arboc, have identical endowments of all resources.
   c. Nationalistic Arbezani politicians, concerned about the loss of sovereignty caused by a free-trade area, have successfully passed restrictions on the flow of labour and other inputs between Arbez and Arboc.

2. The nations of Noil and Regit produce loaves and fishes. The labour supply is 12 000 labour units per year in Noil while, in Regit, the labour supply is 72 000 labour units per year. Assume that labour is the only input and that costs are constant within each economy. The costs of producing loaves and fishes, in labour units, are given in the following table.

| Units of Labour Supply Needed to Produce 1 Unit of: | Noil | Regit |
|---|---|---|
| Loaves | 2 | 3 |
| Fishes | 1 | 3 |

   a. Calculate the maximum output levels of loaves and fishes for each economy and enter your results in the following table.

| Maximum Units Produced | Noil | Regit |
|---|---|---|
| Loaves | | |
| Fishes | | |

   b. Draw the production possibility frontiers for each nation.

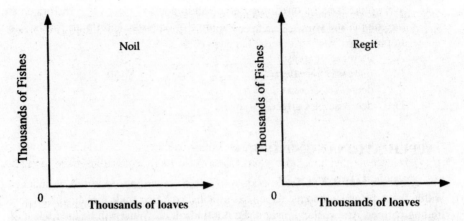

c.  When questioned about the possibility of establishing trade between the two nations, the Regitani Minister of Trade states his government's official line—trade cannot benefit Regit because Regit has an advantage in the production of each good. Is the Regitani view correct?

In both nations, the custom is to consume two loaves with each fish.

d.  Assume that no trade takes place. Calculate the annual production of loaves and fishes that will most satisfactorily meet demand in each country separately. Also determine the total production of loaves and fishes for the two countries without trade.

| Maximum Units Produced | Noil | Regit | Total |
|---|---|---|---|
| Loaves | ___ | ___ | ___ |
| Fishes | ___ | ___ | ___ |

e.  Yielding to pressure, the Regitani government opens its borders to trade with Noil. Based on comparative advantage, which good should Noil specialize in producing? Explain.

f.  Assuming that specialization and trade flows are dictated by comparative advantage, determine the quantity of loaves and fishes that can be produced.

g.  Suppose that the terms of trade are established at 3 fishes = 2 loaves. Determine the consumption of loaves and fishes in each country.

| Units Consumed | Noil | Regit |
|---|---|---|
| Loaves | ___ | ___ |
| Fishes | ___ | ___ |

h.  Has trade been mutually beneficial in this case?

i.  Suppose that the terms of trade are established at 1 fish = 1 loaf. Determine the consumption of loaves and fishes in each country.

| Units Consumed | Noil | Regit |
|---|---|---|
| Loaves | ___ | ___ |
| Fishes | ___ | ___ |

j. Has trade been mutually beneficial in this case?

k. Suppose that the terms of trade are established at 2 fishes = 1 loaf. Determine the consumption of loaves and fishes in each country.

| Units Consumed | Noil | Regit |
|---|---|---|
| Loaves | _____ | _____ |
| Fishes | _____ | _____ |

l. Has trade been mutually beneficial in this case?

m. Determine the "price" of a loaf (in terms of fish) necessary to have mutually beneficial two-way trade.

3. The domestic price of Arbocali cloth is 4 opeks a yard. The domestic price of Arbezani leather is 12 bandu per hide. Arboc sells cloth to Arbez and Arbez sells hides to Arboc. The opek : bandu exchange rate is 2 opeks per bandu.

Ignoring transportation and other such costs, calculate the price in Arbez of a yard of imported Arbocali cloth and the price in Arboc of an imported Arbezani hide.

4. Use the diagrams below to answer this question.

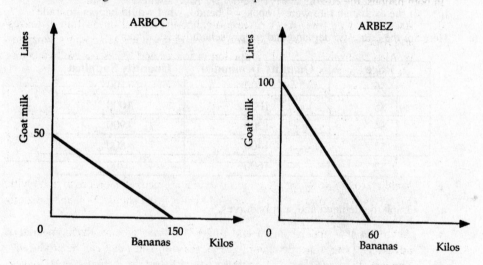

a. What is the opportunity cost of one kilo of bananas in Arboc?
b. What is the opportunity cost of one kilo of bananas in Arbez?
c. Which country has a comparative advantage in the production of bananas?
d. What is the opportunity cost of one litre of goat milk in Arboc?
e. What is the opportunity cost of one litre of goat milk in Arbez?
f. Which country has a comparative advantage in the production of goat milk?
g. If the terms of trade were 1.0 litre of goat milk/kilo of bananas, which country would want to export goat milk?
h. If the terms of trade were 3 litres of goat milk/kilo of bananas, Arboc should produce _____ and Arbez should produce _____.
i. Suppose that the terms of trade were 1 kilo of bananas/1.5 litres of goat milk. _____ would export bananas and _____ would export goat milk.

5.  Arboc and Arbez produce wine and cheese, and each has constant costs of production. The domestic prices for units of the two goods are given in the table. At the moment 1 Arbocali opek is traded for 1 Arbezani bandu.

| | Arboc | Arbez |
|---|---|---|
| Wine | 40 opeks | 120 bandu |
| Cheese | 20 opeks | 30 bandu |

a.  Which country has a comparative advantage in cheese production?
b.  Which country has a comparative advantage in wine production?
c.  At the present exchange rate (1 opek = 1 bandu), will two-way trade occur? Explain.
d.  Which country will have a balance of trade deficit?
e.  What should happen to the value of the opek, relative to the bandu?
f.  If the exchange rate is 1 opek = 2 bandu, what would happen to trade?
g.  Cheese making is capital-intensive, and wine making is labour-intensive. Which country should have the relatively abundant supplies of labour, if the Heckscher-Ohlin theory is correct?
h.  If the exchange rate were 1 opek = 4 bandu, what would happen to trade?

6.  Here are the domestic demand and supply schedules for diapers.

| Price | Quantity Demanded | Quantity Supplied |
|---|---|---|
| $6 | 800 | 1100 |
| $5 | 1000 | 1000 |
| $4 | 1200 | 900 |
| $3 | 1400 | 800 |
| $2 | 1600 | 700 |

a.  Graph the demand and supply curves.

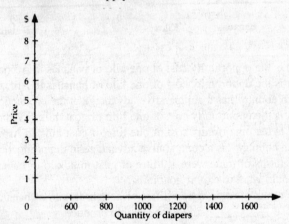

b.  The equilibrium price is $ _____ and quantity is _____.
c.  The world price for diapers is $3. Show this on the diagram as Pw. What will be the levels of domestic consumption and domestic production?

In order to preserve employment, diaper manufacturers contend successfully that theirs is an "infant industry" and should be protected.

d. A tariff is imposed that raises the price of imported diapers to $4. Show this on the diagram as Pt.

e. The tariff causes an increase in price and an increase in domestic production of _____ units. Consumption will fall to _____ units.

f. Imports will be _____ units. The tariff will yield $_____ in tax revenues.

g. Shade in the areas representing the net welfare loss caused by the tariff.

h. The loss in welfare is $_____.

# ANSWERS AND SOLUTIONS

## PRACTICE TEST

### I. SOLUTIONS TO MULTIPLE CHOICE QUESTIONS

1. B. See p. 402.

2. C. See p. 402.

3. C. Arbez might be relatively inefficient in producing both goods but relatively less inefficient in producing goat milk. Because Arbez has a comparative advantage in producing goat milk, its opportunity cost of producing goat milk must be less.

4. B. As the Arbezani currency increases in value, Arbocali goods will become cheaper when calculated in terms of the Arbezani currency.

5. C. See p. 412.

6. A. Remember that comparative advantage is a relative concept. It requires that we compare two producers and two goods.

7. C. In voluntary trade, we expect each trader to gain something more than she or he traded.

8. C. Goat milk is relatively cheap to produce in Arbez and bananas require relatively few resources in Arboc. In a two-good, two-country situation, one party can never have a comparative advantage in both goods.

9. C. .5 labour hour gives 1 kilo of bananas in Arbez—1 hour gives 2 kilos. .2 labour hour gives 1 litre of milk in Arboc—1 hour gives 5 litres.

10. C. The terms of trade must lie in the range from 1 litre of goat milk : 3/5 kilo of bananas to 1 litre of goat milk : 3 kilos of bananas. If Arbez has 6 hours of labour, it could produce 20 litres of goat milk or 12 kilos of bananas—a ratio of 1 : 3/5. If Arboc has 6 hours of labour, it could produce 10 litres of goat milk or 30 kilos of bananas—a ratio of 1 : 3.

11. C. Tariffs impose welfare losses in two ways. Consumers pay a higher price and, as mentioned in this question, marginal producers are allowed to survive. Option B is incorrect—imports don't increase, they decrease. See p. 418.

12. B. See p. 420.

13. A. See p. 415 for a discussion of trade barriers.

14. D. A country with an absolute advantage in the production of Good A and Good B may have a comparative advantage in the production of Good A and, therefore, a comparative disadvantage in Good B. Similarly, a country with a comparative advantage in the production of Good A might have an absolute disadvantage relative to its partner in producing either good.

15. B. A tariff is a tax that provides revenues; a quota merely restricts the number of units that may be imported.
16. C. 125 yen equal $1. 500 yen equal $4.
17. B. 125 yen equal $1. 500 yen equal $4. 250 yen equal $1. 500 yen equal $2.
18. C. See p. 412.
19. A. Dollars are becoming relatively more valuable.
20. A. A tariff will drive up the price of the import, increasing demand for domestic substitutes whose price will then increase.

## II.    SOLUTIONS TO APPLICATION QUESTIONS

1.    a.    Heckscher-Ohlin assumes that inputs are mobile within an economy. Such restrictions will work against trade flows because, as an economy begins to specialize and trade, it will wish to reallocate inputs.

b.    According to Heckscher-Ohlin, comparative advantage is dependent upon differences in factor endowments. No differences in factor endowments, no comparative advantage: no comparative advantage, no trade. Arbez and Arboc should have no basis for trade.

c.    The new restrictions should not affect the pattern of trade. The Heckscher-Ohlin theorem assumes that inputs are not mobile between countries. (In real economies restrictions on factor movements may increase trade as goods move instead of the workers who produce the goods.)

2.    a.

| Maximum Units Produced | Noil | Regit |
|---|---|---|
| Loaves | 6 000 | 24 000 |
| Fishes | 12 000 | 24 000 |

b.    See the following diagrams.

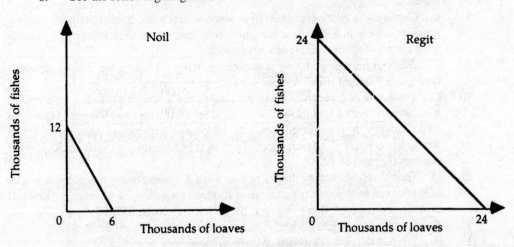

c.    The Regitani view is mainly incorrect. Regit does have an absolute advantage in the production of both loaves and fishes, but it does not have a comparative advantage in both, and it is comparative advantage that determines whether or not trade is advantageous.

d.

| Maximum Units Produced | Noil | Regit | Total |
|---|---|---|---|
| Loaves | 4800 | 16 000 | 20 800 |
| Fishes | 2400 | 8 000 | 10 400 |

One way to obtain these numbers for each country is to find where the production possibility frontier intersects with the line from the origin with slope 1/2 (corresponding to one fish for every two loaves).

e.    Noil should produce fishes. In Noil, the cost of producing 1 loaf is 2 fishes while the cost of producing 1 loaf in Regit is 1 fish. Loaves are less costly in Regit. Regit has a comparative advantage in loaves; Noil has a comparative advantage in fishes.

f.    Noil can produce 12 000 fishes and Regit can produce 24 000 loaves.

g.

| Units Consumed | Noil | Regit |
|---|---|---|
| Loaves | 6000 | 18 000 |
| Fishes | 3000 | 9 000 |

Noil can produce 12 000 fishes and export 9000, earning 6000 loaves in return. Regit can produce 24 000 loaves and export 6000, earning 9000 fishes in return. Noil can produce 12 000 fishes. It could keep them all, or it could export them all in return for 8000 loaves, or it could choose anywhere in between on its "consumption possibility frontier" which is the straight line that joins the point (0 loaves, 12 000 fishes) to the point (8000 loaves, 0 fishes). Because of the custom of consuming two loaves per fish, it will choose the point along that line in which there are two loaves per fish (i.e., the point where the consumption possibility frontier intersects the line from the origin with slope 1/2). By graphical methods or calculation you can show this point to be 6000 loaves, 3000 fishes: That is Noil will export 9000 of the 12 000 fishes it produces and earn 6000 loaves in return. Regit will give up 6000 of the 24 000 loaves it produces to leave 18 000 loaves to consume with the 9000 fishes it imports from Noil.

h.    Yes.

i.

| Units Consumed | Noil | Regit |
|---|---|---|
| Loaves | 8000 | 16 000 |
| Fishes | 4000 | 8 000 |

Noil can produce 12 000 fishes and export 8000, earning 8000 loaves in return. Regit can produce 24 000 loaves and export 8000, earning 8000 fishes in return.

j.    Trade has benefited Noil, but Regit's standard of living is unchanged.

k.

| Units Consumed | Noil | Regit |
|---|---|---|
| Loaves | 4800 | 19 200 |
| Fishes | 2400 | 9 600 |

Noil can produce 12 000 fishes and export 9600, earning 4800 loaves in return. Regit can produce 24 000 loaves and export 4800, earning 9600 fishes in return.

l.    Trade has benefited Regit, but Noil's standard of living is unchanged.

m.    The terms of trade need to be between 1 loaf = 1 fish and 1 loaf = 2 fish.

3. A yard of imported Arbocali cloth will cost 2 bandu in Arbez. An imported Arbezani hide will cost 24 opeks in Arboc.

4.    a.    1/3 litre of goat milk.
      b.    1-2/3 litres of goat milk.
      c.    Arboc.
      d.    3 kilos of bananas.
      e.    6/10 kilo of bananas.
      f.    Arbez.
      g.    Arbez, because it can produce a litre of goat milk at a cost of less than one kilo of bananas and, therefore, can gain through this specialization.
      h.    bananas, bananas. One kilo of bananas can be sold for 3 litres of goat milk. Both Arboc and Arbez can produce bananas more cheaply than this (1/3 litre of goat milk and 1-2/3 litres of goat milk, respectively).
      i.    Arboc, Arbez. One kilo of bananas can be sold for 1.5 litres of goat milk. Arboc can produce bananas more cheaply than this (1/3 litre of goat milk) and so will produce bananas. One litre of goat milk can be sold for 2/3 kilo of bananas. Arbez can produce goat milk more cheaply than this (6/10 kilo of bananas) and so will produce goat milk.

5.    a.    Arbez. Wine is four times as expensive as cheese in Arbez, but only twice as expensive in Arboc.
      b.    Arboc. No country can have a comparative advantage in both goods.
      c.    No. Because Arboc can produce both goods more cheaply, the Arbezanis will import both. The Arbocalis will not wish to buy either Arbezani product.
      d.    Arbez, because it has some imports and zero exports.
      e.    The Arbocali currency (the opek) should be heavily demanded (by Arbezanis seeking to buy Arbocali goods). The demand for the bandu will be low. The opek will rise in value; the bandu will fall in value.
      f.    At a price of 30 bandu (15 opeks), Arbezani cheese will now be cheaper than Arbocali cheese (at a price of 20 opeks). Arboc will import cheese. Arbez will continue to import Arbocali wine. At a price of 40 opeks (80 bandu), Arbocali wine is still cheaper than that produced in Arbez (at a price of 120 bandu).
      g.    Arboc.
      h.    At a price of 30 bandu (7.50 opeks), Arbezani cheese will be cheaper than Arbocali cheese (at a price of 20 opeks). Arboc will import cheese. At a price of 40 opeks (160 bandu), Arbocali wine will be more expensive than that produced in Arbez (at a price of 120 bandu). Arboc will import wine. Arboc will have a trade deficit and Arbez a surplus.

6.    a.    See the diagram below.

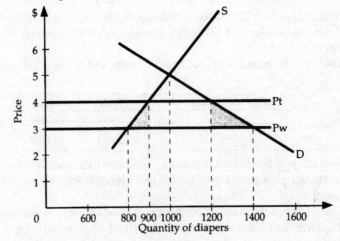

b. $5, 1000.
c. See the diagram above. 1400, 800.
d. See the diagram above.
e. 100, 1200.
f. 300, $300.
g. See the diagram above. The left triangle corresponds to the extra cost of the 100 extra diapers (between 800 and 900) that could have been purchased at the world price, but instead have cost more to produce by firms protected by the tariff. The right triangle corresponds to the loss to those consumers who would have purchased 200 extra diapers if they could have purchased at the world price but did not purchase because of the higher tariff-protected price.
h. $(50 + 100) (the areas of the two shaded triangles).

# 21 Open-Economy Macroeconomics: The Balance of Payments and Exchange Rates

## OBJECTIVES: POINT BY POINT

After completing this chapter, you should be able to accomplish the objectives listed below.

### OBJECTIVE 1: Outline the components of the balance of payments. Distinguish between the current and capital accounts.

When goods, services, or assets are bought and sold, or transfer payments are made internationally, currencies flow between nations. These flows of foreign exchange (that is, all currencies other than that of the home country) are recorded in the *balance of payments*.

(page 427)

The balance of payments, which must "balance" (equal zero) is split into two parts:

a. the *current account*, which includes imports and exports of goods and services, net investment income, and net transfer payments, and

b. the *capital account*, which includes the "export" and "import" of Canadian and foreign assets—i.e., capital inflows and capital outflows. It also includes official net capital movements by the Bank of Canada.

If, on the current account, total credits are greater than (less than) total debits, the economy has a current account surplus (deficit). Funds from a current account surplus can be used to buy foreign assets, such as foreign government bonds or real estate. A current account deficit must be financed by attracting funds from overseas (capital inflows) by selling Canadian assets (capital). The current and capital accounts must sum to zero.

> **Tip:** Any transaction that brings in foreign exchange is a credit item; any transaction causing a loss of foreign exchange is a debit.

> **Tip:** The capital account is difficult to conceptualize. The easy way into this topic is to imagine a nation (Japan) with a current account surplus. What happens to the extra foreign earnings? The Japanese can use the funds to buy other countries' assets and companies. A nation that runs a current account deficit must sell off some of its assets to raise the foreign currency needed to buy imports. Counterintuitively perhaps, capital inflows are rather like exports (in the sense that the country is "exporting" IOUs), and capital outflows can be thought of as similar to imports (funds flow out to "import" foreign securities). A large capital account surplus (the same thing as a large current account deficit) may be a concern, as it may mean a country is borrowing too

much or selling off too many domestic assets, although it may not be a problem if the borrowing is supporting investment that will yield future returns.

**Tip:** A Japanese purchase of a Canadian factory is a capital *inflow* for Canada (funds flow in). A Canadian purchase of a Brazilian coffee plantation is a capital *outflow* for Canada (funds flow out). Focus on which country receives payment, not which receives the asset.

## OBJECTIVE 2: Explain why the sum of the trade balances for all nations is zero.

Because one nation's export is another's import, all the trade balances of the nations of the world must add to zero.

## Practice

1. The sum of the trade balances of all the countries in the world equals
   A. the sum of money balances.
   B. the sum of all exports.
   C. the sum of all imports.
   D. zero.

   **ANSWER:** D. A country's trade balance is its exports of goods and services less its imports of goods and services. But one country can only be exporting more than it imports if another is importing more than it exports. See p. 431.

2. The price of Canada's currency in terms of that of the United States is the
   A. foreign exchange.
   B. exchange rate.
   C. balance of payments.
   D. currency ratio.

   **ANSWER:** B. See p. 426.

3. The balance of payments is split into the
   A. current account and the merchandise trade account.
   B. capital account and the foreign exchange account.
   C. capital account and the current account.
   D. current account and foreign exchange account.

   **ANSWER:** C. See p. 429.

4. Which of the following would be included in the current account?
   A. The purchase by a Canadian resident of stock in Sony, the Japanese company.
   B. The sale by a Canadian resident of a French government security.
   C. The sale of a Canadian-built airplane to Germany.
   D. The sale of Seagram stock to a German citizen.

   **ANSWER:** C. This is an export.

5. The Canadian capital account is
   A. the sum of private net capital movements and official net capital movements.
   B. the sum of net investment income and net transfer payments.
   C. net investment income.
   D. the inflow of foreign exchange from sales of Canadian assets to nonresidents.

   **ANSWER: A.** See p. 430. Option D is incorrect because from this inflow must be subtracted the outflow of foreign exchange from Canadian purchases of foreign assets.

6. Which of the following is not an item in the capital account?
   A. Change in private Canadian assets abroad.
   B. Change in Canadian government assets abroad.
   C. Net investment income.
   D. Change in foreign private investment in Canada.

   **ANSWER: C.** See Table 21.1 on p. 428. Items in the current account show income from earnings (on exports), expenditures (on imports), net transfers, and net investment income—no financial or real productive assets change hands. It is the capital account that shows the effects of the purchase or sale of financial and real productive assets.

## OBJECTIVE 3: Derive the spending multiplier when imports depend on income.

Recall $AE = C + I + G + EX - IM$.

Foreign demand for Canadian goods is influenced mainly by foreign factors—exports are assumed to be constant as domestic output increases. Imports, however, increase as Canadian income increases. The marginal propensity to import (MPM) is positive. The expenditure multiplier is smaller in an open economy than it is in a closed economy because imports represent a leakage of spending power away from domestically produced goods. This effect was discussed briefly in Chapter 10 and an algebraic example was given in Appendix 10C.

In the open economy, the multiplier formula is $1 / [1 - (MPC - MPM)]$.    (page 433)

## Practice

Use this basic Keynesian cross model and the following information to answer the next three questions. In the closed economy of Arbez, the marginal propensity to consume is .75. Arbez opens its borders to trade and finds that its marginal propensity to import is .15.

7. The Arbezani multiplier was _____ for the closed economy and is _____ for the open economy.
   A. 4, 2.5.
   B. 4, 10.
   C. 5, 2.5.
   D. 5, 10.

   **ANSWER: A.** In the closed economy, the multiplier is $1 / [1 - MPC]$. In this case, $1 / [1 - MPC] = 1 / [1 - .75] = 4$. In the open economy, the multiplier is $1 / [1 - (MPC - MPM)]$. In this case, $1 / [1 - (MPC - MPM)] = 1 / [1 - (.75 - .15)] = 1 / .4 = 2.5$. In general, the open-economy multiplier is less than the closed economy multiplier, so Options B and D must be incorrect.

8.  Arbez finds that net exports are zero. As a result of world trade, the Arbezani economy has become _____ stable. If its economy expands due to an increase in investment spending, Arbez will experience a trade _____.
    A.  more, surplus.
    B.  more, deficit.
    C.  less, surplus.
    D.  less, deficit.

    **ANSWER:** B. In the open economy, the multiplier is smaller. Shifts in the components of planned aggregate expenditure will result in smaller changes in equilibrium income level—the economy is more stable. Currently, exports and imports are equal. An economic expansion will increase imports (MPM is .15), but exports, which depend on foreign demand, will not change, and a trade deficit will occur.

9.  The Arbezani government increases government spending by 100. Equilibrium output will _____ and net exports will _____.
    A.  increase by 100, increase by 15.
    B.  increase by 100, decrease by 15.
    C.  increase by 250, increase by 37.5.
    D.  increase by 250, decrease by 37.5.

    **ANSWER:** D. As G increases, the economy will expand by 250 because the multiplier is 2.5—see question 7. Exports do not change, but imports will increase. MPM is .15, so imports will increase by 250 × .15, or 37.5, and net exports (EX – IM) will decrease.

10. The quantity of Canadian exports depends directly on
    A.  the output level in Canada.
    B.  the output level in other countries.
    C.  the size of the multiplier in Canada.
    D.  the size of the multiplier in other countries.

    **ANSWER:** B. The demand for our exports depends on the output (income) level of foreign purchasers. A *change* in their income will affect our exports through their marginal propensity to import.

11. Arboc opens its economy to world trade. Its net exports are negative. Compared with its AE function before world trade, the function now will be
    A.  higher and steeper.
    B.  higher and flatter.
    C.  lower and steeper.
    D.  lower and flatter.

    **ANSWER:** D. Net exports are negative, so the level of expenditure on domestic goods is lower than before. Because the marginal propensity to import is a positive value, some part of any increase in income will be spent abroad, so the rise in domestic expenditures will be less—a flatter function.

## OBJECTIVE 4: Explain how net exports are affected by the Canadian price level, and explain the trade feedback effect.

Canadian imports depend on income, but also on the other factors that influence domestic demand, such as interest rates. Both exports and imports depend on the relative prices of goods. Canadians would buy more Volvos if they were cheaper. Americans would buy more Canadian-made Moosehead beer if it were cheaper. Canadian net exports depend on the relative price of Canadian goods and services compared to foreign goods and services, and hence on the Canadian price level, the price levels in other countries, exchange rates, and any trade barriers.                                     (page 433)

Canadian exports depend on the level of economic activity in other countries, particularly in the United States. This leads to a *trade feedback effect*. A $1 billion jump in Canadian exports to the U.S. will stimulate the Canadian economy (through the multiplier effect), and this will lead to increased Canadian imports from the United States. But Canadian imports are U.S. exports, so this will have a stimulative effect on the U.S. economy and the resulting higher U.S. incomes will feed back into an additional (albeit much less than $1 billion) jump in Canadian exports to the U.S. Trade feedback effects are largest for the large economies and can lead to the spread of economic expansions and contractions across the world. For example, the recession in Japan and Southeast Asia beginning in the spring of 1998 had trade feedback effects on the rest of the world as these countries reduced their imports.　　　　　　　　　　　　　　　　　　　　　　　(page 434)

## Practice

12. Because the U.S. economy is large and there is a trade feedback effect,
    A. an increase in economic activity in the United States results in an increase in U.S. net exports.
    B. an increase in U.S. imports results in an increase in U.S. exports.
    C. an increase in U.S. imports reduces the imports of other countries.
    D. an increase in U.S. exports reduces the imports of other countries.

    **ANSWER:** B.　See p. 434.

13. Canadian exports tend to increase when
    A. economic activity abroad is relatively low.
    B. Canadian prices are relatively low.
    C. Canadian prices are relatively high.
    D. Canadian inflation is relatively high.

    **ANSWER:** B.　When Canadian prices are relatively low, Canadian goods become more competitive overseas.

14. Canadian net exports will usually increase if there is
    A. a rise in the U.S. price level.
    B. an appreciation of the Canadian dollar.
    C. a rise in the Canadian dollar price of Canadian-made goods.
    D. an increase in barriers to Canadian imports to the United States.

    **ANSWER:** A.　This will make Canadian goods more competitive in the United States. All the other options would usually lead to a decrease in Canadian net exports.

## OBJECTIVE 5: Identify how the Canadian dollar exchange rate is determined.

In the foreign exchange market, Canadian dollars are traded for other currencies. Most commonly the value of the Canadian dollar is expressed in terms of U.S. currency. The demand curve for the Canadian dollar is negatively sloped because, as the price of the Canadian dollar rises relative to other currencies, Canadian goods, services, and assets become more expensive than those in other countries, and hence there is less demand for Canadian dollars. Similarly, the supply curve for the Canadian dollar is positively sloped because, as the price of the Canadian dollar rises, foreign goods, services, and assets become cheaper to Canadians, and they are more likely to trade their Canadian dollars for other currencies in order to make foreign purchases.

The market-determined exchange rate is determined where the supply curve meets the demand curve. If the Canadian dollar were above the market-determined rate, there would be more desire to sell the Canadian dollar at that price than to buy it, and if the Canadian dollar were below the market-determined rate, there would be more desire to purchase the Canadian dollar than to sell it. (pages 435-438)

> **TIP:** The easiest example is tourism. If the Canadian dollar is strong relative to other currencies, this will increase the supply of the Canadian dollar as many Canadians trade their Canadian dollars for U.S. dollars so that they can go to Florida or Arizona. But the high value of the Canadian dollar will discourage tourists from the United States from travelling to Banff or Montreal, and hence there will be less demand for the Canadian dollar from holders of U.S. dollars. However, while this kind of example may help you straighten out the basic issues, remember that, in the short run, the strongest influence on exchange rates comes from the relative interest rates in various countries, and not from trends in trade or tourism.

> **TIP:** The supply and demand for the Canadian dollar includes purchases and sales by the Bank of Canada (*official net capital movements*). Under fixed exchange rates, such purchases and sales will be necessary to maintain the fixed price of the Canadian dollar. Some economists, knowing that the overall balance of payments must be zero (as sales of the Canadian dollar must equal purchases of the Canadian dollar), instead call "the balance of payments" the net sales of the Canadian dollar by the Bank of Canada, where a balance of payments surplus means there are net positive sales, and a balance of payments deficit means there are net purchases. When a balance of payments deficit is very large under a fixed exchange rate regime (e.g., Hong Kong in 1997), there may be a danger that the central bank will run out of foreign exchange to continue the necessary purchases of the domestic currency. This is called a "balance of payments crisis."

**Comment:** Is it better to have a "strong" dollar or a "weak" dollar? You might think that a strong dollar must be an "improvement," but it depends on your viewpoint.

Suppose that the dollar experiences a substantial appreciation in value. Who will gain? Consumers, because foreign goods will now be cheaper. But will anyone lose? Exporters will, because they will find it tougher to compete overseas; producers of domestic substitutes (North American car makers, for instance) for imported goods will also be hurt.

## Practice

15. A nation whose price level is rising relatively fast will see its exports become _____ attractive unless its currency _____.
    A. more, appreciates.
    B. more, depreciates.
    C. less, appreciates.
    D. less, depreciates.

    **ANSWER:** D. As the price level rises, exports become more expensive (less attractive). This may be offset by a depreciating currency.

16. A nation whose interest rate is rising relatively fast will see its securities become _____ attractive. Its currency will _____.
    A. more, appreciate.
    B. more, depreciate.
    C. less, appreciate.
    D. less, depreciate.

    **ANSWER:** A. As our interest rate rises, our assets become more attractive. As the demand for Canadian securities increases, so does the demand for dollars.

17. More French companies begin to invest in Canada. This will
    A. increase the demand for dollars and increase the supply of euros.
    B. decrease the demand for dollars and increase the demand for euros.
    C. increase the demand for dollars and decrease the supply of euros.
    D. increase the supply of dollars and decrease the demand for euros.

    **ANSWER:** A. Holders of euros will place this currency on the foreign exchange market (increasing the supply of euros) to demand more dollars.

18. The demand for dollars in the foreign exchange market is downward sloping partly because, when the price of a dollar (the exchange rate) decreases, _____ because they have become relatively _____.
    A. Canadians demand more foreign goods, less expensive.
    B. Canadians demand fewer foreign goods, more expensive.
    C. foreigners demand more Canadian goods, less expensive.
    D. foreigners demand fewer Canadian goods, more expensive.

    **ANSWER:** C. A good becomes less expensive to a British buyer if the dollar weakens (and the pound strengthens). Each pound can buy more dollars, so the demand for Canadian goods (and Canadian currency) increases.

## OBJECTIVE 6: Explain purchasing power parity and interest rate parity.

The law of one price (purchasing power parity) suggests that, with minimal transportation costs, similar goods in different countries should have similar prices, and that the exchange rate should reflect this. If Canadian prices rise, the exchange rate should compensate (the dollar would depreciate in value). Similarly, interest rates in different countries (on bonds of comparable risk and term) can differ only if the exchange rate is expected to change. (pages 438–442)

> **TIP:** Just as competition in the goods market will tend to bring about purchasing power parity, competition in the financial markets will cause a similar phenomenon—interest rate parity—to arise. Interest parity suggests that the Canadian interest rate can be less than the U.S. interest rate if the Canadian dollar is expected to appreciate and hence compensate holders of Canadian bonds.

**Practice**

19. A TV set costs 20 000 yen in Japan and a similar set costs $300 in Canada. The exchange rate is 100 yen per dollar. We would expect the demand for Japanese TV sets to _____ and, if purchasing power parity holds, the yen will _____.
    A. increase, appreciate.
    B. increase, depreciate.
    C. decrease, appreciate.
    D. decrease, depreciate.

    **ANSWER: A.** The Canadian TV costs 30 000 yen. It is more expensive than the Japanese set; therefore, the demand for Japanese TV sets and Japanese currency will increase.

20. The foreign exchange market is in equilibrium, with each British pound trading for $2.30. Now the overall Canadian price level increases. We would expect an excess demand for
    A. pounds. The pound will appreciate.
    B. pounds. The pound will depreciate.
    C. dollars. The pound will appreciate.
    D. dollars. The pound will depreciate.

    **ANSWER: A.** The British will wish to buy fewer Canadian goods, services, and assets. Canadians will demand more pounds in order to buy the relatively cheaper British goods, services, and assets.

21. In Table 1 of the Global Perspective Box entitled "McParity" on page 440, it can be seen that in April 2000 the price of a Big Mac varied from a low of $1.77 in China to a high of $5.13 in Switzerland, in each case converting local currency prices into Canadian dollar prices. Purchasing power parity theory would predict a(n) _____ of Chinese currency and a(n) _____ of Swiss currency.
    A. appreciation, appreciation.
    B. appreciation, depreciation.
    C. depreciation, appreciation.
    D. depreciation, depreciation.

    **ANSWER: B.** Purchasing power parity theory predicts that exchange rates will move to equalize prices so the Chinese yuan (or renminbi) will appreciate and the Swiss franc will depreciate.

22. If the Canadian dollar were expected to appreciate steadily by 2% relative to the U.S. dollar and the rate of interest on secure Canadian bonds was 4% per year, we would expect the rate of interest paid by similar U.S. bonds to be approximately
    A. 6%.
    B. 4%.
    C. 2%.
    D. 1%.

    **ANSWER: A.** If the U.S. dollar is losing value to the Canadian dollar at a rate of 2% per year, we would expect that holders of U.S. dollar securities would have to be compensated for that with interest rates 2% higher. Otherwise, U.S. bondholders would want to switch to Canadian bonds. This is the basis of the interest rate parity condition given on page 442, namely that the Canadian interest rate + the expected rate of appreciation of the Canadian dollar = the U.S. interest rate. Of course, this works for other pairs of currencies as well.

23. If the Canadian dollar were expected to depreciate steadily by 1% relative to the U.S. dollar and the rate of interest on secure Canadian bonds were 5% per year, we would expect the rate of interest paid by similar U.S. bonds to be approximately
    A.  6%.
    B.  4%.
    C.  2%.
    D.  1%.

    **ANSWER:** B.  Use the interest rate parity condition given in the answer to the previous question. In this case U.S. interest rates are lower: Canadian bonds must pay a premium interest rate to compensate holders for the depreciation of the Canadian dollar.

## OBJECTIVE 7: Describe the interactions between monetary and fiscal policy and the exchange rate.

This is largely an extension of earlier analysis in Chapters 12, 13, and 14. Those earlier chapters showed that exchange rate effects weakened the effects of an expansionary fiscal policy on aggregate demand, because such a policy leads to higher interest rates and an appreciating exchange rate, and these changes "crowd out" investment and net exports. In the model presented in this chapter, the long-run effects on aggregate demand are in fact zero, because this crowding out continues until aggregate demand and money demand return to their initial levels, consistent with interest rates at their world-determined levels. Contractionary fiscal policy also has zero effects in this case.          (pages 442-443)

Under fixed exchange rates, there can be no higher interest rates or exchange rate changes, so there is no crowding out and fiscal policy has strong effects.          (page 445)

Under flexible exchange rates, monetary policy expands output by depreciating the exchange rate (or contracts output through exchange rate appreciation), but under fixed exchange rates, monetary policy cannot be used because it would change ("unfix") the exchange rate.          (page 443, page 445)

## Practice

24. With flexible exchange rates in the model in this chapter, fiscal policy has zero long-run effect on all of the following variables except
    A.  aggregate demand.
    B.  interest rates.
    C.  the exchange rate.
    D.  money supply and money demand.

    **ANSWER:** C.  An expansionary fiscal policy will lead to an exchange rate appreciation which will lead to a net export decrease enough to offset the expansionary effects of the fiscal policy itself. After perhaps an initial increase, aggregate demand must fall back to its initial level, so that money demand will fall to its initial level equal to the money supply at the world-determined interest rate.

25. An increase in Canadian government spending will _____ the interest rate and cause the dollar to _____.
    A.  increase, appreciate.
    B.  increase, depreciate.
    C.  decrease, appreciate.
    D.  decrease, depreciate.

    **ANSWER:** A.  Higher government spending increases transactions, the demand for money, and the interest rate. A higher Canadian interest rate draws funds from abroad, increasing the demand for dollars and leading to an appreciation.

26. The effect on output of an increase in Canadian government spending is offset because the dollar
    A. appreciates, increasing net exports and increasing aggregate demand.
    B. appreciates, decreasing net exports and decreasing aggregate demand.
    C. depreciates, increasing net exports and increasing aggregate demand.
    D. depreciates, decreasing net exports and decreasing aggregate demand.

    **ANSWER:** B. An increase in government spending results in an appreciation in the value of the dollar. Exports are relatively more expensive and imports are less expensive in Canada.

27. An increase in the Canadian money supply will _____ the interest rate and cause the dollar to _____.
    A. increase, appreciate.
    B. increase, depreciate.
    C. decrease, appreciate.
    D. decrease, depreciate.

    **ANSWER:** D. An increased money supply will decrease the interest rate. A lower Canadian interest rate will cause Canadian investors to buy foreign securities, decreasing the demand for dollars and leading to a depreciation.

28. An expansionary monetary policy will lead the dollar to
    A. appreciate, increasing net exports and increasing aggregate demand.
    B. appreciate, decreasing net exports and decreasing aggregate demand.
    C. depreciate, increasing net exports and increasing aggregate demand.
    D. depreciate, decreasing net exports and decreasing aggregate demand.

    **ANSWER:** C. An increase in the money supply (which increases aggregate demand) results in a dollar depreciation. Exports are relatively less expensive and imports are more expensive in Canada. Net exports increase. Aggregate demand rises.

## OBJECTIVE 8: Explain the "J-curve effect" of exchange rate changes on net exports.

A depreciating dollar makes exports more competitive abroad (less expensive to foreigners) and imports less attractive domestically (more expensive to Canadians). The balance of trade should improve, but the *J-curve effect* indicates that the trade balance may worsen before it improves, if the short-term demand for imports is relatively unresponsive. In the longer term, a depreciation, which makes imports more expensive and increases the demand for exports, will increase net exports. (page 445)

## Practice

29. The J-curve effect suggests that a depreciation in the value of the dollar may
    A. lead to an appreciation in the value of the dollar.
    B. increase Canadian imports and decrease Canadian exports.
    C. decrease Canadian imports and increase Canadian exports.
    D. cause the balance of trade to worsen before it improves.

    **ANSWER:** D. See p. 445.

30. A depreciation in the value of the dollar is more likely to improve the Canadian balance of trade if the demand for Canadian exports is _____ to price and the Canadian demand for imports is _____ to price.
    A. responsive, responsive.
    B. responsive, unresponsive.
    C. unresponsive, responsive.
    D. unresponsive, unresponsive.

    **ANSWER:** A. If the price of exports falls, the effect will be stronger if the demand for exports is responsive to price. A currency depreciation increases the price of Canadian imports—the effect will be stronger if the demand for imports is responsive to price.

    > **Tip:** The end-of-chapter problem set in the textbook is highly recommended.

# PRACTICE TEST

**I. MULTIPLE CHOICE QUESTIONS.** Select the option that provides the single best answer.

Use the following information to answer the next two questions. Arboc and Arbez are economies of similar size. Arboc's growth rate is 3% while Arbez is growing at a rate of 7%. The marginal propensity to import is the same positive value for both economies.

_____ 1. It is likely that Arbocali exports will _____ and that Arbocali imports will _____.
    A. increase, increase.
    B. increase, decrease.
    C. decrease, increase.
    D. decrease, decrease.

_____ 2. *Ceteris paribus*, we would expect to see the _____ currency depreciating. The new exchange rate will _____ Arbocali consumers.
    A. Arbocali, hurt.
    B. Arbocali, benefit.
    C. Arbezani, hurt.
    D. Arbezani, benefit.

_____ 3. Relative to Japan, the U.S. price level rises. The United States can expect to see a(n) _____ in its balance of trade and, all other things equal, a(n) _____ in the value of its dollar.
    A. increase, depreciation.
    B. increase, appreciation.
    C. decrease, appreciation.
    D. decrease, depreciation.

_____ 4. The current account includes all of the following except
    A. merchandise exports.
    B. capital flows.
    C. tourism.
    D. shipping.

_____ 5. The balance on current account
  A.  will be zero when merchandise exports equal merchandise imports.
  B.  shows the direction and amount of gold flows between the nation and its trading partners.
  C.  includes capital inflows but not capital outflows.
  D.  equals net exports plus net investment income plus net transfer payments.

_____ 6. Three of the following statements can be true at the same time. Which statement is the odd one out?
  A.  Arbez has neither capital inflows nor outflows.
  B.  The Arbezani capital account is equal to zero.
  C.  The Arbezani current account is equal to zero.
  D.  The current account and capital account sum to one.

_____ 7. The multiplier in an open economy is likely to be _____ than in a closed economy because, as income level increases, _____.
  A.  greater, there is a wider market available.
  B.  smaller, some of the increase will be used to buy imports.
  C.  greater, exports become more attractive to foreigners.
  D.  smaller, consumers buy goods that had previously been sent abroad.

_____ 8. Suppose Canada would have a current account balance of zero except for a trade deficit of $5 billion with Japan. Suppose further that there is only one transaction on the capital account. This transaction might be that Canadians
  A.  buy $5 billion worth of Japanese government securities.
  B.  sell $5 billion worth of previously purchased private Japanese securities—e.g., those issued by Sony or Honda.
  C.  lend $5 billion to the Japanese government.
  D.  buy $5 billion worth of Japanese goods on credit next month.

_____ 9. The marginal propensity to consume is .75 and the marginal propensity to import is .15. _Ceteris paribus_, the value of the multiplier is
  A.  10.
  B.  2.5.
  C.  5.
  D.  .9.

_____ 10. The British pound depreciates relative to the dollar. We should expect
  A.  an increase in the number of British tourists visiting Canada.
  B.  an increase in the Canadian demand for British goods.
  C.  an increase in the British demand for Canadian goods.
  D.  a decrease in the number of Canadian tourists visiting Britain.

_____ 11. The trade feedback effect shows that, for a large economy such as the United States, an increase in _____ will result in a subsequent _____.
  A.  exports, depreciation in exchange rates.
  B.  imports, appreciation in the exchange rate.
  C.  income, increase in imports and increase in exports.
  D.  trade, reduction in income in the United States.

_____ 12. A one-dollar increase in income will _____ imports by _____ than one dollar.
  A.  increase, more.
  B.  increase, less.
  C.  decrease, more.
  D.  decrease, less.

_____ 13. The Canadian interest rate rises relative to that of the United Kingdom. We would expect to see the demand for
A. Canadian securities rising, and the dollar appreciating.
B. Canadian securities falling, and the dollar appreciating.
C. British securities rising, and the dollar depreciating.
D. British securities falling, and the dollar depreciating.

_____ 14. Suppose a Montreal software company borrows 10 million Swiss francs from a Zurich bank. This would show up as a
A. credit on the current account.
B. debit on the current account.
C. credit on the capital account.
D. debit on the capital account.

_____ 15. A transaction brings foreign exchange into Canada. This will be recorded as
A. a debit on the balance of trade.
B. a debit on the balance of payments.
C. a credit on the balance of trade.
D. a credit on the balance of payments.

_____ 16. Suppose nations of the former Soviet Union have increased their purchases of Canadian harvesting equipment by $200 million. As a result the Canadian economy has _____ and its net exports have _____.
A. expanded, grown by $200 million.
B. expanded, grown by less than $200 million.
C. contracted, grown by $200 million.
D. contracted, grown by less than $200 million.

_____ 17. The _____ the marginal propensity to consume and the _____ the marginal propensity to import, the larger the multiplier.
A. larger, larger.
B. larger, smaller.
C. smaller, larger.
D. smaller, smaller.

Use the following information to answer the next four questions. The exchange rate is assumed flexible. Note the diagram is drawn so that the exchange rate is the price of a Brazilian currency unit (a "real") in Canadian dollars, not the price of a Canadian dollar in reals. The marginal propensity to import is assumed to be the same in both economies. The current equilibrium exchange rate is assumed to be  $1.00 = 1.25 reals (1 real = $.80).

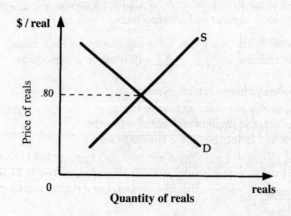

_____ 18. If trade increases between Canada and Brazil, we would expect the demand curve for reals to shift to the _____ and the supply curve for reals to shift to the _____.
   A.   right, right.
   B.   right, left.
   C.   left, right.
   D.   left, left.

_____ 19. If, all other things equal, the worldwide popularity of Brazilian coffee declines, we would expect the real to _____. The price of a Canadian dollar in reals would _____.
   A.   appreciate, rise.
   B.   appreciate, fall.
   C.   depreciate, rise.
   D.   depreciate, fall.

_____ 20. If there is an increase in the interest rate on Canadian government bonds, we would expect the demand curve for reals to shift to the _____ and the supply curve for reals to shift to the _____.
   A.   right, right.
   B.   right, left.
   C.   left, right.
   D.   left, left.

_____ 21. If there is an increase in the interest rate on Canadian government bonds, we would expect the real to _____. The price of a Canadian dollar in reals would _____.
   A.   appreciate, rise.
   B.   appreciate, fall.
   C.   depreciate, rise.
   D.   depreciate, fall.

_____ 22. One reason supply of dollars in the foreign exchange market is upward-sloping is that, when the price of a dollar (the exchange rate) decreases, _____ because they have become relatively _____.
   A.   Canadians demand more foreign goods, less expensive.
   B.   Canadians demand fewer foreign goods, more expensive.
   C.   foreigners demand more Canadian goods, less expensive.
   D.   foreigners demand fewer Canadian goods, more expensive.

_____ 23. As an economy becomes more open (assuming flexible exchange rates), the effectiveness of fiscal policy is _____ and the effectiveness of monetary policy is _____.
   A.   increased, increased.
   B.   increased, decreased.
   C.   decreased, increased.
   D.   decreased, decreased.

## II.   APPLICATION QUESTIONS

1.   Suppose that the price of a Big Mac is $1.50 in the U.S. and £1.00 in the U.K. (For this question, a dollar ($) is a U.S. dollar.) Assume the $/£ exchange rate is $1 = £1.
   a.   Calculate how much (in pounds) a Big Mac would cost a British tourist in the United States.
   b.   Is this more or less expensive than the price in the United Kingdom?
   c.   Calculate how much (in dollars) a Big Mac would cost an American tourist

in the United Kingdom.

    d.    Is this more or less expensive than the price in the United States?

    e.    Assuming Big Mac prices reflect overall price levels, what will happen to the demand for pounds (to buy U.K. goods)? What will happen to the demand for dollars to buy American goods?

    f.    Which currency will appreciate in value?

Suppose the \$/£ exchange rate moves to \$2 = £1. (Confirm that this is a dollar depreciation!)

    g.    Calculate how much (in dollars) a Big Mac would now cost an American tourist in the United Kingdom.

    h.    Is this more or less expensive than the price in the United States?

    i.    Calculate how much (in pounds) a Big Mac would cost a British tourist in the United States.

    j.    Is this more or less expensive than the price in the United Kingdom?

    k.    Again assuming Big Mac prices reflect overall price levels, what should happen to the demand for pounds (to buy U.K. goods)? What should happen to the demand for dollars to buy American goods?

    l.    Which currency will appreciate in value?

    m.    Somewhere between \$1 = £1 and \$2 = £1 an equilibrium exchange rate will occur. Where does purchasing power parity suggest that it will be?

2.    a.    "An expansionary monetary policy by the Bank of Canada will cause the dollar to appreciate against other currencies." Is this true or false? Explain.

    b.    "Short-term interest rates fall in Europe. The dollar should appreciate against the euro." Is this true or false? Explain.

3.    The domestic price of Arbocali cloth is 4 opeks per metre. The domestic price of Arbezani leather is 12 bandu per hide. Arboc sells cloth to Arbez; Arbez sells hides to Arboc. The exchange rate is 2 opeks per bandu. The exchange rate is flexible.

    a.    Ignoring transportation and other such costs, calculate the price in Arbez of a metre of imported Arbocali cloth.

    b.    Calculate the price in Arboc of an imported Arbez hide.

    c.    Calculate the number of units of the domestic currency per unit of foreign currency from the Arbocali perspective.

    d.    Now the exchange rate changes to 4 opeks per bandu. For Arboc, does the exchange rate change represent an appreciation or a depreciation?

4.    The exchange rate between Regit and Noil is 4 Regitani sponduliks per Noilian bonga.

    a.    A bottle of Regitani sherry sells at home for 50 sponduliks. Calculate its price in Noil.

    b.    A bottle of Noilian honey wine sells at home for 20 bonga. Calculate its price in Regit.

    c.    Find the price of a bottle of wine relative to a bottle of sherry in Regit.

Suppose that costs rise in the Noilian honey wine industry. The domestic price of honey wine rises from 20 bonga to 25 bonga. The exchange rate remains at 4 Regitani sponduliks per Noilian bonga.

    d.    Calculate the Regitani price of imported honey wine.

    e.    Find the relative price of wine to sherry in Regit.

    f.    Is wine now relatively more or less expensive in Regit?

    g.    Predict what will happen to Regitani imports and exports.

    h.    What will happen to the trade balance for Noil?

    i.    What will happen to Regit's aggregate demand curve?

5.    In each of the following cases, should the Arbezanis expect an appreciation or a

depreciation in the value of their currency?

    a.    Because of financial uncertainty at home, Arbezani citizens find it more attractive to buy stock in the neighbouring economy of Arboc.

    b.    Arbezani income levels increase.

    c.    The central bank, ArbeFed, increases the money supply.

6.    Suppose the economy is described by the following model. Assume net international transfers and net international flows of investment income are zero.

    (1)  $C$  $=$  $30 + .8Y_d$
    (2)  $I$  $=$  $50$
    (3)  $G$  $=$  $100$
    (4)  $EX$  $=$  $60$
    (5)  $IM$  $=$  $.3Y_d$
    (6)  $T$  $=$  $80$
    (7)  $Y_d$  $=$  $Y - T$

    a.    Calculate the equilibrium level of income (where $Y = C + I + G + EX - IM$).

    b.    Calculate the value of the expenditure multiplier.

    c.    Calculate the value of imports.

    d.    The trade balance is a _____ (surplus/deficit) of _____.

    e.    The government has a budget _____ (surplus/deficit) of _____.

Suppose that government spending is increased by 25.

    f.    What will happen to the equilibrium income level?

    g.    What will happen to imports?

    h.    *Ceteris paribus*, what effect will this import change have on (1) the current account and (2) the capital account?

Suppose imports are fixed at their new level (through the use of quotas). Now the government increases spending again, by 25.

    i.    What will happen to the equilibrium income level?

Go back to the original economy (no quotas, G is at 100).

    j.    If exports were to increase by 36, indicate the effect this would have on:

        i.   income level _____

        ii.  imports _____

        iii.  the current account deficit _____

    k.    Given the original current account deficit, how much would exports have to rise to achieve a trade balance of zero? _____

7.    Suppose that two goods, Canadian moccasins and Mexican tequila, are traded between Canada and Mexico: The exchange rate is 20¢ = 1 peso (exchange rate 1).

    a.    If the exchange rate moves to $1.00 = 10 pesos (10¢ = 1 peso) (exchange rate 2), with which rate is the dollar "stronger"?

    b.    In their home countries, moccasins sell at $10.00 a pair and tequila sells at 40 pesos a bottle. Calculate the price of tequila, in dollars, at the two exchange rates.
        Exchange rate 1 _____ Exchange rate 2 _____

    c.    At which exchange rate will tequila be more attractive to Canadian consumers?

    d.    As the exchange rate moves from $1.00 = 5 pesos (20¢ = 1 peso) to $1.00 = 10 pesos (10¢ = 1 peso), what will happen to the quantity demanded of pesos?

    e.    Show this demand curve on a graph, with vertical axis as "dollars/pesos" and horizontal axis as "quantity of pesos." Note this graph is drawn to show the price of a peso in dollars, not the price of a dollar in pesos.

    f.    Calculate the price of moccasins, in pesos, at the two exchange rates.

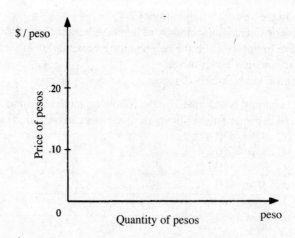

$/ peso

Price of pesos

.20

.10

0

Quantity of pesos    peso

Exchange rate 1 _____    Exchange rate 2 _____

g. At which exchange rate will Canadian moccasins be more attractive to Mexican consumers?

h. As the exchange rate moves from $1.00 = 5 pesos (20¢ = 1 peso) to $1.00 = 10 pesos (10¢ = 1 peso), what will happen to the quantity supplied of pesos?

i. Show this supply curve on the graph. Draw it so the equilibrium exchange rate for one peso is between 10¢ and 20¢.

j. Assume that the diagram is a fair representation of the demand and supply of pesos for purchases of exports and imports. If the exchange rate were fixed at $1.00 = 5 pesos (20¢ = 1 peso), would Mexico have a current account surplus or deficit? Assume no net investment income or net transfers.

k. What can you say about the balance on capital account?

8. Indicate whether each of the following transactions should be included in the current account or the capital account. Indicate whether it is a credit (+) or a debit (−).

9. Use the following table to answer the questions below. Government spending,

| | Account | ± | Transaction |
|---|---|---|---|
| a. | _____ | _____ | Canadian residents buy new shares issued by Sony Corporation. |
| b. | _____ | _____ | Sony Corporation sells a Discman to a Canadian. |
| c. | _____ | _____ | Joe, who works in Japan, sends some money home to his mother in Saskatchewan. |
| d. | _____ | _____ | A Canadian insurance company sells a policy to a Japanese resident. |
| e. | _____ | _____ | Joe's mother goes to visit him in Japan on a Japanese airline. |
| f. | _____ | _____ | A drug dealer smuggles some cocaine into Canada. |
| g. | _____ | _____ | A Japanese purchases some Canadian Treasury bills. |
| h. | _____ | _____ | A Saudi oil sheik buys a chunk of Northern Ontario real estate. |
| i. | _____ | _____ | Ford Canada sells a consignment of vans to the Japanese. |

investment, and exports do not change as output level changes.

a.   Calculate the marginal propensity to consume _____ and the marginal

| GDP (Y) | Domestic Aggregate Expenditure (C + I + G) | Exports (EX) | Imports (IM) | Total Aggregate Expenditure |
|---|---|---|---|---|
| 5000 | 5500 | 400 | 300 | _____ |
| 6000 | 6400 | 400 | 400 | _____ |
| 7000 | 7300 | 400 | 500 | _____ |
| 8000 | 8200 | 400 | 600 | _____ |
| 9000 | 9100 | 400 | 700 | _____ |
| 10 000 | 10 000 | 400 | 800 | _____ |

propensity to import _____. (Assume only consumption and imports vary with Y.)

b.   Calculate the expenditure multiplier.

c.   Complete the table.

d.   The equilibrium income level is _____.

10.  If the Canadian dollar were freely floating at C$1 = US$0.70, what is likely to happen if the Bank of Canada attempts to fix the exchange rate at C$1 = US$0.75, without changing monetary policy? Why might that be more difficult than fixing the exchange rate at C$1 = US$0.65?

11.  Suppose you borrow US $1000 at a rate of interest of 6 percent per year with the intent of converting the money into Canadian dollars. At the time the comparable interest rate in Canada is 4%.

a.   Using the interest rate parity condition, what is expected to happen to the value of the Canadian dollar over the one-year loan period?

b.   Assume that the Canadian dollar was initially at C$1 = US$0.70 at the time of the loan. How many Canadian dollars have you borrowed?

c.   Now assume that, as it happens, the value of the Canadian dollar changes over the year exactly as predicted in part a. Work out the new value of the Canadian dollar, how many Canadian dollars you must repay, and the effective interest rate you have paid.

12.  While Canadians focus on the exchange rate with the U.S. dollar, the exchange rates with other currencies matter as well, although less so.

a.   On April 1, 2001, the exchange rate for the Canadian dollar was C$1 = US$.6347, the exchange rate for the British pound was £1 = US$1.4161 and the exchange rate for the U.S. dollar in terms of euros was US$1 = 1.1406 euros. What was the Canadian dollar exchange rate with the pound and the euro?

b.   Suppose Canada only traded with two countries, 80% with the United States and 20% with Japan. Assume that the Canadian dollar depreciated 5% against the U.S. dollar and appreciated 20% against the yen. What do you think would be the net result in terms of Canadian trade?

## PRACTICE TEST

### I. SOLUTIONS TO MULTIPLE CHOICE QUESTIONS

1. A. Because Arbez is growing, it will increase its imports from Arboc. Similarly, because Arboc is growing, it will import more.

2. D. Because Arboc and Arbez are about the same size, Arbezani imports are growing more quickly than its exports. This imbalance will make the Arbezani currency depreciate. As the Arbezani currency loses its value, the Arbocali currency increases in value. Arbocali consumers will benefit from the greater purchasing power of their currency overseas.

3. D. If U.S. prices increase, exports will decrease and imports will increase because foreign goods are relatively cheaper. The balance of trade will decrease, and the dollar will decrease in value.

4. B. Capital flows are in the capital account. See p. 429.

5. D. See p. 429. The balance on current account includes merchandise exports and imports (Option A), but other items too. Capital inflows and outflows are reflected in the capital account (Option C).

6. D. The current account and the capital account must sum to zero.

7. B. The multiplier is smaller. See p. 433.

8. B. Roughly speaking, if an economy spends more than it takes in, it must sell off some assets to make up the difference. More correctly, if Canadians are buying more goods and services from the rest of the world than they are selling to the rest of the world, and there are no offsetting flows of investment income or transfers, then Canadians must also be selling off some assets to make up the difference. Note that such assets could include Canadian bonds or IOUs (that is, the difference could be borrowed). Also note that, just because the trade deficit is with Japan, it does not mean that Canadians would have to sell Japanese securities or borrow from the Japanese. Answer B would still have been correct if Canadians were selling to any nonresidents (Japanese or otherwise) $5 billion worth of any Canadian-owned assets, from Bell Canada shares to Indonesian mining property.

9. B. Multiplier $= 1 / [1 - (\text{MPC} - \text{MPM})] = 1 / [1 - (.75 - .15)] = 2.5$. See p. 433 for a discussion of the formula.

10. B. A depreciation of the pound is the equivalent of an appreciation of the dollar. Because the dollar can now buy more pounds, British goods become cheaper to Canadian buyers.

11. C. As U.S. economic activity increases, the positive marginal propensity to import will cause greater U.S. imports. The economic activity of exporting countries will be stimulated and, as a consequence, their imports of U.S. goods will increase.

12. B. Given a positive marginal propensity to import, imports will increase but by less than one dollar. See p. 431.

13. A. Canadian securities are offering a higher reward, relative to British securities. The demand for Canadian securities, and the dollars to buy them, will increase. As the demand for pounds decreases and the supply of pounds (to buy dollars) increases, the pound will depreciate and the dollar will appreciate.

14. C. The transaction brings in foreign exchange and hence is a credit.

15. D. If foreign currency flows in, the transaction is a credit. If the transaction involved is an export, it is recorded on the balance of trade. However, the transaction could be, for example, the sale of a government security, which would be recorded on the capital account. In either case, however, the credit would show up on the balance of payments.

16. B. The increase in exports increases net exports by $200 million, and increases Canadian output. As output increases, imports increase and net exports are reduced.

17. B. The multiplier formula is $1 / [1 - (MPC - MPM)]$. The greater the proportion of income being consumed rather than saved or lost overseas, the larger the multiplier.

18. A. Trade increases, so more reals are both demanded and supplied.

19. C. The demand for reals will fall; the real will depreciate so that the value of the Canadian dollar in terms of reals will rise.

20. C. More Brazilian investors will wish to buy Canadian securities and will supply more reals to buy dollars. Fewer Canadian investors will wish to buy Brazilian securities and will demand fewer reals.

21. C. As demand decreases and supply increases for the Brazilian currency, its "price" will decrease—a depreciation. A depreciating real will now be worth less than $.80, so that a Canadian dollar will now be worth more than 1.25 reals.

22. B. See p. 436.

23. C. An increase in government spending increases the demand for money and the interest rate, so that in a more open economy, the expansionary effects on aggregate demand are offset as the exchange rate appreciates, encouraging imports and discouraging exports. Spending power leaks abroad, offsetting the increase in expenditures on domestic production. An increase in money supply decreases the interest rate. In a more open economy, the effects on output through investment spending will be augmented as the exchange rate depreciates, discouraging imports and encouraging exports. This adds to the increase in expenditures on domestic production.

## II.  SOLUTIONS TO APPLICATION QUESTIONS

1. a. $1.50 × £1 = £1.50$.
   b. It is more expensive. A Big Mac in the U.K. costs £1.00.
   c. £1.00 × $1 = $1.00$.
   d. It is less expensive.
   e. The demand for pounds will increase. The demand for dollars will decrease.
   f. The pound will appreciate.
   g. £1.00 × $2 = $2.00$.
   h. more. A Big Mac in the United States costs $1.50.
   i. $1.50 × £0.50 = £0.75$.
   j. This is less expensive than in the United Kingdom.
   k. The demand for pounds will decrease. The demand for dollars will increase.
   l. The dollar will appreciate.
   m. $1.50 = £1$.

2. a. False. An increased money supply will decrease the domestic interest rate, making foreign currency (needed to buy foreign securities) more demanded. An explanation is provided on p. 443.
   b. True. If interest rates fall in Europe, investment in Europe will be less attractive. The demand for euros will decrease and, as Europeans seek to invest in other economies, the supply of euros will increase. These changes will cause the euro to decrease in value (depreciate) and the value of the dollar to increase in value (appreciate).

3. a. A metre of imported Arbocali cloth will cost 2 bandu in Arbez.
   b. An imported Arbezani hide will cost 24 opeks in Arboc.
   c. In Arboc, the number of units of the domestic currency per unit of foreign currency is 2 opeks per bandu.
   d. Arboc has experienced a depreciation and Arbez has experienced an appreciation.

4.   a.   Regitani sherry sells for 12.5 (50 / 4) bonga in Noil.

      b.   Noilian honey wine sells for 80 (20 × 4) sponduliks in Regit.

      c.   The price of a bottle of wine relative to a bottle of sherry in Regit is 1.6 (80 / 50).

      d.   With the new costs in Noil, honey wine will cost 100 sponduliks in Regit.

      e.   The price of a bottle of wine relative to a bottle of sherry in Regit is 2.0 (100 / 50).

      f.   Noilian wine is now relatively more expensive.

      g.   Regitani imports of wine will decrease since they are relatively more expensive, while sherry exports to Noil will increase.

      h.   The Noilian trade balance will worsen; Noil will see its exports become less competitive while (relatively) cheaper imports will enter the country in greater numbers.

      i.   Regit's aggregate demand curve will shift to the right as its exports increase and its imports decrease.

5.   a.   Arbezani currency will depreciate as the demand for foreign currency increases and the supply of Arbezani currency increases.

      b.   Arbezani currency will depreciate. Arbezanis, wishing to buy more imports, will increase the supply of Arbezani currency.

      c.   Arbezani currency will depreciate. An increase in the money supply will depress domestic interest rates. Lower interest rates will lead to a lower demand for Arbezani currency by foreign investors and an increased supply of Arbezani currency by domestic investors who wish to seek higher interest rates abroad.

6.   a.

$$
\begin{aligned}
Y &= C + I + G + EX - IM \\
&= 30 + .8Y_d + 50 + 100 + 60 - .3Y_d \\
&= 240 + .8(Y - T) - .3(Y - T) \\
&= 200 + .5Y \\
Y &= 400.
\end{aligned}
$$

      b.   Multiplier = $1 / [1 - (MPC - MPM)] = 1 / [1 - (.8 - .3)] = 2.00$.

      c.   $IM = .3(400 - 80) = 96$.

      d.   $EX - IM = 60 - 96 =$ deficit of 36.

      e.   $G - T = 100 - 80 =$ deficit of 20.

      f.   Income will increase by 50 because the multiplier is 2.00.

      g.   Imports will increase by 15. $IM = .3(450 - 80) = 111$.

      h.   With no transfers or net investment income, the current account is equal to the trade balance, $EX - IM$, which will decrease by 15 to $60 - 111 = -51$. (That is, the trade deficit will increase from 36 to 51.) The capital account surplus will increase by 15 to 51. Recall that the current account and the capital account must sum to zero.

      i.   The marginal propensity to import is zero (because of the quotas). The multiplier will be 5.00. Income will increase by 125.

      j.   i.   income will increase by $36 \times 2 = 72$.

             ii.   imports will increase by $.3 \times 72 = 21.6$ to 117.6.

             iii.   Again, with no transfers or net investment income, the current account is equal to the trade balance, $EX - IM$, which will increase to $96 - 117.6 = -21.6$ (that is, the trade deficit will decrease from 36 to 21.6).

      k.   Exports would have to rise by 90.

7.  a.  Exchange rate 2. $1.00 = 10 pesos (10¢ = 1 peso) shows a dollar appreciation.
    b.  Exchange rate 1: $8, i.e., 40 × 20¢.
        Exchange rate 2: $4, i.e., 40 × 10¢.
    c.  Exchange rate 2 (10¢ = 1 peso).
    d.  Quantity demanded will increase because Canadians will wish to buy more of the (cheaper) Mexican tequila.
    e.  See the diagram below.

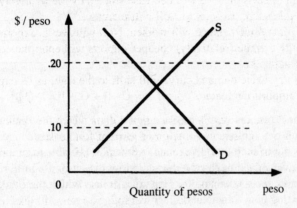

    f.  Exchange rate 1: 50 pesos, i.e., 10 × 5 pesos. If 20¢ = 1 peso, 5 pesos = $1.
        Exchange rate 2: 100 pesos, i.e., 10 × 10 pesos. If 10¢ = 1 peso, 10 pesos = $1.
    g.  Exchange rate 1 (20¢ = 1 peso).
    h.  Quantity supplied will decrease because the Mexicans will be less keen on Canadian purchases.
    i.  See the diagram above.
    j.  As shown above, Mexico would have a deficit on its current account because Mexican exports are less than Mexican imports.
    k.  The balance on capital account will be showing a surplus equal in size to the current account deficit.

8.  See the table below.

|     | Account | ± | Transaction |
| --- | --- | --- | --- |
| a. | capital | debit | Canadian purchase of foreign assets |
| b. | current | debit | import of merchandise |
| c. | current | credit | private transfer |
| d. | current | credit | export of service |
| e. | current | debit | tourism |
| f. | capital | debit | statistical discrepancy |
| g. | capital | credit | foreign purchase of Canadian assets |
| h. | capital | credit | foreign purchase of Canadian assets |
| i. | current | credit | export of merchandise |

9.  a.  MPC = $\Delta C / \Delta Y$ = 900 / 1000 = .9. MPM = $\Delta IM / \Delta Y$ = 100 / 1000 = .1.
    b.  Multiplier = 1 / [1 − (MPC − MPM)] = 1 / [1 − (.9 − .1)] = 5.00

c.

| GDP (Y) | Domestic Aggregate Expenditure (C + I + G) | Exports (EX) | Imports (IM) | Total Aggregate Expenditure |
|---|---|---|---|---|
| 5000 | 5500 | 400 | 300 | 5600 |
| 6000 | 6400 | 400 | 400 | 6400 |
| 7000 | 7300 | 400 | 500 | 7200 |
| 8000 | 8200 | 400 | 600 | 8000 |
| 9000 | 9100 | 400 | 700 | 8800 |
| 10 000 | 10 000 | 400 | 800 | 9600 |

    d.    8000. Equilibrium occurs where Y = C + I + G + EX – IM.

10.    There will be an excess supply of Canadian dollars which the Bank of Canada must buy up, using U.S. dollars or some other form of foreign exchange. If the Bank of Canada runs out of such foreign exchange, it will not be able to support the Canadian dollar. However, if the exchange rate is below the current equilibrium, it is likely there will be an excess demand for Canadian dollars which the Bank of Canada can meet by creating new Canadian dollars to sell.

11.    a.    The interest rate parity condition is that the Canadian interest rate + the expected rate of appreciation of the Canadian dollar = U.S. interest rate, so here the Canadian dollar must be expected to appreciate by 2 percent per year.

    b.    US$1000 / .70 = $1428.57 in Canadian funds.

    c.    The new value of the Canadian dollar will be 1.02 × .70 = US$0.714. You must repay US$1060 which will be 1060 / .714 = C$1484.59 which is 3.9% greater than $1428.57. This is essentially equal to the 4% interest you would have paid if you had borrowed in Canada. (It does not work out exactly because the interest rate parity condition given in the book and in the answer to part a is actually only an approximation, but, as you can see, it is a very close approximation in this case.)

12.    a.    You can calculate the exchange rate of the Canadian dollar to the pound by noting that one Canadian dollar will buy US$0.6347 and US$0.6347 will buy 0.6347 / 1.4161 = £0.4482. Not surprisingly, this was the exact price in the direct Canadian dollar/pound sterling market, because otherwise there would be an easy profit by what is called *arbitrage*. Suppose, for example, the price in these markets was different, and one Canadian dollar could be purchased for £0.30. Then there would be an easy arbitrage profit: One could start with a Canadian dollar, convert it to a U.S. dollar, then to a British pound, and have £0.4482, then buy a Canadian dollar for £0.30. You would have your original Canadian dollar back, plus a riskless profit of £0.4482 – £0.30 = £0.1482. Exchange markets, where billions of dollars are potentially available for arbitrage, always operate to keep exchange rates in line, so such easy profits are not available. There can be a slight difference, however, because of transactions costs.

        Working out the exchange rate with the euro, one Canadian dollar would buy US$0.6347, which will buy 0.6347 × 1.1406 = 0.7239 euros, which was almost the exact Canadian dollar/ euro exchange rate.

b. The results of the two exchange rate changes would tend to cancel each other. One might put a weight of .8 on the appreciation of –5% against the U.S. dollar and .2 on the appreciation of 20% against the yen and .8 × –5 + .2 × 20 = 0. Therefore a depreciation of the Canadian dollar against the U.S. dollar can be offset by appreciation against currencies such as the euro and the yen.

# 22 Economic Growth in Developing Countries

## OBJECTIVES: POINT BY POINT

After completing this chapter, you should be able to accomplish the objectives listed below.

### General Comment

The focus of this chapter is the ways in which developing countries might become developed and the problems that they might encounter along the way. If you study by making lists, be careful in this chapter, because three separate topics are covered—a description of the Third World, how development might be promoted, and some Third World problems. Make up lists using each of these headings.

### OBJECTIVE 1: Distinguish between economic growth and economic development.

Economic growth is the increase in total output (real GDP) or output per capita (real GDP per capita). Economic development is a much broader concept and it includes improvement in average material well-being (measured perhaps by real GDP per capita) but also by health, education, the degree of poverty and perhaps less tangible but important considerations such as political and economic freedom.

In the past, the nations of the world have been roughly divided into three groups: the First World (western, industrialized), the Second World (ex-Socialist, whose future is now uncertain), and the Third World (poor, largely agricultural). There is some mobility—Taiwan, Korea, and Brazil, for instance, are breaking away from others in the Third World category, while a number of nations are lagging so far behind that they have been called the "Fourth World" group. The main characteristic of a Third World country is that the great majority of its inhabitants are poor. Other dimensions that distinguish the "haves" from the "have nots" are: health care, educational facilities, and the percentage of the population engaged in agriculture. (page 452)

> **Comment:** There's no single, unambiguous term that distinguishes the "developing nations" as the textbook deals with them. After all, in one sense, Canada is a developing economy, too. "Third World" tends to have some political undertones. Remember that these nations are a pretty varied group, including countries as diverse as Mexico and Mali, Taiwan and Togo.

## Practice

1. The poorest of the developing nations are sometimes known as the
   A. First World.
   B. Second World.
   C. Third World.
   D. Fourth World.

   **ANSWER:** D. See p. 452.

2. Most of the Fourth World nations are to be found in
   A. Central America.
   B. sub-Saharan Africa.
   C. South America.
   D. the former republics of the Soviet Union and its satellites.

   **ANSWER:** B. Most of the very poorest nations are found to the south of the Sahara desert in Africa. See p. 452.

3. The developing nations of the world contain 75% of the world's population. They are estimated to receive _____ of the world's income.
   A. 5%.
   B. 20%.
   C. 25%.
   D. 33%.

   **ANSWER:** C. See p. 454.

4. Per capita GDP is _____ in developed countries, and infant mortality is _____.
   A. higher, higher.
   B. higher, lower.
   C. lower, higher.
   D. lower, lower.

   **ANSWER:** B. See Table 22.1 on p. 453 of the textbook.

## OBJECTIVE 2: Describe the role of capital, human capital, and social overhead capital in economic growth and development.

No single theory has emerged to explain the development process, but various factors have been identified as potential constraints on development. These include a low rate of accumulation of physical capital, a lack of human capital, and a lack of social overhead capital (infrastructure). All of these problems constrain productivity and economic growth. Moreover, a lack of basic infrastructure (e.g., access to water, electricity and health and education facilities) can reduce the quality of life more generally. (page 459)

> **Tip:** Pay attention to what is happening in your own locality. Many of the sources and strategies discussed in this chapter are not limited to poor foreign regions. Debates on economic development are frequent at all levels of government.

**Comment:** As the textbook notes, economic growth and economic development are not the same phenomenon. Simply because a nation is growing economically doesn't mean that it is also developing. However, you may find it helpful to refer to Chapter 19 in *Principles of Macroeconomics* and locate the factors that promote growth.

**Practice**

5.  The vicious-circle-of-poverty hypothesis suggests that development is stunted by the dependence of
    A.  a potentially fast-growing industrial sector on a slow-growing agricultural sector.
    B.  growth on the limited savings possible in a poor country.
    C.  a developing nation on developed countries as markets for its output.
    D.  a fast-growing agricultural sector on an undermechanized manufacturing sector.

    **ANSWER:** B.  See p. 455.

6.  The brain drain refers to
    A.  the movement of talented personnel from a developing country to a developed country.
    B.  the absence of skilled entrepreneurs in the developing countries.
    C.  declining literacy rates.
    D.  the loss of human capital through the ravages of malnutrition.

    **ANSWER:** A.   See p. 456.

7.  Each of the following has been advanced as a plausible constraint on development except
    A.  the quantity of available capital.
    B.  the quantity of available labour.
    C.  the quantity of infrastructure.
    D.  the quantity of entrepreneurial ability.

    **ANSWER:** B.  The typical developing country has adequate numbers of workers, although specific skills may be limited.

8.  Capital shortages are a typical problem for developing countries. Each of the following is a plausible cause of capital shortages except
    A.  lack of incentives leading to low saving rates.
    B.  the inherent riskiness of investment in a developing nation.
    C.  government policies, such as price ceilings and appropriation of private property.
    D.  widespread poverty resulting in little surplus after consumption needs are met.

    **ANSWER:** D.   The vicious-circle-of-poverty hypothesis fails to account for the success of previously poor nations like Japan. See p. 459.

## OBJECTIVE 3: Describe three tradeoffs affecting strategies for economic development.

At least three types of planning decisions must be made:

1.  Agriculture or industry? Development used to be equated with industrialization; many Third World nations sought to move away from agriculture and toward industrial production. However, merely trying to replicate the structure of the developed nations does not guarantee development. Opinion now favours a balanced growth in both agricultural and industrial sectors—"walking on two legs."

2.  Exports or import substitution? *Import substitution* calls for the encouragement of home-grown substitutes for imported goods. This strategy has failed in almost every case; it results in high-cost production protected by trade barriers. *Export promotion* calls for producing goods for the export market and

has seen some measure of success (e.g., Japan), although it depends on the willingness of the developed nations to import Third World production.

3.  Central planning or the market? Finally, the economy must choose the appropriate balance between free enterprise and central planning. Planning permits coordination of economic activities that private actors in the economy might not undertake (e.g., disease and pest control, literacy training) and the channelling of funds into investment, but is difficult to administer.

(pages 457-459)

Throughout the developing world it appears to be increasingly recognized that market forces can be valuable in allocating scarce resources.

## Practice

9.  Experience suggests that, of the following, the development approach most likely to succeed is
    A.  rapid industrial mechanization coupled with labour migration to the industrial centres.
    B.  intensive training of human capital to occupy technologically advanced positions in import-substitution industries.
    C.  a balanced promotion of both the agricultural sector and the manufacturing sector.
    D.  slow, careful industrial growth combined with rapid expansion in food provision to improve human capital.

    **ANSWER:** C.  This is the "walking on two legs" strategy. See p. 458.

10. Suppose Noil is a small sub-Saharan nation with few sophisticated resources. However, it constructs an airport and hotel with lavish Western facilities and offers safari trips into its beautiful mountain ranges to groups from the developed countries. Noil is best described as having opted for a(n) _____ development strategy.
    A.  import substitution.
    B.  export promotion.
    C.  rural exploitation.
    D.  balanced growth.

    **ANSWER:** B.  Tourism is an export.

11. Generally, import substitution policies have
    A.  failed in almost every case.
    B.  succeeded, but only while the cost of imported oil was held down.
    C.  not been an unqualified success, but have had a better track record than export promotion policies.
    D.  succeeded in Latin America, but failed in Africa and had mixed results in Asia.

    **ANSWER:** A.  Import substitution policies reduce exports and foster inefficient, inappropriate (i.e., capital-intensive) production methods.

12. The small hypothetical Asian nation of Regit chooses to follow an import substitution strategy, and builds a fertilizer plant to serve its rice farmers. Based on similar experiments elsewhere, we would expect to see all of the following except
    A. high fertilizer production costs.
    B. the imposition of tariffs to protect domestic fertilizer production.
    C. capital-intensive fertilizer production techniques.
    D. a rise in the international competitiveness of the nation's rice farmers.

    **ANSWER:** D.  High-cost fertilizer will reduce the ability of the rice farmers to compete with foreign rice.

13. Which would not be an export promotion strategy?
    A. Reducing the value of the domestic currency relative to other currencies.
    B. Increasing the nation's ability to compete domestically with the exports of other nations.
    C. The provision of subsidies to exporters.
    D. The provision of preferential investment tax breaks to exporting firms.

    **ANSWER:** B.  This is typical of import substitution. See p. 458.

## OBJECTIVE 4: Outline how rapid population growth affects economic development.

The Third World death rate has tumbled sharply because of better medical treatment, but the birth rate has declined much more slowly. Although large families may provide a cheap labour pool today and support in old age tomorrow, rapid expansion in the population places burdens on public services and may be undesirable from the viewpoint of society. In some nations, economic incentives (particularly those that expanded labour market alternatives for women) have been applied successfully to encourage smaller families.

(page 460)

## Practice

14. Birth rate minus death rate equals the
    A. fertility rate.
    B. mortality rate.
    C. natural rate of population increase.
    D. development rate.

    **ANSWER:** C.  See p. 462.

15. Malthus predicted that the world population would grow at a(n) _____ growth rate while the production of food would increase more _____.
    A. increasing, rapidly.
    B. increasing, slowly.
    C. constant, rapidly.
    D. constant, slowly.

    **ANSWER:** D.  See p. 461.

16. High fertility rates may cause all of the following except
    A. falling saving rates.
    B. reduced availability of social programs for each individual.
    C. labour shortages.
    D. food shortages.

    **ANSWER:** C.  As the population expands, there should be no labour constraint.

**O**BJECTIVE **5:** Outline the main agricultural policy issues in less-developed economies.

The key issue is whether food shortages are inevitable or due to policy mistakes. A nation that chooses to hold down prices for the benefit of consumers may see its farmers cutting back production, making it more vulnerable to famine. However, policies such as those associated with the so-called "Green Revolution"—the use of high-yield, resilient plants—increase productivity and food supply.                    (page 464)

## Practice

17. Government establishment of low food prices is usually meant to
    A.    discourage farming.
    B.    make domestic farm production competitive with imports.
    C.    please the small, but politically powerful, urban population.
    D.    make domestic farm production more efficient.

    **ANSWER:** C.   Urban dwellers may be more educated and organized—a bigger threat to the longevity of the government in power. See p. 464.

18. Policies that may alleviate Third World food shortages include all but
    A.    introducing Green Revolution techniques.
    B.    land reform.
    C.    imposing price ceilings for farm outputs.
    D.    removing price ceilings for farm outputs.

    **ANSWER:** C.   See p. 465.

## **O**BJECTIVE **6:** Explain why the Third World debt is of global concern.

Between 1970 and 1984, capital-starved developing countries' combined debt increased by 1000% to almost US$700 billion. In the late 1970s, the world economy faltered and Third World export revenues shrank. Interest on the loans became (and remains) hard to pay. Some nations threatened to default. Many sought to reschedule their debt repayment in exchange for promises of economic austerity designed to cut back on imports and to increase exports.                    (page 465)

## Practice

19. Under a debt rescheduling agreement, the borrowing country is expected to increase incentives to _____ and to reduce _____.
    A.    consumers, export spending.
    B.    consumers, imports.
    C.    exporters, the federal government deficit.
    D.    exporters, imports.

    **ANSWER:** D.  A debt rescheduling agreement will require the country to increase exports and reduce imports. Only by increasing its foreign earnings can a nation hope to reduce its debt burden.

## **O**BJECTIVE **7** (**A**PPENDIX **22A**): List six basic terms in Marxian economics. Define tragedy of the commons and explain its implications for an economy with collective ownership.

Six terms in Marxian economics (all defined in the glossary in the appendix) are *alienation, capitalist economy, communism, means of production, socialist economy*, and *surplus.*

Capitalist economies and socialist economies are at the two ends of the economic spectrum; democracy and communism are at the two ends of the political spectrum. Economic systems are classified on the basis of where the ownership of the means of production resides—in capitalism, it's with the private individual; in socialism, it's with the government. (page 469)

No economic system adheres to pure socialism or to pure capitalism—each economy is a blend of the two extremes. China is "socialist" but has (increasing) private ownership; the United States and Japan are "capitalist" but each contains a public sector.

Marx argued that economies generated a surplus, that is the amount of output in excess of what was required to maintain workers at a subsistence level and to replace capital used up in the production process. In Marx's view, this surplus was entirely attributable to the efforts of labour, but nonetheless capitalists unjustly capture most of it. Capitalists are more powerful than workers because they own the means of production and can consume their wealth if need be; workers cannot make a living if they cannot sell their labour to capitalists, who use the threat of unemployment to keep wages down. Workers suffer alienation in that they lose their sense of purpose because their main life activity, work, is under the control of their employer. Marx predicted that eventually workers would rise up and overthrow an ever more repressive capitalist system.

> **Tip:** For Marx, production becomes less labour-intensive as capitalists substitute capital for labour; with relatively less labour to exploit, the rate of profit will fall. To compensate, capitalists increase the rate of exploitation and wages are driven to the subsistence level. Eventually the system becomes unbearable, is overthrown, and is replaced by socialism and, ultimately, communism.

> **Tip:** You may have noted the adjective "Marxian." Marxian, rather than Marxist, is the correct term to use when referring to Marx's economic ideas.

Marxian theory is much different than theory elsewhere in the book, which has assumed the capitalist mixed economy as a given. Instead Marx viewed capitalism as a stage in a path from feudalism to communism. Remember, when Marx was writing in the mid-nineteenth century, almost all workers in the world were at a near-subsistence state. Now, in modern economies such as Canada's, most workers are well above subsistence, although modern Marxists would argue that this is not a stable situation.

The *tragedy of the commons* is an important idea in economics. If grazing land is held in common, individual farmers have the incentive to overgraze because the costs of the overgrazing are borne collectively, not individually as they would be if the farmer owned the land herself/himself. (When the land is owned collectively, each farmer knows that even if she or he tries to save some grass for future grazing, another farmer will likely graze it first.) Similarly the bison of Western Canada were a common resource that individuals did not own; there was no incentive for an individual to decide not to kill a bison to conserve the resource, because most likely that would simply give an opportunity for another to kill the animal and obtain its meat and hide. (It is sometimes remarked that the native peoples of Canada managed the resource of the bison for many centuries, and near-extinction did not occur until a few decades after the arrival of Europeans.)

What does this all have to do with centrally-planned economies? Every economy faces "tragedy of the commons" problems ranging from fishing rights to air pollution, but the effect is still more forceful in an economy of collective ownership. Collectively-owned farms may pay little attention to their profits and hence do not have to worry what they pay for inputs, which may be allocated by quota rather than by a market. Managers may try to get as much as possible of any available input (capital, materials, skilled labour), an effect very much like overgrazing. More generally, managers and workers have little incentive either to economize on inputs or to maximize output, because they will receive little direct reward. Under private ownership, the owners of the firm have a strong incentive to monitor managers to insure that inputs are used efficiently to produce as much output as possible, because this will maximize the financial return.

## Practice

20. In a _____ economy, most capital is privately owned.
    A. democratic.
    B. communist.
    C. capitalist.
    D. socialist.

    **ANSWER:** C. Note that "democracy" refers to a political system, not an economic one.

21. In a true _____ economy, the people would own the means of production directly and plan as a collective, without state intervention.
    A. feudal.
    B. communist.
    C. capitalist.
    D. socialist.

    **ANSWER:** B. In a true communist economy, it was argued, the state would wither away. In fact, the communist economies of the world have really been socialist— e.g., the former Union of Soviet *Socialist* Republics.

22. For Marx, the "means of production" include
    A. only capital.
    B. only capital and labour.
    C. only capital and land.
    D. capital, land, and labour.

    **ANSWER:** C. The means of production are not equivalent to the "factors of production" you met in Chapter 3.

23. Which statement does not represent Marx's views?
    A. Unemployment is used by capitalists to keep wages down.
    B. Human beings should be thought of primarily as consumers, not workers.
    C. The internal conflicts in capitalism will eventually lead to its demise.
    D. Capital embodies the past efforts of labour; owners of capital have no moral claim to a share of the surplus.

    **ANSWER:** B. See p. 470.

24. In Marxian analysis, which of the following statements is true?
    A. The rate of profit tends to fall over time.
    B. Additional capital accumulation increases the rate of profit.
    C. Additional capital accumulation increases surplus value.
    D. As wages fall, production will become more labour-intensive.

    **ANSWER:** A. Capital must be paid for but can't be exploited. Profits derive from the ability of the capitalist to exploit workers and hence fall as, over time, capital replaces labour in production.

25. The notion that collective ownership of resources may be inefficient because individuals do not bear the full cost of their own decisions is called
    A. exploitation.
    B. the tragedy of the commons.
    C. surplus value.
    D. the externality effect.

    **ANSWER:** B.  See p. 471.

26. Each of the following is an example of the tragedy of the commons except
    A. pollution in the Great Lakes.
    B. overgrazing of shared tribal land.
    C. the decimation of the bison by nineteenth-century settlers.
    D. the slaughtering of an entire herd by a rancher.

    **ANSWER:** D.  The herd is private property.

## PRACTICE TEST

**I.  MULTIPLE CHOICE QUESTIONS.** Select the option that provides the single best answer.

_____ 1. Which of the following are characteristics of the average developing country?
    A. Large populations and high savings rates.
    B. Low levels of human capital and low per capita GDP.
    C. High infant mortality but high life expectancy.
    D. Low health standards and high literacy rates.

_____ 2. Import substitution occurs when a country
    A. becomes developed.
    B. erects trade barriers.
    C. no longer has sufficient foreign exchange to buy imports.
    D. strives to produce goods that were previously imported.

_____ 3. Economic development occurs when there is an increase in the
    A. per capita nominal GDP.
    B. per capita real GDP.
    C. material well-being of the nation's citizens.
    D. labour force.

_____ 4. Lack of economic development might be caused by
    A. a low marginal propensity to consume.
    B. an excess supply of private overhead capital.
    C. a high literacy rate.
    D. inadequate amounts of social overhead capital.

_____ 5. Which of the following is an example of an improvement in social overhead capital?
    A. A multinational corporation opens a new plant.
    B. A worker builds a house for his family.
    C. There is an increase in the rate of growth of per capita real GDP.
    D. A national adult literacy program is established by the government.

_____ 6. Labour is relatively abundant in Arboc. Arboc might best be able to develop by
    A. using production techniques that are capital-intensive.
    B. using production techniques that employ labour and capital in fixed and equal proportions.
    C. specializing in the production of labour-intensive commodities which should therefore be relatively cheaper to produce.
    D. specializing in the production of capital-intensive commodities, which should therefore be marketable at relatively higher prices.

_____ 7. Local firms in developing countries are unlikely to drain malarial swamps because
    A. the government provides sufficient pest control.
    B. labour shortages are typical.
    C. the "free-rider" problem will result in a low (or zero) rate of return.
    D. international agencies such as the World Bank and the IMF prefer short-term projects.

_____ 8. Adopting the strategy of "walking on two legs" means that
    A. men and women should be treated equally in the workplace.
    B. import substitution and export promotion should be attempted simultaneously.
    C. attention must be paid to developing both the industrial sector and the agricultural sector.
    D. the dependent links with old colonial nations should be severed.

_____ 9. Import substitution might fail to promote economic development if
    A. producers use domestic inputs that are lower in cost than imported inputs.
    B. firms make use of capital-intensive production methods that fail to reduce unemployment.
    C. such goods require labour-intensive methods of production.
    D. after establishment, these industries are subsidized by the state.

_____ 10. The "export promotion" strategy calls for
    A. the running of a balance of trade deficit.
    B. the production of goods that are demanded by consumers in the developed countries.
    C. the production of export goods for domestic consumers.
    D. the domestic production of goods that previously had been imported.

_____ 11. Sending savings from the imaginary Third World nation of Arboc to the developed countries _____ to growth in Arboc's physical capital. New Arbocali import controls will tend to _____ investment in Arboc.
    A. leads, increase.
    B. leads, decrease.
    C. does not lead, increase.
    D. does not lead, decrease.

_____ 12. Between 1970 and 1984, developing countries' combined debt increased
    A. 1000%.
    B. 100%.
    C. 10%.
    D. 1%.

_____ 13. IMF stabilization policies might call for
   A. cutbacks in government spending and a currency devaluation.
   B. nationalization of foreign investment.
   C. higher subsidies to importers of capital goods.
   D. tax cuts and a currency devaluation.

_____ 14. The poorest 20% of the world's population is estimated to receive
   _____ of the world's income.
   A. .5%.
   B. 2.0%.
   C. 2.5%.
   D. 5.0%.

_____ 15. Which of the following variables tends to be high in the developing coun-
   tries?
   A. Life expectancy.
   B. Literacy rates.
   C. Infant mortality.
   D. Proportion of the population in urban areas.

_____ 16. Under a debt rescheduling agreement, the borrowing country may be
   expected to _____ the value of its currency in order to _____
   exports.
   A. increase, increase.
   B. increase, decrease.
   C. decrease, increase.
   D. decrease, decrease.

_____ 17. All of the following discourage Third World development except
   A. the lack of skilled entrepreneurs.
   B. insufficient social overhead capital.
   C. insufficient labour-saving technological innovation.
   D. inadequate amounts of human capital.

_____ 18. _____ is a development strategy that is designed to encourage sales
   abroad.
   A. Import substitution.
   B. Export promotion.
   C. "Walking on two legs."
   D. Dependency.

_____ 19. Permanently higher birth rates may cause all of the following except
   A. an eventual increase in the proportion of working-age adults in the
      population.
   B. an increase in the number of dependents.
   C. decreases in the rate of capital formation.
   D. decreases in savings rates.

_____ 20. Governments may set food prices low in order to
   A. encourage greater food production.
   B. make domestic producers competitive with foreign producers.
   C. stimulate a willingness to adopt more efficient farming methods.
   D. maintain the political support of urban consumers.

_____ 21. According to Marx, the rate of profit has a tendency to _____, causing capitalists to _____ the rate of exploitation.
   A.  rise, increase.
   B.  rise, decrease.
   C.  fall, increase.
   D.  fall, decrease.

_____ 22. For Marx, the conflicts in capitalism include all of the following except
   A.  inflation and an increasing government deficit.
   B.  alienation and increasing exploitation.
   C.  progressively more violent business cycles.
   D.  the emiserization of the workers.

_____ 23. Capitalism and socialism are distinguished primarily by
   A.  the ownership of labour.
   B.  the number of political parties.
   C.  the ownership of capital.
   D.  the distribution of income throughout society.

_____ 24. According to Marx, the wage is largely determined by
   A.  the surplus value of labour.
   B.  the cost of the bare essentials of subsistence.
   C.  the marginal revenue product of labour.
   D.  the marginal physical product.

_____ 25. To Marx, the profit earned by the owner of a machine was
   A.  an illegitimate return to an exploiter of labour.
   B.  a legitimate return to "the means of production."
   C.  compensation for alienation.
   D.  the price of the final good produced by the machine.

_____ 26. The "tragedy of the commons" exemplifies the problem of _____ that can occur in the case of resources that are owned _____.
   A.  inefficiency, privately.
   B.  inequity, privately.
   C.  inefficiency, collectively.
   D.  inequity, collectively.

_____ 27. Surplus, in the Marxian sense, is
   A.  equal to the wage rate paid to the worker.
   B.  the difference between the subsistence wage and the actual wage received.
   C.  the rate of emiserization.
   D.  the difference between the value of production and what is needed for subsistence consumption by workers and to replace capital used in the production process.


## II.  APPLICATION QUESTIONS

1.  Suppose that 10 units of food are required per person per year in the imaginary developing nation of Arboc. Due to improved crops and farming techniques, food production will increase by a fixed amount every 10 years—suppose this amount is 1000 units of food so that, in 2000, food production will be 11 000 units. Arboc currently exports its surplus food production. Because of high birth rates and decreasing death rates, Arboc's population increases by 50% every 10 years.

a.  Given the conditions specified, complete the table below.

| Year | Food Production | Population | Food Requirements | Food Surplus/Deficit |
|------|-----------------|------------|-------------------|----------------------|
| 1990 | 10 000 | 400 | 4000 | +6000 |
| 2000 | 11 000 | | | |
| 2010 | | | | |
| 2020 | | | | |
| 2030 | | | | |

b.  What happens in or about the year 2020?
c.  Other things unchanged, what will happen to Arboc's balance of trade?
d.  Given the situation in 2030, what do you think will happen to Arboc?

2.  Some Marxian scholars focus on what is called the *labour theory of value*. Commodities are thought of as the physical embodiment of the labour that produced them; a capital good (e.g., a machine) is the physical embodiment of past labour that was used to produce it. Capitalists hire "labour power" to make products and make a profit by selling the products for more than *the value of labour power* (that is, the wages) used to produce them. The question below provides numerical illustrations of calculations empirical Marxian economists could use to analyze an economic system.

In the Marxian economy of Arboc, 500 units of value are produced. Production requires current labour and machinery, which embodies 100 units of past labour.
a.  Calculate the value of current labour used in units of value.
b.  If workers are paid 300 units of value, how many units of profit will capitalists derive?
c.  Calculate the rate of exploitation (surplus value/value of current labour).
d.  Calculate the rate of profit (surplus value/value of production).

Now suppose that output doubles with labour and capital inputs are unchanged.
e.  Output is _____ units of value.
f.  Calculate the value of current labour used in units of value.
g.  If the wage rate is unchanged, how many units of value will the workers receive?
h.  Surplus value is _____.
i.  Calculate the rate of exploitation (surplus value/value of current labour).
j.  Calculate the rate of profit (surplus value/value of production).

Now suppose that relative to the initial situation, output has doubled but, to achieve this, the production technique has become more capital-intensive. Machinery is worth 400 units of past labour.
k.  Calculate the value of current labour used in units of value.
l.  If the wage rate is unchanged, how many units of value will the workers receive?
m.  Surplus value is _____.
n.  Calculate the rate of exploitation (surplus value/value of current labour).
o.  Calculate the rate of profit (surplus value/value of production).

Suppose that the subsistence wage is 200 units of value, given the current level of output. Machinery is worth 400 units of past labour.
p.  Calculate how many units of surplus value capitalists can expropriate.
q.  Calculate the rate of exploitation (surplus value/value of current labour).
r.  Calculate the rate of profit (surplus value/value of production).

# ANSWERS AND SOLUTIONS

## PRACTICE TEST

### I.   SOLUTIONS TO MULTIPLE CHOICE QUESTIONS

1.   B.   See p. 453 for a full discussion of the characteristics of developing nations.
2.   D.   Import substitution is a strategy that attempts to establish a domestic industry that can provide goods to replace imports. See p. 458.
3.   C.   Improvements in per capita GDP do not guarantee development. See p. 452.
4.   D.   To grow, an economy needs an adequate quantity and quality of resources, including socially provided resources.
5.   D.   Social overhead capital includes projects that cannot be undertaken privately.
6.   C.   Incidentally, this is an application of the Heckscher-Ohlin theorem from Chapter 20.
7.   C.   See p. 457.
8.   C.   The Chinese phrase "walking on two legs" describes the need to have both agricultural and industrial sectors developing together. See p. 458.
9.   B.   To be effective, the strategy must play to the strengths of its own economy—typically labour-intensive production. See p. 458.
10.  B.   See p. 459.
11.  D.   See p. 455.
12.  A.   See p. 466.
13.  A.   See p. 467.
14.  A.   See p. 454.
15.  C.   See p. 453.
16.  C.   If the borrowing country reduces the value of its currency, its exports will be cheaper for foreigners to buy.
17.  C.   The quantity of labour is not a significant constraint in the Third World. Labour-saving technology, then, is not critical to successful development.
18.  B.   See p. 458.
19.  A.   As more children are born, even as the population ages, the proportion of adults will decrease.
20.  D.   See p. 464.
21.  C.   As additional capital is accumulated the rate of profit falls. This decline prompts capitalists to increase exploitation of workers. See p. 470.
22.  A.   Marx did not focus on inflation and the government deficit in his writings.
23.  C.    In a capitalist system, ownership of the means of production (capital and land) is in the hands of capitalists and in the hands of the state under a communist system.
24.  B.   Capitalists, in search of profits, will try to drive down the wage to the minimum (subsistence) level. See p. 470.
25.  A.   See p. 470.
26.  C.   Commons (commonly-owned land) are often treated inefficiently. See p. 471.
27.  D.   See p. 470.

## II.   SOLUTIONS TO APPLICATION QUESTIONS

1.  a.   See the table below.

| Year | Food Production | Population | Food Requirements | Food Surplus/Deficit |
|------|-----------------|------------|-------------------|----------------------|
| 1990 | 10 000 | 400 | 4000 | +6000 |
| 2000 | 11 000 | 600 | 6000 | +5000 |
| 2010 | 12 000 | 900 | 9000 | +3000 |
| 2020 | 13 000 | 1350 | 13 500 | −500 |
| 2030 | 14 000 | 2025 | 20 250 | −6250 |

b.   Food requirements outstrip food production.

c.   As the food surplus decreases, less will be available for export and the balance of trade will become less favourable. Sometime just before 2020, the trade surplus in food will become a deficit if it is able to import the required food.

d.   This is an open question. Arboc will be heavily in debt, and will need to import food to feed its population. Imports of industrial goods would slacken. Reduced health care (per person) might cause famine and disease, reducing the population. Arboc might borrow to finance its overseas spending and might have to receive ongoing foreign aid. Population control policies would have to be considered.

2   a.   500 − 100 units of past labour value = 400 units of labour value.

b.   400 units of labour value − 300 = 100 units of profit.

c.   Rate of exploitation = surplus value/value of current labour = 100/400 = .25.

d.   The rate of profit = surplus value/value of production = 100/500 = .2.

e.   500 × 2 = 1000.

f.   1000 − 100 units of past labour value = 900 units of labour value.

g.   Still 300.

h.   Surplus value = 900 − 300 = 600.

i.   Rate of exploitation = surplus value/value of current labour = 600/900 = .67.

j.   Rate of profit = surplus value/value of production = 600/1000 = .6.

k.   1000 − 400 units of past labour value = 600 units of labour value.

l.   Still 300.

m.   Surplus value = 600 − 300 = 300.

n.   Rate of exploitation = surplus value/value of current labour = 300/600 = .5.

o.   Rate of profit = surplus value/value of production = 300/1000 = .3.

p.   Surplus value = 600 − 200 = 400.

q.   Rate of exploitation = surplus value/value of current labour = 400/600 = .67.

r.   Rate of profit = surplus value/value of production = 400/1000 = .4.